Advanced Studies of Financial Technologies and Cryptocurrency Markets

Lukáš Pichl · Cheoljun Eom ·
Enrico Scalas · Taisei Kaizoji
Editors

Advanced Studies of Financial Technologies and Cryptocurrency Markets

Springer

Editors
Lukáš Pichl (Deceased)
Department of Natural Sciences
International Christian University
Mitaka, Tokyo, Japan

Cheoljun Eom
Department of Business Administration
Pusan National University
Busan, Korea (Republic of)

Enrico Scalas
Department of Mathematics
University of Sussex
Brighton, UK

Taisei Kaizoji
Department of Economics and Business
International Christian University
Mitaka, Tokyo, Japan

Lukáš Pichl is Deceased

ISBN 978-981-15-4497-2 ISBN 978-981-15-4498-9 (eBook)
https://doi.org/10.1007/978-981-15-4498-9

This Springer imprint is published by the registered company Springer Nature Singapore Pte Ltd.
The registered company address is: 152 Beach Road, #21-01/04 Gateway East, Singapore 189721, Singapore

Contents

Financial Innovations and Blockchain Applications: New Digital Paradigms in Global Cybersociety

Lukáš Pichl, Cheoljun Eom, Enrico Scalas, and Taisei Kaizoji

Abstract Cryptocurrencies—digital assets—are discussed from the viewpoint of the medium of exchange and the store of value with a focus on Bitcoin. The issue of trust towards the unit of accounts is viewed in the perspective of historical events including fiat currency reforms in the past all over the world. It is argued that a major test of the present global financial system and its emerging new technology alternatives has not occurred yet. The notion of intrinsic value of currency is strongly attached to the stability of the social and economic system, which landscape will be probably drastically altered in the next few decades due to the rise of artificial intelligence. The chapters in this book which are focusing on the current aspects of financial innovations also point out the possible directions and dilemmas the future may bring us.

Keywords Money · Cryptoasset · Cryptocurrency · Blockchain · Currency reform · Financial crisis · Time series prediction · Machine learning

---

L. Pichl (✉) · T. Kaizoji
Graduate School of Arts and Sciences, International Christian University, Osawa 3-10-2, Mitaka, Tokyo 181-8585, Japan
e-mail: lukas@icu.ac.jp

T. Kaizoji
e-mail: kaizoji@icu.ac.jp

C. Eom
School of Business, Pusan National University, Busan 46241, Republic of Korea
e-mail: shunter@pusan.ac.kr

E. Scalas
Department of Mathematics, School of Mathematical and Physical Sciences, University of Sussex, Brighton BN1 9QH, UK
e-mail: E.Scalas@sussex.ac.uk

L. Pichl et al. (eds.), *Advanced Studies of Financial Technologies and Cryptocurrency Markets*, https://doi.org/10.1007/978-981-15-4498-9_1

1 Introduction

The origins of numeracy, the ability to count and work with numbers, are historically documented by archeological findings of tally sticks (Ifrah 2000). Scientific progress has always transformed the society—in the example of the tally, where the number of objects is represented by the (count of) notches on the tally stick—not only the tally served as a number representation object, it often had the transaction function of being convertible in the counted object. This has been especially the case when the tally was endorsed by a high-ranking member of the society. The material form of money, as is well known, is therefore tightly related to the current level of science and technology and goes hand in hand with trust. In our example of the tally stick money precursor, it is the trust that at a later point of time the tally can be converted to the underlying object (store of value) or would be accepted as a means of payment instead of the physical delivery of the represented goods. One feature of money the individual tally stick does not necessarily have is however the *general unit* of accounts property—the universal application of the same counting unit, i.e. the emergence of money in the modern sense of the word as a mediator of all economic transactions (see, e.g. Weatherford 1998).

The requirement for mediating all economic transactions can be met by using a highly marketable asset, which first naturally appeared in the form of grain or livestock, before it was substituted with precious metals. The latter step would not be possible without social hierarchy in which the objects of desire were set by the upper class that controlled the community and the use of its technology. About three thousand years ago in China, bronze models replicating cowrie shells appeared as money (Kerr 2013). In the Iron Age, coins minted from precious metals that represented the notion of economic value appeared in the ancient Mediterranean area (Pavlek et al. 2019), where system of a commodity-based legal tender has prevailed through the medieval times. Our discussion this far was based on the history of numeracy and its relation to money; however, numeracy goes hand in hand with literacy. Promissory notes to deliver money, based on trust and the legal system framework, have first been documented in China during the Han dynasty (von Klaproth 1823), and first precursors of paper money appeared as early as in the seventh century during the Tang dynasty (Pickering 1844). This abstraction of financial value from the underlying value of coin metal asset decoupled the trust in the economic system from the asset value of the legal tender—money went even more abstract and modern currencies were born. Still, the promissory note feature of paper money by the obligation to convert banknotes to gold on demand persisted in the world for quite a long time—convertibility of US dollar to gold was officially terminated by the US President Richard Nixon as late as in 1971 (cf. Zoeller and Bandelj 2019). Instead, the national motto "In God We Trust" on the US dollar banknotes illustrates the truth of the incomplete human control framework and the uncertain future that has been a part of money notion since its inception.

Whom is it therefore that we trust considering the store of value function of fiat currencies? A mainstream answer would perhaps emphasize the role of the government and the role of the central bank in each country; in today's interconnected world, a true cyberworld of computerized financial system, perhaps also a rising global financial order. In the gold standard world, it was the Bretton Woods system at global scale; at present, various institutions influence the dynamics of the intertwined competing world financial system, such as the International Monetary Fund, the World Bank, but also European Central Bank, Asian Infrastructure Investment Bank, and others, based on the region and viewpoint.

What does money mean today? Here is the quotation of Petr Sýkora, co-founder of the charitable foundation Good Angel in the Czech Republic (Petka 2013):

> Money today is just stored as the ones and zeros in a computer system. It does not have to be there tomorrow…

Let us take Czechoslovakia as a historical example how a sudden currency reform can ruin personal savings—there is an infamous quotation by a local spokesman of communist party in the city of Pilsen (May 29, 1953) (Ule 1965)

> Our currency is firm. Trust the party, Comrades. The rumors about a reform have no justification…

followed the next day by the official public announcement of currency reform on May 30th, 1953, which largely deprived the population of cash and bank savings and resulted in local rebellions against the regime. The conversion rates of the old currency to the new one varied from 1:5 to 1:50, based on the amount; the government also realized a bankruptcy as the obligation from all government bonds to their holders was cancelled.

Since currency reforms feature nonlinear conversion between the old and new currency based on the deposited amount leading to arbitrary relocation of financial resources (Krishna and Leukhina 2019), they are popular with totalitarian regimes such as the one during the socialist regime period in Czechoslovakia. Similar loss of savings occurred in Russia during the currency reform of the summer 1993 which wiped out the value of savings of general population using a combination of conversion restrictions with high rate of inflation (cf. Desai 2005).

The global financial crisis of 2008 has resulted in trillion dollar losses all over the world, be it in the house value and related personal mortgage bankruptcies when the US housing bubble burst; or the evaporated retirement savings of US citizens; the extreme losses of European Banks that naively propelled the sub-prime mortgage financial derivative prices; in brief the whole world sank into an aftermath, a recovery from which has been particularly long and painful in Europe (cf. Farmer 2012).

The above-mentioned currency reforms and financial crises serve us here to claim that the probability of major disruption in the time value of fiat currencies, even if it were to be once in a lifetime—is not negligible. Times of hyperinflation, such as the current one in Venezuela, attest to the loss of public trust in the official currency, and the need for an alternative solution—be it a foreign currency, a commodity, or, as we discuss in the next section—perhaps even a cryptocurrency.

2 Algorithmic Innovations in Digital Finance

Money in the world moves to the cyberspace by getting digital form. The consequences of such a change include detailed expenditure and revenue traces in databases of financial institutions, and the shift towards the cashless society, a trend especially pronounced in Scandinavian countries such as Sweden, where cards and mobile apps in smartphones are by far the most common means of payment. Proposals for citizen accounts directly with the central bank are also popular as discussed in the following.

2.1 Fiat Currencies—Pros and Cons

When a fiat currency goes completely digital, which has not yet occurred in the world nevertheless, the central financial institution gains the technical means to cut each individual off the economic system. They also gain the full financial record of individual behavior. Information has become the most valued commodity of our times and its possession results in power. This asymmetric relation of an individual and the financial institution may be convenient when privacy is protected, and general security measures function but turns to a disaster in cases of successful cyberattacks. It is in the very nature of the trusted bookkeeping party that digital money cannot be proved completely secure. Technically, redistribution of financial wealth can easily be implemented by altering the financial records according to any algorithm deemed as legal, be it for instance (nonlinear) negative interest rates to fight deflation in the form of instantaneous currency reforms using central bank digital currency (Bindseil 2019). As the sophistication of the digital financial systems increases, the risks associated with the malfunction of the centralized financial system gradually deepen.

2.2 Cryptocurrencies—Pros and Cons

The year 2008 is not only known for the Great Recession; it is the year when a breaking article entitled "Bitcoin: A Peer-to-Peer Electronic Cash System" published under the name of Satoshi Nakamoto appeared (Nakamoto 2008). The work solved the double spending problem of digital money—how to guarantee that digital money is not spent several times—by publishing the ever-growing entire record of all transactions protected by encryption in the form of blockchain. According to Nakamoto, "The network timestamps transactions by hashing them into an ongoing chain of hash-based proof-of-work, forming a record that cannot be changed without redoing the proof-of-work". Incentive to maintain the cryptographic integrity of the blockchain is given by rewarding the creator of the new block with a fixed amount of Bitcoin (mining process) or by using transaction fees. As long as the majority of the computational nodes participates in the blockchain consensus mechanism, the system is robust to attackers possibly attempting to alter the blockchain records (Nakamoto 2008). The distinguishing features of Bitcoin as cryptocurrency are the lack of any regulatory financial institution, fixed supply of coins, and availability of the complete record of all transactions among (in principle anonymous) addresses.

Bitcoin has found its place in the alternative financial system and remains the leading cryptocurrency. As of January 26, 2020, the price of Bitcoin in USD is about 8367 and the market capitalization is 152 billion USD, out of 230 billion for the entire cryptocurrency market with thousands of altcoins (Coinmarketcap 2020). The major reservation against Bitcoin and cryptocurrencies based on the same concept is that they do not have any underlying economic value unlike from fiat currencies. In other words, the lack of trust in the financial system of fiat currencies which are prone to political etc. interventions should not necessarily imply trust in such an ad hoc built digital asset. The highly fluctuating values of Bitcoin prices over time and various cryptocurrency exchanges attest to the fact that Bitcoin intrinsic value is not in the goods and services available in an economy for which it would be a legal tender. To date, the decentralized nature of Bitcoin has yet to gain its broader acceptance among the public. Cryptocurrencies also face the environmental problem of enormous power consumption for the hash calculations that bear a substantial carbon footprint. The criticisms as well as expectations can be summarized in the following two quotations on Bitcoin (CNBC 2018, 2019).

> Bitcoin has no unique value at all.
>
> —Warren Buffet

> There will be one online equivalent to gold, and the one you'd bet on would be the biggest.
>
> —Peter Thiele

This book treats various aspects of cryptocurrency markets, ranging from efficiency, proportion of informed traders, arbitrage opportunities in short- and long-time span, predictability with machine learning algorithms, causality in the cryptocurrency exchange rate time series, etc. We purposefully leave the issue of the social acceptance of Bitcoin and cryptocurrencies in general open to the future.

2.3 *Time Series Analysis of Fiat Currencies and Crypto Assets*

In order to analyze dynamics of asset prices, including digital assets, the available theoretical models typically rely either on statistics (econometric algorithms, cf. (Martin et al. 2012), such as the GARCH model of volatility (Bollerslev 1986)) or more recently booming methods of machine learning in data science. These algorithms, such as the Elman Recurrent Neural Network in the past (Elman 1990), or more recently Long Short-Term Memory Network (LSTM) (Hochreiter and Schmidhuber 1997) and its derivatives are motivated from the developments in the field of Natural Language Processing (cf. Sagheer and Kotb 2019). Predictions beyond the level of random coin tossing can then be used in algorithmic trading, for instance for dynamic portfolio management. A recent hot topic, focused on the spatial structure of the underlying economic subjects, such as banks or firms, is network science (cf. Barabási 2016), which builds on the network structure models and algorithms for sets of objects connected by edges. Such a formalism allows to study the propagation of initial network shocks, or estimate parametric features distinguishing the behavior of various groups in the economic models. The next section provides examples of such approaches in the following chapters of this book.

3 Financial Technologies and Cryptocurrency Markets

In the first part of the book, there are four chapters related to general financial topics, such as portfolio selection, asset price prediction, and network structure of default risk among financial institutions.

Jun Sakazaki and Naoki Makimoto in Chapter "Financial Contagion Through Asset Price and Interbank Networks" study propagation of shocks caused for instance by regulatory effects through different topologies of network structures. They vary the composition of banks' portfolio and observe its effects upon outbreaks and spreads of a financial contagion.

Adeola Oyenubi in Chapter "Optimal Portfolios on Mean-Diversification Efficient Frontiers" uses genetic algorithm, an evolutionary computing method, for obtaining mean-variance efficient frontiers and portfolios that optimize the trade-off between returns and risk measures.

Ken Matsumoto and Naoki Makimoto in Chapter "Time Series Prediction with LSTM Networks and Its Application to Equity Investment" use the Long and Short-Term Memory algorithm from among the recent recurrent neural network methods to conduct an empirical stock return prediction study for TOPIX Core 30 with applications to portfolio selection problem.

Masato Hisakado and Takuya Kaneko in Chapter "A Response Function of Merton Model and Kinetic Ising Model" consider the contagious defaults of banks created by a network structure based on lending and borrowing relations. In their mathematical description built on a model originating from physics they show that the thermodynamic notion of temperature can be attributed to asset volatility.

The second part of the book contains eight chapters related to crypto-assets, and Bitcoin in particular, focusing on features ranging from security and major player identification through the analysis of crypto-asset forks, cointegration models of crypto-currency time series, triangular arbitrage, estimates of proportion of informed traders, and other advanced topics.

Naoyuki Iwashita in Chapter "Bitcoin's Deviations from Satoshi's World" examines the reasons why Bitcoin has not yet become a major means of payment, focusing on the security issues, and making the point of the difficulty that that ordinary investors cannot manage their secret keys in a secure way.

Yoshi Fujiwara and Rubaiyat Islam in Chapter "Hodge Decomposition of Bitcoin Money Flow" study how money flows among users of Bitcoin based on an algorithm that partially identifies anonymous users from addresses, and construct a dynamic directed graph of Bitcoin transaction flow. Graph theory then serves them as a tool understand the dynamics on the complex network of Bitcoin transactions, including some indirect consequences on Bitcoin price in the exchange markets.

Takeshi Yoshihara et al. in Chapter "Time Series Analysis of Relationships Among Crypto-asset Exchange Rates" investigate market efficiency (Fama 1970, 1991) in crypto-asset exchange rates through the application of several kinds of unit root tests and the Johansen procedure. They also elucidate the causal relation between the cryptocurrency exchange rates and the foreign exchange rates.

Zheng Nan and Taisei Kaizoji in Chapter "The Optimal Foreign Exchange Futures Hedge on the Bitcoin Exchange Rate: An Application to the U.S. Dollar and the Euro" propose the use of FX futures to hedge the risk of currency exchanges based on the bitcoin exchange rate. The time-dependent optimal hedge ratio for the resulting portfolio is calculated from the conditional covariance matrix of the two returns.

Lukáš Pichl et al. in Chapter "Time Series Analysis of Ether Cryptocurrency Prices: Efficiency, Predictability, and Arbitrage on Exchange Rates" compute the Hurst exponent for Ether(eum) related time series, explore the predictability margin of daily returns with Support Vector Machine based techniques, and compute the triangular arbitrage characteristics between Ether and fiat currency pairs selected from among USD, JPY, GBP, EUR, CNY, and CAD.

Ping Chen Tsai and Shou Huang Dai in Chapter "Estimating the Proportion of Informed Traders in BTC-USD Market Using Spread and Range" identify a proxy—a spread-to-range ratio—for the unobserved proportion of informed traders in a market based on the classic Glosten-Milgrom model. They show that for a USD-BTC market the proportion of the informed traders can be as high as 6%.

Vasily Derbentsev et al. in Chapter "Forecasting of Cryptocurrencies Prices Using Machine Learning" use the machine learning algorithms of Binary Auto Regressive Trees, Random Forests, and Artificial Neural Network for short-term prediction of three crypto-assets with major capitalization.

Walter Bazán-Palomino in Chapter "Bitcoin and Its Offspring: A Volatility Risk Approach" examines the risk-return relationship between the return on Bitcoin and the returns on its forks (Litecoin, Bitcoin Cash, Bitcoin Gold, Bitcoin Diamond, and Bitcoin Private). He provides the evidence that there is a transmission of the risk from Bitcoin forks to Bitcoin.

4 Summary and Outlook

In this book, we have collected a number of articles from finance with a focus on the recently trending topic of crypto-currencies or crypto-assets. We believe these are of broad general readership interest. The future will show whether crypto-assets are a viable option to fiat currencies, or rather an obscure portfolio diversification complement, or even a dead-end outcry of blockchain technology. Nevertheless, given the excitement, tensions and controversies that recently accompanied the announcement of planned introduction of the Facebook's Libra digital currency or the project of digital yuan in China, we feel the time is ripe for further substantial breakthrough brought by information technology-based innovations in finance.

References

Barabási, A.-L. (2016). *Network science*. Cambridge: Cambridge University Press.

Bindseil, U. (2019). Central bank digital currency: Financial system implications and control. *International Journal of Political Economy, 48*(4), 303–335.

Bollerslev, T. (1986). Generalized autoregressive conditional heteroskedasticity. *Journal of Econometrics, 31*(3), 307–327.

CNBC. (2018, 2019). https://www.cnbc.com/video/2019/02/25/warren-buffett-bitcoin-has-no-unique-value-at-all.html; https://www.cnbc.com/2018/03/15/peter-thiel-is-betting-on-bitcoin-to-be-the-online-equivalent-to-gold.html.

Coinmarketcap. (2020). *Cryptocurrency Market Capitalizations*. https://coinmarketcap.com/. Accessed January 26, 2020.

Desai, P. (2005). Russian retrospectives on reforms from Yeltsin to Putin. *The Journal of Economic Perspectives, 19*(1), 87–106.

Elman, J. L. (1990). Finding structure in time. *Cognitive Science, 14*(2), 179–211.

Fama, E. F. (1970). Efficient capital markets: A review of theory and empirical work. *The Journal of Finance, 25*, 383–417.

Fama, E. F. (1991). Efficient capital markets: II. *The Journal of Finance, 46*, 1575–1617.

Farmer, R. E. A. (2012). The stock market crash of 2008 caused the Great Recession: Theory and evidence. *Journal of Economic Dynamics and Control, 36*(5), 693–707.

Hochreiter, S., & Schmidhuber, J. A. (1997). Long short-term memory. *Neural Computation, 9*(8), 1735–1780.

Ifrah, G. (2000). *The universal history of numbers: From prehistory to the invention of computer*. New York: Wiley.

Kerr, G. (2013). *A short history of China: From ancient dynasties to economic powerhouse*. Pocket Essentials.

Krishna, R. V., & Leukhina, O. (2019). On the benefits of currency reform. *Journal of Economic Dynamics and Control, 102*, 81–95.

Martin, V., Hurn, S., & Harris, D. (2012). *Econometric modelling with time series; specification, estimation, and testing*. Cambridge: Cambridge University Press.

Nakamoto, S. (2008). *Bitcoin: A Peer-to-Peer Electronic Cash System*. https://bitcoin.org/bitcoin.pdf.

Pavlek, B., Winters, J., & Morin, O. (2019). Ancient coin designs encoded increasing amounts of economic information over centuries. *Journal of Anthropological Archaeology, 56*, 101103.

Petka. (2013). Information Monthly for Residents of Prague District 5, No 11/2013, p. 18. www.ipetka.cz (in Czech).

Pickering, J. (1844). The history of paper money in China. *Journal of the American Oriental Society, 1*(2), 136–142.

Sagheer, A., & Kotb, M. (2019). Unsupervised pre-training of a deep LSTM-based stacked autoencoder for multivariate time series forecasting problems. *Scientific Reports, 9*, 19038.

Ule, O. (1965). Pilsen: The unknown revolt. *Problems of Communism*, January–February issue.

von Klaproth, H. J. (1823). *Origin of paper-money* (tr. from the Fr.). Treuttel and Wurtz.

Weatherford, J. (1998). *The history of money*. New York: Three Rivers Press.
Zoeller, C. J. P., & Bandelj, N. (2019). *Crisis as opportunity: Nixon's announcement to close the gold windows* (Vol. 5, pp. 1–14). Socius: Sociological Research for a Dynamic World.

Financial Contagion through Asset Price and Interbank Networks

Jun Sakazaki and Naoki Makimoto

Abstract In a financial network where mark-to-market accounting rules apply, the sale of assets enforced by behavioral constraints such as minimum capital requirements can induce an amplification effect of additional asset sales that further depresses the market price. This paper explores these contagious processes through simulation exercises under some different sets of network structures. We introduce a complete graph, clusters and core periphery while varying the composition of banks' portfolios and observing their effects on outbreaks and the spread of a financial contagion. This paper also investigates ex ante conditions that could prevent a contagion and examines some ex post measures that could restrain the propagation of a contagion. Securing a certain level of liquidity in a financial system that includes large-scale banks can be an effective ex ante regulatory measure. Additionally, certain ex post operations, such as a price-supporting purchase of risky assets and/or a capital injection into a bank, could be effective countermeasures to prevent the contagion from spreading under some limited conditions.

Keywords Behavioral constraints of financial institutions · Mark-to mark accounting rules · Deleverage · Liquidity · Interbank network structure

1 Introduction

The 2007 to 2008 financial crisis (the crisis) exerted a negative influence on the global economy through far-reaching propagation of investment losses. Funds that had circulated globally during the time of credit expansion in the early 2000s drastically counterrotated with the eruption of the crisis and elicited the propagation of negative externalities throughout the world. In describing the crisis, Brunnermeier

J. Sakazaki (✉)
2-24-24, Higashi-cho, Koganeii, Tokyo, Japan
e-mail: sakazaki@joy.ocn.ne.jp

N. Makimoto
University of Tsukuba, 3-29-1 Otsuka, Bunkyo, Tokyo, Japan
e-mail: makimoto@gssm.gsbs.tsukuba.ac.jp

L. Pichl et al. (eds.), *Advanced Studies of Financial Technologies and Cryptocurrency Markets*, https://doi.org/10.1007/978-981-15-4498-9_2

and Pedersen (2009) introduce a model that links an asset's market liquidity (i.e., the ease with which it is traded) and funding liquidity (i.e., the ease with which traders can obtain funding). Brunnermeier (2009) notes that the mechanisms that explain why liquidity can suddenly evaporate function through the interaction between market liquidity and funding liquidity.

To understand financial contagion through asset price, Adrian and Shin (2009) explain that in a financial system where balance sheets are continuously marked to market, asset price changes immediately appear as changes in net worth. These changes elicit responses from financial intermediaries who adjust the size of their balance sheets particularly in cases where the financial intermediaries are subject to behavioral constraints such as minimum capital requirements. In terms of the influence of the accounting system on the contagion, Eboli (2010) notes that for any network and any shock, the flow of losses generated with the mark-to-market rule is greater than the losses generated by accounting at historical cost. The author indicates that a financial network is more exposed to default contagion, both in terms of scope and threshold of contagion, under the marking-to-market accounting regime than with the historical cost regime.

Regarding contagion through network structure, Watts (2002) notes that the threshold rules of global cascades have local dependencies that is, the effect that a single infected neighbor will have on a given node depends critically on the state of the node's other neighbors, and the threshold is the corresponding fraction of the neighborhood. Additionally, the cascade conditions are induced from the degrees of the vulnerable vertices. Eisenberg and Noe (2001) indicate that one of the most pervasive aspects of the contemporary financial environment is the rich network of interconnections among firms, where the value of firms is dependent on the payoffs they receive from their claims on other firms. The author describes this feature of financial systems as cyclical interdependencies and shows, via a fixed-point argument, that there always exists a "clearing payment vector" that clears the obligations in the clearing system under mild regularity conditions.

Acemoglu et al. (2015) introduce an economy composed of financial institutions that lasts for three periods and examine the extent of financial contagion as a function of the interbank liability structure. The authors investigate the robustness of financial networks and provide the results including the fact that as the magnitude or the number of negative shocks crosses certain thresholds, the types of financial networks that are fragile against contagions change drastically. Fricke and Lux (2014) consider an interbank network as directed and valued linkage among banks. Using overnight interbank transaction data for the Italian interbank market from January 1999 to December 2010, the authors investigate the market situation before and after the global financial crisis and show that the core-periphery structure may well be a new "stylized fact" of modern interbank networks. Elliott et al. (2014) consider that financial contagions can propagate through cross-holdings of shares, debt, or other liabilities and investigate the influence by introducing the notion of integration (mutual holdings of equities) and diversification (the extent of the holding). The authors also consider contagion through asset holdings and price by simulation.

Cifuentes et al. (2005) extend Eisenberg and Noe (2001) and combine the discussions on contagion through interbank networks and asset prices as described above. Considering the effectual validity of the model of Cifuentes et al. (2005), this paper extends the model and examines some realistic factors that might contribute either to the occurrence or the arrest of contagion. First, we explore contagious processes under some different sets of network structures such as a complete graph, clusters, and a core periphery through simulation exercises while attempting to quantify the implication of the contagion and to examine some factors that might assume significant importance concerning a contagion outbreak. Second, we investigate some countermeasures to prevent a contagion from spreading, such as a price-supporting purchase of risky assets in the market and a capital injection to a bank. We examine the validity of these measures quantitatively. The results show that the form of outbreaks and contagion processes differ depending on the network structure, and it is suggested that the location and linkages of large-scaled nodes within the network assume some importance concerning the occurrence of contagion. Some ex ante regulatory measures, such as securing a certain level of liquidity in a financial system including the asset holdings of large-scale banks, can be effective in preventing contagion. Similarly, ex post measures such as a price-supporting purchase of risky assets in the market and capital injection to a bank can be effective ex post countermeasures to containing contagion.

This paper is organized as follows. Section 2 illustrates the model. Section 3 describes the algorithm and simulation. In Sect. 4, we analyze the effect that interbank networks have on financial contagion. Section 5 discusses the effectiveness of countermeasures for contagion. Finally, Sect. 6 concludes the paper.

2 Model

Our model is based on that of Cifuentes et al. (2005) with some modifications. We assume N linked financial intermediaries (for simplicity, here considered as banks) and their balance sheets. Each bank has a balance sheet described in Table 1 and forms an interbank network with mutual financial relationships each other (here considered as an $N \times N$ debts and credits matrix). On the liability side, bank i has deposit liability denoted by d_i. The interbank liability of bank i to bank j is denoted by L_{ij} with $L_{ii} = 0$. The total liability of bank i is then $\overline{x}_i = \sum_{j=1}^{N} L_{ij}$.

On the asset side, bank i's endowment of risky assets is given by e_i. The price p of the risky asset is determined in equilibrium as described in Sect. 2.2. Bank i also has liquid asset holdings given by c_i. Liquid assets have a constant price of 1. Let $\pi_{ij} = L_{ij}/\overline{x}_i$. Interbank claims are of equal seniority, so that if the market value falls short of the notional liability, the bank's payments are proportional to the notional liability. Then, the payment by j to i is given by $x_j \pi_{ji}$ where x_j is the market value of bank j's interbank liabilities. This can be different from the notional value because the debtor may be unable to repay these liabilities in full. Accordingly, the total payment received by bank i from all other banks is $\sum_{j=1}^{N} x_j \pi_{ji}$.

In the interbank network, the ability to clear the debt of the respective banks is interdependently determined according to the simultaneous equation below.

$$x_i = \min\left\{\overline{x}_i + d_i,\ pe_i + c_i + \sum_{j=1}^{N} x_j \pi_{ji}\right\},\quad i = 1, \ldots, N. \tag{1}$$

As shown in Eisenberg and Noe (2001), a unique clearing vector $\mathbf{x}$ is determined as fixed point of (1) under suitable conditions on the liability matrix $\mathbf{L} = (L_{ij})$.

2.1 Minimum Capital Requirements

Assets held by banks attract a regulatory minimum capital ratio, which stipulates that the ratio of the bank's equity value to the mark-to-market value of its assets must be above a pre-specified ratio r^*. This constraint is given by

$$\frac{pe_i + c_i + A_i + \sum_{j=1}^{N} x_j \pi_{ji} - (x_i + d_i)}{pe_i + c_i + \sum_{j=1}^{N} x_j \pi_{ji}} \geq r^* \tag{2}$$

where A_i denotes the units of cash received as the proceeds of both risky and liquid assets sales. In Cifuentes et al. (2005), it is assumed that the assets are sold for cash, and cash does not constitute a risky asset under the minimum capital requirements. In the simulation process, cash is consecutively accumulated in balance sheets as the proceeds of the asset sales and thus affects the respective banks' capital adequacy status. In this paper, we, therefore, explicitly incorporate the process of cash accumulation in the algorithm. When a bank finds itself violating this constraint, it must sell some of its assets to reduce the size of its balance sheet. That is, bank i sells s_i units of risky assets and t_i units of liquid assets to satisfy

$$\frac{pe_i + c_i + A_i + \sum_{j=1}^{N} x_j \pi_{ji} - (x_i + d_i)}{p(e_i - s_i) + (c_i - t_i) + \sum_{j=1}^{N} x_j \pi_{ji}} \geq r^*. \tag{3}$$

Table 1 Balance sheet

e_i	d_i
c_i	$\bar{x}_i$
$\sum_{j=1}^{N} x_j \pi_{ji}$	
	Net worth

As in Cifuentes et al. (2005), we assume that bank i first sells liquid assets, and in the case where bank i cannot achieve r^* with the sale of liquid assets only, it is forced to additionally sell risky assets in the amount required to satisfy (3).

2.2 *Equilibrium Price*

By rearranging the minimum capital requirements (2) together with the condition that $s_i > 0$ only if $t_i = c_i$, the sale s_i can be written as a function of p:

$$s_i(p) = \min\left\{ e_i, \frac{x_i + d_i - (1 - r^*)\left(\sum_{j=1}^{N} x_j \pi_{ji} + p e_i\right) - c_i - A_i}{r^* p} \right\}. \tag{4}$$

Hence, $s(p) = \sum_{i=1}^{N} s_i(p)$ is the aggregate sale of the risky assets given price p. To satisfy the minimum capital requirements, bank i sells the risky assets at the amount of $s_i(p) \times p$ at the price level p, thus, $s_i(p)$ is a decreasing function of p. Accordingly, the aggregate supply function $s(p)$ is also decreasing in p.

The inverse demand curve for the risky asset is assumed to be of exponential form

$$p = d^{-1}\left(\sum_{i=1}^{N} s_i\right) = e^{-\alpha\left(D + \sum_{i=1}^{N} s_i\right)} \tag{5}$$

where $\alpha > 0$ is a positive constant and D is the accumulated number of risky assets sold after the initial shock. We impose the condition whereby when the price of the risky asset is its highest price no bank is required to sell its risky assets. Accordingly, we have $s(1) = d(1) = 0$ and there is at least one equilibrium price at $p = 1$. This is the price where no exogenous shock exists. If banks are forced to sell risky assets, the amount of units to sell exceeds the demand so that the price is decreased from 1 and the new equilibrium price $p^* < 1$ is formed at the intersection $s(p^*) = d(p^*)$. Since the two curves are both convex, we must ascertain whether the equilibrium price is determined uniquely or not in the following simulation experiments. Let $\underline{p} = d(\sum_{i=1}^{N} e_i)$ be the floor price of the risky asset when all of the risky assets are sold in the market. In our experiments, we choose α to satisfy the prescribed $\underline{p}$.

2.3 *Contraction of an Interbank Debts and Credits Matrix*

In the case where bank i becomes insolvent, the bank is forced to exit from the interbank network. As a result, the interbank assets are assumed to be redirected or redistributed at face value proportionally among the holders of the bank's liabilities in the model. This process is materialized as a stepwise contraction process of the interbank debts and credits matrix **L**.

3 Simulation

Given the level of the minimum capital ratio r^*, the algorithm checks the capital adequacy ratio of each bank; that is, whether it satisfies condition (2) or not. Failure to comply with this requirement triggers a resizing of the bank's balance sheet and possibly the liquidation of the bank. If the bank violates the minimum capital requirements and needs to liquidate assets, depending upon the size of its equity capital, the bank can resize its balance sheet by scaling down the size of its assets to a new level consistent with the actual level of equity capital available. Alternatively, if this is not possible, the bank is liquidated. Accordingly, the bank will assume one of the following four statuses depending upon its condition and whether it satisfies the minimum capital requirements or falls insolvent.

- status $= 0$: insolvent (minimum capital requirements cannot be satisfied or the bank already has excessive liability).
- status $= 1$: minimum capital requirements are satisfied if all the liquid assets and certain units of risky assets are sold.
- status $= 2$: minimum capital requirements are satisfied if certain units of liquid assets are sold.
- status $= 3$: minimum capital requirements are satisfied without any action taken.

After a bank experiences an initial shock, the statuses of all the banks are judged according to the flow below.

1. Initial shock.
2. Judgment of the status (status $= 0/1/2/3$).
3. Loop until all the banks are $s = 0$ or all the surviving banks are status $= 3$:

    (1) if any status $= 0$ exists (liquidation routine)

    - All holdings of liquid and risky assets are sold.
    - Interbank debts and assets are divided proportionally and redistributed, and the interbank liability network is contracted.
    - The equilibrium price is calculated.
    - Mark-to-market the surviving banks' asset holdings.

    else if any status $= 1$ exists (resizing routine 1)

    - All liquid asset holdings and the amount of risky assets necessary to achieve minimum capital requirements are sold.
    - The equilibrium price is calculated.
    - Mark to market the surviving banks' asset holdings.

    else if any status $= 2$ exists (resizing routine 2)

- The amount of liquid assets necessary to achieve minimum capital requirements are sold.

end

(2) Judgment of status

In the case where the numbers of the banks with status $= 0$ is greater than one, the liquidation routine is applied to only one bank per loop. Hereinafter, one loop is called one round. In the simulation, we set the liquidity ratio and the initial shock. Each represents a market condition where the contagion breaks out and spreads along with the shock that triggered the contagion. The liquidity ratio (hereinafter, LR) is $c/(c+e)$ of each bank's risk (e) and liquid (c) asset holdings. Thus, $c/(c+e)$ of the aggregated amount represents the LR of the whole financial system in this model. The initial shock (hereinafter, IS) is an idiosyncratic loss on the liquid asset holdings (c) of a bank.[1] The size of IS is hereinafter represented as a percentage of the initially shocked bank's equity capital. In the simulation, we vary the level of LR gradually and observe the occurrence of the contagion at the respective LR level. The IS level is either varied or fixed depending on the purpose of the experiments, but in most of the cases unless indicated otherwise, we fix IS as 100% to measure the influence of LR. In the experiments in Sects. 4 and 5, we set the minimum capital requirement $r^* = 7\%$. Additionally, the initial price of risky asset is 1, and the floor price of the risky asset is set at $\underline{p} = 0.6$.

4 Network Structure and Contagion

While varying the composition of banks' portfolios, the effects on the outbreaks and the spread of the financial contagion are observed. The processes and consequences of the contagion are measured by the number of insolvent banks, equilibrium price, and the capital adequacy ratios of the respective banks. Cifuentes et al. (2005) analyzed the case where all banks are homogeneous, that is, they all have identical balance sheets at the outset, and an interbank network constitutes a complete graph. To investigate the effect of the difference in network structures on risk contagion, we examine other types of networks such as clusters and a core periphery with differently sized nodes as described in Fig. 1. A complete graph expresses the base case where every bank has a direct financial relationship with each other. Clusters are composed of two large banks and several smaller banks in the respective clusters while only the two large banks constitute a sole direct linkage between the clusters. A core-periphery structure has been adopted from the models of Imakubo (2009) and Imakubo and Soejima (2010) that describes real international finance networks

[1]The liquid assets here can possibly be considered a money market fund (MMF). MMFs are basically traded at their notional values, but in cases where the prices of the investment objects, for example, bonds values decrease, the value of the MMF can go under per. Such a case occurred in Japan in 2001 when the price of the bond issued by ENRON Corporation sharply declined.

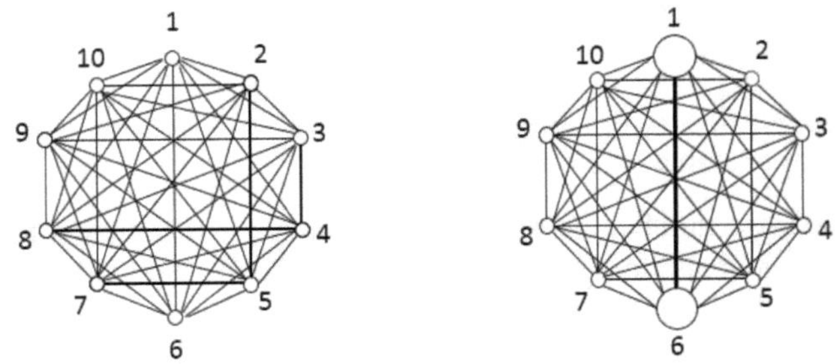

Identical (CG-I) Large and Small (CG-LS)

(a) Complete Graphs

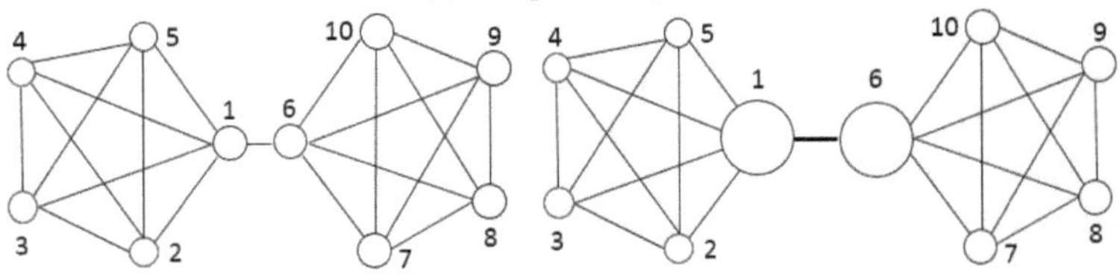

Identical (CL-I) Large and Small (CL-LS)

(b) Clusters

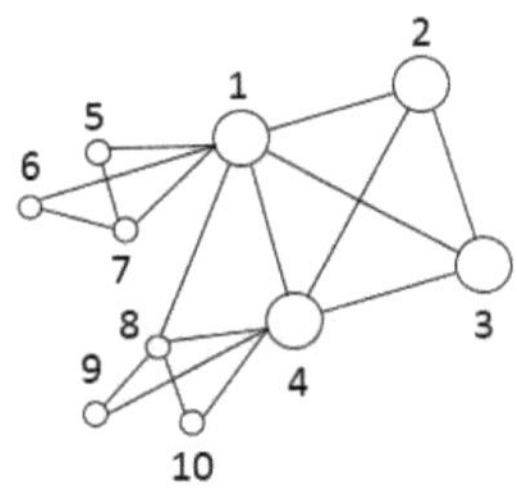

(c) Core periphery (CP)

Fig. 1 Configuration of interbank networks

at the time immediately prior to the 2007 to 2008 crisis. According to the studies, this is the structure that (i) has a two-tier structure of a core and periphery, (ii) nearly all nodes in its core are linked to every other node in what is close to a complete network, (iii) the core serves as a hub for the periphery, and (iv) the periphery has clustering. In this section, we identify each of these networks using an abbreviated notation described in Fig. 1 such as CG-I for complete Graph with identical nodes.

In Fig. 1, each node shows the size of a bank's balance sheet, and each link shows the financial relationships (lending and borrowing) between two banks. To represent the network of the financial relationship, we set up a debts and credits matrix **L** for the simulation. To form the matrix, we set the size of the balance sheet of each bank and the proportion of the difference in size between the large and small banks,

Table 2 Balance sheets of small (left) and large (right) banks

$e_i + c_i$	70	d_i	63	$e_i + c_i$	700	d_i	630
		$\overline{x}_i$	30			$\overline{x}_i$	300
$\sum_{j \neq i} x_j \pi_{ji}$	30	Net worth	7	$\sum_{j \neq i} x_j \pi_{ji}$	300	Net worth	70

if applicable, considering the degrees of respective nodes. This assures the utmost consistency[2] of the matrix with the characteristic structure of the respective networks.

4.1 The Difference Between the Complete Graph and Clusters

The first set of examinations is the comparison between a complete graph and clusters in terms of the LR level where the first full-scale (all banks go insolvent) contagion breaks out. To assure the comparability of the difference, we compare the two types of networks with identical balance sheets among the banks in the respective networks; that is, the comparison between CG-I and CL-I and between CG-LS and CL-LS. In the case of CL-I, because of the difference in the degree of hub nodes and peripheral nodes, we set the balance sheets with the utmost identity. As for the CG-LS and CL-LS, the size of a large bank's balance sheet is 10 times as much as that of a small bank,[3] as shown in Table 2. IS is given for bank number 1 for CG-I in Fig. 1. For the debts and credits matrix **L** of CG-LS, we set the financial relationship between the large nodes as the largest of 236 with each other considering the prominent size of their balance sheets. The second largest is the relationship between the large and small nodes which accounts for eight, and the smallest is between the small banks of which there are two. In the case of CL-LS again, the financial relationship between the large nodes are the largest of 240, and the second largest is 15 between the large and the small, lastly five is between the smallest.

Figure 2 depicts the number of insolvent banks as the LR changes. As LR is reduced by 10 percentage points from 90%, in case of CG-I in the left panel, full-scale contagion breaks out at LR = 30%, and all banks go insolvent in the case of CL-I, a slightly higher LR = 40%. On the other hand, in the case of CG-LS in the right panel of Fig. 2, in case that IS is given on a large node, the first contagion breaks out at an LR as high as 90%, which spreads to all the small nodes except the other large node and spreads to the entire network at LR = 60%. The robustness of

[2]In case of CL-1, the difference in the degree of nodes in a network makes it impracticable to set an entirely identical balance sheet among the corresponding nodes. In this case, we set the balance sheet as identical as utmost.

[3]As the difference in total asset size between the mega financial groups and the regional financial groups in Japan is around this range or larger, we believe the assumption here is not considerably unrealistic.

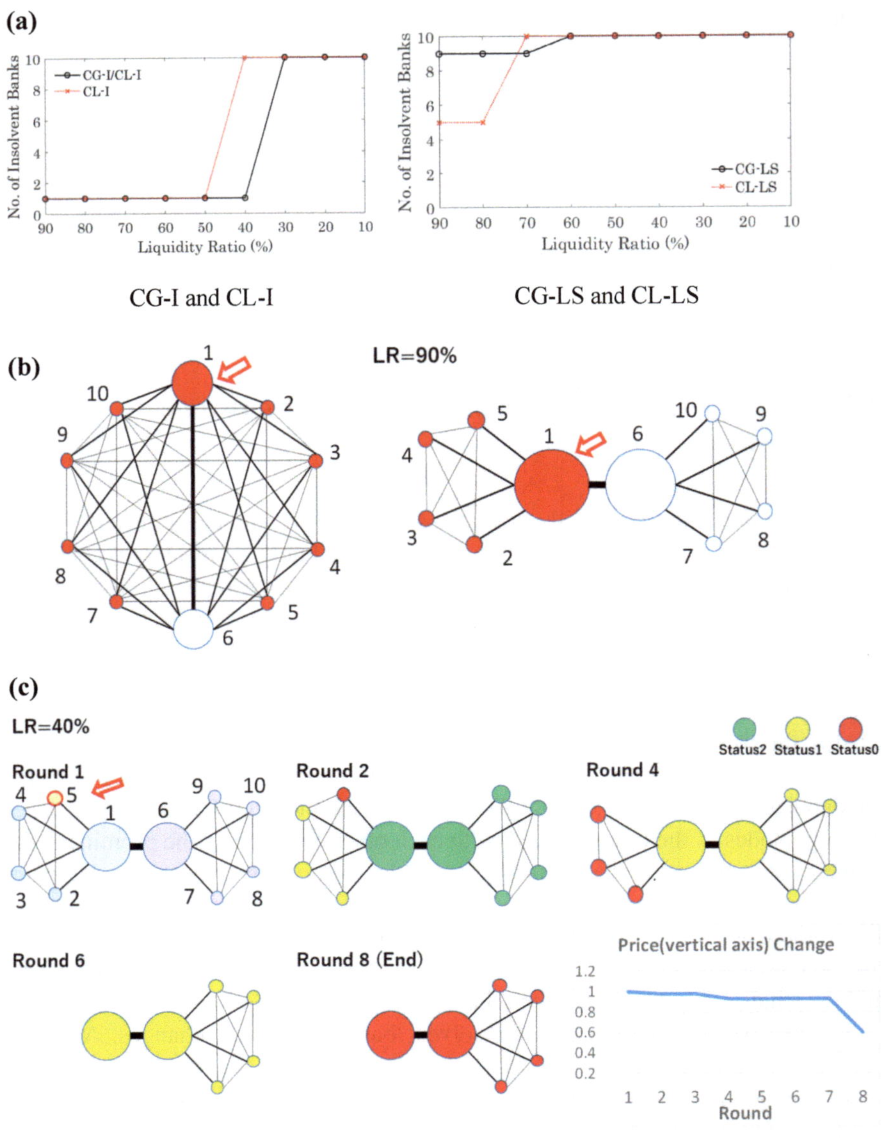

Fig. 2 **a** Number of insolvent banks. **b** Extent of contagion (Initially shocked are shown in (⇐) and insolvent banks are shown in red circles) . **c** Status transitions in each round (initially shocked node is shown by (⇐) and color of each circle represents status of the node) and price change by the sale of risky asset

a complete graph is commonly recognized as indicated by Allen and Gale (2007). From the result, under the coexistence of large and small nodes, such characteristics were not particularly observed. In the case of CL-LS, in case that IS is given on a large node, the first contagion breaks out at LR = 90%, the same level as CG-LS, but the extent of the contagion differs. In case of CL-LS, five nodes go insolvent at LR = 90%, but contagion exists within the same cluster of the initially shocked large node, while CG-LS contagion spreads to all the small banks in the network (Fig. 2b). The result indicates the possibility that the location of a large node could matter for the robustness of the network against contagion.

On the contrary, when IS is given to a small node, the LR level where a full-scale contagion is observed for the first time is much lower. In the case that IS is given to a small node number 5, a full scale contagion breaks out for the first time at LR = 40% with IS = 70% in CL-LS (Fig. 2c). However, it is the sale of risky assets by large nodes that plays a critical role in eventually triggering a full-scale contagion. In Fig. 2c, the sale of risky assets at round 7, of which 83.3% are made by large nodes (number 1 and 6), triggers a sharp decline in price, thus cause the full-scale contaign.

Additionally, the LR level at which the first full-scale contagion breaks out in the two panels in (Fig. 2a) shows a significant difference between the left and right panels. While the left panel shows robust-yet-fragile characteristics in terms of networks' LR with identical nodes, the right panel shows that the LR level of the first full-scaled contagion outbreak is much higher. Considering the prominent difference in the size of the large bank's balance sheet in CG-LS and CL-LS, under the financial system composed of the coexistence of mega-sized and small-sized institutions, the result here suggests that to maintain a certain level of liquidity in the financial system can be an effective ex ante regulatory measure to prevent contagion.

4.2 *Core periphery*

As explained in Sect. 4, core periphery is adopted from the studies of Imakubo (2009) and Imakubo and Soejima (2010), where the authors conjecture the core periphery structure by analyzing the linkages among the respective regions through the distribution of the degree of links and clustering coefficient. Here, we set up the composition and the proportion of balance sheets by calculating the least common multiple of the degrees of respective nodes; that is, 2, 3, 4, 6, and 7 degree. We allocate the least common multiple 42 among the interbank asset (and liability) holdings of the large nodes in the core domain while the units distributed to the nodes in the peripheral domain are mostly proportional. Lastly the fraction is adjusted at node number 8. Table 3 shows the result and we form the matrix **L** accordingly.[4] Here, we implement

[4]Imakubo (2009) defines the degree of nodes as indegree when calculating the clustering coefficient. Here, we calculate the clustering coefficient by defining the sum of indegree and outdegree as the degree of nodes as we assume that all banks are mutually lending and borrowing in the financial system.

Table 3 Balance sheets of core-periphery networks

No. 1–4

$e_i + c_i$	98	d_i	88.2
		$\overline{x}_i$	42
$\sum_{j \neq i} x_j \pi_{ji}$	42	Net worth	9.8

No. 5, 6, 9, 10

$e_i + c_i$	4.67	d_i	4.2
		$\overline{x}_i$	2
$\sum_{j \neq i} x_j \pi_{ji}$	2	Net worth	0.47

No. 7

$e_i + c_i$	7	d_i	6.3
		$\overline{x}_i$	3
$\sum_{j \neq i} x_j \pi_{ji}$	3	Net worth	0.7

No. 8

$e_i + c_i$	11.67	d_i	10.5
		$\overline{x}_i$	5
$\sum_{j \neq i} x_j \pi_{ji}$	5	Net worth	1.17

three different experiments giving IS for three different nodes: numbers 1, 3, and 8. Number 1 is the hub in the core domain while number 3 is the non-hub, and number 8 is a peripheral node.

Figure 3a shows the number of insolvent banks at various levels of LR. As we can see, the LR level of the full-scale contagion outbreak is mostly proportional to the location and size of the initially shocked nodes. Status transitions at each round in the cases that IS is given to number 1 (a hub in the core domain) and to number 3 (a non-hub in the core domain) respectively are shown in Fig. 3b. These status transitions describe the cases of number 1 and number 3 at LR = 60% level in Fig. 3a. For a comparsion, insolvent banks remain denoted in Fig. 3b in red circles even after being forced out of the network. In the case that IS is given to number 1, a full-scale contagion propagates throughout the network at around 9. On the contrary, in the case that IS is given to number 3, no contagion breaks out. Again, this indicates importance of the location of a large node in the network.

4.3 Overall Description of Results

We implemented the same simulation in other types of networks while varying the composition of the banks' portfolios and the size of the initial shock. We measured the liquidity ratio and the size of the initial shock given where the full-scale contagion breaks out. The overall results are given in Table 4.

Table 4 shows that in cases where the large nodes are initially shocked, full-scale contagion (all 10 banks become insolvent) breaks out at comparatively high levels of LR (e.g. complete graph L/S with shock on a large node = 90%, clusters L/S with shock on a large hub node = 70%, core periphery with shock on a large hub node = 60%). On the contrary, in cases where the initial shock is given to small and/or peripheral nodes, the full contagion breaks out only at the lower LR levels of 20% or less (e.g., complete L/S with shock on a small node = 20%, core periphery with

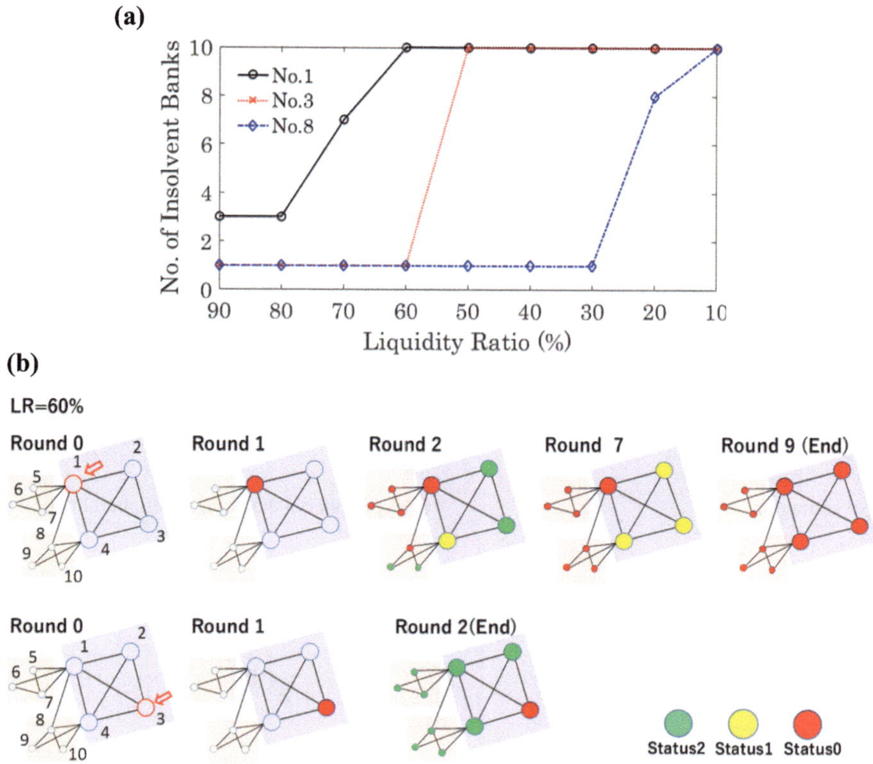

Fig. 3 **a** Number of insolvent banks in the core and periphery network. The initial shock is given for numbers 1, 3, and 8. **b** Status transitions in each round (initially shocked node is shown by (⇐) and color of each circle represents status of the node)

shock on a small hub node = 10%), and no contagion occurs in the case of core periphery shocked on a small peripheral node.

Additionally, we compared the extent of contagion at each level of LR while the initial shock is fixed at 100% for the sake of simplicity. In Fig. 4, no full-scale contagion breaks out at all while only three cases (in shadowed boxes) out of 11 show a contagion. Within these three cases, two are partial contagions (the contagion spreads only within the same cluster of initially shocked nodes). In these cases, one large node is initially shocked, and in all the other cases no single contagion is observed regardless of the position or size of a node where the initial shock is given. On the contrary, at the extremely low LR of 10% (Fig. 5), a full-scale contagion appears in as many as 10 cases except for a single case where the initial shock is given on a small peripheral node (shown in a shadowed box).

The figures show that as long as liquidity is maintained abundantly in the financial system, the robustness of the financial networks is assured as no full-scale contagion is observed. Although some partial contagions are observed, the occurrence of those

Table 4 Levels of LR where the first full-scale contagion breaks out

LR (%)	Network structure types
90	Complete L/S (shock on a **large** node)
80	n.a.
70	Cluster L/S (shock on a **large** hub node)
60	Core periphery (shock on a **large** hub node)
50	Core periphery (shock on a **large** non hub node)
40	Cluster L/S (shock on a **small** peripheral node), cluster identical (shock on a peripheral node)
30	Complete identical, cluster identical (shock on a hub node)
20	Complete L/S (shock on a **small** node), core periphery (shock on a **small** hub node)
10	n.a.
No contagion	Core periphery (shock on a peripheral node)

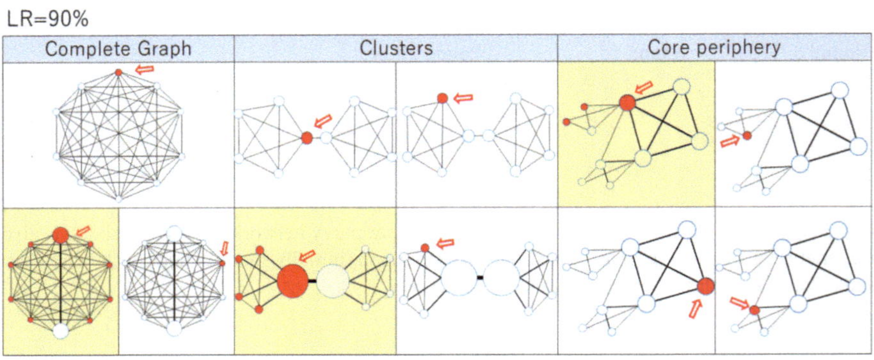

Fig. 4 The arrows show the nodes where the initial shocks were given, and the shadowed circles show the nodes that became insolvent

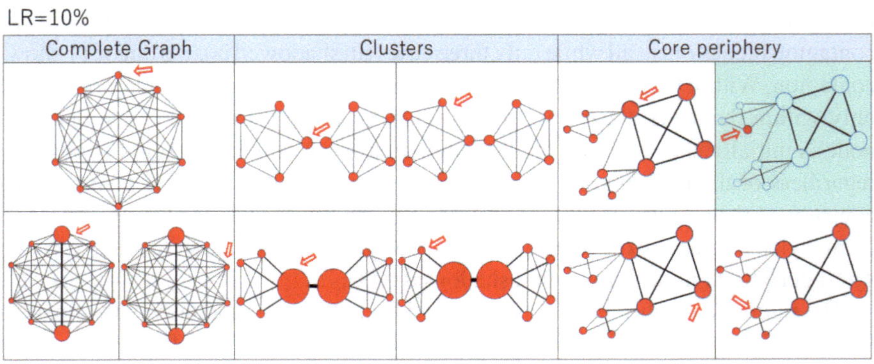

Fig. 5 Same as the above

contagions are limited to cases where a fatal shock (in this case, 100% of net worth) is given to a large node, particularly a hub (Fig. 4).

On the other hand, in a system with extremely limited liquidity, the difference in network structures including the position and size of nodes has less relevance to the extent of a contagion as full-scale contagion propagates in almost all cases (Fig. 5).

One possible interpretation for the phenomenon is that the effect of an asset price decrease caused by the forced sales by banks in the system described in Sects. 2 and 3 surpasses the potential robustness embedded in a network structure under the condition of limited liquidity in the system, and this construction is intuitively understandable. To this extent, our observation suggests that a major path of a contagion may as well depending on market conditions in this case, particularly in terms of liquidity.

5 Effectiveness of Countermeasures against Contagion

According to the observations in Sect. 4.3, in cases where the liquidity in a market is abundant (=higher LR), the extent of a contagion differs depending on the network structure and the position of a large node matters. In this regard, the observations suggest that to maintain a sufficient level of liquidity in respective banks' balance sheets can be an effective ex ante measure to prevent a full-scale contagion from occuring.

On the other hand, cases where risk asset holdings on banks' balance sheets are large, in other words when the risk appetite of market participants is elevated, the asset price effect promotes the propagation of a contagion regardless of the difference in network structures. A negative spiral effect of forced sale abruptly appears in the financial system as a whole and can lead to a full-scale contagion. What, then, are the possible ex post countermeasures[5] against a contagion that is ready to break out?

We examine the effectiveness of some virtual remedial actions taken by governments or financial supervisory authorities to prevent financial contagion from propagating, such as price-supporting purchase of risky assets in the market and capital injection into a bank.

5.1 *A Price-Supporting Purchase in the Market*

The process of a price-supporting purchase and its effects are described as follows.

[5]Ex post countermeasures here are measures to be taken to prevent the possible occurrence of a contagion in response to the fact that an initial shock has been given to a certain bank.

Table 5 Balance sheets of complete graph (identical nodes, large and small nodes) and core periphery for 20 banks

Large nodes				Small nodes/Identical nodes			
$e_i + c_i$	70	d_i	63	$e_i + c_i$	7	d_i	6.3
		$\overline{x}_i$	30			$\overline{x}_i$	3
$\sum_{j \neq i} x_j \pi_{ji}$	30	Net worth	7	$\sum_{j \neq i} x_j \pi_{ji}$	3	Net worth	0.7

5.1.1 The Process of a Price-Supporting Purchase

Let p_{n-1} be a price of the risky assets at the termination of Round $n-1$. If it is the case that any sales of assets are implemented at Round n, the number of units sold is denoted as f_n and the equilibrium price is $\widehat{p}_n < p_n$. If we set Q_n as the amount of funds disposable for the price-supporting purchase at Round n, the price increase per unit of the risky assets at the full disposal of Q_n for the purchase is calculated by Q_n/f_n. Here, we set the price cap at p_{n-1} as we consider that an unrealistically excessive price increase should be excluded. Thus, the price-supporting purchase is implemented with the upper limit of p_{n-1} at the price level of

$$p_n = \min\left\{p_{n-1},\ \widehat{p}_n + \frac{Q_n}{f_n}\right\}. \tag{6}$$

As the amount of funds necessary for the supporting purchase is denoted by $(p_n - \widehat{p}_n) f_n$, the total amount of funds disposable for the purchase at the following round is depicted as $Q_{n+1} = Q_n - (p_n - \widehat{p}_n) f_n$. The price-supporting purchase is consecutively implemented at every round where the risky assets are sold to the extent that $Q_n = 0$ is achieved, except at the round where no risky assets are sold as the withdrawal procedure of the failed bank from the network is implemented.

We selected three types of networks from Sect. 4; complete graph with identical nodes, complete graph with large and small nodes, and core periphery. Additionally, we extended the size of the networks to 20 nodes to add reality to the simulations to some extent.

For the complete graph with large and small nodes again, each of two large nodes (numbers 1 and 11) has interbank assets (and liabilities) of 30, and all the small nodes have interbank assets of three (Table 5). Each of the two large nodes has a financial relationship of 18.3 with each other and has financial relationships of 0.65 with all the small banks while all the small banks have financial relationships of 0.1 with each other. For the complete graph with identical nodes, we adopted the same balance sheet as the small nodes above and every node has a financial relationship with each other of 19/3. For the core periphery, each node within the same domain (either core or periphery) has a mutually identical balance sheet. Accordingly, the composition of the matrix L is comparatively simple. A large node has interbank assets (and liabilities) of 30, and has a financial relationship of eight with three other large nodes and a relationship of 1.5 with four small nodes within its own cluster. The small nodes have a relationships of 1.5 with one small node and with one large node in its own cluster.

5.1.2 Effects of the Price-Supporting Purchase

To quantify the effectiveness of the price-supporting purchase, we measured the number of insolvent banks at the termination of each simulation. The common initial shock of IS = 100% is given for node number 1 shown in Fig. 6, which is one of the large nodes in the case of the complete graph with large and small nodes and one of the large hub nodes in the case of the core periphery. While setting the amount of disposable funds to purchase the risky assets in three different amounts of 10, 50, and 100, we examined the effects of the purchase implemented at various levels of LR from 90 to 10% and observed the effectiveness of the operation, particularly at lower levels of liquidity. We executed two sets of the simulation to examine the differences in effectiveness in terms of purchase timing. In Case one, the purchase starts from Round 1, and the purchase commences from Round 2 in Case two.

Figure 7 shows that the early commencement of the purchase at Round 1 has remarkable effects in restraining a contagion from spreading to the entire network regardless the network configuration. Without the supporting purchase ($Q_0 = 0$), full-scale contagion breaks out at various levels from LR 90% (complete graph with L/S nodes[6]) to LR 20% (Complete graph with identical nodes). On the contrary, the supporting purchase with the smallest fund $Q_0 = 10$ restrains the contagion from spreading in every case; that is, the sole insolvent bank is only the initially shocked bank in the case of complete graph with identical nodes and core periphery while in the case of complete graph with large and small nodes, the initially shocked banks also escape insolvency. The operation shows its effectiveness even at the lowest level of LR 10%.

On the other hand, the purchase starting in Round 2 has somewhat different consequences. Even with larger amount of purchasing fund of 50 or 100, full-scale contagion cannot be prevented in the cases of complete graph with large and small nodes and core periphery. Figure 8 shows the comparison of the number of insolvent banks in cases with a purchasing fund of $Q_0 = 10, 50$, and 100. In every network structure, the purchase with fund size $Q_0 = 10$ shows results completely identical to $Q_0 = 0$, which means the supporting purchase is ineffectual. $Q_0 = 50$ is valid in the case of complete graph with identical nodes, but in cases of complete graph with large and small nodes and core periphery, even $Q_0 = 100$ is not valid to prevent contagion.

[6]In simulation settings here, the initial shock IS = 100% to the large node in the complete graph with L/S is fatal to the whole system. Thus, the price-supporting purchase is not effective regardless of the LR level or the size of the fund. We adopted the marginal IS level where the supporting purchase is effective; that is, IS = 70% in this case.

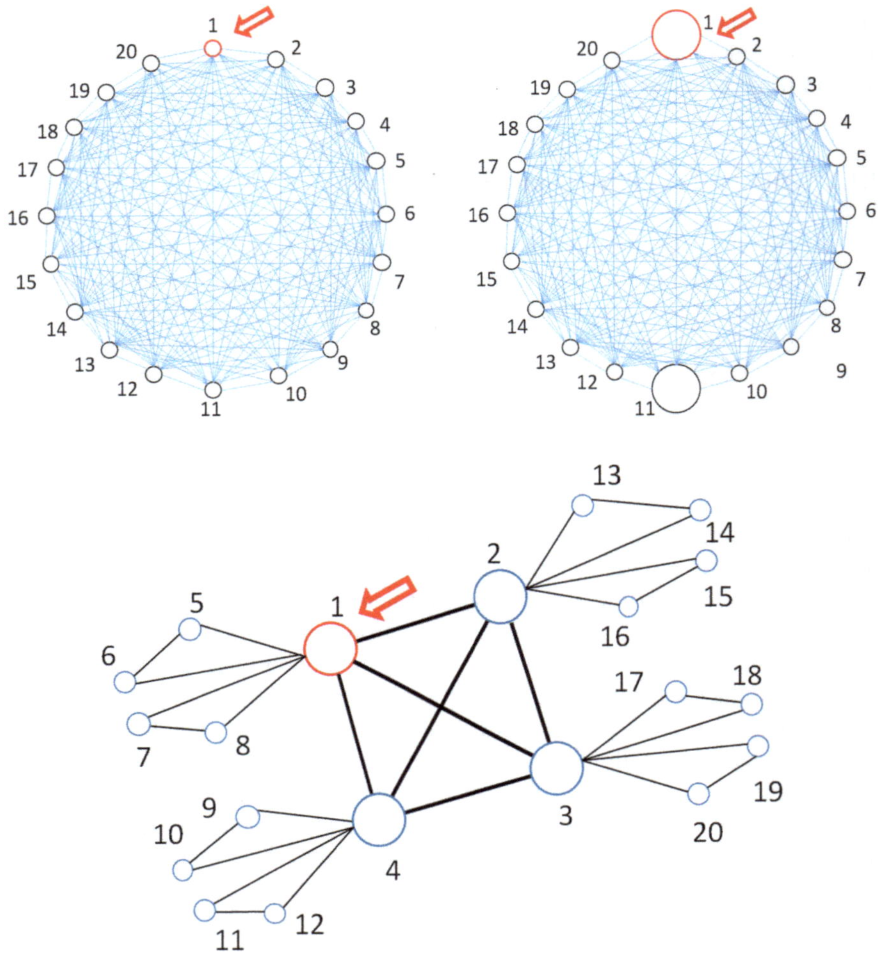

Fig. 6 Configuration of interbank networks (20 banks) and location of intially shocked nodes (⇐)

Figure 9 shows the transition of the price of the risky assets (Upper-left), the number of risky assets sold (upper-right), and the net support amount (lower) at the fixed purchasing fund at $Q_0 = 10$ to examine the effects of purchasing timing and the influence of LR. Here, we examine the case of core periphery with regard to (i) purchase at Round 1 under LR = 10%, (ii) purchase at Round 2 under LR = 60% and (iii) purchase at Round 2 under LR = 50%. The net support amount represents $(p_n - \widehat{p}_n) f_n$ in Sect. 5.1.1. We see that the early purchase at Round 1 is valid at the extremely low LR = 10% (lower panel) as it can support the price level at 1 (upper-left panel) while the purchase at Round 2 is only valid at LR = 60%, (lower panel). At LR = 50%, the supporting purchase is ineffectual (all of 20 banks go insolvent). The results suggest that initiating a supporting purchase in the early stages of a crisis

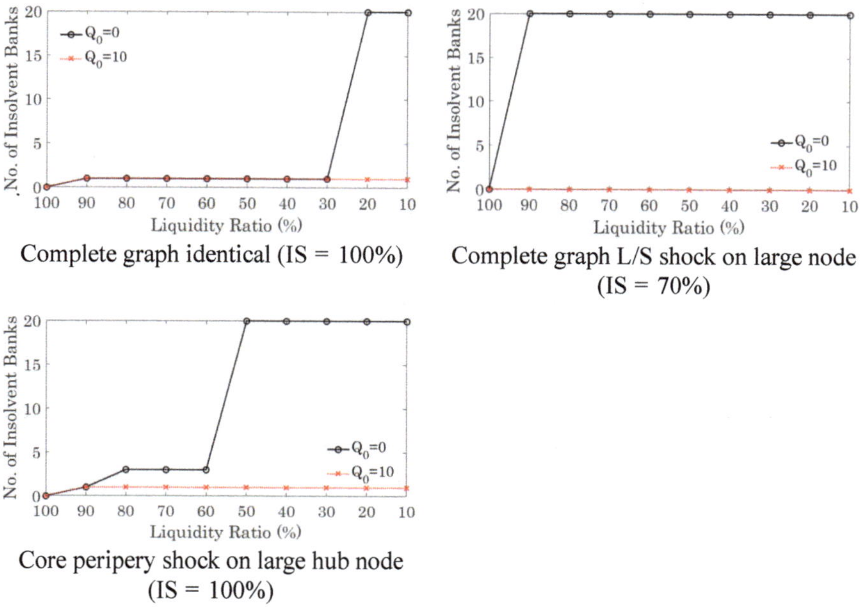

Complete graph identical (IS = 100%)

Complete graph L/S shock on large node (IS = 70%)

Core peripery shock on large hub node (IS = 100%)

Fig. 7 Number of insolvent banks and LR in case of purchase in round 1

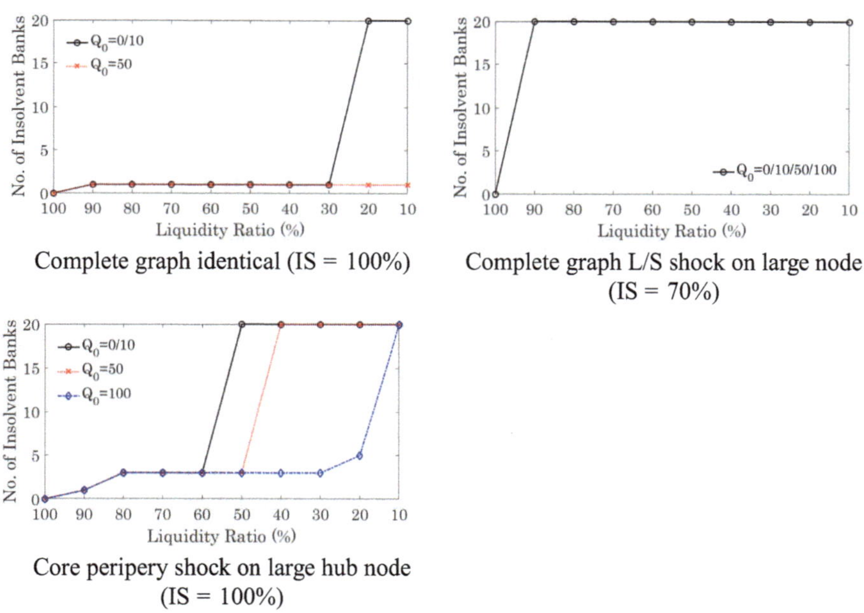

Complete graph identical (IS = 100%)

Complete graph L/S shock on large node (IS = 70%)

Core peripery shock on large hub node (IS = 100%)

Fig. 8 Number of insolvent banks and LR in case of purchase in round 2 (fig DD case 2)

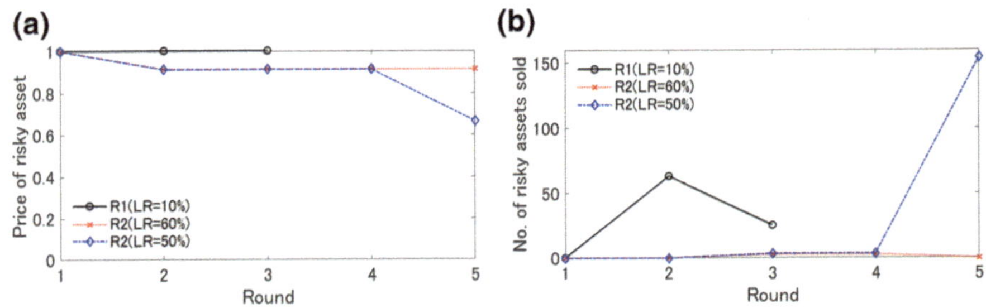

Fig. 9 Price transition, number of units sold, net support and number of insolvent banks in case of $Q_0 = 10$

could considerably improve the effectiveness of the countermeasure in preventing a contagion, and it could be an effective ex post measure to restrain contagion.

5.2 Capital Injection into a Target Bank

We also examined the effectiveness of a capital injection as a countermeasure against a contagion. The same set of networks and parameters are used as in Sect. 5.1. The nodes receiving the initial shock are shown with arrows aside, and the nodes where funds are injected are shown as shadowed circles in Fig. 10. We measure the effectiveness of a capital injection by counting the number of insolvent banks after injecting the funds to enlarge the net worth of the injected node to reach twice, five times, and 10 times its original size. We inject the funds in the cases where the first full-scale contagions are observed in terms of LR at the level of IS $= 100\%$. The cash injected is registered as a liquid asset on the balance sheet of the injected bank as we consider it is unlikely that the capital injected bank would immediately invest the funds in risky assets.

The results for capital injection are distinctive. The successful cases are limited to those where the node where the capital is injected is identical to the node initially shocked. All the other cases of capital injection failed regardless of the size of injection.[7] We can interpret this in the following way; (i) the amount of injected capital is limited (even 10 times the original net worth of a bank is comparatively small compared to the entire asset holdings in the system) and (ii) the limited capital is not used to purchase risky assets (see the balance sheet registration described above); thus, there is no price lifting effect. Figure 11 shows the injection failure cases except for the nodes that were initially shocked. Even in the case that IS is much lower than

[7]In some cases of large capital injections (e.g., five or 10 times as much as the net worth), the injected bank can survive until all the other banks are insolvent. But in the simulation here, we define such cases as insolvent for the injected bank also. If all the other banks are insolvent, the entire financial relationships of the bank have also ceased to exist, and we consider the entire system extinct.

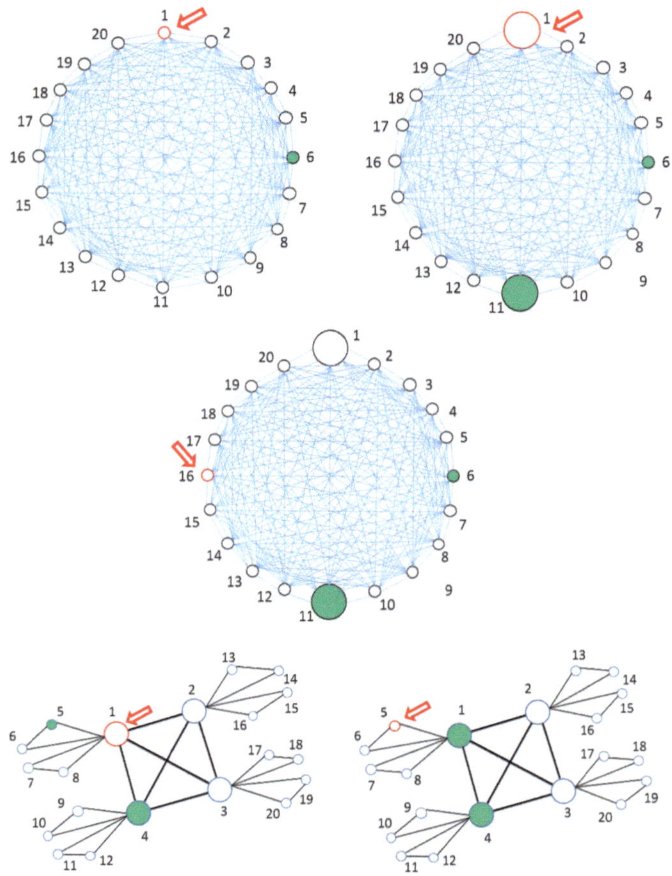

Fig. 10 Location of initially shocked nodes (⇐) and capital-injected nodes (shadow)

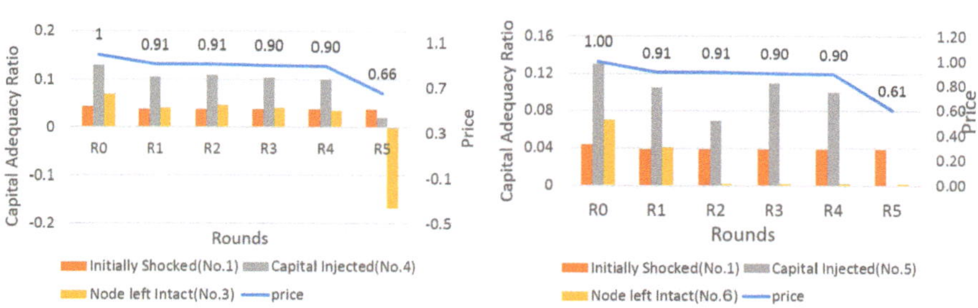

Fig. 11 Capital injection failure cases

100 % (in Fig. 11, IS = 40% at LR = 50% which is the threshold level for a full scale contagion), we see a sharp decrease in the price which leads a substantial decline in the captial adequency ratio of the banks.

Table 6 Capital injection success cases

LR for the first full contagion (%)	Network structure	IS (%)	Injected capital	Percentage of initial net worth
90	Complete L/S (shock on a **large** node)	100	2.591	37.0
50	Core periphery (shock on a **large** node)	100	4.546	65.0
20	Complete identical	100	0.413	59.0
10	Core periphery (shock on a **small** peripheral)	100	0.293	41.9
10	Core periphery (shock on a **small** peripheral)	40	0.014	2.0
10	Complete L/S (shock on a **small** node)	100	0.425	60.6
10	Complete L/S (shock on a **small** node)	60	0.004	0.6
10	Core periphery (shock on a **large** hub node)	100	6.508	93.0

The success cases are shown in Table 6. We see that the full-scale contagion caused by an initial shock to small nodes does break out, if the case occurs under lower LR levels. In those cases, a capital injection into small banks can save the entire system from contagion. The percentage of injected capital to the bank's original net worth is comparatively high, but the absolute amount necessary for the injection is much smaller compared to cases where injection were administered to larger banks under similar liquidity conditions (see LR = 10% in Table 6).[8] Some argue the legitimacy of spending tax money to bail out troubled mega financial institutions at times of financial crisis, but our observation suggests the possibility that even under lower liquidity (the risk appetite is elevated in the case here), a comparatively small capital injection to a small bank could prevent a collapse of the entire financial system. If that is the case, the countermeasure is socially meaningful.

6 Conclusion

The path of a contagion may vary depending on market conditions, particularly in terms of liquidity. When liquidity is abundant in a market, the form of the outbreak

[8] At each LR level, if the injection could be implemented at a smaller IS; that is, before the entire market condition had worsened to the level of an initial shock of IS = 100%, the amount of purchasing fund necessary to prevent a full-scale contagion could be much more limited. Examples are in Table 6 at LR = 10%. Here, at IS = 40% for core periphery shock on a small peripheral and at IS = 60% for complete L/S shock on a small node, the first full-size contagion breaks out at LR = 10%. If the injection at these IS levels is implemented, the amount of fund necessary to prevent a full-scale contagion could be much smaller at 0.0014 and 0.004, compared to the cases of where IS = 100% (the amount of fund necessary is 0.293 and 0.425, respectively). We consider that recognizing the early warning signs is important despite its difficulties.

and the process of the contagion differ depending on the network structure, and the location and linkages of large-scale banks have critical significance. On the other hand, when the risky asset holding in banks' balance sheets are large, in other words the risk appetite of market participants is elevated, the asset price effect could promote the propagation of a contagion, and the difference in network structures including the position and size of nodes has less relevance to the extent of a contagion.

Thus, maintaining a sufficient level of liquidity in financial institutions' balance sheets can be an effective ex ante measure to prevent a contagion. For ex post countermeasures, the results here suggest that to initiate a price-supporting purchase at the early stages of the crisis could be effective in restraining a contagion. When lower liquidity exists in the market, a limited capital injection into a shocked small bank could protect the entire financial system by preventing a full-scale contagion.

Acknowledgements The authors would like to thank the editors and the participants at The 23rd Annual Workshop on Economic Science with Heterogeneous Interacting Agents for helpful suggestions and comments. This research was supported by JSPS KAKENHI Grant Number 16K01234 and 16H01833.

References

Acemoglu, D., Ozdaglar, A., & Tahbaz-Salehi, A. (2015). Systemic risk and stability in financial Networks. *American Economic Review, 105*(2), 564–608.

Allen, F., & Gale, D. (2007). *Understanding financial crises*. Oxford University Press.

Adrian, T., & Shin, H. S. (2009). *Financial intermediaries and monetary economics*. Federal Reserve Bank of New York Staff Report No. 398.

Brunnermeier, M. (2009). Deciphering the liquidity and credit crunch 2007–2008. *Journal of Economic Perspectives, 23*(1), 77–100.

Brunnermeier, M., & Pedersen, L. H. (2009). Market liquidity and funding liquidity. *The Review of Financial Studies, 22*(6), 2201–2238.

Cifuentes, R., Ferrucci, G., & Shin, H. S. (2005). Liquidity Risk and Contagion. *Journal of the European Economic Association, 3*(2/3), 556–566.

Eboli, M. (2010). Direct contagion in financial networks with mark-to-market and historical cost accounting rules. *International Journal of Economics and Finance, 2*(5), 27–34.

Eisenberg, L., & Noe, T. (2001). Systemic risk in financial systems. *Management Science, 47*(2), 236–249.

Elliott, M., Golub, B., & Jackson, M. O. (2014). Financial networks and contagion. *American Economic Review, 104*(10), 3115–3153.

Fricke, D., & Lux, T. (2014). Core-periphery structure in the overnight money market: evidence from the e-MID trading platform. *Computational Economics, 45*, 359–395.

Imakubo, K. (2009). The global financial crisis from the view point of international finance networks. *Bank of Japan Review* (in Japanese).

Imakubo, K., & Soejima, Y. (2010). The transaction network in Japan's interbank money markets. *Monertary and Economic Studies, Bank of Japan*, 107–150.

Watts, D. (2002). A simple model of global cascades on random networks. *Proceedings of the National Academy of Sciences of the United States of America, 99*(9), 5766–5771.

Optimal Portfolios on Mean-Diversification Efficient Frontiers

Adeola Oyenubi

Abstract Recent research has seen increasing use of risk/diversification based approach to portfolio optimization. Under the risk-based approach, returns are ignored, and a diversification or risk measure is optimized in portfolio construction. This approach has been criticized for lacking a clearly defined objective like the trade-off between returns and risk in the Markowitz's Mean-variance set up. Optimizing risk/diversification alone is a single objective optimization approach to portfolio construction. This is in contrast to the usual bi-objective optimization that yields the portfolio that optimizes the trade-off between return and risk. In this paper, we note that portfolios that optimize the trade-off between returns and diversification measures exist (i.e. portfolios that replace variance with other risk measures). In theory, these mean-diversification optimal portfolios should dominate risk-based portfolio on a risk-adjusted basis. Using genetic algorithm, mean-diversification efficient frontiers are drawn for various diversification measures and portfolios that optimize the trade-off between returns and the diversification measures are identified. We argue that these portfolios are better candidates to be compared with the portfolio that is constructed to be mean-variance optimal since they sensitive to returns. Our results suggest that mean-diversification optimal portfolios are useful alternatives in terms of risk-reward trade-off based on their in-sample and out-of-sample performance.

Keywords Diversification · Genetic algorithm · Portfolio optimization

JEL Classification G11 · C61 · C63

A. Oyenubi (✉)
School of Economics and Finance, University of the Witwatersrand, Johannesburg, South Africa
e-mail: adeola.oyenubi@wits.ac.za

L. Pichl et al. (eds.), *Advanced Studies of Financial Technologies and Cryptocurrency Markets*, https://doi.org/10.1007/978-981-15-4498-9_3

1 Introduction

There has been a proliferation of portfolio construction approaches that focus on risk and/or diversification reduction. Lee (2011) refer to these portfolios as risk-based portfolios. One feature of the risk-based approach is that it excludes returns forecast and use only risk forecast in portfolio optimization. However, the performance measure used with the resulting portfolio is often based on risk-adjusted returns (e.g. Sharpe ratio). Furthermore, risk-based portfolios have been shown to outperform portfolios that are constructed to be mean-variance optimal on a risk-adjusted basis. The rationale behind this approach to portfolio construction is that risk-based portfolios provide better diversification than the conventional mean-variance optimal portfolio.

However, Lee (2011) argued that the objective function ex-ante, and the performance evaluation ex-post, of risk-based portfolios, are inconsistent. This is a valid point since one should not expect a portfolio constructed to minimize risk to outperform a portfolio constructed to optimize the trade-off between risk and returns on a risk-adjusted basis. This, however, has been the practice in the literature (see the discussion in Lee (2011)). In terms of portfolios on efficient frontiers, a risk-based portfolio is a solution on the mean-diversification frontier that places zero weight on returns (much like the minimum variance portfolio in the mean-variance space). The implication of this is that the mean-variance optimal portfolio should be compared with mean-diversification optimal portfolios while risk-based portfolios should be compared with the minimum variance portfolio. This correct matching of portfolio construction objective, ex-ante, and portfolio evaluation metric ex-post is more appropriate.

This paper seats at the intersection of Lee (2011) and Tsao and Liu (2006). Lee (2011) criticized risk-based portfolios for lacking a clearly defined objective. On the other hand, Tsao and Liu (2006) show that it is possible to incorporate a risk measure where traditional optimization technique (such as the delta method) is not applicable. The authors use value-at-risk (VaR) as a risk measure in portfolio selection, and recover the mean-VaR frontier using a heuristic approach. The reason for the heuristic approach is that the objective function that trades-off returns for VaR cannot be presented as a quadratic form (Tsao and Liu 2006). We note that this is also the case for most of the diversification measures that are used to construct risk-based portfolios. Based on the approach in Tsao and Liu (2006), one way to answer Lee (2011)'s criticism is to incorporate returns into the optimization of risk-based portfolios. This way, portfolios that optimally trades-off returns for these risk measures will be recovered.

In this study, we consider portfolios that are mean-diversification optimal. We use various diversification measures to draw mean-diversification efficient frontiers, and on these frontiers, optimal portfolios (i.e. portfolios that optimally trades-off returns for gains in diversification) are identified. In theory and by definition, mean-diversification optimal portfolios should dominate the portfolio that optimizes the corresponding diversification measure alone on a return-diversification adjusted basis. We examine the in-sample and out-of-sample performance of risk-based portfolios relative to mean-diversification optimal portfolios. Unsurprisingly, our empirical result follows the theoretical prediction; on a risk-adjusted basis mean-diversification optimal portfolios dominate risk-based portfolios in-sample. However, out-of-sample performance show that any portfolio strategy can out-perform another one irrespective of its objective function.

Our main point is that irrespective of how risk is measured, risk-based portfolios should be compared with other risk-based portfolios. Furthermore, portfolios that trades-off risk for returns should be compared with other portfolios that utilize similar trade-off. Given the position of these portfolios on the efficient frontier, this is the only justifiable and theoretically coherent comparison that can be made. While this does not rule out the possibility of a risk-based portfolio dominating a risk-return optimal portfolio out-of-sample, this should be seen as an exception and note a rule.

We acknowledge up front that the method used in this study (Genetic algorithm) may not be the most ideal method to get precise results. However, the fact that the objective function associated with some of the risk measures considered cannot be presented as a quadratic form and may have discontinuities in the objective function space means that we have to use a method that can handle these characteristics. Using a heuristic method also allow the results to be comparable across risk measures. We have taken steps to mitigate the effect of the heuristic method on our results, and we believe that our main points remains valid despite this limitation.

The rest of the paper is organized as follows. Section 1.1 describes the theoretical framework, Sects. 2 and 3 review the literature on Evolutionary Algorithms and Diversification measures. Section 4 presents our result for the mean-variance frontier while Sect. 5 present results for the mean-diversification frontiers. In Sects. 6 and 7 we compare the performance of various portfolios using Treynor and Information ratio measures (in-sample). We also compare the performance of the portfolios (out-of-sample). Section 8 concludes.

1.1 Bi-objective Optimization and the Efficient Frontier

Scherer (2011) noted that minimization of risk on its own is meaningless; risk needs to be traded-off against returns. Even though it is unlikely, one may choose to optimize a single objective (risk/diversification in this case) rather than consider a bi-objective optimization given a particular set of preferences. It is, however, problematic (at least from a theoretical standpoint) to expect a risk-based portfolio to outperform the return-risk optimal portfolio on a risk-adjusted basis.

In the mean-variance (MV) framework, one can decide how much risk is to be traded-off for returns. Candidate portfolios like the minimum variance portfolio (MVP) and the mean-variance optimal portfolio (MVO) are members of the efficient frontier that satisfy some condition that may be of interest to an investor. Instead of minimizing variance, other risk-based approaches attempt to optimize some diversification measure directly. In this case, the diversification measure is the objective function to be optimized. When a risk-based approach is used in portfolio optimization, the result is the portfolio that optimizes that objective function as against an entire set of solutions referred to as the efficiency frontier in a bi-objective optimization problem.

For example, the Most Diversified Portfolio (MDP) (Choueifaty and Coignard 2008) optimizes diversification as measured by Diversification Ratio (DR), Maximum Diversification index (MDI) maximizes the Portfolio diversification Index (PDI) (see Diyarbakirlioglu and Satman (2013) and Rudin and Morgan (2006)). Similar to the minimum variance portfolio, portfolios that optimize a diversification measure will be on a mean-diversification efficient frontier. However, the portfolio will be the solution that places zero weight on returns. The question of interest here is: if returns is incorporated in the construction of these risk-based portfolios so that we have the full mean-diversification efficient frontier, what difference will it make? To be more precise what will be the answer to the following questions in light of Lee (2011)'s criticism of risk-based approaches

(i) What would a Mean-Diversification efficient frontier of various diversification measures look like?
(ii) If it is possible to draw such frontiers, are there other potentially attractive options in terms of return-diversification trade-off other than the portfolio that ignores returns?[1]

Obviously, the answer to the first question will depend on the diversification measure used to construct the mean-diversification frontier. Since there is no universally accepted way of defining diversification (Meucci 2009), this paper explores selected diversification measures to answer the proposed questions. To implement this, a heuristic approach namely the Non-Dominated Sorting Genetic Algorithm (NSGA II) (Deb et al. 2002) is used. This optimization method is based on the Multi-Objective Evolutionary Algorithm (MOEA). We choose this approach because of our interest in the entire Pareto front and the fact that optimizing some diversification measures require optimizing a function that is non-convex or/and has discontinuity in the objective function space.

In terms of the second question, similar to the optimal portfolio on the mean-variance frontier (that optimizes the Sharpe ratio) interest is in the portfolio that yields the highest return-diversification trade-off. We argue that portfolios that are optimal in the mean-diversification space are better candidate portfolio to be compared with portfolios that are constructed to be mean-variance optimal. This is in contrast to the practice in the literature which Lee (2011) criticized. By construction, mean-diversified portfolios should dominate risk-based portfolios on a risk-adjusted basis.

[1]In other words, will there be alternatives that are more mean-diversification efficient than the portfolio that ignores returns.

2 Evolutionary Algorithm and Portfolio Optimization

An evolutionary algorithm (EA) is a class of metaheuristic that relies on emulating Darwinian's theory (i.e. "survival of the fittest" approach). Formulation of a multi-objective EA can be written as

$$\begin{aligned} &\min \vec{F}(\vec{x}) = \{f_1(\vec{x}), f_2(\vec{x}), \ldots f_k(\vec{x})\} \\ &\text{Subject to} \\ &g_i(\vec{x}) \leq 0 \; and \; h_i(\vec{x}) = 0 \end{aligned} \tag{1}$$

where $\vec{x} = [x_1, x_2, \ldots x_n]^{\mathrm{T}}$ is a vector of decision variables for example portfolio weights in a portfolio optimization problem, $f_i : R^n \to R, \; i = 1 \ldots k$ are objective functions, for example summary measures of asset returns that we wish to optimize (e.g. mean and variance). g_i, h_i are constraints (Ponsich et al. 2013). One way to find the solution to this problem is to aggregate the objective functions i.e.

$$\begin{aligned} &F = \beta_1 f_1(\vec{x}) + \beta_2 f_2(\vec{x}) + \cdots + \beta_k f_k(\vec{x}) \\ &\text{Subject to} \\ &g_i(\vec{x}) \leq 0 \; and \; h_i(\vec{x}) = 0 \end{aligned} \tag{2}$$

F is a single objective function that represent the k objectives and β_i are weights that depicts the trade-off between the objectives. Note that these weights are subjective in that they depend on the preference of the decision maker.[2] This aggregated objective can be solved using a Single Objective Evolutionary Algorithm (SOEA), this results in one solution to the optimization problem. It is however possible to get a set of Pareto optimal results, each corresponding to a different weighting (i.e. different sets of $\beta_i s$). Therefore, in these types of problems, one may extend the result by uncovering a set of solutions representing the best possible trade-offs between the objectives as against identifying one point on the optimal solution space (Ponsich et al. 2013). For example, the portfolio that optimizes the Sharpe ratio is the one that yields the best trade-off between two objectives i.e. mean and variance. The entire solution set is referred to as the Pareto front. Being aware of the entire spectrum of solutions can be useful in that it helps decision makers to pick the solution that fits their preference. This argument is applied to diversification based optimization problems and this paper explores other solutions that may be of interest in the return-diversification efficient space.

While one could run multiple SOEA with different weights each time, it is preferred to use the Multi-Objective Evolutionary Algorithm (MOEA) approach to uncover the Pareto front. With this approach, the entire Pareto front is uncovered in one run.

[2]This is the usual language in the evolutionary algorithm literature. In this case the decision maker is the investor or portfolio manager.

An example of how portfolio optimization can be described as a single or multiple objective optimization problem is the case of Markowitz (1952) portfolio optimization. The problem is set up in the following way

$$\min_{n_i}\{w'Rw\}$$
$$\max_{n_i}\{w'\mu\}$$
$$\text{Subject to}$$
$$\sum_{i=1}^{p} w_i = 1 \tag{3}$$

Here w_i is the weight of asset i, p is the number of assets i.e. $i = 1, 2 \ldots p$, R represents the variance-covariance matrix and μ is the vector of returns. In the language of evolutionary algorithm, this problem is a bi-objective optimization problem with conflicting[3] decision criteria (Lin and Liu 2008). The resulting frontier gives the best risk (as measured by variance) to reward (as measured by returns) trade-off for every level of risk. In other words, each solution represents a particular weighting of risk against returns. In this context, the weighting reflects the risk profile of the decision maker. One such weighting is the minimum variance portfolio that places all its weight on variance (the risk measure) thereby ignoring the return objective.

Equation 3 above can be written as Eq. 4 below. In this formulation, the efficient frontier can be recovered by changing the value of λ (risk preference of the decision maker).

$$\max_{w_i}\{\lambda w'\mu - w'Rw\} \tag{4}$$

Portfolio theory predicts that all decision-makers should seek to hold the portfolio that maximizes the Sharpe ratio irrespective of their risk preference i.e.

$$\max_{w_i}\left\{\frac{r_p - r}{\sigma_p}\right\} \tag{5}$$

where r is the return on a risk free asset, $r_p = w'\mu$ is the portfolio's expected return and $\sigma_p = \sqrt{w'\Sigma w}$ is the portfolio's standard deviation (Sharpe 1966). In this framework, risk preference is only important when deciding the weight that should be allocated to the risky portfolio as against the risk free asset. However, the prediction that favours the portfolio that maximizes Sharpe ratio has been challenged. For example, Clarke et al. (2006) found that the minimum variance portfolio (which optimizes variance alone) outperform the Market portfolio (which is a proxy for the portfolio that maximizes the Sharpe ratio) in their sample of 1000 largest capital stocks in the

[3]Conflicting in the sense that increase in expected return (which is desirable) inadvertently leads to increase in variance (which is undesirable).

U.S. from 1986 to 2005. The result of Clarke et al. (2006) suggests that there might be reasons or conditions under which some decision makers may prefer this single objective optimal point to the portfolio that maximizes the Sharpe ratio.

As mentioned earlier the optimization method used in this study is a metaheuristic one. Unlike an exact method like quadratic programming (QP), genetic algorithm (GA) converges to a near optimal solution to the problem (Kalayci et al. 2017). Furthermore, heuristic methods are often sensitive to parameters. The implication of this is that it might be tricky to use these methods for actual portfolio construction. This approach is however useful in this case because when portfolio variance is replaced with some of the risk measures considered in this study, the objective function is such that the weight of stocks in the portfolio is endogenous and analytical solution to the optimization problem does not exist. Therefore, the heuristic method allows for credible comparison of portfolios across frontiers (mean-diversification and mean-variance efficient frontiers).[4] This removes the possibility that the methodology will influence the results. To mitigate the effect of sensitivity to parameters, we use a set of parameters that approximate QP's mean-variance efficient frontier. Therefore, the imperfection of the heuristic method is mitigated since all portfolios are sketched with the same method and the same set of parameters.

A genetic algorithm starts by postulating a population of random solutions (in our case optimal portfolio weights). The weights in each individual solution are referred to as the gene. These solutions are assessed based on a fitness or objective function and ranked in order of their desirability. To form a new generation of solutions, the existing population undergoes stochastic transformation using genetic operators such as crossover and mutation. Crossover combine solutions from the old population to form new solutions (offsprings) while mutation randomly changes genes in existing solutions to form new solutions. This process of creating a new generation from the old one is repeated until the algorithm converges to a solution that meets certain criteria (e.g. number of iterations) or cannot be improved further. Another important component of the algorithm is Elitism, this means some of the best (non-dominated) solution in the current population are allowed to go into the next generation as they are. These genetic operations tend to improve average fitness of each successive generation. For more details on the genetic algorithm as it relates to portfolio optimization see Kalayci et al. (2017)

3 Diversification Measures

This section gives a brief description of the diversification measures used in this study and their merits and demerits.

---

[4]As noted earlier, in addition, optimization of some of the diversification measures considered in this study requires a method that can handle non-convexity and/or discontinuity in the objective function space.

The first measure is the diversification ratio (DR). DR quantifies diversification by measuring the "distance" between two volatility measures of the same portfolio, namely, volatility in a world where diversification is assumed not to exist and volatility in a world where there is diversification (Lee 2011). It is given by

$$DR = \frac{\sum_{i=1}^{p} w_i \sigma_i}{\sqrt{w' R w}} \tag{6}$$

where σ_i is the standard deviation of asset i and the other parameters are as defined earlier. Although this measure is straightforward to construct, it is not without flaw. Meucci (2009) pointed out that the DR is a differential diversification measure and not one that measures diversification in absolute terms. The measure is bounded below by 1, and it is unbounded from above. Higher values reflect better diversification. Finally, $DR = \sqrt{p}$ if all assets are perfectly uncorrelated.

The second measure is the PDI. PDI evaluates the effective number of independent variation components in a portfolio. Introduced by Rudin and Morgan (2006), PDI attach weights to the principal components of a portfolio's returns in the following way;

$$PDI = 2\sum_{k=1}^{p} k W_i - 1$$
$$W_i = \frac{\lambda_i}{\sum_{k=1}^{p} \lambda_i} \tag{7}$$

where p is the number of assets in the portfolio and W_i are the ordered and normalized covariance or correlation eigenvalues (λ_i). Diyarbakirlioglu and Satman (2013) noted that maximizing PDI to achieve better diversification is similar to maximizing R^2 in econometrics. PDI is a monotonically non-decreasing function of the number of stocks. This may create a problem when PDI is the criterion for optimizing a portfolio. A portfolio P_1 may be preferred to a portfolio P_2 if P_1 has more stocks (or assets). However, this becomes a problem when the marginal effect of the stocks in P_1 that are not in P_2 on diversification is minimal. To deal with the sensitivity to the number of stocks, Diyarbakirlioglu and Satman (2013) introduced an upper limit such that the problem is that of selecting a subset of assets from a given number of assets i.e. portfolios are indexed by the maximum number of stocks allowed.[5] Like DR the higher the value of PDI the higher the level of diversification in the portfolio.

We also consider Information complexity of the covariance matrix (ICOMP), this measure was proposed by Oyenubi (2010, 2016) and it is given by

$$\text{ICOMP} = \frac{p}{2}\log\left[\frac{tr(R)}{p}\right] - \frac{1}{2}\log|R| \tag{8}$$

[5]For example, in a universe of 20 stocks one may preselect 10 as the highest number of stocks allowed in a portfolio. The portfolio can then be optimized by selecting the portfolio with the maximum PDI out of all possible portfolios that have 10 stocks or less.

where $|R|$ and $tr(R)$ denote the determinant and trace of the variance-covariance matrix of returns. ICOMP can be thought of as a measure of return correlation concentration (Oyenubi 2016). Unlike PDI that quantifies the number of independent factors in a portfolio, ICOMP quantifies the level of dependency or variation redundancy among the returns of assets that make up a portfolio. The value of ICOMP reduces as the level of diversification increases. Similar to PDI, ICOMP is a non-decreasing function of the number of stocks, therefore; it is sensitive to the number of stocks.

The last measure considered is based on the trade-off between ICOMP and PDI. Oyenubi (2016) use this approach to estimate the optimum number of stocks in a given universe of stocks. The idea is that both ICOMP and PDI are sensitive to the number of stocks, but the direction of this sensitivity is opposed to each other. PDI tend to include stocks whose marginal contribution to diversification may be minimal to optimize diversification while ICOMP tends to pick the portfolio with the smallest size to achieve the same objective. One way to mitigate the sensitivity of both measures to the number of stocks is to consider the trade-off between PDI and ICOMP i.e. construct a portfolio that maximizes (the absolute value of) the difference between PDI and ICOMP i.e. |PDI-ICOMP|. The portfolio that maximizes this difference should have the optimum number of stocks for the universe under consideration because marginal ICOMP equals marginal PDI. This means that the number of independent sources of variation (measured by PDI) cannot be improved without incurring heavier cost in terms of the complexity of the portfolio (measured by ICOMP). This way the choice of the number of stocks is data-driven. In this study, we use this trade-off as another diversification measure.

4 Mean-Variance GA and QP Efficient Frontiers

We use weekly returns data of 80 randomly selected stocks from S&P 500. The data spans January 2005 to November 2013 (Details of the stocks in the universe are presented in the appendix[6]).

To mitigate the problem of sensitivity to parameters we follow Tsao and Liu (2006) by using genetic algorithm to sketch the mean-variance efficient frontier that replicates the result produced by quadratic programming. This exercise is used to narrow down reasonable parameters that can be used when variance is replaced with the proposed diversification measures. The result of the mean-variance frontier is shown in Fig. 1. The result agrees with the one in Tsao and Liu (2006), the mean-variance frontier drawn using the NSGA II algorithm (blue in Fig. 1) is able to approximate the mean-variance Pareto front (red in Fig. 1) drawn using quadratic programming.

On the graph, the position of the portfolio that optimizes the Sharpe ratio (labelled "OPTIMAL") and the portfolio that minimizes variance (labelled "MVP") are very

[6]The R code to reproduce the result is also available on request.

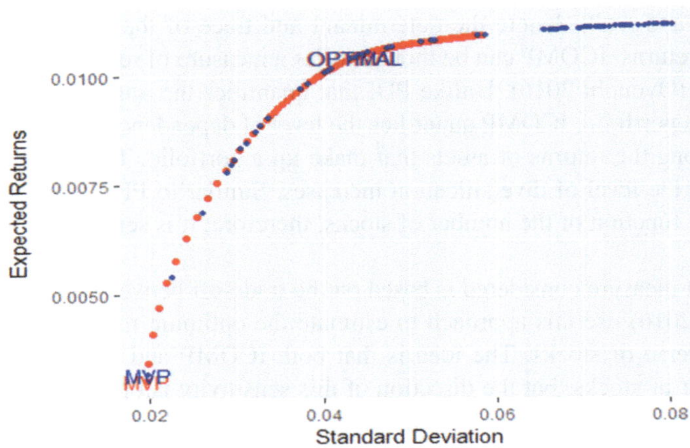

Fig. 1 Mean-variance efficient frontiers (blue NSGA II, red QP). "OPTIMAL" is the location of the portfolio that optimizes the Sharpe ratio. MVP is the portfolio that places zero weight on returns i.e. the minimum variance portfolio

similar under the quadratic programming and the Genetic Algorithm methods.[7] Sharpe ratio for the MV frontier is calculated using Eq. 5 where we set $r = 0.007$ (this represent the average discount rate for the United States for the period covered by the data i.e. 2015–2013[8]).

It is clear that these two sets of portfolios have similar expected returns and variance under the two methods. Figures 12 and 13 in the appendix show the weights allocated to the stocks for the optimal and the minimum variance portfolios while Figs. 14 and 15 shows the cumulative returns and the drawdown for the portfolios. These graphs show that the performance of the OPTIMAL and MVP portfolios are very similar under the two approches so that one can conclude that the choice of method does not matter. The conclusion here is that the NSGA II approach provides a good approximation for the result under the QP optimization.[9]

For the mean-diversification frontiers, we use Shape-like ratios depending on how the diversification measure quantifies diversification. High values of ICOMP means lower diversification so for ICOMP we replace σ_p with $ICOMP_p$ (where $ICOMP_p$ is the covariance-complexity of the portfolio) in Eq. (5). In the case of the other measures, higher values means better diversification. Therefore, the Sharpe-like ratios are constructed by replacing σ_p in Eq. (5) with the inverse of the diversification

[7]In Sect. 6 we compare these portfolios.

[8]The information used for the calculation is available at "https://fred.stlouisfed.org/series/INTDSRUSM193N".

[9]In the case of the optimal portfolio, the same stocks were picked by both optimization methods. Furthermore, the weight allocated to each stock is approximately equal. For the minimum variance portfolio there are 3 stocks that have weights under the QP approach but have no weight under NSGA II. However the weight allocated to these 3 stocks are very small. This is probably due to the threshold parameter (details in Sect. 5) used under the NSGA II approach.

measure. This effectively means that the optimal portfolio is the one where the product of the excess return and the diversification value is maximized.

The NSGA II algorithm is implemented with the R package "nsga2R" (Tsou and Lee 2013). The main programme uses fast non-dominated sorting, and a crowding distance approach to maintain the diversity of solutions. The programme also uses tournament selection and binary crossover.

4.1 Details of the Algorithm and Parameters

The parameters used in Fig. 1 are as follows, the population size is 300, tournament size is 4, number of iterations or generations is 500. The crossover probability is 0.02, and mutation probability is 0.2 (these parameters are needed to operationalize the genetic operators mentioned in Sect. 2 see Tsou and Lee (2013) for details on these parameters). Mutation and crossover distribution indices are set to 5. Since these parameters work well to approximate the mean-variance efficient frontier produced by the quadratic programming in Fig. 1, the same set of parameters is used for the mean-diversification frontiers.

This study follows Tsao and Liu (2006) in setting up the NSGA II algorithm. For the initiation of random solutions, random numbers, $\{\upsilon_i,\ i = 1, 2, \ldots p\}$ from a uniform distribution $U\{0, 1\}$ are simulated. Portfolio weights $\{w_i,\ i = 1, 2, \ldots p\}$ are obtained by normalizing υ_i i.e. $w_i = \upsilon_i / \sum \upsilon_i$, the weights therefore satisfy $\sum_i w_i = 1$. To make sure that each portfolio contains at least 2 assets we implement a general restriction (across all frontiers) that guarantees this.

Tsao and Liu (2006) use a threshold parameter D to set an upper limit for the weights allocated to each stock. In other words, if $\upsilon_i > D$ then υ_i is replaced with zero. Tsao and Liu (2006) reported that threshold set at 0.1 help the NSGA II to approximate the efficiency frontier generated by quadratic programming. We did not encounter this problem, in this study, the NSGAII algorithm (as implemented in the R package) performs reasonably well without the ceiling constraint on weights. We however implement a different threshold to guard against having small weights on every stock. Therefore, in this study, a floor constraint is used to eliminate small weights.[10] When $\upsilon_i < D$ then υ_i is replaced with zero, where $D = 0.01$. After the floor constraint is imposed the weights are re-normalized so that $\sum_i w_i = 1$. This device also allows for the possibility that some stocks have zero weight in the optimal portfolio. Apart from the floor constraint, the rest of our algorithm is similar to the one described in Tsao and Liu (2006).

Kirchner and Zunckel (2011) noted that PDI does not deal with weights attached to assets and Oyenubi (2016) noted that the same is true for ICOMP. This makes it difficult to use these measures in portfolio construction. For example, Crezée and Swinkels (2010) use PDI to pick stocks in portfolios that are equally weighted

[10]This did not affect our result in any significant way, the only impact was instead of having very small weight for some stocks these stocks are allocated zero weight in the portfolio.

(perhaps because in an equally weighted portfolio weights can be ignored). To deal with this problem, Kirchner and Zunckel (2011) suggested that weights could be incorporated with these measures by considering weighted returns. This will require using the covariance matrix of the fractional contributions of stocks. This suggestion is implemented in the following way to construct portfolios that optimizes PDI and ICOMP.

Let

$$V = \begin{bmatrix} \sigma_{11} & \cdots & \sigma_{1p} \\ \vdots & \ddots & \vdots \\ \sigma_{p1} & \cdots & \sigma_{pp} \end{bmatrix}$$

be a $p \times p$ covariance matrix of stock returns. Then $V(w)$ the covariance matrix of the weighted returns can be written as

$$V(w) = \begin{bmatrix} w_1^2\sigma_{11} & \cdots & w_1 w_p \sigma_{1p} \\ \vdots & \ddots & \vdots \\ w_p w_1 \sigma_{p1} & \cdots & w_p^2 \sigma_{pp} \end{bmatrix}$$

Note that the portfolio variance is given by

$$\sigma^2(w) = l' V(w) l$$

where l is a $p \times 1$ vector of ones. This means that[11]

$$\sigma^2(w) = w' V w$$

Therefore, one can set $V(w) = R$ in Eq. (8) to compute ICOMP. Furthermore, the eigenvalues of $V(w)$ can be used in Eq. (7) to compute the PDI measure. This way the weights used to calculate PDI and ICOMP does not have to be uniformly distributed as in Crezée and Swinkels (2010).

5 Mean Diversification Efficient Frontiers

In this section, the results of the mean-diversification frontiers are discussed. Figures 2, 3, 4, 5, 6 and 7 show the efficient frontiers. As mentioned earlier, the parameters used for the mean-variance frontier in Fig. 1 are used for the mean-diversification frontiers. Unlike the mean-variance frontier where in general increase in returns

[11] Similar calculations can be found in "A critical review of Correlation-based measures of portfolio diversification" http://www.northinfo.com/documents/616.pdf. Randy O'Toole is the author of the document.

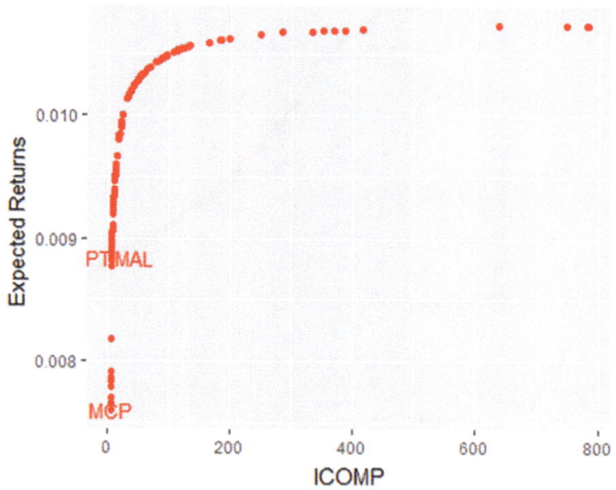

Fig. 2 Mean-ICOMP frontier for 10 stocks

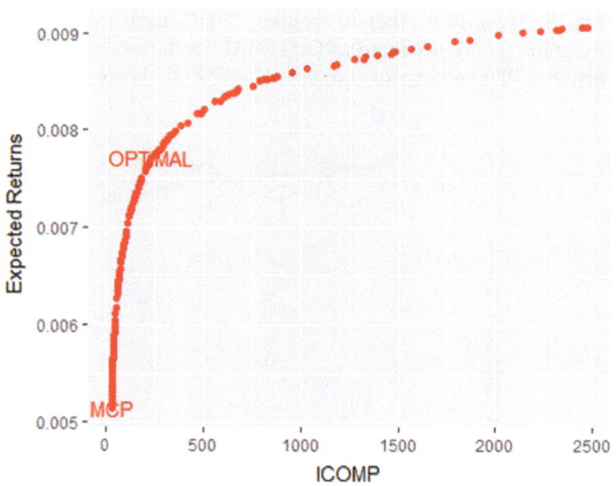

Fig. 3 Mean-ICOMP frontier for 40 stocks

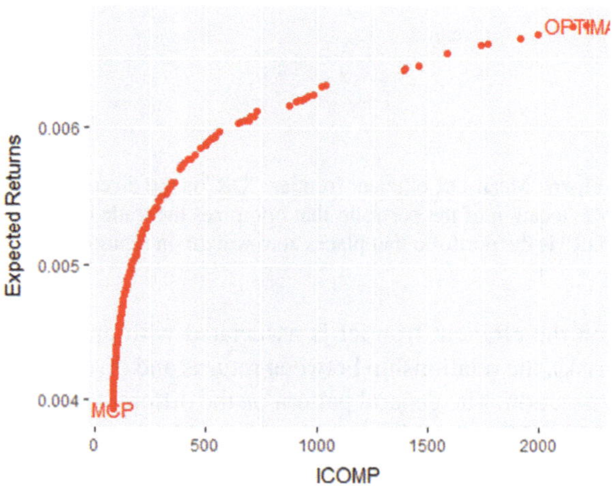

Fig. 4 Mean-ICOMP frontier for 80 stocks. ICOMP is the covariance complexity of weighted covariance matrix. "OPTIMAL" is the location of the portfolio that optimizes the trade-off between ICOMP and expected returns. "MCP" is the portfolio that places zero weight on returns i.e. minimizes ICOMP

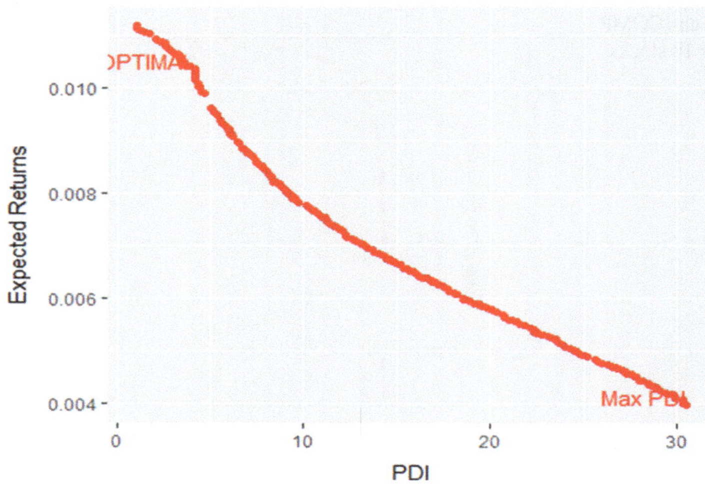

Fig. 5 Mean-PDI efficient frontier. "PDI" measures the portfolio diversification index of the weighted covariance matrix. "OPTIMAL" is the location of the portfolio that optimizes the trade-off between PDI and expected returns. "Max PDI" is the portfolio that places zero weight on returns

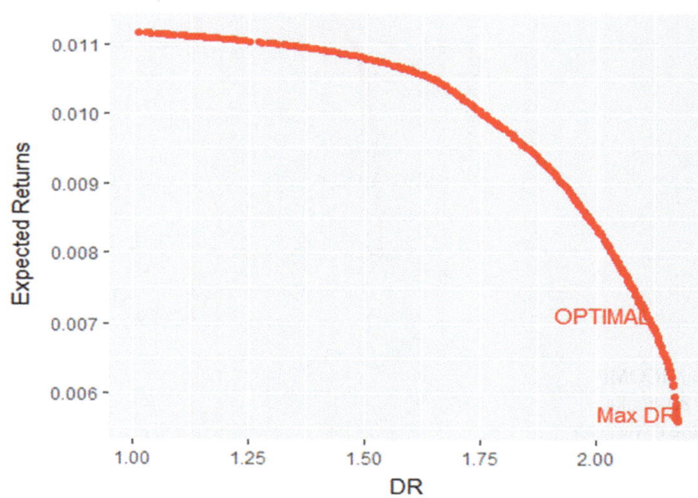

Fig. 6 Mean-DR efficient frontier. "DR" is the diversification ratio of portfolios. "OPTIMAL" is the location of the portfolio that optimizes the trade-off between DR and expected returns. "Max DR" is the portfolio that places zero weight on returns

on the efficient frontier is associated with an increase in variance (the measure of risk), the relationship between returns and diversification measures is in the opposite direction. The general pattern on the different frontiers (ICOMP, PDI, DR, and |PDI-ICOMP|) is that higher return (desirable) is associated with lower diversification (not desirable) as one would expect.

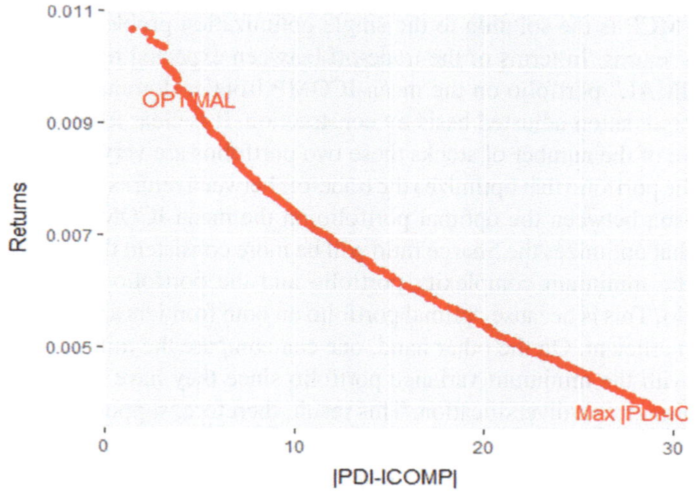

Fig. 7 Mean-|PDI-ICOMP| efficient frontier. "|PDI-ICOMP|" is the difference between PDI and ICOMP of portfolios. "OPTIMAL" is the location of the portfolio that optimizes the trade-off between "|PDI-ICOMP|" and expected returns. "Max |PDI-ICOMP|" is the portfolio that places zero weight on returns

Figures 2, 3 and 4 show the mean-ICOMP efficient frontiers. We have three separate frontiers for this measure to show the effect of the sensitivity of ICOMP to the number of stocks. Figures 2, 3 and 4 show the frontier when the minimum number of stocks allowed is 10, 40 and 80 respectively (i.e. the general constraint of at least 2 stock is changed to 10, 40 and 80 respectively for Figs. 2, 3 and 4). As mentioned earlier, because portfolios that optimize ICOMP always tend to be the one with the smallest size, for each of the frontiers, all the portfolios on the efficient front contain the same number of stocks and this number is equal to the minimum number of stocks allowed in the NSGA II algorithm. Therefore this is somewhat a stock picking exercise with a restriction on the number of stocks allowed.

This is because under ICOMP portfolio with the lowest covariance complexity is always the most diversified because complexity is sensitive to the number of stocks. Therefore, portfolios with two stocks always dominate other portfolios when the optimization is not constrained. To mitigate this effect the minimum number of stocks is restricted in the optimization.

The first thing to note is that as the minimum number of stocks increase (from 10 to 80) the maximum expected return on the frontier decreases (from approximately 0.011 to 0.007) and the maximum complexity increases from (800 to 2500). This agrees with the statement made earlier i.e. there is a negative relationship between diversification and expected returns.

In terms of Lee's criticism of optimizing diversification measure alone, the figures show the position of the optimal complexity portfolio (OPTIMAL) and the minimum complexity portfolio (MCP). The former minimizes the Sharpe-like ratio for this frontier i.e. the ratio of excess returns to ICOMP while the latter minimizes ICOMP only. The MCP is the solution to the single optimization problem that places zero weight on returns. In terms of the trade-off between expected returns and ICOMP, the "OPTIMAL" portfolio on the mean-ICOMP frontier dominates the MCP on a mean-diversification adjusted basis by construction. It is clear from the figures that irrespective of the number of stocks these two portfolios are very different.

Since the portfolio that optimizes the trade-off between returns and ICOMP exists, a comparison between the optimal portfolio on the mean-ICOMP frontier and the portfolio that optimizes the Sharpe ratio will be more consistent than the comparison between the minimum complexity portfolio and the portfolio that optimizes the Sharpe ratio. This is because optimal portfolio on both frontiers are constructed to be risk-return efficient. On the other hand, one can compare the minimum complexity portfolio with the minimum variance portfolio since they have the same objective i.e. to minimize risk/diversification. This result, therefore, supports Lee's criticism.

Figure 5 shows the mean-PDI frontier. Although this measure is also sensitive to the number of stocks, its sensitivity is not as strong as that of ICOMP. Therefore, the general restriction of a minimum of 2 stocks works well for this measure. One possible explanation for this is that while ICOMP tries to optimize diversification by selecting the minimum number of stocks given their correlations, optimizing PDI often entail selecting the highest number of stocks possible for each return level. Therefore, for each return level, the portfolio that maximizes PDI need not be the one with the largest size since marginal PDI decreases with the number of stocks (Rudin and Morgan 2006; Oyenubi 2016).

In terms of Lee (2010)'s criticism, the portfolio that optimizes PDI alone (Max PDI) is also different from the one that optimizes the trade-off between PDI and returns. Again, this result suggests that there is a viable option that does not place all its weight on PDI (when one is interested in diversification-adjusted returns) and this option is a better candidate to compare with the mean-variance optimal portfolio.

Figure 6 shows the mean-DR efficient frontier. Just like the other diversification measures. The portfolio that optimizes the diversification measure is not optimal when the trade-off between the mean and the DR is considered.

Lastly, following Oyenubi (2016), the trade-off between PDI and ICOMP is used as a diversification measure. The rationale for this measure is that it helps mitigate the sensitivity of ICOMP (and PDI to some extent) to the size of the portfolio. PDI acts such that to increase the diversification of a portfolio more stocks are needed (i.e. adding stocks is a way to increase the number of independent sources of variation). However, the marginal contribution of the last stock added may be so small that it does not justify the addition. Contrasting PDI with ICOMP will guarantee that the last stock is added only if its benefit in terms of improvement in diversification is more than its cost in terms of its marginal complexity. This creates a data-driven mechanism that selects portfolio in such a way that the sensitivity of these measures to the number of stocks is curtailed.

Diversification increase as the difference between PDI and ICOMP increases. Figure 7 shows the result; again, the portfolio that optimizes the diversification measure alone is different from the one that optimizes the trade-off between expected returns and the diversification measure.

In summary, all the results agree. There are portfolios that place some weight on return while optimizing the diversification measures. In theory, these mean-diversification optimal portfolios are more efficient and more comparable with the portfolio that optimizes the Sharpe ratio than risk-based portfolios that ignore returns. Furthermore, while one may struggle to understand why an investor will want to optimize risk or diversification alone the mean-diversification optimal portfolio offers a better option i.e. it has a clearly defined objective of maximizing returns while minimizing lack of diversification.

6 In-Sample Comparison of Portfolios

By construction mean-diversification optimal portfolios should dominate the risk-based portfolios on their respective frontiers. Figures 8, 9, 10 and 11 supports this expectation. Figures 8, 9, 10 and 11 show the cumulative returns and the drawdown for the optimal mean-diversification portfolios and the portfolio that optimizes the diversification measure.

In all cases, the result shows that portfolios that optimize the trade-off between returns and diversification have better returns and recover quicker from the 2008/2009 financial market crises than the corresponding portfolio that optimizes diversification alone. Although in comparison to the other portfolios, the portfolio that optimizes the DR perform better, the DR portfolio's return is much closer to the return of the portfolio that optimizes the trade-off between DR and returns (especially before the crises) and the drawdown result suggests that this portfolio also recovered well from the 2008/2009 crash.

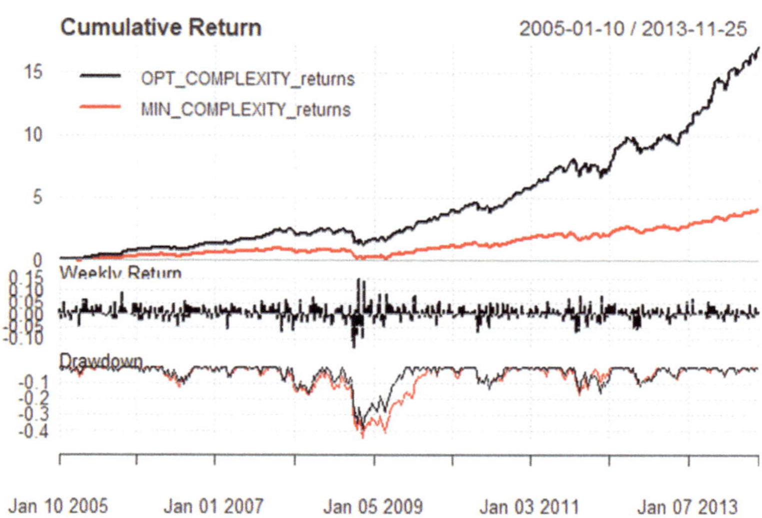

Fig. 8 Complexity (ICOMP) portfolios

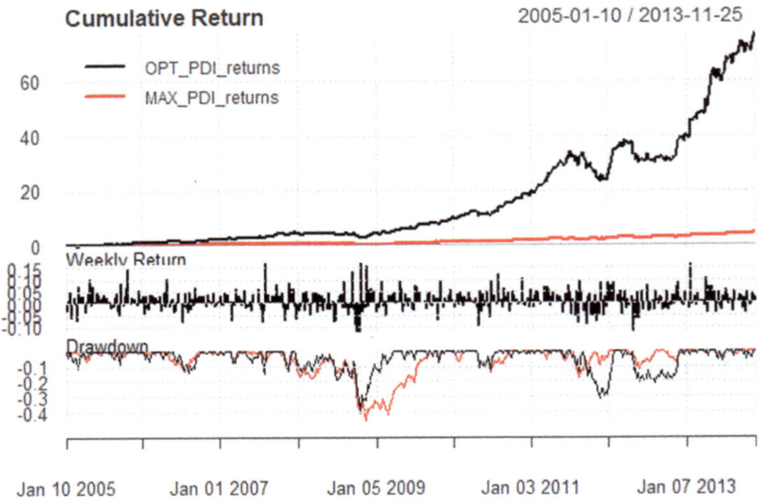

Fig. 9 PDI portfolios. OPT_COMPLEXITY_returns and OPT_PDI_returns represent the optimal mean-ICOMP and mean-PDI portfolio respectively. MIN_COMPLEXITY_returns and MAX_PDI_returns represent the portfolio that minimizes ICOMP and the portfolio that maximizes PDI respectively

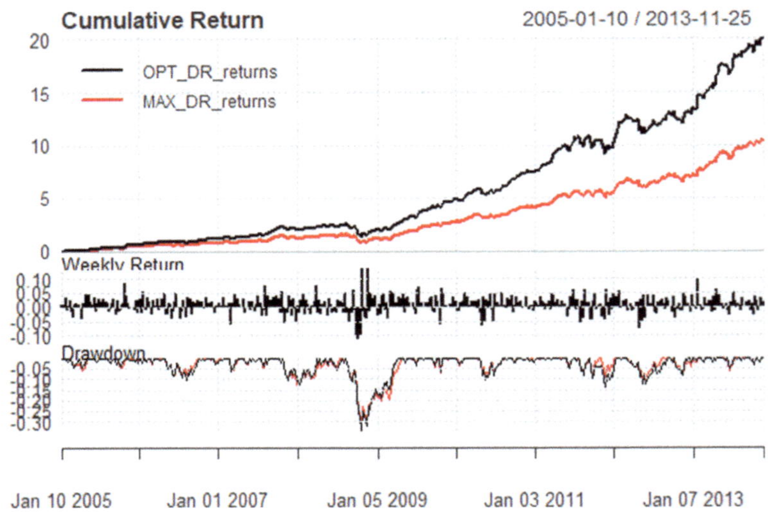

Fig. 10 DR portfolios

This result is expected, the risk-based portfolios place zero weight on returns so it is not surprising that their performance in terms of returns is lower than the performance of the corresponding return-diversification optimal portfolio. On the other hand, one would expect the risk-based measure to perform better in terms of

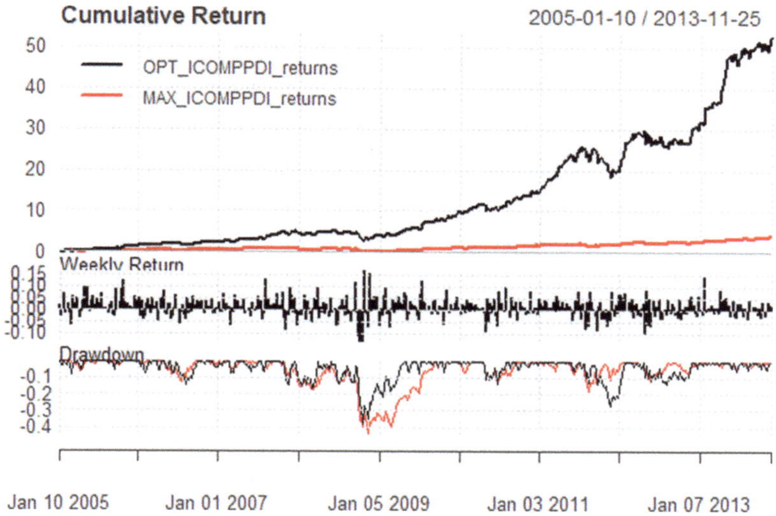

Fig. 11 PDI-ICOMP portfolios. OPT_DR_returns and OPT_ICOMPPDI_returns represent the optimal mean-DR and mean-|PDI-ICOMP| portfolio respectively. MAX_DR_returns and MAX_ICOMPPDI_returns represent the portfolio that maximizes DR and |PDI-ICOMP| respectively

minimizing risk alone, however, the drawdown in Figs. 8, 9, 10 and 11 suggests that during crises period risk-based portfolios take longer to recover.

To properly compare the portfolios (especially the mean-variance optimal portfolio with the mean-diversification optimal portfolios) we use a use Treynor ratio and Information ratio. These measures are given by

$$TR_i = \frac{\hat{\alpha}_i}{\hat{\beta}_i}$$

$$IR_i = \frac{\hat{\alpha}_i}{\hat{\alpha}(\varepsilon_i)}$$

where TR_i and IR_i represent the Treynor and Information ratio of portfolio i respectively. $\hat{\alpha}_i$ (Jensen's alpha) is the abnormal excess return of portfolio i, $\hat{\beta}_i$ is the beta of portfolio i (a measure of systemic risk) and $\hat{\sigma}(\varepsilon_i)$ is the standard deviation of portfolio i's residual returns (a measure of specific risk). The motivation for choosing these performance measures is that they will be less bias than the sharpe ratio or any other measure that utilize one of the risk measures that has been used to sketch the efficient frontiers. These measures also allow for the comparison of the portfolios with reference to two components of risk i.e. systemic and specific risks.

Table 1 shows the results. We start by noting that across panels A (optimal portfolios) and B (risk-based portfolios) in Table 1, all the portfolios that trade-off returns for risk/diversification (Panel A) outperform corresponding portfolios that optimize diversification/risk alone. This is consistent with the results in Figs. 8, 9, 10 and 11.

Table 1 In-sample comparison of mean-diversification optimal, mean-variance optimal and risk-based portfolios using Sharpe ratio

	NSGAII MV	QP MV	OCP (80)	OCP (40)	OCP (10)	OCP (5)	PDI	|PDI-ICOMP|	DR
Optimal portfolios									
Panel A									
Information ratio	2.3999	2.4124	3.0237	3.0581	2.9256	2.3331	2.45	2.5038	2.7238
Treynor ratio	0.1949	0.1948	0.0091	0.0567	0.1137	0.1811	0.1901	0.1387	0.0323
Jensen alpha	0.0095	0.0095	0.0059	0.0069	0.008	0.0094	0.0094	0.0086	0.0053
Number of stocks	5	5	80	40	10	5	5	7	16
Maximum risk/diversification portfolios									
Panel B									
Information ratio	1.2733	1.22033	2.27008	2.7838	2.7529	2.169	2.2632	2.2934	2.3945
Treynor ratio	−0.2346	−0.2435	−0.1231	−0.067	0.064	0.1211	−0.121	−0.126	−0.052
Jensen alpha	0.0004	0.0003	0.0031	0.0045	0.006	0.0085	0.0032	0.0031	0.0036
Number of stocks	13	16	80	40	10	5	76	76	17

NSGAII MV: Mean-variance optimal and minimum variance portfolio using genetic algorithm. QP MV: Mean-variance optimal and minimum variance portfolio using quadratic programming. OCP (n): Optimal complexity portfolio when a minimum of n stocks are allowed in the portfolio. MCP (n): Minimum complexity portfolio when a minimum of n stocks are allowed in the portfolio. PDI: Optimal and maximum PDI portfolio. PDI-ICOMP: optimal maximum diversification portfolio on the frontier that uses PDI-ICOMP as a diversification measure. DR: Optimal and the most diversified portfolio

For the risk-based measures, the portfolios that optimize other risk/diversification measures perform better than the one that optimizes variance (i.e. the minimum variance portfolio). Lastly, for the optimal portfolios, the mean-variance optimal portfolio dominates the mean-diversification optimal portfolios when using the Treynor measure and the portfolio that optimizes the trade-off between complexity and returns (with a minimum of 40 stocks) performs better when the performance is based on the information ratio.[12] In other words, when systemic risk is the biggest threat mean-variance optimal portfolio performs better but when specific risk is the main concern optimal complexity portfolio with 40 stocks performs better than other portfolios. Which suggests that different diversification measures focus on different aspects of risks.

We also report the Jensen's alpha for all the portfolios, the implied estimate of $\hat{\beta}_i$ and $\hat{\sigma}(\varepsilon_i)$ based on the value of $\hat{\alpha}_i$ suggests that the portfolios with lower performance (as measured by Treynor and Information ratio) does have better risk properties i.e. lower systemic or/and specific risk. However, the portfolio with better performance have excess returns that more than compensate for their higher risk.

This result is instructive when it comes to understanding the relationship between mean-diversification optimal portfolios and risk-based portfolios. The former performs better than the latter because its excess return compensates better for its level of risk than the excess return of the former. This goes to the heart of Lee (2011)'s criticism of risk-based portfolio construction. Without a clearly defined objective like the trade-off between returns and the diversification measure, there is no way of knowing that the mean-diversification optimal portfolio offers a better risk-reward trade-off. Our result suggests that by incorporating returns into the optimization of the new risk measures, the resulting portfolio becomes riskier but the excess return is such that the higher risk is better compensated (we note that this is at least true for the data we used, confirming this for other periods and data is a question for future research).

If in-sample, optimal portfolios on mean-diversification frontiers outperforms risk-based portfolios on a risk-adjusted basis, then it is more reasonable (theoretically) for one to expect them to repeat the same performance out of sample. This expectation is at least more reasonable than the alternative of expecting a risk-based portfolio to outperform the mean-variance optimal portfolio on a risk-adjusted basis. This suggests that the body of research that has focused on showing that risk-based portfolio outperforms the mean-variance portfolio may have better justification if it was comparing mean-diversification optimal portfolios with the mean-variance optimal portfolio. Note that while it is not impossible for a risk-based portfolio to outperform a portfolio that is constructed to be risk-reward optimal this should be an exception and not the rule.

Apart from this main point, there are other points we wish to highlight. Portfolios that are based on the complexity measure tend to perform well when they are constrained (i.e. when there is a lower limit to the number of stocks). Across the rows of

[12]In other words the order of dominance is mean-variance or mean-complexity optimal portfolio, other mean-diversified optimal portfolios, risk-based portfolios and minimum variance portfolio.

Table 1 complexity portfolio tend to be the best or second best (i.e. the complexity portfolio with 40 or 5 stocks). We explore this option for the complexity measure because it is highly sensitive to the number of stocks. However, these results confirm the idea that portfolio diversification depends not only on the correlation structure of the stocks but also the number of stocks (Oyenubi 2016). Clearly curtailing the number of stocks for the complexity measure improves its performance. Perhaps this effect exists for other diversification measures like the PDI (which is also known to be sensitive to the number of stocks).

The number of stocks reported in Table 1 suggests that different diversification measures chose different number of stocks to optimize their objective (in the presence or absence of returns). Apart from the cases where the number of stocks is constrained, risk-based portfolios (Panel B) tend to select more stocks than optimal risk-reward portfolios (Panel A). The point here is that in portfolio optimization the choice of the number of stocks is important. However, this choice is often implicitly determined by the objective function. This means that flaws in the way the objective function react to the number of stocks will affect the performance.

7 Out-of-Sample Performance

It is known that the mean-variance optimal portfolio does not perform well out-of-sample, one reason for this is that mean-variance efficient portfolio weights can be extremely sensitive to changes in returns (Best and Grauer 1991; Hurley and Brimberg 2015). The literature also suggests that portfolios that optimizing risk alone can somehow outperform the mean-variance optimal portfolio on a risk-adjusted basis. Given the result in this paper, it will be interesting to compare the performance of mean-diversification optimal portfolios with the mean-variance optimal portfolios out of sample. Since these portfolios place some weight on returns, the expectation is that they should have better risk-adjusted returns.

To do this, we divide the total period in our data (i.e. 2005–2013) into two periods. The first period is from "2005-01-10" to "2011-01-03" (313 weeks) while the second period is from "2011-01-10" to "2013-11-25" (151 weeks). The various portfolios discussed so far are re-estimated using the first period's data to obtain the optimal portfolio weights for each portfolio. These portfolio weights are then applied at the beginning of the second period and the portfolios are allowed to grow over the second period (note that this means there is no rebalancing). The performance of the different portfolios are compared at the end of the second period, For the comparison we use the ratio of returns to the standard deviation of the portfolios i.e. risk adjusted return (note however that we did not use the risk free rate as in Sharpe ratio). The result is shown in Table 2, the first row show the result of an equally weighted portfolio as a baseline.

For the optimal portfolios, the mean-variance optimal portfolio has the worst performance. This should not be surprising since the mean-variance optimal portfolio is optimized to be optimal in-sample and there is no guarantee that that performance

Table 2 Out-of-sample performance of Risk adjusted return of portfolios

	Equal	NSGA MV	OCP	PDI	|PDI-ICOMP|	DR
Optimal portfolios						
Returns	0.004331	0.007024	0.004929	0.006325	0.006048	0.004899
SD	0.02455	0.052406	0.030792	0.035095	0.032846	0.026497
Return risk ratio	0.176421	0.134039	0.160068	0.180234	0.184133	0.184882
Risk-based portfolio						
Returns	0.004331	0.004282	0.00418	0.004205	0.004175	0.004906
SD	0.02455	0.018522	0.023972	0.023878	0.023878	0.024322
Return risk ratio	0.176421	0.231194	0.174372	0.176085	0.174867	0.201699

will be repeated out-of-sample (note that this also applies to all the other portfolios). The implication here is that the optimal mean-variance portfolio performs worse than all the mean-diversification optimal portfolios. However, we note that this need not be the case for every period or and every universe of stocks. The point here is that under the right conditions incorporating returns in the optimization of diversification measures can be useful. Lastly, the equally weighted portfolio perform better than the mean-variance optimal and the mean-complexity optimal portfolios.

Furthermore, the result also show that the minimum variance portfolio also outperform the mean-variance optimal portfolio out-of-sample, this is similar to the results reported by DeMiguel et al. (2009). For the risk-based portfolios, the minimum variance portfolio has better return-risk ratio than other portfolios. In second place is the portfolio that maximizes DR followed by the equally weighted portfolio. Again it is hard to predict which portfolio will perform better out-of-sample.

This underscores the point of Lee (2011), any portfolio strategy can outperform another one (out-of-sample) under the right set of conditions. All portfolio strategies can be thought of as a special cases of the mean-variance optimal framework, for example when all assets have equal returns, volatility and correlation the equally weighted portfolio is equivalent to the mean-variance optimal portfolio. Lee (2011) also show that when expected returns of all assets are identical the minimum variance portfolio is equivalent to the mean-variance optimal portfolio.

In conclusion these results show that there is value in incorporating returns when optimizing diversification measures. As shown in Table 2 such return-diversification optimal portfolio can outperform the mean-variance optimal portfolio out-of-sample. We also note that the result suggests that risk-based portfolios can outperform portfolios that trade-off returns for risk or diversification measures (i.e. compare each return-risk optimal portfolio in Table 2 with the corresponding risk-based portfolio). While this is the case for this sample, like Lee (2011) there is no guarantee that this performance can be repeated on a different data set.

8 Conclusion

Studies have compared the performance of risk based portfolios with the mean-variance optimal portfolio. As noted by Lee (2011) irrespective of the result of this comparison there is no theory that predicts ex-ante that a risk based portfolio will outperform the optimal portfolio on the mean-variance frontier. Lee (2011) criticized risk and or diversification based approaches to portfolio optimization for not having a clearly defined objective like the Sharpe ratio. In other words, risk/diversification approach involves single objective optimization rather than trading off one objective for the other to find the optimal portfolio.

In this paper, we incorporate return as a second objective to be optimized with diversification. We explore optimization on mean-diversification space for selected diversification measures and identify portfolios that are mean-diversification optimal. Our result suggests that while incorporating returns is costly in terms of higher level of risk relative to risk-based portfolios, the higher risk is well compensated for in the optimal mean-diversification portfolio (in-sample). We argue that while this result may not be applicable out of sample or with dataset from other periods, without exploring the whole frontier it will be naïve to assert that a risk-based portfolio is the optimal choice. In addition, we argue that portfolios that trade-off diversification for returns are more justifiable (theoretically) as competitors to the mean-variance optimal portfolio, unlike portfolios that place zero weight on return. Our out-of-sample result confirm that it is hard to predict the performance of different portfolio strategies but it also shows that incorporating returns in the optimization of risk based portfolios can be valuable.

The main contribution of this paper is at the intersection of Lee (2011) who criticized risk based approaches and Tsao (2010) who use an heuristic method to estimate the mean value-at-risk frontier. We show that by using the method of Tsao (2010) one can empirically shed some light on the criticism in Lee (2011). In this study we find that Lee (2011)'s criticism is justified.

Acknowledgements This research is made possible by the research price awarded under the Young Investigator Training Programme (YITP) during the Third Annual Conference of the International Association for Applied Econometrics (IAAE 2016). The author is also grateful to Prof. Claudio Morana and Università di Milano-Bicocca for hosting the research. Lastly, the assistance of David Mcclelland on calculating out-of-sample performance is acknowledged.

Appendix 1

	Symbol	Company		Symbol	Company
1	AAPL	Apple Inc.	43	KLAC	KLA-Tencor Corp.
2	ADBE	Adobe Systems	44	LBTYA	Liberty Global Plc.
3	ADI	Analog Devices	45	LLTC	Linear Technology Corp.
4	ADP	Automatic Data Processing Inc.	46	MAT	Mattel Inc.
5	ADSK	Autodesk Inc.	47	MCHP	Microchip Technology
6	AKAM	Akamai Technologies Inc.	48	MDLZ	Mondelez International, Inc.
7	ALTR	Altera Corp.	49	MNST	Monster Beverage Corporation
8	ALXN	Alexion Pharmaceuticals, Inc.	50	MSFT	Microsoft Corp.
9	AMAT	Applied Materials	51	MU	Micron Technology
10	AMGN	Amgen	52	MXIM	Maxim Integrated Products, Inc.
11	AMZN	Amazon Corp.	53	MYL	Mylan Inc.
12	ATVI	Activision Blizzard, Inc.	54	NFLX	Netflix, Inc.
13	BRCM	Broadcom Corporation	55	NTAP	NetApp
14	CA	CA, Inc.	56	NUAN	Nuance Communications, Inc.
15	CELG	Celgene Corp.	57	NVDA	Nvidia Corporation
16	CERN	Cerner Corporation	58	ORLY	O'Reilly Auto Parts
17	CHKP	Check Point Software Technologies Ltd.	59	PAYX	Paychex Inc.
18	CHRW	C. H. Robinson Worldwide	60	PCAR	PACCAR Inc.
19	CMCSA	Comcast Corp.	61	PCLN	The Priceline Group Inc.
20	COST	Costco Co.	62	QCOM	QUALCOMM Inc.
21	CSCO	Cisco Systems	63	REGN	Regeneron Pharmaceuticals, Inc.
22	CTSH	Cognizant Technology Solutions	64	ROST	Ross Stores Inc.
23	CTXS	Citrix Systems	65	SBAC	SBA Communications Corp.
24	DLTR	Dollar Tree, Inc.	66	SBUX	Starbucks Corp.
25	DTV	DIRECTV Group Inc.	67	SHLD	Sears Holdings Corporation
26	EBAY	eBay Inc.	68	SIAL	Sigma-Aldrich
27	EQIX	Equinix, Inc.	69	SIRI	Sirius XM Holdings Inc.
28	ESRX	Express Scripts	70	SNDK	SanDisk Corporation
29	EXPD	Expeditors Int'l	71	SPLS	Staples Inc.

(continued)

(continued)

	Symbol	Company		Symbol	Company
30	FAST	Fastenal Co.	72	SRCL	Stericycle Inc.
31	FFIV	F5 Networks, Inc.	73	STX	Seagate Technology Public Limited Company
32	FISV	FIserv Inc.	74	SYMC	Symantec Corp.
33	FOSL	Fossil Group, Inc.	75	TXN	Texas Instruments
34	FOXA	Twenty-First Century Fox, Inc.	76	VOD	Vodafone Group Plc.
35	GILD	Gilead Sciences	77	VRTX	Vertex Pharmaceuticals Incorporated
36	GMCR	Keurig Green Mountain, Inc.	78	WDC	Western Digital
37	GOLD	Randgold Resources Limited	79	WFM	Whole Foods Market, Inc.
38	GOOG	Google Inc.	80	WYNN	Wynn Resorts Ltd.
39	GRMN	Garmin Ltd.			
40	HSIC	Henry Schein, Inc.			
41	INTU	Intuit Inc.			
42	ISRG	Intuitive Surgical Inc.			

Data downloaded using "get.hist.quote" command in R, spans Oct 10, 2005, to Nov 25, 2013

Appendix 2

See Figs. 12, 13, 14, 15, 16 and 17.

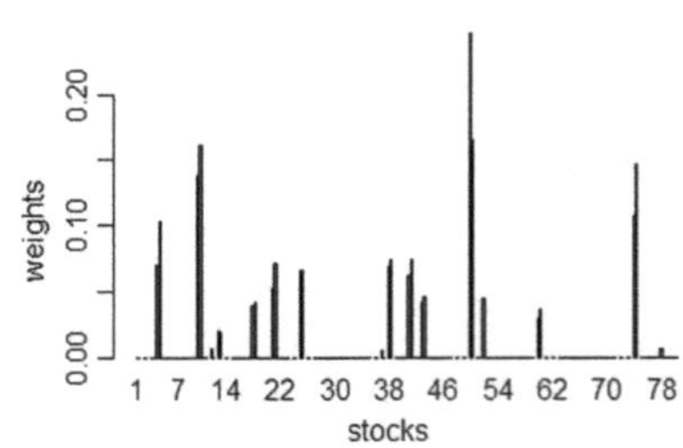

Fig. 12 Weight of stocks in the minimum variance portfolio under QP (red) NSGAII (blue)

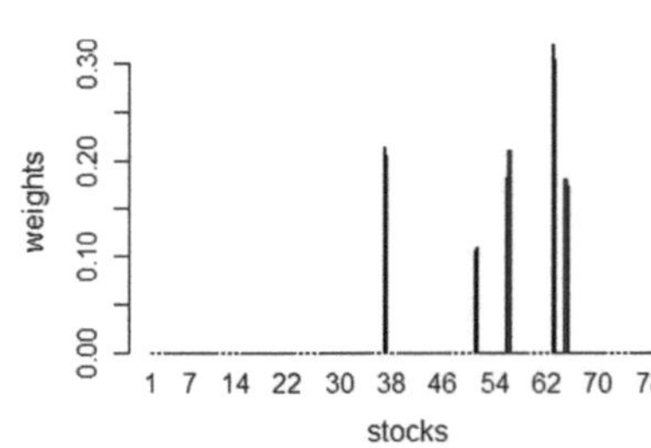

Fig. 13 Weight of stocks in the optimal mean-variance optimal portfolio under QP (red) NSGAII (blue)

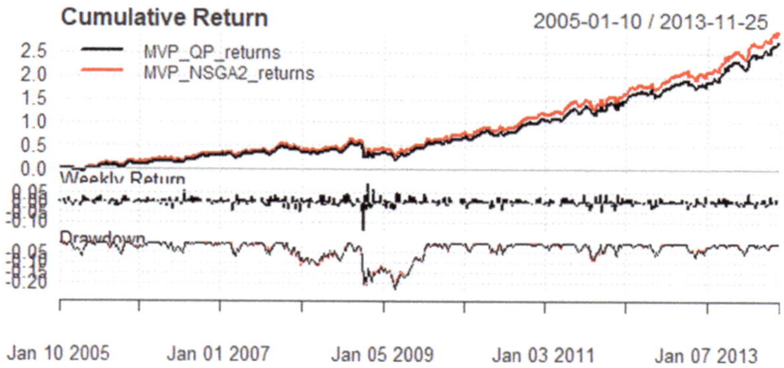

Fig. 14 Cumulative returns and drawdown of minimum variance portfolios (QP and NSGA2). MVP_QP_returns is the cumulative return for the minimum variance portfolio under quadratic programming while MVP_NSGA2_returns is the cumulative returns for the minimum variance portfolio under the genetic algorithm method

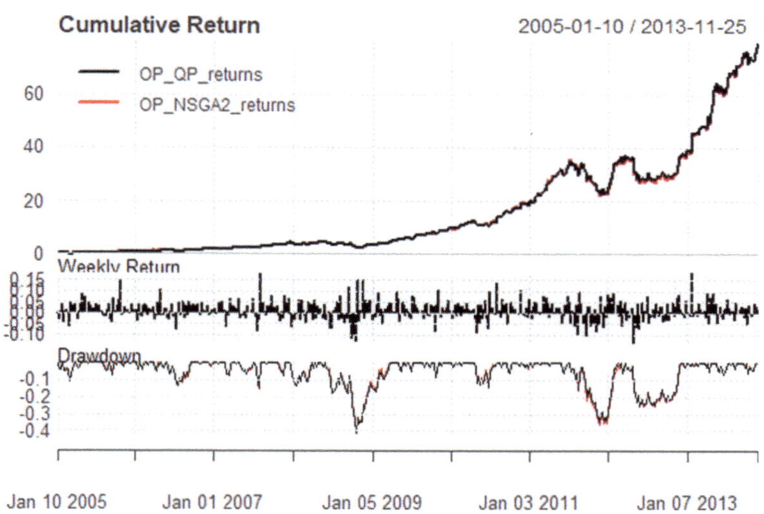

Fig. 15 Cumulative returns and drawdown of mean variance optimal portfolios (QP and NSGA2). OP_QP_returns is the cumulative returns for the mean variance optimal portfolio under quadratic programming while OP_NSGA2_returns is the cumulative returns for the mean variance optimal portfolio under the genetic algorithm method

Fig. 16 Weight of stocks in the optimal PDI portfolio

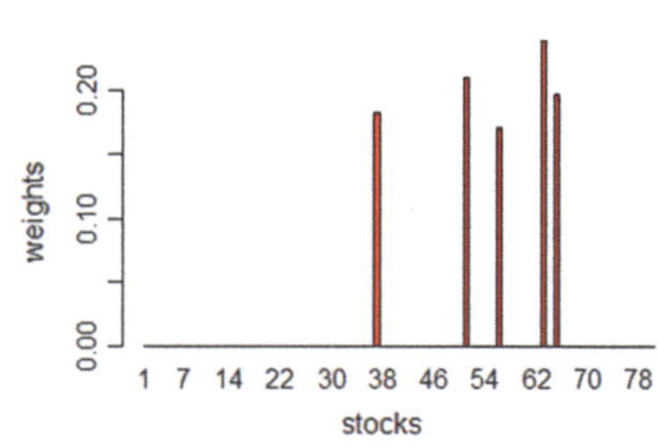

Fig. 17 Weight of stocks in the optimal COMPLEXITY portfolio with 5 stocks

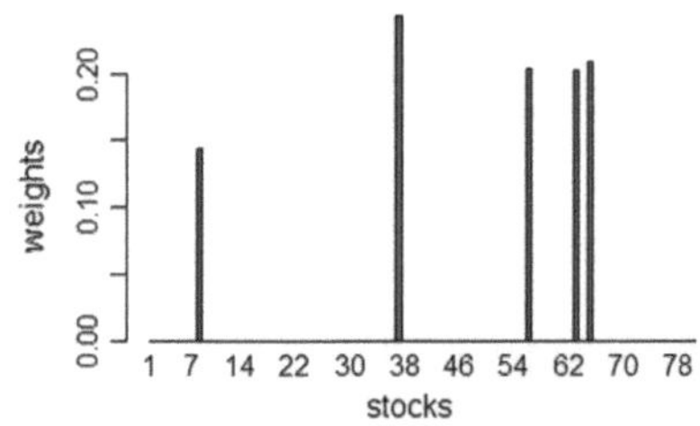

References

Best, M. J., & Grauer, R. R. (1991). On the sensitivity of mean-variance-efficient portfolios to changes in asset means: Some analytical and computational results. *Review of Financial Studies, 4*(2), 315–342.

Clarke, R., De Silva, H., & Thorley, S. (2006). Minimum-variance portfolios in the US equity market. *Journal of Portfolio Management, 33*(1), 10.

Choueifaty, Y., & Coignard, Y. (2008). Toward maximum diversification. *The Journal of Portfolio Management, 35*(1), 40–51.

Crezée, D. P., & Swinkels, L. A. (2010). High-conviction equity portfolio optimization. *The Journal of Risk, 13*(2), 57.

Deb, K., Pratap, A., Agarwal, S., & Meyarivan, T. (2002). A fast and elitist multiobjective genetic algorithm: NSGA-II. *IEEE Transactions on Evolutionary Computation, 6*(2), 182–197.

DeMiguel, V., Garlappi, L., & Uppal, R. (2009). Optimal versus naive diversification: How inefficient is the 1/N portfolio strategy? *The Review of Financial Studies, 22*(5), 1915–1953.

Diyarbakirlioglu, E., & Satman, M. H. (2013). The maximum diversification index. *Journal of Asset Management, 14*(6), 400–409.

Hurley, W. J., & Brimberg, J. (2015). A note on the sensitivity of the strategic asset allocation problem. *Operations Research Perspectives, 2*, 133–136.

Kalayci, C. B., Ertenlice, O., Akyer, H., & Aygoren, H. (2017). A review on the current applications of genetic algorithms in mean-variance portfolio optimization. *Pamukkale University Journal of Engineering Sciences, 23*(4).

Kirchner, U., & Zunckel, C. (2011). *Measuring Portfolio Diversification.* arXiv preprint arXiv: 1102.4722.

Lee, W. (2011). Risk-based asset allocation: A new answer to an old question? *Journal of Portfolio Management, 37*(4), 11.

Lin, C.-C., & Liu, Y.-T. (2008). Genetic algorithms for portfolio selection problems with minimum transaction lots. *European Journal of Operational Research, 185*(1), 393–404.

Markowitz, H. (1952). Portfolio selection*. *The Journal of Finance, 7*(1), 77–91.

Meucci, A. (2009). *Risk and asset allocation.* Springer Science & Business Media.

Oyenubi, A. (2010). *Information theoretic measure of complexity and stock market analysis: Using the JSE as a case study* (Master's thesis). University of Cape Town. http://open.uct.ac.za/handle/11427/10967.

Oyenubi, A. (2016). Diversification measures and the optimal number of stocks in a portfolio: An information theoretic explanation. *Computational Economics*, 1–29.

Ponsich, A., Jaimes, A. L., & Coello, C. A. C. (2013). A survey on multiobjective evolutionary algorithms for the solution of the portfolio optimization problem and other finance and economics applications. *IEEE Transactions on Evolutionary Computation (IEEE), 17*(3), 321–344.

Rudin, A. M., & Morgan, J. S. (2006) A portfolio diversification index. *The Journal of Portfolio Management (Institutional Investor Journals), 32*(2), 81–89.

Scherer, B. (2011). A note on the returns from minimum variance investing. *Journal of Empirical Finance, 18*(4), 652–660.

Sharpe, W. F. (1966). Mutual fund performance. *The Journal of Business, 39*(1), 119–138.
Tsao, C.-Y. (2010). Portfolio selection based on the mean–VaR efficient frontier. *Quantitative Finance, 10*(8), 931–945.
Tsao, C.-Y., & Liu, C.-K. (2006). Incorporating value-at-risk in portfolio selection: An evolutionary approach. *JCIS*.
Tsou, C. S. V., & Lee, M. M. C. A. (2013). Package 'nsga2R'.

Time Series Prediction with LSTM Networks and Its Application to Equity Investment

Ken Matsumoto and Naoki Makimoto

Abstract Forecasting financial time series has been traditional and important theme for market analysis and investment strategy. However, it is not easy to capture the statistical characteristics of the data due to high noise level and volatile features. On the other hand, technological innovation by artificial intelligence is progressing rapidly in various fields. Especially, long short-term memory (LSTM) has been widely used in natural language processing and speech recognition. In this paper, we study prediction performance of LSTM by comparing it with other machine learning models such as logistics regression and support vector machine. The characteristics of these models were first investigated by applying them to predict different types of simulated time series data. We then conducted an empirical study to predict stock returns in TOPIX Core 30 with application to portfolio selection problem. Overall, LSTM showed favorable performance than other methods, which is consistent with Fischer and Krauss (Eur J Oper Res 270(2):654–669, 2018) for S&P500 data.

Keywords Time series model · Stock return prediction · Portfolio selection · LSTM networks · TOPIX Core30

1 Introduction

It is an important issue to accurately forecast returns of stocks or other financial assets from the viewpoints of both market analysis and investment. Traditional approaches based on the econometric time series analysis such as autoregressive (AR) model usually assumes linear relation between past and future returns. Although these basic models have been extended to describe the stylized facts observed in the market such

K. Matsumoto (✉)
Ebisu Lab, 6-28-2-107 Otsuka, Bunkyo, Tokyo, Japan
e-mail: matsumoto.ken.xj@alumni.tsukuba.ac.jp

N. Makimoto
University of Tsukuba, 3-29-1 Otsuka, Bunkyo, Tokyo, Japan
e-mail: makimoto@gssm.gsbs.tsukuba.ac.jp

L. Pichl et al. (eds.), *Advanced Studies of Financial Technologies and Cryptocurrency Markets*, https://doi.org/10.1007/978-981-15-4498-9_4

as volatility clustering and regime switching, the predictability of time series models are still limited mainly due to the weak linear dependence of return data.

On the other hand, predictions using machine learning and artificial intelligence models have attracted considerable attention in recent years. For example, recurrent neural network (RNN) (Robinson 1994; Bengio et al. 2013) contributes greatly to the improvement of recognition accuracy by effectively capturing the features of sound waves and word strings. In addition, long short-term memory (LSTM), one kind of the RNN with feedback links, was proposed to resolve the drawback of RNN by retaining time related information for longer time period (Olah 2015; Palangi et al. 2016). LSTM and other deep learning-based models drastically improved the accuracy of the prediction in the field of, for example, natural language processing (Sutskever et al. 2014) and speech recognition (Hinton et al. 2012). In contrast to the traditional time series models that assume linear relationship, these models are able to flexibly represent nonlinear relation between input and output. In this regard, an application of these models is expected to improve forecasting accuracy if the past returns have nonlinear effect on future returns.

The main purpose of this paper is to confirm prediction capability of LSTM and other machine learning models for two types of time series data. At first, we use the simulation data sampled from AR and AR with volatility clustering to understand the characteristics of each model and evaluate predictability. The second set of data is daily returns of TOPIX Core 30, the Japanese stock market, for which we check the predictability of positive/negative return. We also evaluate the performance of the portfolio constructed based on model predictions.

This paper is organized as follows. Section 2 gives a brief overview of previous researches on financial time series analysis which is classified into two categories: econometric approach and artificial intelligence approach. In Sect. 3, we examine LSTM and other models to predict simulated data from AR and AR + GARCH process and compare the accuracy. In Sect. 4, we conduct empirical application to stock return data of TOPIX Core 30. An application to portfolio selection problem is also discussed. Finally, Sect. 5 summarizes and concludes the paper.

2 Related Literatures

There are a huge number of literatures on the time series analysis of financial data and its application to investment strategy. The most widely used model is autoregressive integrated moving average (ARIMA) that is utilized for analyses based on the econometric theory. On the other hand, recent technology innovations enhance development of other types of analysis such as machine learning and artificial intelligence. In this section, we briefly summarize the literatures related to those approaches.

2.1 Econometric Approach

ARIMA model is an integrated process of ARMA model that decomposes time series data into AR and MA terms. Since AR model has a natural structure that the future data is more affected by the recent data than the past, AR and related models have been deeply studied in the econometric analyses of time series data. These models are generalized to some directions. A VARIMA model is developed for analyzing multi-variate time series data. Another direction of extension is to develop time series models that are able to describe stylized facts observed in financial markets such as volatility clustering or regime switch.

ARCH (Engle 1982) and GARCH (Bollerslev 1986) models are developed to represent volatility clustering. Another type of model that describes fluctuation of volatility is a stochastic volatility model by Heston (1993) where the volatility is modeled by a AR process. These models explicitly include dependent structure of the variance of error terms so that, once the level of volatility jumps up, high level of volatility continues for some time. Many empirical studies have shown that GARCH and stochastic volatility models well capture the structure of market volatility.

The regime switching model is a times series model where a set of model parameters changes when the underlying state changes. The underlying state is called regime and represents, for example, business cycle or market circumstances. For example, Ang and Bekaert (2002) have proposed a two-regime switching model to describe the relation between asset correlation and volatility that the correlation between returns on international assets tends to increase as the market becomes more volatile.

To construct an investment strategy based on econometric approach, we first select a time series model such as AR or AR + GARCH, forecast the return and risk of assets based on the model, then make an investment decision. For example, Komatsu and Makimoto (2015) proposed a regime switching factor model to predict asset returns and derived optimal investment strategy for a mean-variance based utility function. Also, their empirical studies show that 2 and 3 regime models exhibit superior performance of the portfolio over the single regime model.

2.2 Machine Learning and Artificial Intelligence Approach

Recently, an increasing number of literatures apply machine learning and artificial intelligence approach to financial time series. Moritz and Zimmermann (2014) conducted an empirical analysis of U.S. stock returns from the Center for Research in Security Prices (CRSP). A random forest model is trained to predict the return of each stock, and a quantile trading strategy is developed based on tree-based conditional portfolio sorts. Takeuchi and Lee (2013) also analyzed CRSP data and proposed an enhanced momentum strategy by stacked autoencoders constructed from some restricted Boltzmann machine (RBM). The RBM performs feature abstraction from input feature vectors, then the encoder is employed as a classifier to calculate the probability for each stock to outperform the cross-sectional median return.

Zhang (2003) proposed a hybrid model combining the statistical model with the artificial intelligence model. An ARIMA model is fitted to the time series data, and the residuals are then fitted with neural networks instead of the widely-used volatility fluctuation model. The result shows that the hybrid model has higher accuracy than the ARIMA model or the neural network alone.

Most relevant literatures to this paper are researches by Fischer and Krauss (2018) and Krauss et al. (2017) where LSTM together with some other machine learning models such as gradient boosting tree are applied to S&P500 data to predict the probability of each stock to out/underperform the cross-sectional median. One key finding there is that LSTM exhibits higher accuracy of prediction than the other machine learning models. Also, LSTM shows superior performance of the quantile portfolio constructed from model predictions.

Although machine learning and related models have been widely recognized in finance, there is little consensus on which model is effective for predicting financial time series. In particular, research on the application of LSTM in finance is still limited because of a high degree of difficulty in model construction and hyperparameter tuning. In this research, we therefore verify the effectiveness of LSTM and other models through simulational study as well as empirical analysis of financial time series.

3 Simulation Study for Comparison of Prediction Models

In general, the stock return series has a low signal-to-noise ratio. This makes it difficult to properly evaluate the performance of prediction models through empirical studies using actual stock return data. In this section, we therefore conduct a simulation study where LSTM and some other machine learning models are used to predict time series data generated from AR and AR + GARCH models to compare their performances.

3.1 Experimental Time Series Data

To compare prediction models, we generate 6 sets of time series data with different statistical characteristics. Here and in what follows, let R_t denote the return data at time t. Then, 3 sets of simulated return data are generated from AR(p) model

$$R_t = c + \sum_{i=1}^{p} \phi_i R_{t-i} + \varepsilon_t, \qquad \varepsilon_t \sim WN(0, 1^2) \tag{1}$$

Table 1 Parameters for simulation data. For AR(5) model, c is set to either 0 or positive values to adjust given ratio of positive labels

Time series	c	ϕ_1	ϕ_2	ϕ_3	ϕ_4	ϕ_5	α	β	ω
AR(1)	0	0.8							
AR(3)	0	0.3	−0.4	0.2					
AR(5)	$0/c$	0.2	−0.2	−0.2	0.2	0.4			
AR(1) + GARCH(1, 1)	0	0.8					0.0	0.0	1.0
AR(1) + GARCH(1, 1)	0	0.8					0.2	0.2	0.6
AR(1) + GARCH(1, 1)	0	0.8					0.4	0.4	0.2

where c is a constant term, ϕ_i's are autoregressive coefficients, and ε_t is a white noise with mean 0 and variance 1^2.

Although AR(p) is a standard model for financial time series, observed data in financial markets often exhibits volatility clustering that is not described by AR(p) model. To simulate such characteristic of financial data, the remaining 3 sets are generated from AR(1) + GARCH(1, 1) model given as

$$R_t = \phi R_{t-1} + u_t \tag{2}$$

$$u_t = \sqrt{h_t} v_t, \qquad v_t \sim IN(0, 1^2) \tag{3}$$

$$h_t = \omega + \beta h_{t-1} + \alpha u_{t-1}^2 \tag{4}$$

where v_t independently follows standard normal distribution. As can be seen in (4), $\alpha + \beta$ represents the degree of volatility clustering. That is, the volatility clustering is more persistent when $\alpha + \beta$ is close to 1.

Table 1 summarizes the parameters of AR(p) and AR(1) + GARCH(1, 1) used to generate simulation data.

In AR(p) model, we choose $p = 1, 3, 5$. Compared with $\phi_1 = 0.8$ in AR(1), we choose smaller coefficients in AR(3) and AR(5). In general, smaller coefficients make prediction more difficult in AR(p) models since signal-to-noise ratio decreases. In GARCH models, the time stationary mean of h_t is given by $\omega/(1 - (\alpha + \beta))$. The parameters in Table 1 are so chosen that $\omega/(1 - (\alpha + \beta)) = 1$ for all GARCH models.

3.2 Learning Models

In addition to the LSTM model, we evaluate and compare the prediction capability of the following 4 standard machine learning models. For more detailed description, implementation, and framework, see `scikit-learn` (Pedregosa et al. 2011) for machine learning models, and `keras` (Chollet et al. 2015) for deep learning models.

- Regularized logistic regression (**LOG**)
  As most basic but robust model, we prepared the LOG which has regularized method that linearly combines the L1 and L2 penalties (Friedman et al. 2010). The LOG serves as a baseline, so that we can derive the advantage of the more complex and computationally intensive LSTM networks.
- Random forest (**RAF**)
  The RAF is composed of deep decorrelated decision trees built on different bootstrap samples (Breiman 2001). Since various types of weak learners can be combined to perform diverse learning, it is possible to create a strong estimator that has high performance and is less prone to overfitting.
- Gradient boosting decision tree (**GBT**)
  The GBT has boosting method for converting weak learners, i.e. decision trees into one that achieves arbitrarily high accuracy (Friedman 2002). The boosting works by sequentially applying weak learners to repeatedly re-weighted versions of samples.
- Support vector machine (**SVM**)
  The SVM has a solid theoretical background, an intuitive geometrical interpretation, and several properties that link the development of kernel space and convex optimization (Cortes and Vapnik 1995). The algorithm outputs an optimal separating hyperplane which categorizes new examples.

For each simulation data, we generate the feature vector (input data) and the response variable (output data). Let the cumulative return $CR_{t,\,m}$ over m periods be

$$CR_{t,m} = \sum_{i=0}^{m-1} R_{t-i} = R_t + R_{t-1} + R_{t-2} + \cdots + R_{t-(m-1)} \tag{5}$$

For predicting R_{t+1} of AR(p), we input a feature vector $\{CR_{t,1}, CR_{t,2}, \ldots, CR_{t,p}\}$ into each learning model. This means that each model has enough information since the conditional distribution of R_{t+1} is completely determined from those data in AR(p) model.

Next, we prepare a binary true label as the output data for classification. The true label is the sign of one point ahead return R_{t+1} defined by

$$B_{t+1} = \begin{cases} 0 \ (R_{t+1} < 0) \\ 1 \ (R_{t+1} \geq 0) \end{cases} \tag{6}$$

When $c = 0$, the ratio of positive label ($B_{t+1} = 1$) is 50% in both AR(p) and AR + GARCH models. To see this, note that the time stationary mean of the process is given by

$$m = \frac{c}{1 - \sum_{i=1}^{p} \phi_i} \tag{7}$$

which equals 0 when $c = 0$, and that error terms ε_t or u_t are normally distributed with mean 0. If $c \neq 0$, the ratio of positive label deviates from 50% which could affect the prediction capability of each model. We therefore analyze the cases with the ratio of positive label 60 and 70% in AR(5) model where c is adjusted to achieve those ratios.

The prediction capability of each learning model is evaluated by comparing the probability of label 0/1 predicted by each model with the true probability calculated as follows. At time $t-1$, we observe the data R_S up to $s \leq t-1$. Given those data, R_t is normally distributed with the mean $\sum_{i=1}^{p} \phi_i R_{t-i}$, the variance 1 for AR($p$) and h_{t-1} for AR(1) + GARCH(1, 1). Therefore, the true probability of $R_t > 0$ is given by

$$\mathrm{P}\left(c + \sum_{i=1}^{p} \phi_i R_{t-i} + \varepsilon_t > 0\right) = \Phi\left(\frac{c + \sum_{i=1}^{p} \phi_i R_{t-i}}{\sigma}\right) \tag{8}$$

where $\Phi(\,)$ denotes the standard normal distribution function and the standard deviation $\sigma = 1$ for AR(p) or $\sigma = \sqrt{h_t}$ for AR(1) + GARCH(1, 1).

We set the sample size of each simulation dataset to 2000. the datasets are then divided into three subsets: training, validation, and test data. In order to minimize information leakage, the latest 20% of the time series is used as the test data. The remaining 80% of the data is divided into training and validation data by stratified extraction method. Given a hyperparameter group of a certain combination, the model parameters are estimated from training data. Then, the evaluation is performed using validation data. For hyperparameter turning, we adopt Bayesian optimization, which has become mainstream in recent years (Bergstra 2013).

3.3 Results and Discussions

Figure 1 shows the results of predicted probabilities that serve as criteria for label classification. The horizontal axis of each figure shows the theoretical value obtained from Eq. (8), and the vertical axis shows the predicted probability by the model. These histograms are shown outside the scatter plot (top and right, respectively).

When focusing on the predicted and theoretical probabilities of LOG, we find that the slope is almost 1 and the error is small. This is a natural consequence since an AR model is expressed as a linear sum of past data and LOG is a logit transformation of a linear combination of past data. SVM and LSTM are almost the same as LOG. In contrast, the scatter plot of RAF widely spreads along the regression line. Furthermore, the slope decreases for higher probability. The predicted probabilities of GBT is distributed similar to RAF, except that the possible range is not 0 to 1, but the distribution is concentrated at 0.2 or 0.8.

Next, Fig. 2 shows the scatter plots for AR + GARCH data where the results for $\alpha + \beta = 0, 0.4, 0.8$ are shown from the top. The predicted probabilities of LOG, SVM, and LSTM are in good agreement with the theoretical value, and their shapes are almost equal. On the other hand, the predicted probabilities of RAF and GBT are different from the theoretical values, similar to the results of the AR process.

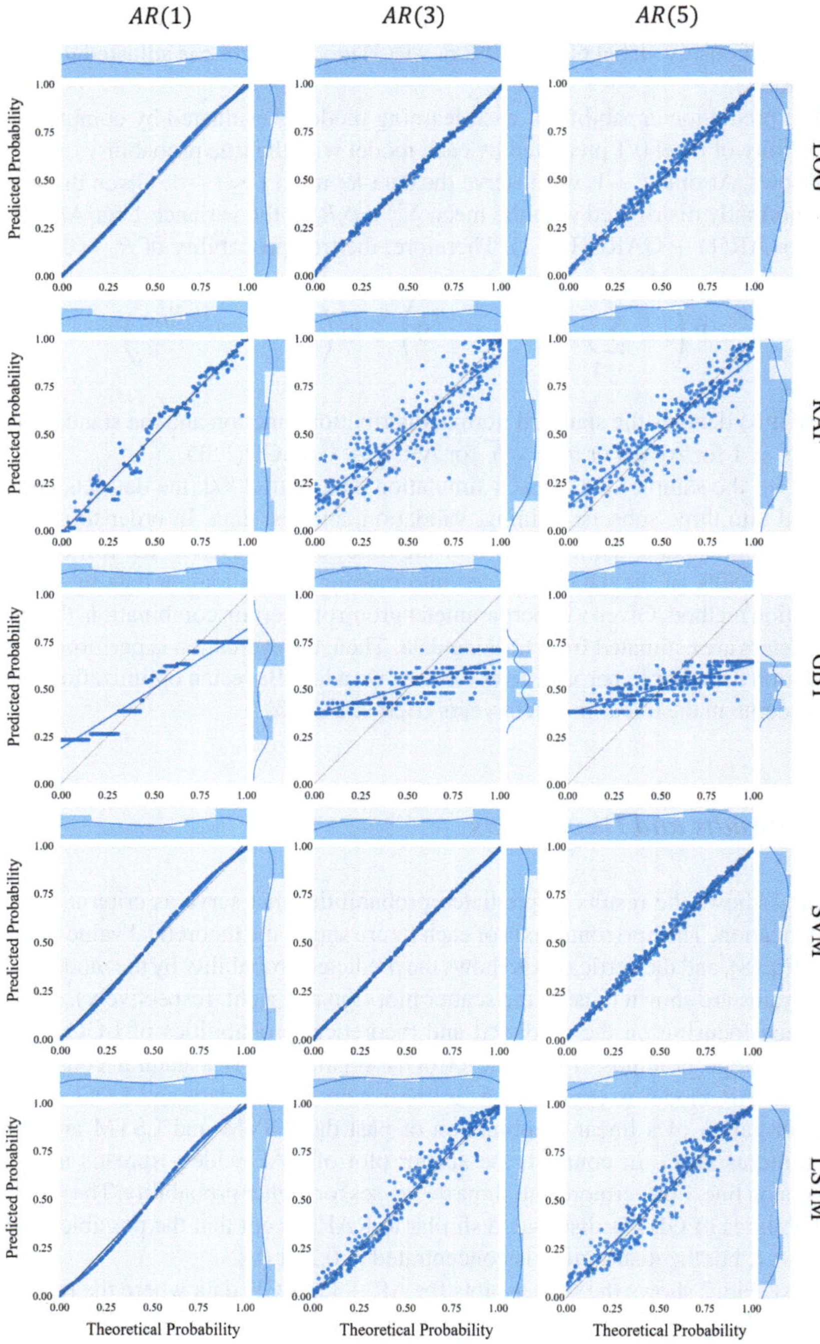

Fig. 1 Comparison of predicted probabilities and theoretical values of each model for AR(p) data. The horizontal/vertical axis shows the theoretical/predicted probabilities with their histograms. AR(1), AR(3), and AR(5) are shown from the left to right. LOG, RAF, GBT, SVM, and LSTM are shown from the top to bottom

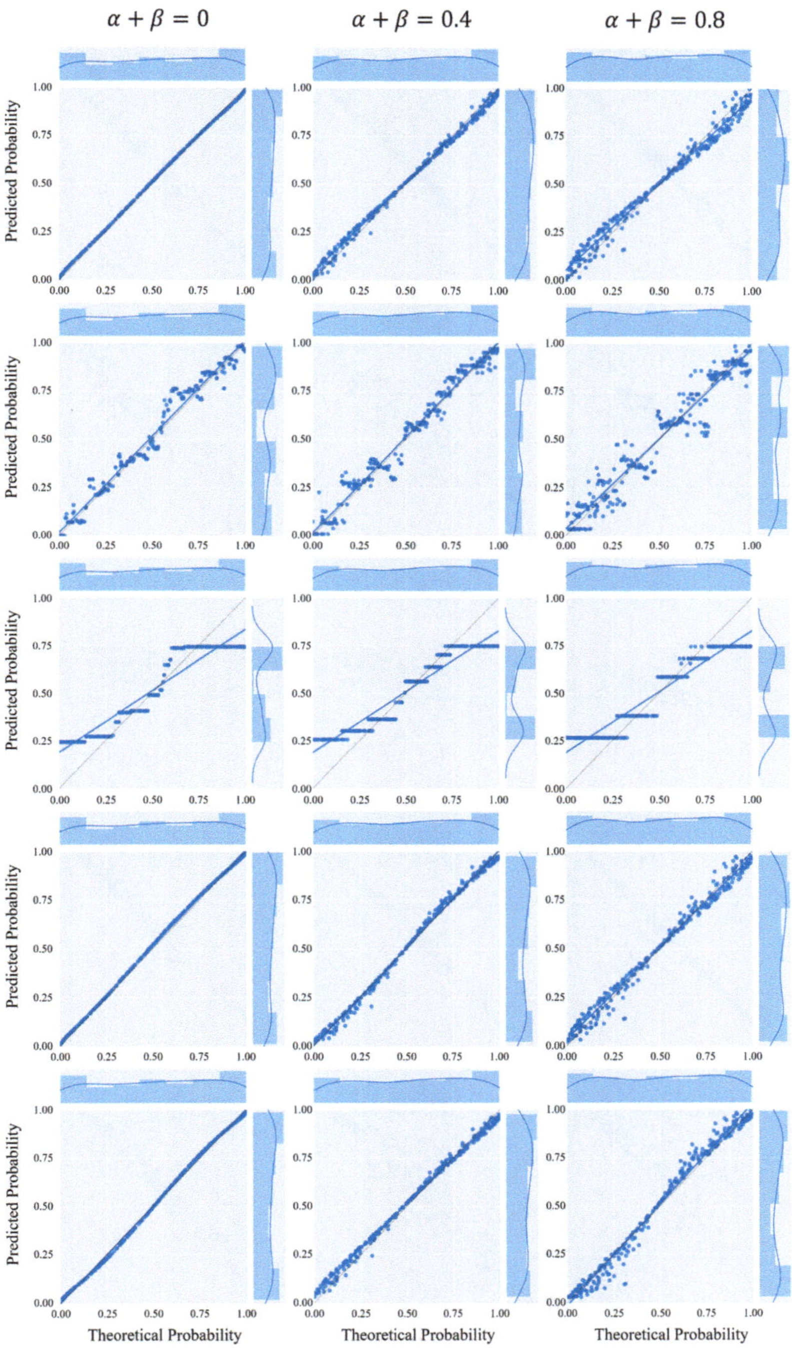

Fig. 2 Comparison of predicted probabilities and theoretical values of each model for AR(1) + GARCH(1, 1) data. The horizontal/vertical axis shows the theoretical/predicted probabilities with their histograms. $\alpha + \beta = 0, 0.4, 0.8$ are shown from the left to right. LOG, RAF, GBT, SVM, and LSTM are shown from the top to bottom

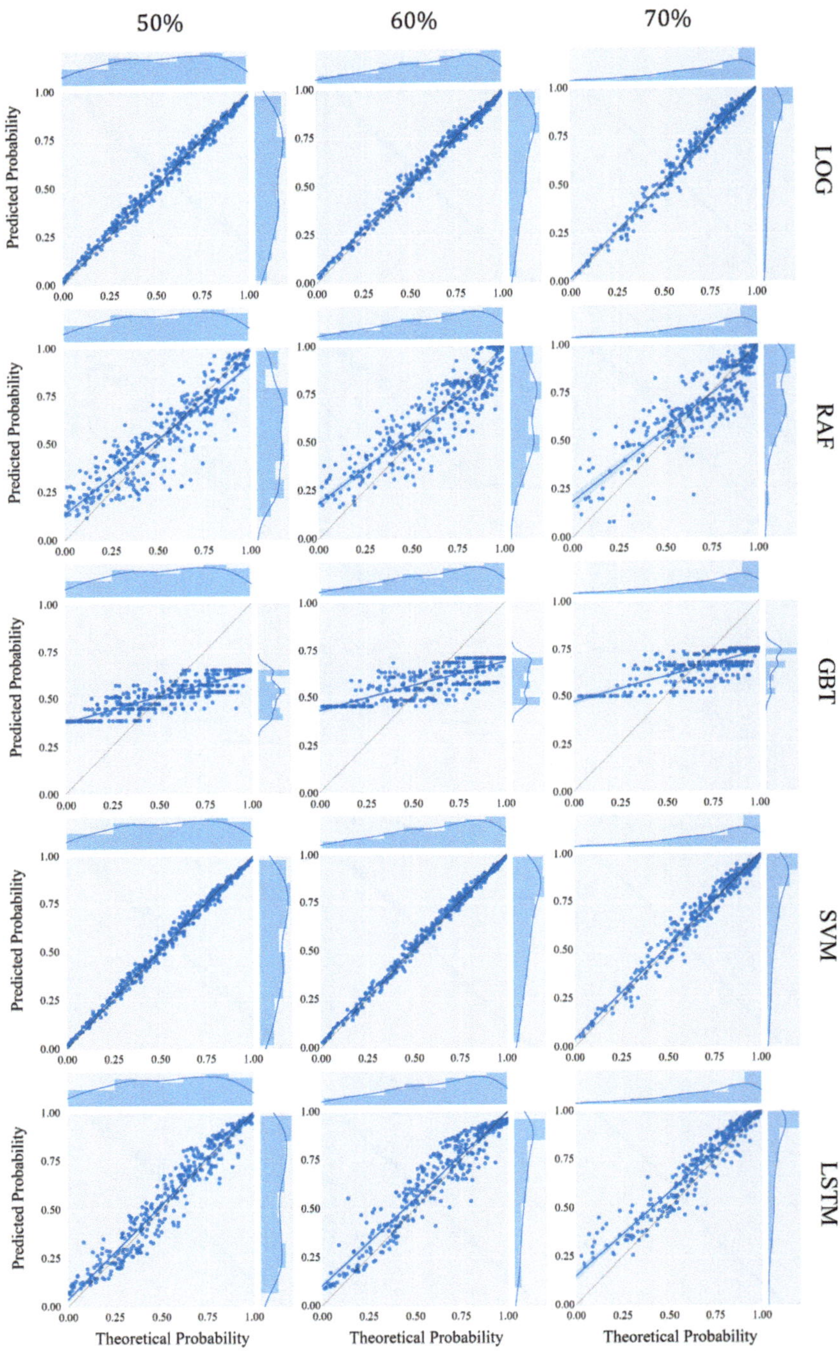

Fig. 3 Comparison of predicted probabilities and theoretical values of each model of AR(5) data. The horizontal/vertical axis shows the theoretical/predicted probabilities with their histograms. The ratios of positive label 50, 60, and 70% are shown from the left to right. LOG, RAF, GBT, SVM, and LSTM are shown from the top to bottom

Based on the experimental results, we discuss the characteristics of each model. The LOG has the fewest hyperparameters and thus robust as expected. Since the predicted probability and the theoretical value are in good agreement, it is notable that the probability can be directly interpreted as the predictability of the model. In contrast, the RAF and the GBT showed poor results. The discrepancy between the predicted probability and the theoretical value may be caused by the use of a decision tree as a weak learner. It is difficult to measure the predictability by the predicted probability, so that some probability calibration process would be required. The result of SVM represents stable performance as well as LOG. However, LOG is an identification model, whereas SVM is an identification function. For this reason, the SVM itself could not calculate the predicted probability. Therefore, in `scikit-learn` framework (Pedregosa et al. 2011), the calibrated probability was generated by Platt scaling for the case of binary classification (Platt et al. 1999). The LSTM achieved almost the same performance as LOG and SVM. Since LSTM is an identification model similar to LOG, the predicted probability could be interpreted as the predictability.

Finally, we consider the case when the ratio of positive label changes from 50% in AR(5) model. Figure 3 shows the scatter plots of 5 models for the ratios of positive label 50, 60 and 70%. As the ratio of positive label increases, the histogram of theoretical values is steadily biased. In LOG and SVM model, the measured values and the theoretical values are in good agreement, so that those models are robust against imbalanced data. As with previous results, RAF and SVM perform poorly. The slope of LSTM gradually decreases as the ratio of positive label increases. The predicted probabilities are distributed approximately from 0.2 to 1 and are more biased than the theoretical distribution. This bias is peculiar to LSTM model and the label ratio is likely to have an impact on the prediction capability.

The evaluation of machine learning models is often discussed by comparing true labels with predicted labels such as accuracy. However, paying attention to predicted probabilities, there were significant differences in the shape of the distribution and the variation. In addition, such a variety of the probabilities is compatible with stacking of ensemble learning. In fact, Krauss et al. (2017) shows an improvement in prediction accuracy by stacking various models.

4 Stock Return Prediction and Its Application to Portfolio Selection

In this section, we apply LSTM and other machine learning models discussed in Sect. 3 to stock return prediction in the Japanese market. In addition, we discuss the performance of the portfolio selection. based on the prediction models.

4.1 Data and Prediction Models

As an empirical analysis, we focused on the daily returns of 30 constituent stocks in the TOPIX Core30 (Japan Exchange Group 2017). The TOPIX Core30 is one of the "TOPIX new index series" and consists of 30 stocks with particularly high market capitalization and liquidity among all stocks in the first section of the Tokyo Stock Exchange. We use the daily log-return of the constituent stocks as of October 2017. Note that the constituents of TOPIX Core30 are reviewed once a year in order to better reflect the current market situation. The length of the data is approximately 2150 days from January 2009 to December 2017.

Let P_t^s and P_t^{TPX} be the time t price of stock s and TOPIX index respectively, and define daily log-returns by $R_t^s = \ln(P_t^s/P_{t-1}^s)$ and $R_t^{TPX} = \ln(P_t^{TPX}/P_{t-1}^{TPX})$. We also denote the cumulative returns in the past m days by $CR_{t,m}^s = \ln(P_t^s/P_{t-m}^s)$ and $CR_{t,m}^{TPX} = \ln(P_t^{TPX}/P_{t-m}^{TPX})$.

For the purpose of stock return prediction, we employ LSTM, LOG, RAF, GBT and SVM that have already been examined for simulation data in Sect. 3. Two cumulative daily returns $CR_{t,m}^s$ and $CR_{t,m}^{TPX}$ within the past year (240 days) are selected as feature vectors. Krauss et al. (2017) pointed out importance of the cumulative returns and suggested that not only the most recent daily returns but also returns in the longer intervals such as 40, 60, and 240 days could contribute to improve return predictability. We therefore construct the feature vectors by $(CR_{t,m}^s, CR_{t,m}^{TPX})$ for $m \in \{1, 2, \ldots, 9, 10, 20, 40, 60, 120, 240\}$ with the total number of timestamps is 15.

Since our main objective here is to outperform the TOPIX, we denote an excess return of stock s by

$$y_t^s = R_t^s - R_t^{TPX} \tag{9}$$

The target positive/negative label for binary classification is then defined by

$$B_t^s = \begin{cases} 0 & (y_t^s < 0) \\ 1 & (y_t^s \geq 0) \end{cases} \tag{10}$$

The data preprocessing and the optimization procedure for hyperparameter tuning conforms to Sect. 3.2.

4.2 Evaluation of Stock Return Prediction

At time t, each model makes 1-day ahead predicted probability of positive label

$$\widehat{p}_{t+1}^s = \mathrm{P}(B_t^s = 1) \tag{11}$$

based on the available feature vectors $(CR^{s}_{t,m}, CR^{TPX}_{t,m})$ for $m \in \{1, \ldots, 10, \ldots, 240\}$ as explained above. The prediction of positive/negative label is then defined by

$$\widehat{B}^{s}_{t+1} = \begin{cases} 0 & (\widehat{p}^{s}_{t+1} < 0.5) \\ 1 & (\widehat{p}^{s}_{t+1} \geq 0.5) \end{cases} \tag{12}$$

The predictability of each model is evaluated from the three viewpoints: prediction capability, predicted probability, and return/risk.

4.2.1 Evaluation of Prediction Capability

The accuracy, F1 score, and Area Under the ROC Curve (AUC) are adopted for evaluating model predictability. The F1 score is interpreted as a weighted average of the precision and the recall. Assuming that predicting a positive label is equally important to that of a negative label, we calculate two F1 scores, then adopt their weighted average by the number of true instances for each label. The AUC is a typical metric for particularly binary classification problem at various thresholds settings. Since the Receiver Operating Characteristic (ROC) is a probability curve, the AUC represents degree or measure of separability.

Table 2 summarizes the mean and standard deviation of accuracy, F1 score, and AUC of the 30 stocks, and Figs. 4, 5 and 6 show the violin plot of their distribution. In those results, LSTM achieves the highest accuracy while LOG is the lowest, which is different from the simulation study in Sect. 3 where both LSTM and LOG show favorable accuracy. We also observe that accuracy of LSTM and GBT is rather stable over 30 stocks as the level of the standard deviation is low. In contrast, F1 scores of RAF and SVM are relatively low and widely spread. Since F1 score indicates the coincidence of positive label between data and prediction, prediction of RAF and SVM has some bias to one side.

The difference of AUC among all models is smaller than accuracy and F1 score. In fact, both RAF and SVM achieve AUC comparable to other models in spite of their poor F1 scores. It is also noted that the value of AUC depends on the classification threshold that is set to 0.5 in our analysis, i.e., $\widehat{B}^{s}_{t+1}$ is determined from whether $\widehat{p}^{s}_{t+1}$ is greater than or equal to 0.5. This means that AUC could be improved by changing the classification threshold from 0.5.

Table 2 Comparison of prediction capability. The mean (standard deviation) of 30 stocks is displayed for accuracy, F1 score, and AUC

	LOG (%)	RAF (%)	GBT (%)	SVM (%)	LSTM (%)
Accuracy	50.7 (2.9)	51.5 (3.3)	51.7 (2.3)	51.6 (2.4)	53.4 (2.3)
F1 score	49.8 (3.1)	44.6 (6.5)	49.4 (3.4)	43.7 (7.4)	50.8 (4.2)
AUC	51.4 (3.5)	51.0 (2.7)	51.6 (3.1)	50.8 (3.3)	52.8 (3.4)

4.2.2 Evaluation of Predicted Probability

This subsection is concerned with positive predicted label $\widehat{B}_t^s$ and probability $\widehat{p}_t^s$. For each stock, we define positive ratio of the true label B_t^s and predicted label $\widehat{B}_t^s$ respectively by

$$b^s = \frac{1}{T}\sum_{t=1}^{T} B_t^s, \qquad \widehat{b}^s = \frac{1}{T}\sum_{t=1}^{T} \widehat{B}_t^s \tag{13}$$

where T denotes the data length. Table 3 summarizes the mean of b^s (1st row) and $\widehat{b}^s$ (2nd row) over the 30 stocks, with the standard deviation in parenthesis. We also calculate the mean and standard deviation of the predicted probability $\widehat{p}_t^s$ by

$$\widehat{\mu}_p^s = \frac{1}{T}\sum_{t=1}^{T} \widehat{p}_t^s, \qquad \widehat{\sigma}_p^s = \sqrt{\frac{1}{T-1}\sum\nolimits_{t=1}^{T} (\widehat{p}_t^s - \mu^s)^2} \tag{14}$$

The 3rd row of Table 3 displays the mean (standard deviation) of $\widehat{\mu}_p^s$ over the 30 stocks, while the 4th row is the mean (standard deviation) of $\widehat{\sigma}_p^s$. Figures 7, 8 and 9 respectively show the violin plot of $\widehat{b}^s$, $\widehat{\mu}_p^s$ and $\widehat{\sigma}_p^s$.

While the standard deviation of b is 2.2%, the standard deviation of $\widehat{b}$ is obviously large, especially in RAF and SVM. When $\widehat{b}^s$ is greatly biased to 0/1, it means that, the predicted return of a certain stock s would be almost negative/positive. The effectiveness of such a biased model would be debatable. For example, if the accuracy is at a very high level of approximately 70%, the model is valuable even though there

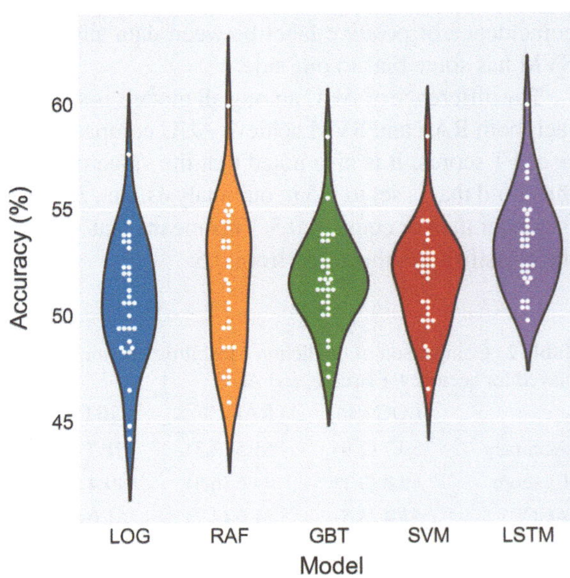

Fig. 4 Comparison of accuracy. Each violin plot represents the distribution of stock s accuracy

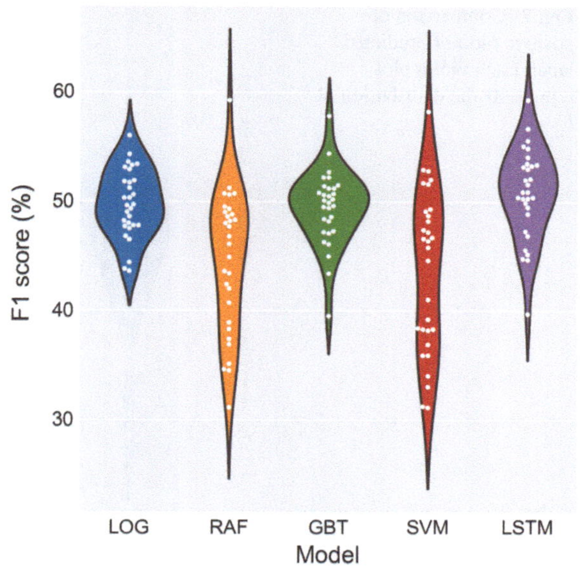

Fig. 5 Comparison of F1 score. Each violin plot represents the distribution of stock *s* F1 score

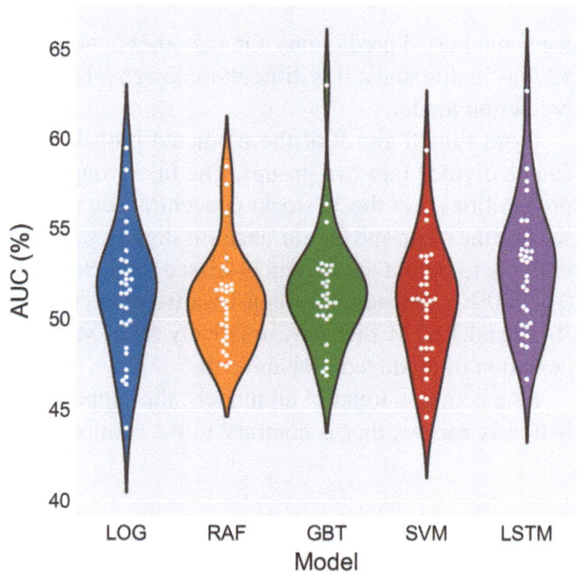

Fig. 6 Comparison of AUC. Each violin plot represents the distribution of stock *s* AUC

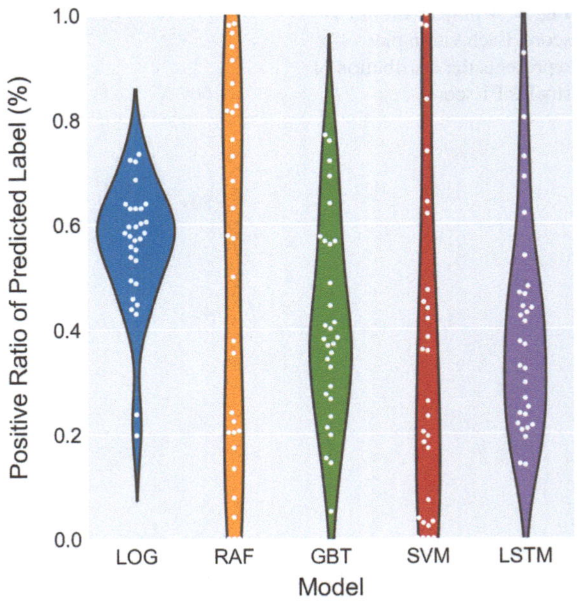

Fig. 7 Comparison of positive ratio of predicted label. Each violin plot represents the distribution of $\widehat{b^s}$

are some biased predictions. On the other hand, if the accuracy is at approximately 52% as in this study, it is difficult to objectively show the effectiveness of the biased prediction model.

From Figs. 8 and 9 of the predicted probability, five machine learning models can be divided into two groups. The first group is GBT and SVM whose predicted probabilities over the 30 stocks concentrate on rather narrow range. Furthermore, we see that the mean and the variance are slightly small. This suggests that the models are unlikely to output an extremely-biased predicted probability such as approximately 0 or 100%, and tend to be a conservative prediction. The 2nd group consists of LOG, RAF, and LSTM that have relatively large variances of both mean and standard deviation of predicted probabilities.

As a common trend of all models, the support of the predicted probability distribution is narrow, that is contrary to the results from the simulation data in Sect. 3.

Table 3 Comparison of true/predicted label and predicted probability. The mean (standard deviation) of 30 stocks is displayed for positive ratio of the true label (b), positive ratio of the predicted label ($\widehat{b}$), the mean ($\widehat{\mu}_p$) and standard deviation ($\widehat{\sigma}_p$) of the predicted probability

	LOG (%)	RAF (%)	GBT (%)	SVM (%)	LSTM (%)
b	48.9 (2.2)	48.9 (2.2) %	48.9 (2.2)	48.9 (2.2)	48.9 (2.2)
$\widehat{b}$	55.7 (12.2)	49.3 (34.7)	41.2 (18.9)	37.1 (33.8)	39.5 (19.9)
$\widehat{\mu}_p$	50.7 (2.1)	49.2 (3.7)	49.9 (0.9)	48.6 (1.7)	48.5 (2.5)
$\widehat{\sigma}_p$	6.3 (3.4)	10.8 (3.8)	1.8 (1.1)	1.7 (1.2)	4.5 (1.9)

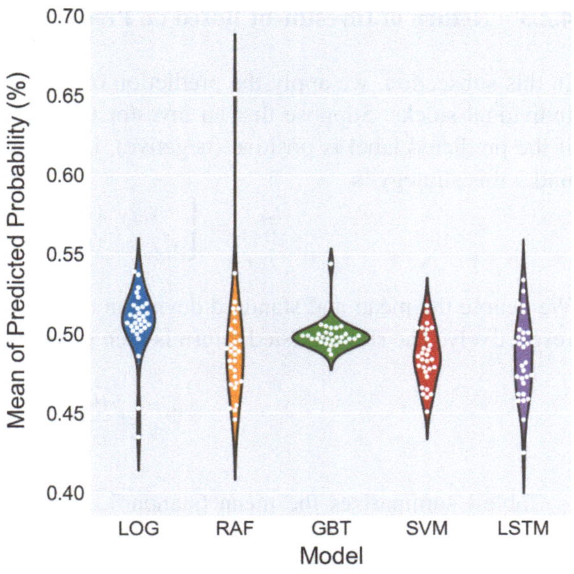

Fig. 8 Comparison of positive predicted probability (mean). Each violin plot represents the distribution of $\widehat{\mu}_p^s$

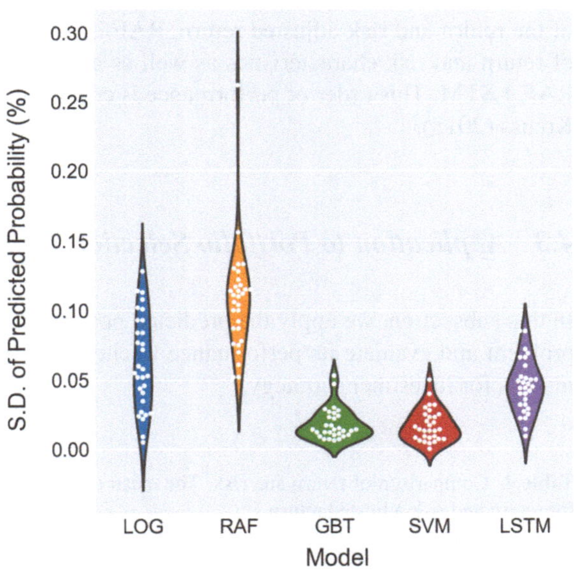

Fig. 9 Comparison of positive predicted probability (standard deviation). Each violin plot represents the distribution of $\widehat{\sigma}_p^s$

There is a possibility that the non-linearity, signal-to-noise ratio, and positive ratio of true label would cause this difference.

4.2.3 Return of Investment Based on Prediction

In this subsection, we apply the prediction of the model to investment decision of individual stocks. Suppose that an investor takes a long (short) position at time t if the predicted label is positive (negative), i.e., $\widehat{B}^s_{t+1} = 1\ (= 0)$. A realized return under this strategy is

$$\widehat{y}^s_{t+1} = \begin{cases} -y^s_{t+1} & (\widehat{B}^s_{t+1} = 0) \\ y^s_{t+1} & (\widehat{B}^s_{t+1} = 1) \end{cases} \tag{15}$$

We denote the mean and standard deviation of $\widehat{y}^s_{t+1}$ over the interval as $\widehat{\mu}^s_y$ and $\widehat{\sigma}^s_y$, respectively. The risk-adjusted return is then given by

$$\widehat{y}^s_{adj} = \frac{\widehat{\mu}^s_y}{\widehat{\sigma}^s_y} \tag{16}$$

Table 4 summarizes the mean (standard deviation) of $\widehat{\mu}^s_y$ and $\widehat{y}^s_{adj}$ over the 30 stocks, and Figs. 10 and 11 show their violin plots. We see that LSTM in which few stocks earn minus returns, exhibits favorable return and risk-adjusted return. In fact, both returns of LSTM are over twice that of the other models. Looking at the variance of the return and risk-adjusted return, RAF is slightly larger. Performance in terms of return and risk characteristics as well as accuracy is good in the order of LOG, RAF, LSTM. This order of performance is consistent with the result of Fischer and Krauss (2018).

4.3 *Application to Portfolio Selection Problem*

In this subsection, we apply the predicted positive probability to portfolio selection problem and evaluate its performance to check the usefulness of LSTM and other models for investment strategy.

Table 4 Comparison of return and risk. The mean (standard deviation) of 30 stocks is displayed for return and risk-adjusted return

	LOG (%)	RAF (%)	GBT (%)	SVM (%)	LSTM (%)
$\widehat{\mu}_y$	0.021 (0.076)	0.028 (0.095)	0.028 (0.072)	0.014 (0.070)	0.082 (0.067)
$\widehat{y}_{adj}$	0.015 (0.056)	0.019 (0.067)	0.019 (0.050)	0.015 (0.044)	0.057 (0.049)

4.3.1 Construction of Prediction-Based Portfolio

Based on the prediction of each classification model, we construct a portfolio in the following way. At time t, all 30 stocks are ranked in the descending order of 1-day ahead positive probability $\widehat{p}^s_{t+1}$. From the definition of $\widehat{p}^s_{t+1}$, the first (last, respectively) stock has the highest (lowest) probability that the stock outperforms TOPIX at $t+1$. For $k = 1, 2, \ldots, 5$, portfolio k is then defined by taking long positions of the first $3k$ stocks and short positions of the last $3k$ stock. For example, Portfolio 1 consists of long positions of the first 3 stocks and short positions of the last 3 stocks. The other 24 stocks are not traded in Portfolio 1. On the other hand, Portfolio 5 trades all 30 stocks with long/short positions of the first/last 15 stocks each.

The sizes of long and short positions of each stock are set to be equal so that the portfolio becomes dollar neutral. To focus on the performance of the portfolio itself, we do not consider any transaction cost and commissions related to trading.

4.3.2 Performance of the Portfolios

We evaluate the performance of the portfolio for each classification model. They are compared from the perspective of accuracy, return, and risk-adjusted return. The accuracy of each portfolio is defined as the percentage of positive daily returns. Table 5 and Fig. 12 show the accuracy for $k = 1, 2, \ldots, 5$.

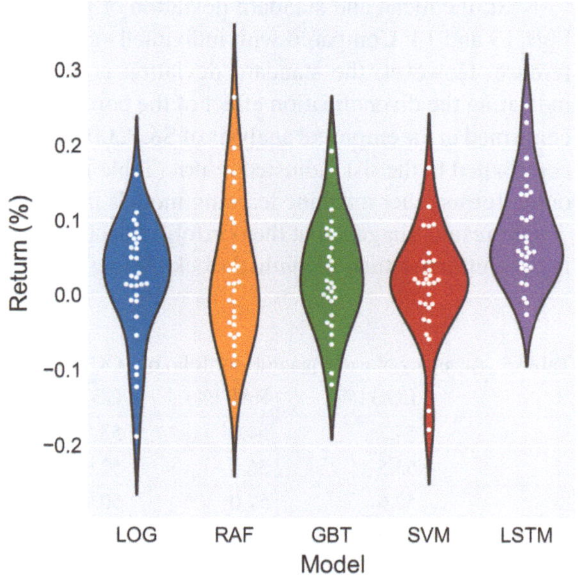

Fig. 10 Comparison of return. Each violin plot represents the distribution of $\widehat{\mu}^s_y$

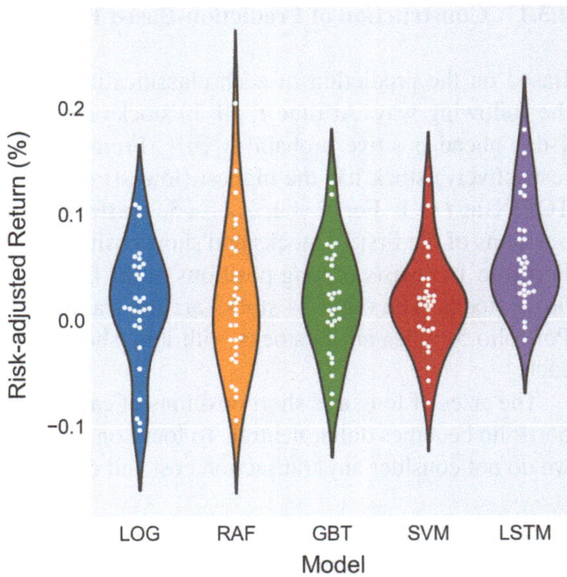

Fig. 11 Comparison of risk-adjusted return. Each violin plot represents the distribution of $\widehat{y}^s_{adj}$

For $k = 1$, we see that the accuracy of all models except SVM is improved compared with the case of individual stock (see Table 2). On the other hand, as k increases, the degree of accuracy improvement varies depending on the models. Namely, the accuracy of SVM improves, but the others do not change and decrease slightly. The differences between these models deserve more than a passing notice.

Next, the mean and standard deviation of portfolio returns are shown in Table 6, Figs. 13 and 14. Compared with individual stock returns, there is no significant difference. However, the standard deviation is the smallest at $k = 5$ in any model, indicating the diversification effect of the portfolio. This phenomenon has also been confirmed in the empirical analysis of S&P500 (Fischer and Krauss 2018) and greatly contributed to the risk-adjusted return (Table 7 and Fig. 15). It is notable that LSTM outperforms other machine learning models irrespective of the size of k.

Our results suggest that the portfolio selection based on the predicted probability is more effective than individual stock trading. However, this simple and transparent

Table 5 Accuracy of each quantile portfolio of LOG, RAF, GBT, SVM, and LSTM

k	LOG (%)	RAF (%)	GBT (%)	SVM (%)	LSTM (%)
1	54.7	54.4	53.5	51.2	58.4
2	53.5	56.1	52.6	54.1	56.1
3	52.6	57.0	50.9	55.2	61.0
4	52.6	52.0	53.5	56.7	58.1
5	52.0	52.6	52.0	56.1	58.4

Table 6 Mean and standard deviation of return for LOG, RAF, GBT, SVM, and LSTM, respectively

k	LOG (%)	RAF (%)	GBT (%)	SVM (%)	LSTM (%)
1	0.039 (0.752)	0.076 (0.709)	0.063 (0.702)	0.012 (0.681)	0.087 (0.627)
2	0.035 (0.532)	0.063 (0.498)	0.032 (0.482)	0.039 (0.538)	0.071 (0.468)
3	0.018 (0.448)	0.039 (0.405)	0.022 (0.376)	0.030 (0.475)	0.074 (0.379)
4	0.013 (0.377)	0.027 (0.342)	0.021 (0.312)	0.036 (0.435)	0.064 (0.348)
5	0.025 (0.326)	0.024 (0.305)	0.021 (0.268)	0.020 (0.378)	0.058 (0.301)

Table 7 Risk-adjusted return of each quantile portfolio for LOG, RAF, GBT, SVM, and LSTM, respectively

k	LOG (%)	RAF (%)	GBT (%)	SVM (%)	LSTM (%)
1	0.052	0.108	0.090	0.017	0.138
2	0.065	0.127	0.067	0.072	0.152
3	0.041	0.096	0.060	0.064	0.195
4	0.035	0.080	0.067	0.083	0.185
5	0.078	0.078	0.077	0.054	0.194

portfolio strategy is not aimed at reducing risk or pursuing returns, i.e., any optimization process is not carried out. Altogether, there is still potential for enhancing the edge of portfolio strategy by any machine learning model as well as the LSTM networks.

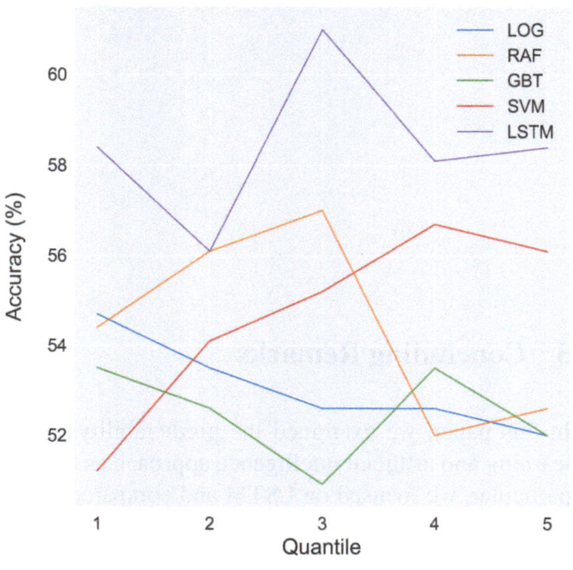

Fig. 12 Comparison of accuracy

Fig. 13 Comparison of return (mean)

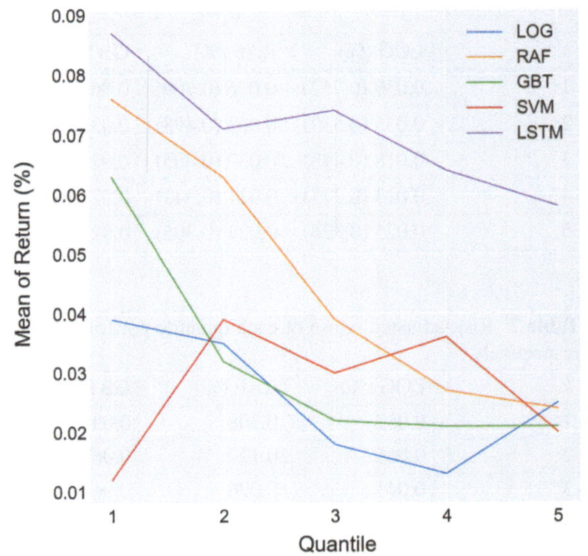

Fig. 14 Comparison of return (standard deviation)

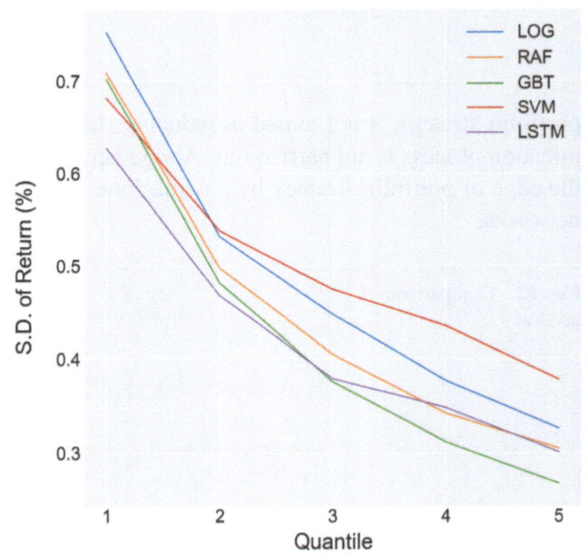

5 Concluding Remarks

In this paper, we examined the predictability for time series data using machine learning and artificial intelligence approach as an alternative to statistical models. In particular, we focused on LSTM and compared its performance with such machine learning models as LOG, RAF, GBT, and SVM.

The model characteristics were first investigated by applying those models to predict several types of simulated data with different statistical characteristics. LSTM

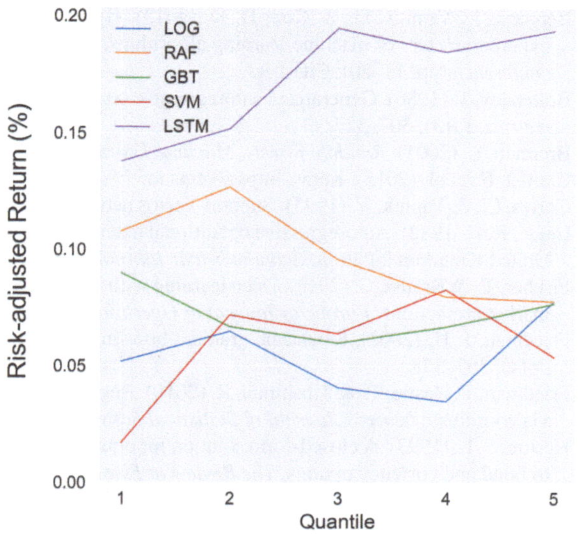

Fig. 15 Comparison of risk-adjusted return

as well as LOG and SVM showed favorable performances in terms of accuracy, F1 score and AUC, though the prediction capability of LSTM deteriorates to some extent when the ratio of positive data deviates from 50%.

From the empirical study to predict positive/negative sign of TOPIX Core 30 stock returns, LSTM showed better performance of risk-adjusted return than other models. We also confirmed the effectiveness of the market neutral portfolio constructed from model predictions as simple quantile portfolios using the predicted probability showed higher risk-adjusted returns than individual stocks. These observations are consistent with those in Fischer and Krauss (2018) for S&P500 returns.

In this paper, we only use past return data as input to each model since statistical time series model for return prediction basically uses only historical data. To further improve the accuracy of prediction, it would be useful to add other information such as news or analysts' report on each stock. In this regard, LSTM has advantages over time series models as it accepts various types of input data other than numeric data.

Acknowledgements The authors would like to thank the editors for helpful suggestions. This research was supported by JSPS KAKENHI Grand Number 19K04899 and 16H01833.

References

Ang, A., & Bekaert, G. (2002). International asset allocation with regime shifts. *The Review of Financial Studies*, *15*(4), 1137–1187.

Bengio, Y., Boulanger-Lewandowski, N., & Pascanu, R. (2013). Advances in optimizing recurrent networks. In *2013 IEEE international conference on acoustics, speech and signal processing* (pp. 8624–8628), IEEE.

Bergstra, J., Yamins, D., & Cox, D. D. (2013). Hyperopt: A python library for optimizing the hyperparameters of machine learning algorithms. In *Proceedings of the 12th Python in science conference* (pp. 13–20), Citeseer.

Bollerslev, T. (1986). Generalized autoregressive conditional heteroskedasticity. *Journal of Econometrics, 31*(3), 307–327.

Breiman, L. (2001). *Random forests. Machine Learning, 45*(1), 5–32.

Chollet, F., et al. (2015). Keras. https://keras.io.

Cortes, C., & Vapnik, V. (1995). Support-vector networks. *Machine Learning, 20*(3), 273–297.

Engle, R. F. (1982). Autoregressive conditional heteroscedasticity with estimates of the variance of United Kingdom inflation. *Econometrica: Journal of the Econometric Society*, 987–1007.

Fischer, T., & Krauss, C. (2018). Deep learning with long short-term memory networks for financial market predictions. *European Journal of Operational Research, 270*(2), 654–669.

Friedman, J. H. (2002). Stochastic gradient boosting. *Computational Statistics & Data Analysis, 38*(4), 367–378.

Friedman, J., Hastie, T., & Tibshirani, R. (2010). Regularization paths for generalized linear models via coordinate descent. *Journal of Statistical Software, 33*(1), 1.

Heston, S. L. (1993). A closed-form solution for options with stochastic volatility with applications to bond and currency options. *The Review of Financial Studies, 6*(2), 327–343.

Hinton, G., Deng, L., Yu, D., Dahl, G., Mohamed, A.-R., Jaitly, N., Senior, A., Vanhoucke, V., Nguyen, P., Kingsbury, B., et al. (2012) Deep neural networks for acoustic modeling in speech recognition. *IEEE Signal Processing Magazine, 29*.

Japan Exchange Group. (2017). TOPIX new index series (TOPIX core30, TOPIX large70 etc.). https://www.jpx.co.jp/english/markets/indices/line-up.

Komatsu, T., & Makimoto, N. (2015). Dynamic investment strategy with factor models under regime switches. *Asia-Pacific Financial Markets, 22*(2), 209–237.

Krauss, C., Do, X. A., & Huck, N. (2017). Deep neural networks, gradient-boosted trees, random forests: Statistical arbitrage on the S&P 500. *European Journal of Operational Research, 259*(2), 689–702.

Moritz, B., & Zimmermann, T. (2014). *Deep conditional portfolio sorts: The relation between past and future stock returns*. LMU Munich and Harvard University Working paper.

Olah, C. (2015). Understanding lstm networks.

Palangi, H., Deng, L., Shen, Y., Gao, J., He, X., Chen, J., et al. (2016). Deep sentence embedding using long short-term memory networks: Analysis and application to information retrieval. *IEEE/ACM Transactions on Audio, Speech and Language Processing (TASLP), 24*(4), 694–707.

Pedregosa, F., Varoquaux, G., Gramfort, A., Michel, V., Thirion, B., Grisel, O., et al. (2011). Scikit-learn: Machine learning in Python. *Journal of Machine Learning Research, 12*, 2825–2830.

Platt, J., et al. (1999). Probabilistic outputs for support vector machines and comparisons to regularized likelihood methods. *Advances in Large Margin Classifiers, 10*(3), 61–74.

Robinson, T. (1994). An application of recurrent nets to phone probability estimation. *IEEE Transactions on Neural Networks, 5*(2).

Sutskever, I., Vinyals, O., & Le, Q. (2014). Sequence to sequence learning with neural networks. *Advances in NIPS*.

Takeuchi, L., & Lee, Y.-Y.A. (2013). Applying deep learning to enhance momentum trading strategies in stocks. In *Technical Report*, Stanford University.

Zhang, G. P. (2003). Time series forecasting using a hybrid arima and neural network model. *Neurocomputing, 50*, 159–175.

A Response Function of Merton Model and Kinetic Ising Model

Masato Hisakado and Takuya Kaneko

Abstract We study contagious defaults of banks by applying a voting model. The network of banks are created by the relation, lending and borrowing among banks. We introduce the response function from Merton model. Using this response function we calculate the probability of default (PD) which includes not only changes of asset values but also the effects of connected banks' defaults using the mean field approximation. If we approximate the normal distribution which Merton model uses by tanh function, we can obtain the kinetic Ising model which represents phase transition. The asset volatility plays the role of temperature. In the low temperature limit, the model becomes the threshold model. We calculate PD which shows the effect of the situations around the bank as the additional PD using the self consistent equation.

Keywords Network · Credit risk management · Default probability · Contagion

1 Introduction

Human beings estimate public perception by observing the actions of other individuals, following which they exercise a choice similar to that of others. This phenomenon is also considered as social learning or imitation and studied several fields (Galam 1990). It is usually sensible to do what other people are doing. Hence, collective herding behavior is assumed to be the result of a rational choice according to public perception. In ordinary situations this is the correct strategy and sometimes erroneous decisions like the beauty contest of Keynes (1936). As a macro phenomenon, large social movement is the absence of central control or public communications.

M. Hisakado
Nomura Holdings, Inc., Otemachi 2-2-2, Chiyoda-ku, Tokyo 100-8130, Japan
e-mail: hisakadom@yahoo.co.jp

T. Kaneko (✉)
International Christian University, Osawa 2-10-2, Mitaka, Tokyo 181-8585, Japan
e-mail: tkaneko@icu.ac.jp

L. Pichl et al. (eds.), *Advanced Studies of Financial Technologies and Cryptocurrency Markets*, https://doi.org/10.1007/978-981-15-4498-9_5

A well-known example of erroneous decisions is the bank run on the Toyokawa Credit Union in 1973. The incident was caused by a false rumor, the process of which was analyzed in detail by Ito et al. (1974a, b). These phenomenon is known as an example of information cascade (Bikhchandani et al. 1992).

Herding behavior is represented as the response function. Threshold rules have been derived for a variety of relevant theoretical scenarios as the influence response function. Some empirical and experimental evidence has confirmed the assumptions that individuals follow threshold rules when making decisions in the presence of social influence. This rule posits that individuals will switch between two choices only when a sufficient number of other persons have adopted the choice. We have studied the voting model including herders. The model was introduced to explain the information cascade. We refer to herders such as the threshold rule as digital herders (Hisakado et al. 2011). From their experiments, they observed that human beings exhibit behavior between that of digital and analog herders (Mori et al. 2012; Hisakado etal. 2012). Analog herders vote for each candidate with probabilities that are proportional to candidates' votes (Hisakado et.al 2010). The analog herder has weaker herding power than the digital herder.

Bank defaults are contagious. The failure of single bank can be spread through financial networks. Over the past years after great recession in 2008, many researchers in various fields have been addressing the question to how to prevent financial contagion. Some of them studied especially inter-bank networks where banks lend to and borrow from each other with the threshold rule (Watts 2002; Gai et al. 2010; Caceioli et al. 2018). On randomly connected networks, a small fraction of initial activated when the network is not too sparse or too dense, a phase transition can be found. It is called the cascade window. The noise is only first fraction and the models are the deterministic model. The model with noise which do not have the cascade window was studied in (Young 2011).

The relations between borrowers and lenders play important role in the contagions. The behavior of banks is similar to the herder. The situation affects the status of the banks and the persons. The relation is represented by the response function in our voting model. We extend the voting model and use Merton model as a response function to apply to the contagious defaults. In this case we can introduce the network between the banks and the change of the asset price naturally. The latter is presented by the correlations of assets (Hisakdo et al. 2015). We show the relation to kinetic Ising model which represent the phase transition and the asset volatility plays the role of temperature (Kitsukawa et al. 2006; Hisakado et al. 2015).

The remainder of this paper is organized as follows. In Sect. 2, we introduce our voting model and mathematically define the herders. In Sect. 3, we construct the response function using Merton model. In Sect. 4, we show the relation to kinetic Ising model. In Sect. 5 we calculate the probability of default affected by the situations around the bank. Finally, the conclusions are presented in the last section.

2 Model

Here we consider a voting model. We model the voting behavior of two candidates, C_{-1} and C_1, at time t, and C_{-1} and C_1 have $c_{-1}(t)$ and $c_1(t)$ votes, respectively. In each time step, one voter votes for one candidate, which means that the voting is sequential. Hence, at time t, the t-th voter votes, after which the total number of votes is t. Voters are allowed to see r previous votes for each candidate; thus, they are aware of public perception. Here r is a constant number.

A voter's vote is based on the number of previous r votes. We call these voters herders. Here the voter refers to the latest r votes. In this paper we consider the network, the lattice case only (Hisakado et al. 2016). Therefore, at time t, r previous votes are the number of votes for C_{-1} and C_1, which is represented by $c^r_{-1}(t)$ and $c^r_1(t)$, respectively. Hence, $c^r_{-1}(t) + c^r_1(t) = r$ holds. If $r > t$, voters can see t previous votes for each candidate. In the limit $r \rightarrow \infty$, voters can see all previous votes. We define the number of all previous votes for C_{-1} and C_1 as $c^{\infty}_{-1}(t) \equiv c_{-1}(t)$ and $c^{\infty}_1(t) \equiv c_1(t)$. Here we specify r to be constant. We define $c(t)^r_1/r = 1 - c(t)^r_{-1}/r = Z(t)$.

A herder's behavior is defined by a response function. We will lead the response function in next section using Merton model. In the voting model the response function is defined by the function $F(Z)$. We have considered the several symmetric function, digital herder $F(Z) = \theta(Z - 1/2)$ where θ is the Heaviside function, analog herder $F(Z) = Z$, and tanh type herder $\tanh(Z - 1/2)$. In this paper we consider the asymmetric function for the response function.

3 A Response Function of Merton Model

3.1 *Balance Sheet*

We constructed the voter's model in previous section. Here we apply the model to the contagion of defaults. The voters correspond to the banks. The bank's state is decided by around banks. $C_{-1}(C_1)$ is the status default (non-default) instead of the candidate for the voting model. The banks decide their status sequentially as the voters.

Here we lead the response function for banks using the balance sheet. On the asset side, bank i holds external risk assets, a_i, inter-bank assets, l_i, and safe assets, b_i. On the liability side, there are deposits, d_i, inter-bank liabilities, $\bar{l}_i$, and net worth, S_i. The balance condition of the bank is $A_i = a_i + l_i + b_i = D_i + S_i = d_i + \bar{l}_i + S_i$. Here we introduce the asset value A_i, and debt value D_i. Here these are present values, not book values.

Banks are connected each other by the relation, lending and borrowing among the banks. The existence of the relation is expressed as the arrow, from the borrower to the lender. The amount of bank j's borrowings from bank i is expressed as δ_{ij}. There are relations $l_i = \sum_j \delta_{ij}$ and $\bar{l}_i = \sum_j \delta_{ji}$.

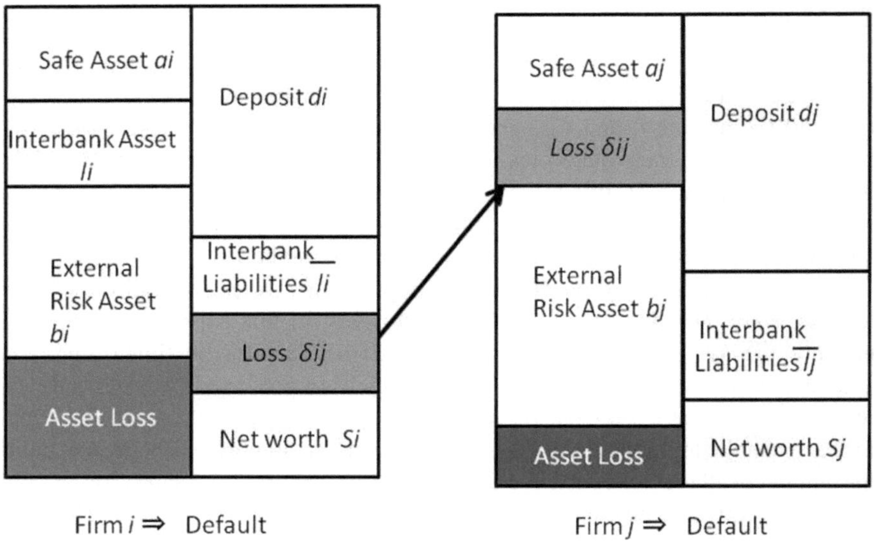

Fig. 1 The balance sheets of the banks. If the bank A is default because of the asset loss, the inter-bank liability from the bank B will be lost and the bank B be will be default contagiously

The solvency condition of bank i is

$$A_i = a_i + l_i + b_i > D_i = d_i + \bar{l}_i. \tag{1}$$

It means that present value of the bank is larger the liability. If the present value of the bank is negative, excess debt, the status of the bank becomes default. We show the balance sheets of the banks and the contagion of defaults in Fig. 1.

3.2 Merton Model

In this subsection we introduce the Merton model to calculate the probability of default (PD). We consider that stock price (market capitalization) is described as follows

$$\mathrm{d}S_t = \mu_S S_t \mathrm{d}t + \sigma_S S_t \mathrm{d}W_t. \tag{2}$$

S_t is the stock price, which corresponds to the present net-worth at time t, μ_S is trend, and σ_S is the volatility of stock price. W_t is the Brownian motion. We omit the index of the firm i. Equation (2) means the returns of stock price is log-normal distribution (Osborne 1959).

We consider the time series of whole balance sheet. The balance condition at time t is

$$A_t = D_t + S_t, \tag{3}$$

where A_t is asset, D_t is debt, and S_t is market capitalization at time t. Here we assume that the price of debt does not change, $D_t = D_0$. The initial condition of the balance sheet is $A_0 = S_0 + D_0$.

Using Eq. (2), we can obtain the stochastic differential equation for the asset A_t.

$$\mathrm{d}A_t = \mu_A A_t \mathrm{d}t + \sigma_A A_t \mathrm{d}W_t, \tag{4}$$

where μ_A is the trend of asst, $\sigma_A$is the volatility of asset.

The default condition is $A_t < D_0$, as the solvency condition Eq. (1). Here we consider the default probability in the term T. We can obtain the probability of default of this bank at time T,

$$\begin{aligned} \mathrm{P}(A_T < D_0) &= \mathrm{N}\left(\frac{\ln D_0 - \left(\ln A_0 + \left(\mu_A - \frac{\sigma_A{}^2}{2}\right)\right)T}{\sigma_A\sqrt{T}}\right) \\ &= 1 - \mathrm{N}(DD_0) = \mathrm{N}(-DD_0). \end{aligned} \tag{5}$$

$\mathrm{N}(x)$ is the cumulative normal distribution[1] and DD is

$$DD_0 = \frac{-\ln D_0 + \ln A_0 + \left(\mu_A - \frac{\sigma_A{}^2}{2}\right)T}{\sigma_A\sqrt{T}}. \tag{6}$$

As DD_0 which becomes larger, the probability of default Eq. (5) decreases. Hence, DD_0 is "Distance to Default". We can observe μ_E and σ_E in the market stock price. The relation between μ_A and μ_E is

$$\mu_A = \frac{E_0}{A_0}\mu_E + \left(1 - \frac{E_0}{A_0}\right)\mu_D, \tag{7}$$

where μ_D is the expected debt growth rate. The relation between σ_E and σ_A is

$$\sigma_E = \frac{A_0 \mathrm{N}(d)}{E_0}\sigma_A, \tag{8}$$

where

$$d = \frac{-\ln D_0 + \ln A_0 + \left(\mu_A + \frac{\sigma_A{}^2}{2}\right)T}{\sigma_A\sqrt{T}}. \tag{9}$$

Using Eqs. (8) and (9) we can estimate σ_A and μ_A.

---

[1] $\mathrm{N}(x) := \int_{-\infty}^{x} \phi(\xi)\mathrm{d}\xi,\ \phi(\xi) = \frac{1}{2}\mathrm{e}^{-\frac{1}{2}\xi^2}$.

3.3 A Response Function with Inter-bank Liabilities

In this subsection we extend the previous subsection and calculate a response function which we use in the voting model from Merton model (Merton 1974). When the borrower j is default, the lender's inter-bank assets $\delta_{ij}(1-R)$ are lost. Here we assume the recovery rate R is constant. DD in the condition that some borrowers defaulted, becomes,

$$DD(s) = \frac{-\ln D_0 + \ln\left[A_0 - \sum_{j=\text{default}}(1-R)\delta_{ij}\right] + \left(\mu_A - \frac{\sigma_A{}^2}{2}\right)T}{\sigma_A\sqrt{T}}. \tag{10}$$

We assume all inter bank assets are equal δ and the number connected banks is r. The total present value of the inter-bank assets is $l = \delta r = \sum_j \delta_{ij}$ and the number of the borrowers is r. In the voting model r is the number of referred voters.

We can rewrite

$$DD(s) = \frac{-\ln D_0 + \ln\left[A_0 - \frac{s(1-R)l}{r}\right] + \left(\mu_A - \frac{\sigma_A{}^2}{2}\right)T}{\sigma_A\sqrt{T}}. \tag{11}$$

$DD(0) > 0$ by the solvency condition, but as s increases DD might be negative.

Here we change the valuable from s to Z, where $Z = s/r : 0 \leq Z \leq 1$.

$$DD(Z) = \frac{-\ln D_0 + \ln\left[A_0 - (1-R)lZ\right] + \left(\mu_A - \frac{\sigma_A{}^2}{2}\right)T}{\sigma_A\sqrt{T}}, \tag{12}$$

and

$$\Phi(Z) = \mathrm{N}(-DD(s)) = \mathrm{N}(-DD(Z)). \tag{13}$$

Equation (13) is the response function which included the status around the bank. When there is no default which the bank lent, DD is

$$DD(0) = \frac{-\ln D_0 + \ln A_0 + \left(\mu_A - \frac{\sigma_A{}^2}{2}\right)T}{\sigma_A\sqrt{T}}, \tag{14}$$

which is stand alone one which corresponds to Eq. (6).

Equation(13) takes several shapes. If we set $\sigma_A \to 0$, the response function becomes steep and the Heaviside function. In the extreme case the response function becomes the threshold model. In this case the contagious defaults risk is stronger than the risk of the change of the asset values. The threshold is $\lfloor (A-D)/\delta \rfloor$ where $\lfloor x \rfloor$ are floor function. The model becomes threshold model in Watts model (Watts 2002). For example, $D/A = 0.9$, $\delta/A = 0.2$, $\sigma_A = 0.01$, $\Phi(i)$ becomes digital. If one of the borrowers is default, the default probability becomes 1, $\Phi(0) = 0$ and $\Phi(i) = 1, i \geq 1$.

We consider the sensitivity analysis to confirm the effects of parameters. When the asset volatility change $\sigma_A \to \sigma_A + \Delta\sigma_A$ and $\sigma_A \gg \Delta\sigma_A$, the change of DD is

$$\Delta DD(Z) = -\left(T + \frac{DD(Z)}{\sigma_A}\right)\Delta\sigma_A \sim -\left(T + \frac{DD(1/2)}{\sigma_A}\right)\Delta\sigma_A. \quad (15)$$

If the volatility of asset increases, the decrease of DD does not depends on Z. Here we assume $l \ll A_0$. It is the parallel shift of DD.

When we consider the change of the inter-bank liability $l \to l + \Delta l$ and $\Delta l \ll l$,

$$\Delta DD(Z) = -\frac{(1-R)Z\Delta l}{(A_0 - (1-R)lZ\sigma_A)\sqrt{T}} \sim -\frac{(1-R)Z\Delta l}{A_0\sqrt{T}}. \quad (16)$$

If the inter bank-liability increases, the decrease of DD is proportional to Z. As Z becomes large, the change of DD becomes large. It is the increasing of steepness of DD about Z.

4 Dynamics of the Model

The state of firms is denoted by the vector $\sigma = (\sigma_1, \ldots, \sigma_{r+1})$ with $\sigma_j = \pm 1$. $\sigma = 1(\sigma = -1)$ means the default(non-default). The i-th agents state at time t is $\sigma_i(t)$. Total number of agents is $(r+1)$. We consider the case where the updated agents is chosen by the rules. The ordering of update is from σ_1 to σ_{r+1}. After the update of σ_{r+1}, we update σ_1 and so on. We repeat this process. Hereafter, we define the updated state of the firm σ_j after n th time as $\sigma_j^{(n)}$. The initial condition is $\sigma_j^{(0)} = 0$. All banks are not default. Time t is the number of updated banks.

The update of a bank is described by response function, Eq. (13). At time t, the bank decides a state by the response function. The bank is connected with other banks by the relations, borrower and lenders. The bank has r borrowers and decides the state of the bank using the state of connected borrowers states. It means all banks are connected by the response function Eq. (13). Here we assume the balance sheets of all banks are the same for the simplicity.

The transition can be written

$$\begin{aligned}\sigma_j = 1 \to -1 &: w_j(\boldsymbol{\sigma}) = \Phi(-DD_j),\\ \sigma_j = -1 \to 1 &: F_j w_j(\boldsymbol{\sigma}) = 1 - \Phi(DD_j) = \Phi(DD_j),\end{aligned} \quad (17)$$

where $\Phi(-DD_j)$ is Eq. (13). Here we approximated normal distribution by logistic function,

$$\begin{aligned}
\Phi(-DD_j) &\sim \frac{1}{1+\mathrm{e}^{\lambda_0 DD_j}} \\
&= \frac{-\ln D_0 + \ln\left[A_0 - \frac{(1-R)l}{2}\right] + \ln\left[1 - \frac{(1-R)l(\frac{s}{r}-\frac{1}{2})}{A_0 - \frac{(1-R)l}{2}}\right] + \left(\mu_A - \frac{\sigma_A{}^2}{2}\right)T}{\sigma_A\sqrt{T}}, \\
&\sim \frac{1}{1+\frac{1-p_{1/2}}{p_{1/2}}\exp\left(-\frac{(1-R)l\lambda_0}{(A_0-(1-R)l/2)\sigma_A\sqrt{T}}\frac{(s-\frac{r}{2})}{r}\right)}, \\
&= \frac{1}{1+\frac{1-p_{1/2}}{p_{1/2}}\exp\left(-\frac{(1-R)l\lambda_0}{2(A_0-(1-R)l/2)\sigma_A\sqrt{T}}\frac{(\hat{c}_1-\hat{c}_{-1})}{r}\right)}, \\
&= \frac{1}{2}\left[1+\tanh\left\{\frac{(1-R)l\lambda_0}{4(A_0-(1-R)l/2)\sigma_A\sqrt{T}}\frac{(\hat{c}_1-\hat{c}_{-1})}{r}+\frac{1}{2}\log\frac{p_{1/2}}{1-p_{1/2}}\right\}\right],
\end{aligned} \tag{18}$$

where

$$p_{1/2} = \frac{1}{1+\mathrm{e}^{DD(1/2)}}, \tag{19}$$

and $\lambda_0 \sim 1.6$. Here we use the approximation $\log(1-x) \sim -x$ when $x \ll 1$ and $A_0 \gg l$. We have changed the variables from s to $\hat{c}_1$ and $\hat{c}_{-1}$. $\hat{c}_{-1}(\hat{c}_1)$ is the number of defaults (non-defaults).

The transition can be written

$$\begin{aligned}
\sigma_j &= 1 \to -1: \\
w_j(\boldsymbol{\sigma}) &= \frac{1}{2}\left[1-\tanh\left\{\frac{(1-R)l\lambda_0}{4(A_0-(1-R)l/2)\sigma_A\sqrt{T}}\frac{(\hat{c}_1-\hat{c}_{-1})}{r}+\frac{1}{2}\log\frac{p_{1/2}}{1-p_{1/2}}\right\}\right], \\
\sigma_j &= -1 \to 1: \\
F_j w_j(\boldsymbol{\sigma}) &= \frac{1}{2}\left[1+\tanh\left\{\frac{(1-R)l\lambda_0}{4(A_0-(1-R)l/2)\sigma_A\sqrt{T}}\frac{(\hat{c}_1-\hat{c}_{-1})}{r}+\frac{1}{2}\log\frac{p_{1/2}}{1-p_{1/2}}\right\}\right].
\end{aligned} \tag{20}$$

The process is nothing but the kinetic Ising model. (see Appendix A) The last term $\log p_{1/2}/(1-p_{1/2})$ corresponds to the outer field. The correspondence to the parameter for Ising model is

$$\frac{(1-R)l\lambda_0}{4(A_0-(1-R)l/2)\sigma_A\sqrt{T}} = \beta J. \tag{21}$$

The condition of no outer field is $DD(1/2) = 0$. We can obtain the condition

$$A_0 - (1-R)l\frac{1}{2} = D_0\exp\left\{-\left(\mu_A - \frac{\sigma_A{}^2}{2}\right)T\right\}. \tag{22}$$

σ_A, volatility of asset, corresponds to the temperature in Ising model. When $\mu_A \sim 0$ and $\sigma_A^2 \sim 0$, the condition of the symmetric is $A_0 - D_0 = E_0 = (1-R)l/2$ which is discussed in (Watts 2002; Gai et al. 2010) where l/E_0 is the threshold. These model are the low temperature limit of our model.

The mean field equation is

$$\tanh\left\{\frac{(1-R)l\lambda_0\hat{Z}}{4(A_0-(1-R)l/2)\sigma_A\sqrt{T}}+\frac{1}{2}\log\frac{p_{\frac{1}{2}}}{1-p_{\frac{1}{2}}}\right\}=\hat{Z}, \tag{23}$$

where $\hat{Z}=2Z-1$. The critical condition of the symmetric case is

$$\sigma_{Ac}=\frac{(1-R)l\lambda_0}{4(A_0-(1-R)l/2)\sqrt{T}}. \tag{24}$$

5 Additional Default Probability

In the ordinal case the default probability (PD) of the bank is calculated $\Phi(-DD_i(0))$ which is stand alone PD. It corresponds to that there is no default in the banks which the bank i lent to. PD depends on the situation of the bank i. If the some of the banks which the bank i lent to are defaults, PD of bank i increases. We calculate the non conditional PD as $\bar{P}=\int\Phi(DD(Z))\mathrm{d}\mu(Z)$ where $\mu(Z)$ is the measure of Z.

The difference to the stand alone PD, which is PD excluded the effects of the other banks, is defined as the additional PD (Kaneko et al. 2019),

$$\Delta P=\bar{P}-\Phi(-DD(0)). \tag{25}$$

We calculate the additional PD using the mean field approximation,

$$\bar{P}=Z=\Phi(-DD(Z)). \tag{26}$$

We show the mean field equation in Fig. 2. If there is only solution of the mean field equation, the intersection is the equilibrium solution in Fig. 2a, b. Hence, the intersection becomes the equilibrium PD, $\bar{P}$. The distribution of Z is $\mu=\delta_{Z_1}$, where $Z_1=\bar{P}$ and δ_x is the delta function. We can obtain the additional PD, $\Delta P=Z_1-\Phi(-DD(0))$.

On the other hand, in Fig. 2c there is three solutions, both ends intersections are the solutions. The mid solution is not stable. The distribution of Z is $\mu=\alpha\delta_{Z_1}+\beta\delta_{Z_2}$, where Z_1 and Z_2 corresponds to the two stable solutions. We can obtain the additional PD, $\Delta P=\alpha Z_1+\beta Z_2-\Phi(-DD(0))$.

In Fig. 3 we show the image of the two solutions case using the image of the physical potential. The ball comes from the left side, and there is no default in the initial condition. The solution oscillates between the two stable solutions Z_1 and Z_2 where $Z_1<Z_2$. When the outer field is the left (right) direction, the potential of the low (high) PD equilibrium Z_1 (Z_2) is deeper than the high (low) PD equilibrium in Fig. 3a, b.

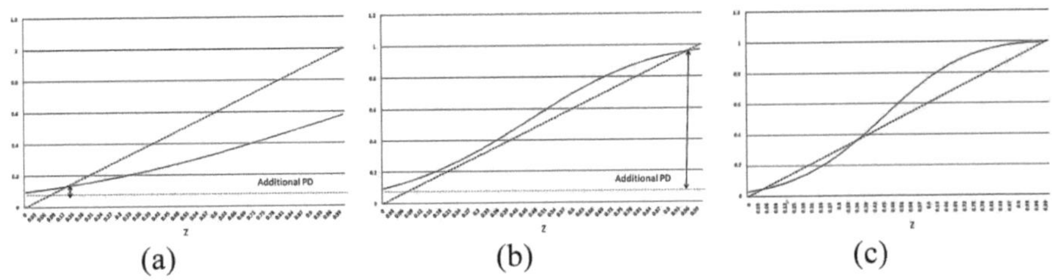

Fig. 2 The mean field equation and the solution of the equilibrium. **a** Is small additional PD case, $D_0/A_0 = 0.91, l/A_0 = 0.1, \sigma_A = 0.07$, **b** is large additional PD case $D_0/A_0 = 0.91, l/A_0 = 0.2, \sigma_A = 0.07$ and **c** is the two solutions case $D_0/A_0 = 0.91, l/A_0 = 0.2, \sigma_A = 0.05$

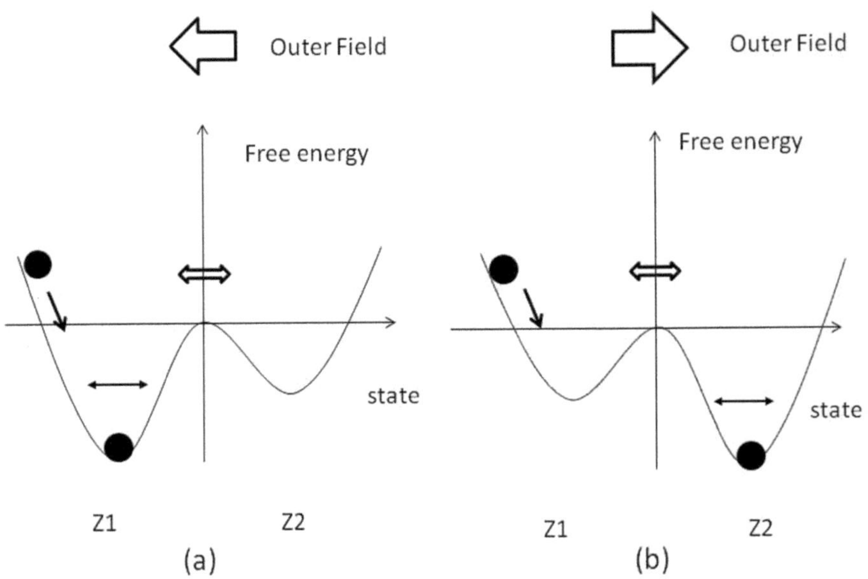

Fig. 3 Illustration of the equilibrium PD when there are two solutions, using the analogy of physical potential. The ball comes from the left side

When there is no outer field, symmetric case, one of the solution of Eq. (26) is $Z = 1/2$. When $\mathrm{d}\Phi(-DD(Z)/\mathrm{d}Z > 1$, there is three solutions. On the other hand, when $\mathrm{d}\Phi(-DD(Z)/\mathrm{d}Z < 1$, there is one solution. There is the phase transition in the limit $r \to \infty$ as Ising model. The condition of the critical asset volatility σ_{Ac} is

$$\sigma_{Ac} = \frac{\Phi'(0)l(1-R)}{(A-(1-R)l/2)\sqrt{T}}. \tag{27}$$

It is consistent with the critical condition of the Ising model Eq. (24), because $\Phi'(0) \sim \lambda_0/4$.

6 Concluding Remarks

We considered contagious defaults of banks and applied a voting model to them. The network of the firms are created by the relation, lending and borrowing. We introduced the response function from Merton model. Using this response function we calculate the PD which includes not only the changes of the asset value but also the effects of other banks' defaults. The temperature corresponds to the asset volatility. When the asset volatility is small, the contingent default is effective for banks. On the other hand, the asset volatility is large, the change of asset price is effective.

In this paper we use the mean field approximation to calculate the PD. In general we have to do numerical simulations. If we use the random number including the correlations, we can simulate the correlation of the asset prices which several banks have.

Merton model uses the cumulative normal distribution. If we approximate the normal distribution by tanh function, we can obtain the kinetic Ising model. If there is no outer field, symmetric case, there is the phase transition. We show the additional PD which corresponds to the effects of the situations of the bank using the mean field approximation.

Appendix A Ising Model

Here we consider the infinite range model. It is one of the most popular model in statistical physics which explains phase transition. In the model spins interact all other spins. Hamiltonian is

$$H(\sigma) = -\frac{J}{r+1}\sum_{i>j}\sigma_i\sigma_j - h\sum_{i=1}^{r+1}\sigma_i, \tag{28}$$

where $(r+1)$ is the number of spins, σ_i is the spin has the value ± 1, J is the parameter of interaction, and h is the outer field. Here we define average of spins, as an order parameter, $m = 1/(r+1)\sum\sigma_i$ which represents the phase transition.

In large $r \to \infty$ limit the self consistent equation is

$$m = \tanh\beta(Jm + h), \tag{29}$$

where $\beta = 1/k_B\hat{T}$. k_B is Bolzman constant and $\hat{T}$ is temperature. When infinite range model, we can obtain the strict solution form the self consistent equation Eq. (29). When the symmetric case, under the transition temperature $\hat{T}_c$, in the low temperature range there are two solutions. The critical point is decided by the equation $\beta_c J = 1$. One of the solution is selected in the two stable solution. On the other hand, above $\hat{T}_c$, in the high temperature range, there are only one solution. This is the phase transition of Ising model. When there is the outer field h, the model becomes the asymmetric model and there is no phase transition.

References

Bikhchandani, S., Hirshleifer, D., & Welch, I. (1992). A theory of fads, fashion, custom, and cultural change as information cascade. *Journal of Political Economy, 100*, 992.

Caceioli, F., Barrucca, P., & Kobayashi, T. (2018). Network models of financial systemic risk: A review. *The Journal of Computational Social Science, 1*, 81–114.

Gai, P., & Kapadia, S. (2010). Contagion in financial networks. *Proceedings of the Royal Society, 466*, 2401–2423.

Galam, G. (1990). Socail praradoes of majority rule voting and renormalization group. *Statistical Physics, 61*, 943.

Hisakado, M., & Kaneko, T. (2015). Financial management methodology No. 595346 Japan patent office.

Hisakado, M., & Mori, S. (2010). Phase transition and information cascade in a voting model. *Journal of Physics A, 43*(3152), 7.

Hisakado, M., & Mori, S. (2011). Digital herders and phase transition in a voting model. *Journal of Physics A, 22*, 275204.

Hisakado, M., & Mori, S. (2012). Two kinds of phase transition in a voting model. *Journal of Physics A: Mathematical and Theoretical, 45* 345002–345016.

Hisakado, M., & Mori, S. (2015). Information cascade, Kirman's ant colony model, and kinetic Ising model. *Physica A, 417*, 63.

Hisakado, M., & Mori, S. (2016). Information cascade on networks. *J. Phys. A, 450*, 570–684.

Ito, Y., Ogawa, K., & Sakakibara, H. (1974a July). *Journalism Quarterly Review, 69*, 70–80 (in Japanese).

Ito, Y., Ogawa, K., & Sakakibara, H. (1974b October). *Journalism Quarterly Review, 70*, 100–111 (in Japanese).

Kaneko, T., & Hisakado, M. (2019). Additional default probability in consideration of firm's network. In *Network Theory and Agent-based Modeling in Economics and Finance* (Vol. 301). Springer-Nature.

Keynes, J. M. (1936). *General theory of employment interest and money*, Macmillan Cambridge University Press.

Kitsukawa, K., Mori, S., & Hisakado, H. (2006). Evaluation of tranche in securitization and long-rang Ising model. *Physica A, 368*, 191–206.

Merton, R. C. (1974) On the pricing of corporate debt: Risk structure of interest rate. *Journal of Finance, 29(2)*, 449–470.

Mori, S., Hisakado, M., & Takahashi, T. (2012). Phase transition to a two-peaks phase in an information-cascade voting experiment. *Physical Review E, 86*, 26109.

Osborne, M. F. (1959). Brownian motion in the stock market*Operation Research, 7*(2), 145–173.

Watts, D. J. (2002). A simple model of global cascade on networks. *Proceedings of the National Academy of Sciences of the United States of America, 99*(9), 5766–5771.

Young, H. P. (2011). The dynamics of social inovation. *Proceedings of the National Academy of Sciences of the United States of America, 108*(4), 21285–21291.

Bitcoin's Deviations from Satoshi's World

Naoyuki Iwashita

Abstract After several years of the proposal and implementation of Bitcoin by Satoshi Nakamoto, people in the world were enthusiastic about crypto-assets. However, the market prices of crypto-assets are too unstable to use as a payment method. After many cyber-attack incidents, the confidence in the security of crypto-asset exchanges has also been compromised. Satoshi proposed Bitcoin to realize anonymous payment to protect individual privacy. Actual crypto-assets have changed from the original concept. The main reason for this deviation was the reality that ordinary investors cannot manage their secret keys securely. In this chapter, the reasons for this deviation are investigated.

Keywords Bitcoin · Crypto-asset · Cyber-attack · Decentralization · Secret key

1 Introduction

Bitcoin gained much attention from the public after a massive rise in 2017. After the crash in 2018, the market prices of crypto-assets have been unstable (Chart 1). However, blockchain technology derived from Bitcoin has attracted attention as a leading-edge technology of the next generation, and various pilot projects are in progress. Nevertheless, until now, the case of a large-scale implementation of blockchain technology accepted by society is almost exclusively an example of crypto-assets (virtual currency) centered on Bitcoin.

N. Iwashita (✉)
School of Government, Kyoto University, Yoshidahonmachi, Sakyo Ward, Kyoto 606-8317, Japan
e-mail: iwashita.naoyuki.7e@kyoto-u.ac.jp

L. Pichl et al. (eds.), *Advanced Studies of Financial Technologies and Cryptocurrency Markets*, https://doi.org/10.1007/978-981-15-4498-9_6

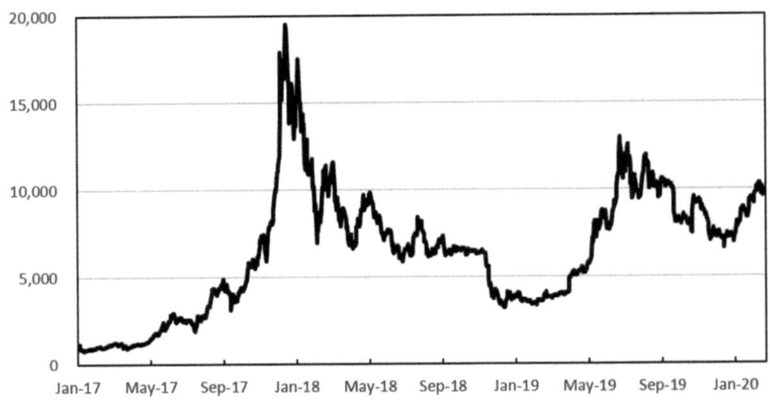

Chart 1 Price of Bitcoin. *Source of data* coinmarketcap.com

Crypto-assets attracted people as a target of a speculative bubble, and it was traded having a financial value of several hundreds of billion dollars at peak time, millions of users participated in this new market.[1]

However, the development of Bitcoin is not just a rosy success story. Earlier investors gained economic benefits by increasing the value of Bitcoin that they purchased at a very low price. However, such a rise came from the fact that Bitcoin was capable of international, anonymous transactions beyond the financial regulation suitable for money laundering and procurement of terrorist funds. And it brought confusion to the global financial order.

Besides, for investors after 2017, when the market price rose, a very large value of crypto-assets was lost by cyber-attacks to many crypto-asset exchanges, and the market price declined. From the viewpoint of information security technology, these experiences of crypto-assets made us aware of how difficult it is for non-experts to securely manage secret keys for digital signature, which is the heart of the security.

Bitcoin employed a new technology called PoW (Proof of Work), as a means to increase the security of transactions even if there was no trusted third party. It was the core of the success of Bitcoin. However, it was a double-edged sword. With the soaring price of Bitcoin, PoW or "mining Bitcoin" was considered to be a high-profit business. As a result, excessive capital investment in the mining business has lead to the distortion of global resource allocation. It caused side effects such as global environmental problems getting worse.

Satoshi Nakamoto was the inventor of Bitcoin and one of the initial core developers. He designed Bitcoin as electronic cash that allows unfamiliar people to exchange

[1]Counting users of crypto-assets is a controversial issue. According to the report of Chainalysis (2018), the Bitcoin blockchain consists of 460 million addresses as of December 2018. Still, only 27 million addresses actually hold Bitcoin, and there is no information on how these addresses link to actual Bitcoin holders. In 2017, Japanese regulation required crypto-asset exchanges in Japan to perform a strict KYC to every customer in Japan. Japan Virtual Currency Exchange Association (JVCEA) aggregated reported numbers of customers of all registered exchanges and disclosed that there are 3.5 million actual crypto-asset holders in Japan (JVCEA 2018).

monetary values anonymously on the Internet. However, Bitcoin had departed from the world that Satoshi would have dreamed of. And it could not realize the original concept. How did the deviation occur?

Will it return to the original?

This chapter focuses on the development of Bitcoin and other crypto-assets that have become social phenomena to society and deals with its impact on society.

2 Prerequisite of Bitcoin

There is no evidence that the person "Satoshi Nakamoto" exists. It is even unknown whether it is the name of a specific individual or not, and its identity is enveloped in mystery. However, let's keep that mystery aside. As you can see in his paper (Nakamoto 2008), it is hard to believe that the author envisioned Bitcoin as the present.

The title of his paper was "Bitcoin: A Peer-to-Peer Electronic Cash System." The concept of electronic cash was to realize a new payment and remittance method which protects privacy by using digital data on the Internet, just like cash provides the anonymity of the transaction in the face-to-face environment. There were various proposals since the 1980s (Chaum 1982; Okamoto and Ohta 1989). The research has been handed down to date as an application of cryptographic technology. Various electronic payment methods have been proposed and used in many countries around the world, and electronic money has become widespread in many countries.

However, such practical electronic money is often regulated by the authorities as a debt of the issuer. There was no anonymity of the transaction at all. That was far from ideal for Satoshi. He proposed a Bitcoin as an electronic payment method with the prerequisite that there is no reliable third-party mediation, and anonymous transactions are possible.

From the viewpoint of information technology, the Bitcoin is only a combination of two known projects. One is Surety.com's electronic notary service (Haber and Stornetta 1991, 1997; Bayer et al. 1993), the other is hashcash (Back 2002). Bitcoin was born by adopting the method of making data tampering difficult by using the hash function link from the former and incorporating the idea of PoW from the latter. Bitcoin was an electronic "cash" because it can anonymously remittable on the Internet without a third-party mediating.

I will not explain the mechanism in detail here, but the important thing is that there is no organization like the Bitcoin issuing company. Bitcoin is based on computer resources provided by individuals or companies who agree with its spirit or intend to profit from it. There is neither an explicit contract nor an institution, and there is only the code (computer program). The code can also be freely rewritten while voluntarily gathered engineers review each other. The code causes significant economic consequences (e.g., price fluctuation of crypto-assets and settlement of contentious leadership battle). From the beginning of the Internet, it was predicted that a "world dominated by the code" will realize. However, it was enough to surprise people that such a world began to realize in the form of a hundreds-of-billion dollar of crypto-assets earlier than anticipated.

3 Bitcoin at the Dawn

On January 3, 2009, the first block of Bitcoin blockchain was generated from the first code written by Satoshi himself. In the early days of Bitcoin seemed to move in the direction Satoshi is envisaging. Only some geeks were interested in Bitcoin. They agreed with the purpose of Bitcoin, provided computing resources of their PCs, and supported the transaction of Bitcoin by mining it. They generated secret and public keys of the digital signature required for the transaction of Bitcoin by themselves. Each user securely kept his secret key to his responsibility.

Some of the Bitcoin came to be exchanged for the legal tender currency, an exchange price was established, but the price was still low. The primary usage of Bitcoin was the settlement of transactions on the Internet, and it was often used for underground transactions such as narcotics and weapons sales. Participants were limited to geeks even around 2012 when transactions expanded to some extent, and the exchange price was around 1 BTC = $10. You can find a lively description of how Bitcoin was used those days in an article of "Silk Road" (Bearman 2015), which was an infamous underground website. There is a symbolic expression "a digital instantiation of the libertarian ideal" in the article. For libertarians who hate government intervention and claim self-determination rights, the appearance of Bitcoin would seem to realize an ideal society. It was such a world that Satoshi must have dreamed of.

4 Deviations from Satoshi's World

4.1 First Deviation: Entry of Amateur Investors

However, this idyllic period soon passed, and in 2013, the market of Bitcoin began to change dramatically. At the Cyprus crisis, the demand for Bitcoin increased instead of the international remittance via banks, which trading stopped, and the market price rose tenfold.

Media coverage over Bitcoin was heating up, and many amateur investors rushed to buy Bitcoin. The crypto-asset exchanges became commonplace to buy Bitcoin. The crypto-asset exchanges have two tasks. The first is to exchange legal tender currency to crypto-assets, and second is to keep crypto-assets for their customers. Instead of intractable digital signature technology, amateur investors can use ordinary ID and password to authenticate their trade request to the exchanges. This is an unavoidable treatment because amateur investors cannot securely manage and operate their secret keys to generate a digital signature. However, this procedure was the first deviation from Satoshi's world.

If both sell-side and buy-side investors are clients of the same crypto-asset exchange, they can make the trade of crypto-asset without blockchain. The settlement can be done within the relational database of the crypto-asset exchange. This kind of transaction is called "off-chain" instead of traditional "on-chain" because the transaction is not written on the blockchain (Table 1). Today, 95% of crypto-asset transactions are said to be off-chain.

Table 1 Pros/cons of on-chain and off-chain transaction (Iwashita 2019a, b)

Type	On-chain transaction	Off-chain transaction
Summary	Transaction method that has been used since the dawn of Bitcoin. A digital signature is generated with a secret key managed by the user himself, and a transaction record including his own address is recorded on the blockchain	Transaction method whose settlement completes within the RDB of a crypto-asset exchange. Users authenticate with ID and password, instead of a secret key
User type	• Geeks who have been using Bitcoin from its dawn, • Users who want anonymous transactions, • Users who remit or pay across borders, • Inter-exchange transactions, Mining companies	• Individual investors who are laypersons about crypto-asset transactions, • Customers of crypto-asset exchanges
Pros	• Transactions recorded on the blockchain are immutable • Transactions can be almost anonymous • Even if there are troubles in the exchange, the crypto-assets recorded on the blockchain are safe	• Nontechnical investors can make transactions with simple authentication such as passwords, and their crypto-assets are at no risk of loss or leakage of secret keys
Cons	• Each user needs to be technologically skilled in managing his secret key of the digital signature securely • Loss or unauthorized use of user's secret key would result in the total loss of his crypto-assets	• Risk of losing crypto-assets if a cyber-attack damages an exchange

4.2 *Second Deviation: Cyberattack to the Crypto-Asset Exchange*

After 2013, many crypto-asset exchange ventures were established, and they began to keep crypto-assets from amateur investors. Due to the soaring price of crypto-assets, the amount of value retained at exchanges increased rapidly. In such circumstances, some crypto-asset exchanges became victims of cyber-attacks. The crypto-asset exchange is quite a new business. The exchanges are all venture companies, and unfortunately, the level of risk management was not high enough. Crypto-asset exchanges around the world were targets of cybercrime (Table 2).

From the viewpoint of attackers, systems of crypto-asset exchanges are built on the cloud, and many are remotely operated, including secret keys. Suppose an attacker targeted a crypto-asset exchange and succeeded in stealing information. The attacker could illegally use the secret key to transfer vast amounts of crypto-assets in the exchange to their accounts. Once transferred, the attacker can abbreviate the characteristics of crypto-assets and remit them anonymously. In that sense, targeting the system of crypto-asset exchange was very rational for attackers.

When a switching company receives a cyber-attack, crypto-assets kept from customers are leaked illegally. In particular, in Japan, large-scale illegal outflow incidents occurred one after another. In 2018, CoinCheck received 58 billion-yen, Tech Bureau was damaged by 7-billion-yen theft. Since both companies compensated for losses to customers, they did not lead to consumer damage, but the attacker was not identified,

Table 2 Major cyber-attack incidents to crypto-asset exchanges (Iwashita 2019a, b)

Attacked exchange	Nationality	Month/year	Estimated loss ($ in millions)	Stolen crypto-assets
Mt.GOX(1)	Japan	June, 2011	9	–
Bitfloor	U.S.	September, 2012	0.25	24,000 BTC
Mt.GOX(2)	Japan	February, 2014	480	850,000 BTC
Poloniex	U.S.	March, 2014	0.55	–
BitStamp	U.K.	January, 2015	5	19,000 BTC
Bitfinex	Hong Kong	August, 2016	66	119,756 BTC
CoinCheck	Japan	January, 2018	530	526,300,010 XEM
BitGrail	Italia	February, 2018	170	1,700 XRB
Coinrail	Korea	June, 2018	40	NXPS, ATC, NPER
Bithumb	Korea	June, 2018	31	XRP?
Zaif	Japan	September, 2018	62	BTC, MONA, BCH
Cryptopia	New Zeeland	January, 2019	3	ETH?

and the leaked cipher assets were not regained. It would not have been included in Satoshi's assumption that such a crime would go wrong.

Let's take a closer look at the CoinCheck incident that occurred in January 2018. In this case, the domestic biggest exchange CoinCheck keeps crypto-asset NEM equivalent to 58 billion yen in fair value from 260,000 customers, but an attacker stole the full amount. The company compensated for the loss by compensating the customer but forced to suspend its business for an extended period and was to be ordered by the Financial Services Agency twice.

The inspection by the Financial Services Agency revealed that the coin check company's system was wholly inadequate as a position to keep customers' assets. CoinCheck managed 266,000 NEMs with only one account. A single encryption key merely protected procedures for transferring crypto-assets from that account. The device stored the secret key was always connected to the Internet. Because this cryptographic key management was risky, the cyber-attack was received, the key was illegally used, and the NEM was remitted (Table 3).

In Table 3, the address "NC3…" is the address of CoinCheck. At this address, NEM, which worth 58 billion yen deposited by customers, was kept. On the other hand, the perpetrators prepared the address "NC4…" The first 10 XEM was remitted at 0:02 am on January 26, then 523,000,000 XEM was remitted in less than 20 min. After that, the perpetrators remitted them to several different addresses. Eventually,

Table 3 NEM transactions in CoinCheck incident

Date/Time	Amount(XEM)	From:	To:
2018/1/26 8:26	800,000	NC3BI3DNMR2	NC4C6PSUW5
2018/1/26 4:33	1,000,000	NC3BI3DNMR2	NC4C6PSUW5
2018/1/26 3:35	1,500,000	NC3BI3DNMR2	NC4C6PSUW5
2018/1/26 3:29	92,250,000	NC4C6PSUW5	NA6JSWNF24Y
2018/1/26 3:28	100,000,000	NC4C6PSUW5	NDDZVE32WB
2018/1/26 3:18	100,000,000	NC4C6PSUW5	NB4QUCLTZW
2018/1/26 3:14	100,000,000	NC4C6PSUW5	NDZZJBH6JZP
2018/1/26 3:02	750,000	NC4C6PSUW5	NBKLQYXFIVF
2018/1/26 3:00	50,000,000	NC4C6PSUW5	NDODXOWFIZ
2018/1/26 2:58	50,000,000	NC4C6PSUW5	NA7SZ75KF67
2018/1/26 2:57	30,000,000	NC4C6PSUW5	NCTWEIOOVIT
2018/1/26 0:21	3,000,000	NC3BI3DNMR2	NC4C6PSUW5
2018/1/26 0:10	20,000,000	NC3BI3DNMR2	NC4C6PSUW5
2018/1/26 0:09	100,000,000	NC3BI3DNMR2	NC4C6PSUW5
2018/1/26 0:08	100,000,000	NC3BI3DNMR2	NC4C6PSUW5
2018/1/26 0:07	100,000,000	NC3BI3DNMR2	NC4C6PSUW5
2018/1/26 0:06	100,000,000	NC3BI3DNMR2	NC4C6PSUW5
2018/1/26 0:04	100,000,000	NC3BI3DNMR2	NC4C6PSUW5
2018/1/26 0:02	10	NC3BI3DNMR2	NC4C6PSUW5

Source Extracted by the author from the public data in the NEM's blockchain information these crypto-assets were laundered and taken somewhere. To date, the perpetrators have been unknown, and no clues have been found to link them.

According to the inspection conducted by the Financial Services Agency, which was carried out as a result of the incident this time, severe problems in organization management were pointed out by most crypto-asset exchanges in Japan, and a business improvement order was issued.

One of the puzzling things in the CoinCheck incident is that everybody can confirm that the crypto-assets were transferred to the perpetrator's address. Still, nobody, even the judiciary, can recover them back. If it had been a bank deposit, it could have been seized by the authorities and finally returned to the victim when the stolen money was found in some bank account.

Since the very beginning of Bitcoin's popularity, it has been noted that there is a unique idea behind it. It is a policy that never places a trusted central agency, a concept called "trustless." Bitcoins are considered to have made it possible for international use by easily crossing the walls of the border due to differences in law and political systems because of these characteristics.

On the other hand, the conventional system in which a reliable central organization is located is called the world of "trust." Since we live in a world built on the premise of reliable central institutions such as governments, central banks, and courts, the world of trustless seems very special and precarious. However, Bitcoin's existence has been recognized, and trust and trustless have continued to coexist.

For example, geek users who are directly connected as Bitcoin nodes live in a world of "trustless." But amateur users who can't connect themselves to the nodes deposit Bitcoin on crypto-asset exchanges and rely on them to trade Bitcoin. In this case, for such users, the exchange is the trusted third party. And the structure of the trust exists there (Chart 2).

The leaked NEM was stolen and money laundered in a world of "trustless." There is no reliable central organization, and no one, including the government, can arbitrarily rewrite information to resume the normal situation. This incident shows that the "trustless" concept of crypto-asset is a double-edged sword.

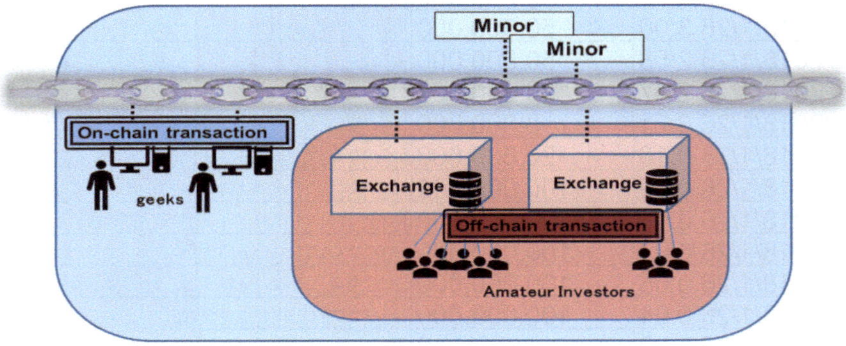

Chart 2 The structure of the "trust" within the structure of "trustless"

4.3 *Third Deviation: Development of Dedicated Mining Companies*

Bitcoin mining equipment evolution and the development of dedicated mining companies ignited the third deviation from Satoshi's world. What Satoshi assumed was that many Bitcoin users provide their own PCs to participate in the mining competition, and lucky people succeed in generating blocks and receive mining rewards. However, miners aiming to win the mining competition changed the rule of the game. They invented new application-specific integrated circuits (ASICs) to calculate SHA-256, and many sophisticated Bitcoin mining machines evolved. The mining competition of Bitcoin was dominated by a few dedicated mining companies. Also, it would have been unexpected for Satoshi that mining consumed much electric power and worsened the global environmental problem.

Bitcoin mining is a process of linking time series of data using hash functions to create a chain of data that is difficult to rewrite. People can use Bitcoin as a way to exchange some value because it was difficult to tamper with data even on the Internet. This technology could be used for electronic cash, but it could also be used for other purposes.

Let's take a closer look at how Bitcoin's data links are constructed when miners mine them. When miners are trying to generate the new block of the chain, they begin by verifying Bitcoin transactions that have not yet been approved. It monitors the trading environment for Bitcoin, including whether the digital signatures used in the transactions are legitimate and if the balance of Bitcoin after the transaction is not negative. Then, a hash value is generated by combining two transactions judged to have no problem, and the hash values are combined to generate a hash value. Repeat these tournament table-like tasks to calculate the Root Hash Value. The workload so far is not so heavy.

A new hash value is created by combining (1) the hash value from the previous block, (2) the Root Hash Value obtained above procedure, and (3) a random number called the nonce. If the hash value satisfies the conditions (For example, if the first 20 bits are 0) determined at that time, the mining is successful. Minor can receive 12. 5 BTC reward and mining fees.[2]

However, in fact, things do not go so well. Since all bits of the generated hash value is randomly set, it can be considered that the possibility that every bit becomes 0 is 1/2. Therefore, this condition is satisfied only with the probability of $(1/2)^{20}$. This is only a probability of about 0.0001% (1/1,048,576). Then, the miner changes the nonce slightly and try to calculate the hash value once again. Then the hash value is totally different, but the probability that it satisfies the condition is also about 0.0001%. If there were only one miner in the world, to have a 50% probability of finding a hash value that satisfies this condition, he needs to repeat about 720,000 trials. This is why they need vast calculation power. For this reason, miners all over the world set up mining machines with many ASICs specialized only for SHA-256 hash

[2]The reward is programmed to decline to 6.25 BTC in mid-May 2020. This event is called "Halving."

function calculation at mining plants, seek rewards and mining fees, and compete with each other for every 10 min.

Miner can earn a reward if they can find the hash value to satisfy the condition even a moment earlier than their competitors. Thus, each minor increases its computational power to search faster. As a result, when the overall computing power increases, the earliest minor can find the hash value within less than 10 min. In that case, Bitcoin has a built-in mechanism that makes it difficult to find the hash value. Instead of the first 20 digits, the number of digits that should be 0 increases to 21 and 22. This keeps competitive mining block generation at an average of 10 min.

These mining machines consume a lot of electric power. The surge in Bitcoin prices in 2017 resulted in a sharp increase in power consumption. A large amount of money was invested in the mining industry, which produced mining machines that affected the silicon cycle of the semiconductor industry.

Digiconomist, a site that has been pointing out the problem, estimates that the amount of electricity used for mining increased from October 2017, and continued to increase until June 2018 despite a crash in the price of crypto-assets. As a result, the annual conversion of power consumption reached approximately 70 TWh (terawatt hour) (Chart 3). Comparing with the power consumption by country, this estimation is closest to Austria, which uses about 70 TWh of electricity per year. The energy spent searching for matching hash values doesn't produce anything useful; it's just wasted. A rise in the price of Bitcoin means additional waste. This is one of the serious problems with Bitcoin.

Moreover, since the mining machine, once manufactured, is a device specialized in the high-speed calculation of a hash function, it cannot be used for other purposes. As a result, the mining ability continues to be enhanced, and the search speed for hash values increases and the difficulty level accordingly becomes difficult, even when the market prices and mining fees drop sharply. This is why mining capacity and

Chart 3 Bitcoin energy consumption trend. *Data source* Cambridge Bitcoin electricity consumption index https://www.cbeci.org/

power consumption did not decline despite a decline in the dollar value of mining reward in 2018.

However, as the earnings environment for miners deteriorated further following the market decline in November 2018, some companies withdrew from mining. Major miners are said to have moved to close unprofitable mining plants. As a result, the estimated power consumption was reduced to about 40 TWh. At current Bitcoin levels, power consumption is unlikely to surge for the time being. According to the pessimistic scenario assumed by Digiconomist.net some time ago, the Bitcoin power consumption was expected to exceed 120 TWh by the end of 2018. This prediction turned out to be in the direction desired by mankind.

Then, in the spring of 2019, the price of Bitcoin soared to $13,750 in June 2019. The rise in global electricity consumption is beginning to rise again as miners that had temporarily suspended operations resume operations.

It's hard to say how the market should move since some people benefit and others lose from the rise and fall of crypto assets. However, if the market overheats and miners start to waste resources, it will be a disadvantage for all mankind in the form of global environmental problems. In this sense, the excessive rise seen in late 2017 is undesirable. There needs to be a shared understanding that such a situation should be avoided in the future.

4.4 Fourth Deviation: Altcoin Appreciation and 51% Attack

The fact that a large number of Bitcoin-like altcoins were issued and their market capitalization surpassed that of Bitcoin was also a major deviation from Satoshi's world. It is well known that Satoshi predicted a 51% attack on Bitcoin, but he also said that it was possible in theory but unrealistic. That's because even if someone had 51% of power to compute hashes, he would"t act to undermine the value of Bitcoin. This logic is correct if Bitcoin is the only crypto-asset in the world, but it is not valid in a world where large and small crypto-assets coexist. As a result, damage from the 51% attack actually appeared. This must have been another unexpected incident for Satoshi.

In May 2018, a crypto-asset called Monacoin was attacked, causing about 100,000 dollars in damage to a Russian operator. Over the next two weeks or so, crypto-assets like Bitcoin Gold, Verge, and ZenCash were reportedly attacked similarly, causing losses of some crypto-asset exchanges.

The attack methods are slightly different, but basically, an attacker involves mining the blockchain with a huge amount of hash calculation power, generating a fork of the chain that is profitable for them, and making newly developed fork to the mainstream of the chain (Chart 4). Variations of the 51% attacks are assumed to occur when the attacker's side hash calculation ability was rich.

Theoretically, the existence of such an attack was pointed out, and the details of the attack method and the necessary hash calculation capability were estimated. Still, it was considered to be very expensive and unlikely to be realized. However, in this

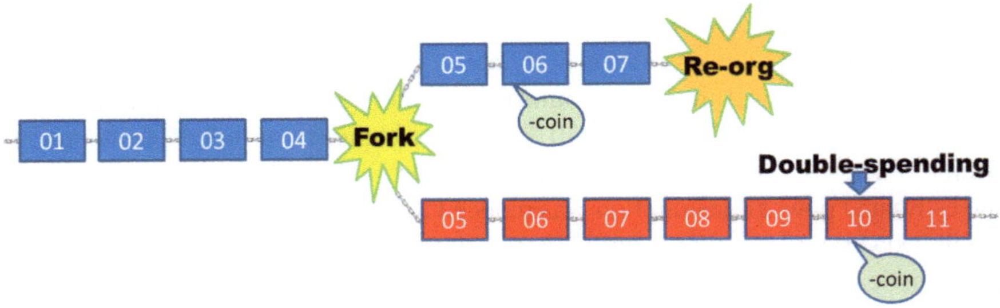

Chart 4 51% attack

place, the damage has occurred one after another. The targets were "non-mainstream" crypto-assets, except for major crypto-assets such as Bitcoin, Ethereum, and Ripple.

Why did these attacks come real? One reason is that non-mainstream crypto-assets have become highly valuable. When you look at the share of the total market capitalization of crypto-assets over a long period, until 2016, Bitcoin accounted for around 90%, and other crypto-assets (altcoins) were of little value. But in 2017, Altcoin's share has soared to 40%.

These altcoins were originally mined by a small number of miners and used relatively little hashing power. Although the difficulty level has been adjusted as prices have risen, there has been a large discrepancy in the computational power of Bitcoin and other mainstream crypto-assets. The attacker took advantage of this disparity in computing power. One of the main reasons for the series of attacks was that the prices of altcoins rose sharply in 2017, increasing the profits gained by the attackers, while the gap in computing power remained.

The designers of these altcoins, many of which mimic Bitcoin, have selected the hash function different from SHA-256 to differentiate them from Bitcoin. If they chose the same hash function as Bitcoin, it would be easy for a Bitcoin miner to monopolize mining rewards due to its massive hash calculation capabilities, and the blockchains of altcoins could be selfishly manipulated. For this reason, non-mainstream crypto-assets had used hash functions that have characteristics that make them difficult for Bitcoin miners to mine.

However, the number of crypto-assets increased, and various entities participated in mining. Furthermore, it became possible to buy and sell the hash capability. For example, at www.nicehash.com, people can trade hashing capability to mine over the Internet. When the hash capability becomes commoditized, and attackers can freely select a hash capability to buy, it becomes impossible to prevent attacks by the traditional strategy that the non-mainstream altcoins have adopted so far. If there is a significant gap in hash capability, the computing resources used for mainstream crypto-assets can be diverted to non-mainstream mining. Instead of investing in the hardware itself, attackers can anonymously purchase hashing capabilities for time lending.

Of course, the attack itself is considered a criminal act, but there are no laws against it nor a law enforcement agency. Many non-mainstream crypto-assets soared in the wake of the big market in late 2017. They have not been thoroughly tested in terms of security and attack readiness.

4.5 Fifth Deviation: Bitcoin Scalability Problem

The Bitcoin is mined after executing the transaction and takes about 10 min to verify. However, from 2016 to 2017, troubles that settlements are not verified for hours are sometimes increased. Blocks that store transaction contents are generated once every ten minutes on average. Still, since the block size has an upper limit (1 MB), as the number of transactions increases, it cannot be stored, and the overflowing transactions are no longer validated. The maximum number of transactions per day was about 400,000. The commission paid for the miner to get the deal approved, which had been almost free until then, had soared. Such a problem is called the scalability problem of Bitcoins.

There were two proposals to solve the problem. Plan A: Deleting redundant signature data in the block, introducing a method called SegWit. Plan B: Raising the upper limit value of the block size. On the other hand, Bitcoin core-developers insisted plan A, and large-scale miners insisted plan B. The campaign of both camps was not buried.

In July 2017, the core developer attracted attention as the day of division August 1, 2017, set to the deadline to introduce plan A. Observations of a sharp drop in the market spread. If SegWit forced without an agreement, there would be two branches of Bitcoins supported by both sides. There was no solution to such a situation. There was a risk that the user suffered a loss.

However, just before the deadline comes, as a compromise between plan A and B, a policy of "SegWit adopts immediately, block size expansion will be discussed again in November again" is proposed, and both sides compromised.

As a result, although initially concerned divisions were avoided, some of the miners expressed creating a new folk of the Bitcoin to create new crypto-assets, and another division occurred. The price of Bitcoin was evaluated as having survived the troubles of the disintegrated but safely, but it was to rise further.

After that, the block size expansion planned for November was postponed because it is not ready, but the soaring market price and busy trading continued even though it is not ready. In particular, at the end of 2017, the market price of Bitcoins temporarily rose to $20,000, and the number of transactions for speculative purposes increased sharply. As a result, the scalability problem became more serious, and at the end of 2017, the fee paid on the day was more than 2 billion yen in total on some days.

However, the decline of the Bitcoins price in 2018 calmed frequent transactions, and the scalability problem naturally disappeared. The block size of the Bitcoin is not stuck to the upper limit, and the trade fees are almost zero. Nonetheless, the fundamental problem was not solved, but if the volume of transactions expanded again, there is a high possibility that the problem will reoccur. On these dangerous infrastructures, trading for speculative purposes is a market of crypto-assets.

4.6 *Sixth Fourth Deviation: A Stable-Coin Tether and the Rise of Bitcoin Price*

Several new factors have affected the price of crypto-assets since the market rose in 2017. This is also the sixth deviation from Satoshi's assumption.

The market capitalization of crypto-assets over the past three years has peaked two times, at the end of 2017 and in mid-2019 (Chart 1). The previous surge in 2017 was caused by the global rise in ICO or Initial Coin Offering, which led to a rise in the price of the underlying Ethereum, which then spread to other altcoins. By contrast, Ethereum and other Altcoins failed to recover from their 2018 slump, while Bitcoin recovered from its 2018 crash and took the lead in the rally in 2019. Although prices declined slightly from autumn 2019 to the end of the year, they have remained at a higher level than at the beginning of the year, indicating that Bitcoin is the only winner.

Various factors have been pointed out as to why Bitcoin soared again in 2019, but the prevailing view is that the massive issuance of stable coins "Tether (USDT)," which had been driving the market rise since the second half of 2017, triggered the current market rise. Tether is a crypto-asset issued by Tether Co, an affiliate of Bitfinex, a major Hong Kong crypto-asset exchange company. Since about 2018, Tether has become the payment method used by the crypto-asset exchange in place of dollars, and its daily transaction value is the largest among all crypto-assets, including Bitcoin.

In April 2019, the New York State Attorney General announced that she had received a court order banning the transfer of funds from Tether to Bitfinex following an investigation into Bitfinex's misuse of its underlying assets to cover its losses. In defiance of the attorney general's announcement, Bitfinex pushed for more Tethers, and its issuance doubled from $2 billion in April to more than $4 billion in July. It was at the same time that the price of Bitcoin soared. There is some speculation that Bitfinex has used the money from its Tether issuance to boost the Bitcoin market. Since July, Tether issuance has leveled off, and Bitcoin fell again toward the end of 2019.

5 Conclusion

Only around 2009–2012, Satoshi's Bitcoin technology was shining, when the initially assumed assumptions were satisfied. Although the price of Bitcoin has risen dramatically since then, the use of electronic cash, which Satoshi had envisioned, didn't realize. In the early days, people expected Bitcoin as a low-cost international remittance service, but now it is not suitable for remittance because fluctuation in market price is intense. If transactions for speculative purposes overflow the upper limit and settlement is delayed. It cannot be convenient for the use of electronic cash.

These deviations were inevitable. Early stakeholders of Bitcoins welcomed the appreciation of price and were not very aggressive in negotiations to raise the systemic upper limit of transactions. Other crypto-assets made by imitating the success of Bitcoins are also almost the same purpose. As a result, the crypto-asset lacked the function as a currency and became a speculative target. As this perception was shared among people, G20 and other international organizations have decided to change the name of virtual currency to crypto-asset.

There are proposals to repair current Bitcoin somehow and use it as a means of payment in the future, but such repair is difficult, and even if technically feasible, it would be almost impossible for parties concerned to agree on a drastic repair. If you need an electronic cash system for use on the Internet, it's much more practical to start from scratch. In considering the future of Bitcoins and crypto-assets, we need to accept actual situations being traded as speculative products. We need to impose regulations from the viewpoint of prohibiting unauthorized use, such as money laundering and consumer protection. Consumer education to prevent misconduct seems to be very important. Information sharing among government agencies to prevent cyber-crime is also important.

The current crypto-assets are incomplete applications because they dump private key management to users. As a practical matter, it is difficult for ordinary users to manage secret keys securely. If so, general users need to trust someone to manage keys and assets. In other words, the catchphrases, such as "decentralization" and "trustless," which the advocate of Bitcoin raised as the ideal, were only an illusion. The current crypto-asset has become a mechanism for the exchange trader to take full responsibility, and if it is, then there is no decentralization nor trustless at all.

It is difficult for ordinary users to judge whether a crypto-asset exchange is reliable or not. In the framework of the current Japanese crypto-asset exchanger regulation system, the registered exchanges are required to conduct risk management in the same manner as banks and other financial institutions. This regulation would also be useful for people who seek a reliable operator.

After all, it seems not always easy or desirable to actually build a world dominated by code that Satoshi would have dreamed of. Ultimately, it is the government of each country that protects the life and property of the citizens from the risks of money laundering and cyber-attacks, The lessons learned from past crypto-asset incidents show that it is safer for economic transactions larger than a certain scale to be checked and backed in some form of the government. The question is how to reconcile the relationship between this reality and the protection of privacy from the government.

References

Back, A. (2002). Hashcash—A denial of service counter-measure. http://www.hashcash.org/papers/hashcash.pdf.

Bayer, D., Haber, S., & Stornetta, W. S. (1993). *Improving the efficiency and reliability of digital time-stamping*.

Bearman, J. (2015). *Silk road: The untold story*. https://www.wired.com/2015/05/silk-road-untold-story/.

Chainalaysis. (2018). *Mapping the universe of Bitcoin's 460 million addresses*. December 19, 2018. https://blog.chainalysis.com/reports/Bitcoin-addresses.

Chaum, D. (1982). Blind signatures for untraceable payments. In *Advances in Cryptology Proceedings of Crypto*, vol. 82.

Haber, S., & Stornetta, W. S. (1991). How to time-stamp a digital document. *Journal of Cryptology, 3*(2), 99–111.

Haber, S., & Stornetta, W. S. (1997). Secure names for bit-strings. In *Proceedings of the 4th ACM Conference*.

Iwashita, N. (2019a). Threats to crypto-assets and counter-measures. *Journal of Digital Practices Information Processing Society of Japan 10*(3) (in Japanese).

Iwashita, N. (2019b). *Regulation of crypto-asset exchanges and the necessity of international cooperation*, T20/TF2 Policy Brief, March 15, 2019. https://t20japan.org/wp-content/uploads/2019/03/t20-japan-tf2-3-regulation-crypto-asset-exchanges.pdf.

Japan Virtual Currency Exchange Association (JVCEA). (2018). *Current status report on virtual currency transaction in Japan*. April 10, 2018 (in Japanese). https://www.fsa.go.jp/news/30/singi/20180410-3.pdf.

Nakamoto, S. (2008). *Bitcoin A peer-to-peer electronic cash system*. https://Bitcoin.org/Bitcoin.pdf.

Okamoto, T., & Ohta, K. (1989). Divertible zero-knowledge interactive proofs and commutative random self-reducibility. *Advances in Cryptology—EUROCRYPT'89, LNCS, 434,* 134–149.

Hodge Decomposition of Bitcoin Money Flow

Yoshi Fujiwara and Rubaiyat Islam

Abstract How money flows among users of Bitcoin is an interesting question in order to understand the dynamics on the complex network of Bitcoin transactions, and also how the transactions are related to the price in the exchange market indirectly. We employ the data of blockchain in the Bitcoin from 2013 to 2018 (compiled by a Hungary research group), utilize a simple algorithm to partially identify anonymous users from addresses, and construct snapshots of temporarily changing network with the users as nodes and the transactions as directed links. In order to understand how users are located in the entire flow, in particular upstream and downstream, we use the so-called Hodge decomposition (or Helmholtz-Hodge-Kodaira decomposition). In addition, we examine the so-called "bow-tie" structure of the binary network disregarding flow to find how the users in the upstream/downstream peripheries (the so-called IN/OUT) are located away from the core of strongly connected component (SCC). We compare the Hodge potential of each node with such a location in the bow-tie structure, and also with the net demand/supply of each node measured from the money flow, to find a significant correlation among the potential, the topological position, and the net demand/supply. We also decompose the flow of each link into potential flow and circular flow to find that circulation of the flow is quite significant. We shall discuss about possible implication of these findings.

Keywords Bow-tie structure · Hodge decomposition · Bitcoin · Cryptoasset · Complex network

1 Introduction

Money is essentially a ledger to record transactions between creditors and debtors (Martin 2014). Flow of money and determination of value or price of currency are fun-

Y. Fujiwara (✉) · R. Islam
Graduate School of Simulation Studies, University of Hyogo, Kobe 650-0047, Japan
e-mail: yoshi.fujiwara@gmail.com

R. Islam
e-mail: rubaiyat.islam1982@gmail.com

L. Pichl et al. (eds.), *Advanced Studies of Financial Technologies and Cryptocurrency Markets*, https://doi.org/10.1007/978-981-15-4498-9_7

damental to the economic activities based on money. It has been a formidable task to study such a flow of money due to the lacking of available data. Cryptocurrency, now called cryptoasset, based on the blockchain technology of non-centralized ledgers (see Antonopoulos 2017 for example), provides an exhaustive record of transactions in the ledger; a quite unique opportunity to study how money flows among users.

It would be interesting to study the structure and its temporal change of a complex network comprising the users as nodes and the money flow as links, because such dynamics is quite possibly related to the users' behaviors during normal and abnormal periods of the cryptoasset's market value. Even if we focus on such studies in the framework of complex network, there are a considerable amount of literature (see Reid and Harrigan 2013; Ober et al. 2013; Ron and Shamir 2013; Kondor et al. 2014a, b; Alvarez-Pereira et al. 2014; Baumann et al. 2014; Fleder et al. 2015; Maesa et al. 2016; Lischke and Fabian 2016; Akcora et al. 2017; Bartoletti et al. 2017; Cachin et al. 2017; Cazabet et al. 2017; Maesa et al. 2017; Ranshous et al. 2017 for example, and references therein).

In this manuscript, we address a specific question of how to identify and quantify the upstream, downstream, or core in the entire money flow. We employ the data of blockchain in the Bitcoin, compiled by a Hungary research group, with addresses converted to users by a well-known algorithm. We shall examined the so-called "bow-tie" structure of the binary network disregarding flow to find how the users in the upstream/downstream peripheries are located away from the core of strongly connected component. On the other hand, we use a combinatorial method of Hodge decomposition, or Helmholtz-Hodge-Kodaira decomposition, to quantify how individual user is located in the upstream and downstream portions of the network by calculating the user's Hodge "potential". We also decompose the flow of each link into potential flow and circular flow to find that circulation of the flow is quite significant.

In Sect. 2, we describe the data of daily aggregation and the construction of network with basic statistics. Then, in Sect. 3, we give the method of bow-tie structure based on the connectivity of the network and show a result for its snapshot. In Sect. 4, we explain the Hodge decomposition with an illustration, and show results for the Hodge potential and others with implications. Two appendices refer to a proof of uniqueness of the potential and to a relevance to de Rham cohomology.

2 Data

A Hungary research group's ELTE Bitcoin Project website and resources (Hungary research group 2020) is used as a comprehensive dataset. The dataset contains all Bitcoin transactions in the first 508,241 blocks, namely from the genesis block approximately up to 9 February 2018. See also (Kondor et al. 2014a, b) for the details. What is important for our analysis of temporally changing networks of money flow among *users*, addresses recorded in the blockchain of Bitcoin are identified as users under the criterion that multiple input addresses in a transaction are regarded as a user. The dataset employs such a criterion (see the original paper Reid and Harrigan 2013 for details) as a minimum but necessary identification in the anonymous system of blockchain, being aware of more sophisticated estimation (see Androulaki et al. 2013; Juháaz et al. 2018 for example and references therein). In addition, the "miners" were deleted from the data.

Let us denote by $G = (V, E)$ the graph or network composed of a set of vertices or nodes as users, E, and of a set of edges or links as flow of money, E. The network changes in time. We shall use the notation of $G_t = (V_t, E_t)$ to denote the snapshot at time t. Time-scale with which one observe the temporal change of the network can be arbitrary depending on the research interest. Here we focus on the daily snapshots for possible comparison with the price of cryptoasset in exchange markets. For this purpose, transactions or money flow from user i to j that took place in each day were aggregated into a single link $i \to j$ with total amount of flow $f_{ij} > 0$. Finally, self-loops were discarded from E.

We select a particular period of time from July 1 to December 31, 2017, which corresponds to the active period of transactions after the revisions of laws concerning

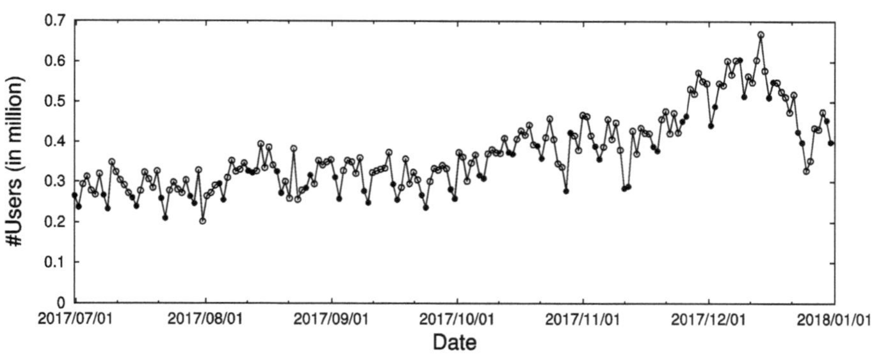

(a) Time-series for the number of users.

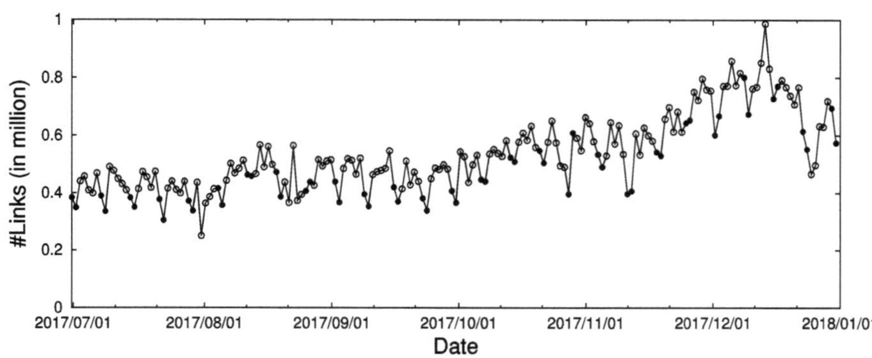

(b) Time-series for the number of links.

Fig. 1 Temporal change of the number of users/links for the period from July 1 to December 31 in the year 2017, **a** users, **b** links. In both plots, the filled dots represent Saturdays and Sundays payment services in several countries, most notably after the revision of Payment Services Act in Japan (April 1, 2017) and the authorized "virtual currency exchange service" as a consequence of the revised regulation.

Figure 1 shows the temporal change of the number of users in V_t and that of the number of links in E_t during the period. The number of users increases with a typical size 0.4M (million), and the number of links is typically 0.6M with an increasing

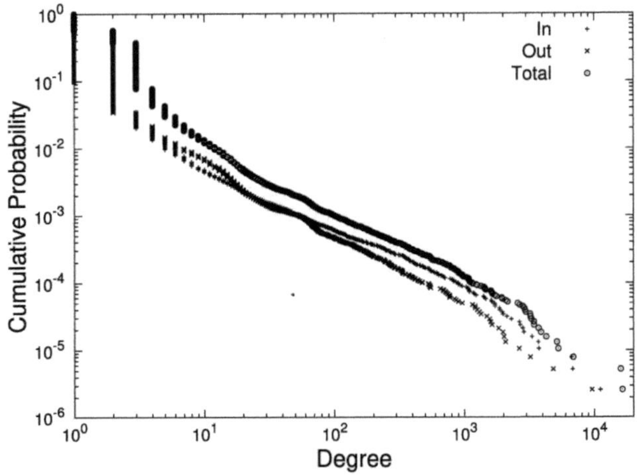

(a) CDF for user's degree; in (+), out (×), and total degree (∘).

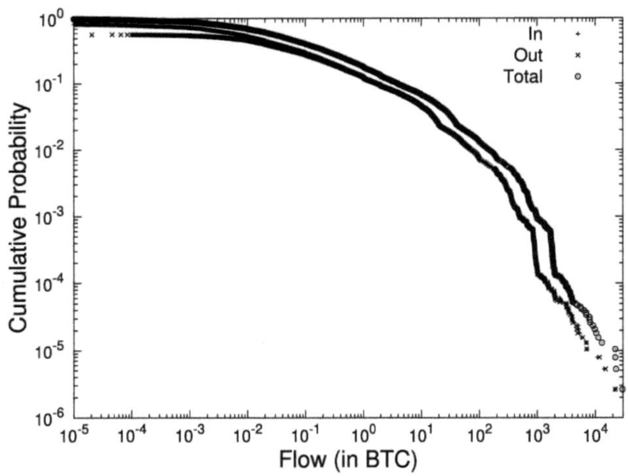

(b) CDF for user's flow; in-coming (+), out-going (×), total flow (∘).

Fig. 2 Cumulative distribution functions (CDF) for **a** user's degree (in, out, and total), **b** user's flow (in the unit of Bitcoin, BTC). Both of the plots are for the date of October 10, 2017 number.[1] In the following, let us randomly select a particular date of October 10, 2017 in order to focus on the topology of and the money flow on a daily snapshot of the temporally changing network with a claim that properties to be shown are quantitatively the same as other snapshots. We shall omit the subscript t for brevity. The number of nodes, denoted by $|V|$, is $|V| = 380{,}792$, while the number of links is $|E| = 551{,}917$.

Figure 2 gives the distributions for the degrees and flows in the network. Figure 2a is the cumulative distribution function (CDF) for the in-degree, out-degree, and total degree, i.e. how many links are in-coming into, out-going from each user, and the sum of them, respectively. The degree distributions have heavy tails; there are users with a huge number of links, like 10^3 or even larger transactions in a day. Figure 2b is the CDF for the amount of flow for in-coming into, out-going from each user, and the total sum of them. The flow distributions are also heavy-tailed; there are users with more than 10^3 BTC. The currency exchange market had the price on the date like 4700 USD per BTC, those daily transactions had considerable market values. Those "big players" can be considered to be exchange markets and financial institutions (see Islam et al. 2020 for more analysis of identification).

3 Bow-Tie Structure

Flow of money on our network $G = (V, E)$ has a flow from upstream to downstream, so to speak, as well as a circulation among users. In this section, we shall identify the location of users V in the upstream, downstream and the core of the network by focusing on the connectivity E alone, that is, ignoring how much money is flowing along the links. For this purpose, we shall use the well-known analysis of "bow-tie" structure (Broder et al. 2000).

Decompose G into weakly connected components (WCC), i.e. connected components when regarded as an undirected graph. We found that there exists a giant WCC (GWCC) with $|V| = 349{,}635$ and $|E| = 529{,}313$, while there are more than a thousand tiny components with a median size $|V| = 3$. Let us focus on the giant WCC (GWCC) in what follows. The GWCC can be decomposed into the parts that are defined as follows:

GWCC Giant weakly connected component: the largest connected component when viewed as an undirected graph. An undirected path exists for an arbitrary pair of firms in the component.

GSCC Giant strongly connected component: the largest connected component when viewed as a directed graph. A directed path exists for an arbitrary pair of firms in the component.

[1] It is interesting to observe that the users and links in the weekends are relatively smaller in comparison with weekdays (see the filled dots in Fig. 1a, b). Such a weekly pattern was found and is discussed in (Islam et al. 2019, 2020). The pattern is likely related to the activities of big players such as currency exchange markets and financial institutions with less activity in weekends.

IN The firms from which the GSCC is reached via a directed path.
OUT The firms that are reachable from the GSCC via a directed path.
TE "Tendrils"; the rest of the GWCC

It follows from the definitions that

$$\text{GWCC} = \text{GSCC} + \text{IN} + \text{OUT} + \text{TE} \tag{1}$$

One can apply graph-search algorithms such as depth-first search and breadth-first search to do the above decomposition (see Cormen et al. 2001 for example). Figure 3 is an illustration. Figure 3a is an example of network, and its decomposition (1) is given in Fig. 3b. The whole of GSCC, IN and OUT looks like a bow-tie, frequently observed in many social and economic networks.

Now we apply the analysis of bow-tie structure to our data. The result is depicted in Fig. 4. In (1), GWCC is decomposed into GSCC (17.5%), IN (29.4%), OUT (23.9%), and TE (29.1%) with percentages in parentheses being the fraction in terms of the number of users contained in each part. GSCC is relatively small, but is present as a core, presumably circulating money mutually among users. IN is the largest portion supplying money to the core from the upstream, while OUT is demanding in the downstream side.

In addition, we calculated the shortest distance from each user to the GSCC. If the user is located in IN, the distance measures how many minimum steps are necessary to go from the user to the GSCC along the directed links. If the user is in OUT, it is the minimum number of steps from the GSCC to arrive at the user. If the shortest distance is long, it means that the user is located in a remote place in the upstream or downstream. In most social and economic networks, such distances are not very long. For example, a study on the supplier-customer links or the production network at nationwide scale in Japan, comprising of a million firms as nodes, shows that such distances are typically very small like 4 steps so that the diameter (the maximum

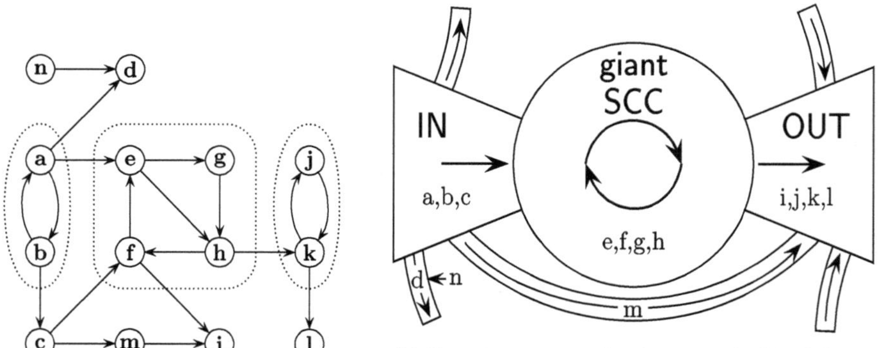

(a) Example of a directed network.

(b) Bow-tie structure for the example. Tendrils are the three nodes d,n,m.

Fig. 3 Example of bow-tie structure

distance between all the pairs of nodes) is quite small, namely and example of the so-called "six-degree of separation" (see Chakraborty et al. 2018 for a recent study on a production network). In contrast, the money flow of Bitcoin has surprisingly long distances as shown in Fig. 4. Actually, the maximum shortest distance for the upstream side of IN is 58, while that for OUT is 85; the bow-tie has an elongated shape! We do not pursue this interesting property further, but can guess that it comes from unique way users were added to the system as suppliers and customers in a decentralized formation of the network.

We have uncovered the bow-tie structure and have located upstream, downstream users in the network with shortest distances from the core of GSCC. This was, however, obtained by merely examining the connectivity of the network, which is different from the money flow. Directed but binary relationship between pairs of users is not sufficient in order to locate users in the entire flow. It would be necessary to take into account the amount of flow, because the distributions for degree and flow have heavy tails as shown in Sect. 2 implying the possible big roles of users with large amounts of money flow. Let us turn our attention to an analysis of flow on the network.

4 Hodge Decomposition

A Helmholtz-Hodge-Kodaira decomposition, or a Hodge decomposition for short, is a combinatorial method to decompose flow on a network into circulation and

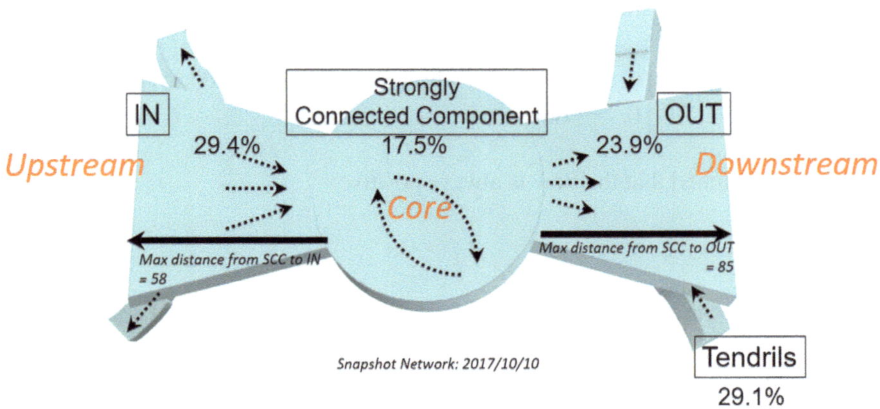

Fig. 4 Bow-tie structure for the network of money flow in the largest weakly connected component (data: October 10, 2017). At the "core" is located the giant strongly connected component (GSCC), which is connected to the IN and OUT component by in-going links into and outgoing links from the SCC, namely "upstream" and "downstream" (see the main text for definitions). The other parts of nodes are called tendrils. The percentage in each portion is the ratio of the number of nodes to the total number $|V| = 349{,}635$. Also shown are the maximum distances from SCC to IN, and from SCC to OUT

gradient flow. Original idea dates back to the so-called Helmholtz theorem in vector analysis, which states that under an appropriate condition any vector field can be uniquely represented by the sum of an irrotational or rotation(curl)-free vector field and a solenoidal or divergence-free vector field. The theorem can be generalized from Euclidean space to graph and other entity as shown by Hodge, Kodaira and others.

In the context of graph, the readers can refer to (Jiang et al. 2008, 2011; Johnson 2013). For recent applications to neural network and economic network, see (Miura and Aoki 2015; Kichikawa et al. 2018) and references therein for example.

For our purpose, the Hodge decomposition can quantify individual user's "potential" to locate the user in upstream and downstream of the entire flow of money, and can decompose individual link's flow into circulation and gradient flow, as we shall see.

4.1 Method

Let us recapitulate the method briefly.

Consider a directed network with an adjacency matrix A_{ij}, i.e.

$$A_{ij} = \begin{cases} 1 & \text{if there is a directed link from node } i \text{ to node } j, \\ 0 & \text{otherwise.} \end{cases} \tag{2}$$

Denote the number of nodes by N. By assumption, $A_{ii} = 0$, i.e. we do not include self-loops. Represent the flow on the network as

$$B_{ij} = \begin{cases} f_{ij} & \text{if there is a flow from node } i \text{ to node } j, \\ 0 & \text{otherwise ,} \end{cases} \tag{3}$$

where it is assumed that the flow is always positive:

$$f_{ij} > 0. \tag{4}$$

Note that there can be possibly a pair of nodes such that $A_{ij} = A_{ji} = 1$ and $f_{ij}, f_{ji} > 0$.

Now let us define a "net flow" F_{ij} by

$$F_{ij} = B_{ij} - B_{ji}, \tag{5}$$

and a "net weight" w_{ij} by

$$w_{ij} = A_{ij} + A_{ji}. \tag{6}$$

Note that w_{ij} is symmetric:

$$w_{ij} = w_{ji}, \tag{7}$$

and non-negative in the sense that

$$w_{ij} \geq 0, \tag{8}$$

for any pair of i and j. It should be mentioned that (6) is simply a convention to take into account the effect of mutual links between i and j; one could multiply (6) by a half or an arbitrary positive weight, which actually has little change to the result for a large network.

The Hodge decomposition is given by

$$F_{ij} = w_{ij}(\phi_i - \phi_j) + F_{ij}^{(\text{loop})}, \tag{9}$$

where ϕ_i is called a *Hodge potential* of node i, and $F_{ij}^{(\text{loop})}$ is divergence-free by definition, namely

$$\sum_j F_{ij}^{(\text{loop})} = 0, \tag{10}$$

for $i = 1, \ldots, N$. The original flow F_{ij} is decomposed into *gradient flow*, $w_{ij}(\phi_i - \phi_j)$, and *circular flow*, $F_{ij}^{(\text{loop})}$.

From (9) and (10), given F_{ij} and w_{ij}, one has simultaneous linear equations to determine ϕ_i:

$$\sum_j L_{ij}\phi_j = \sum_j F_{ij}, \tag{11}$$

for $i = 1, \ldots, N$. Here

$$L_{ij} = \delta_{ij} \sum_k w_{ik} - w_{ij}, \tag{12}$$

and δ_{ij} is Kronecker delta:

$$\delta_{ij} = \begin{cases} 1 & \text{if } i = j, \\ 0 & \text{otherwise}. \end{cases} \tag{13}$$

Obviously, from the symmetry (7), L_{ij} is symmetric:

$$L_{ij} = L_{ji}. \tag{14}$$

Note that simultaneous linear equations (11) are not independent of each other. In fact, the summation over i gives zero. This corresponds to the fact that there is a freedom to change the origin of potential arbitrarily. Let us use the convention in the following that the average is zero:

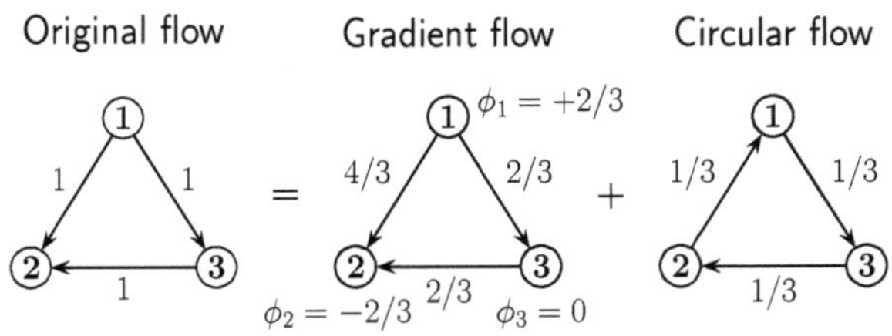

Fig. 5 Example of Hodge decomposition. Original flow among three nodes (*left*). The flow is decomposed into gradient flow (*middle*) and circular flow (*right*). In the gradient flow, each node's Hodge potential ϕ_i is shown. Note that $\phi_i - \phi_j$ gives each gradient flow from node i to j. On the other hand, the circular flow has vanishing divergence

$$\sum_i \phi_i = 0. \tag{15}$$

It is not difficult to prove that if the network is weakly connected, i.e. connected when regarded as an undirected graph, the potential can be determined uniquely up to the choice of the origin of the potential. See Appendix 1 for the proof.

Figure 5 is an illustration of the Hodge decomposition. The adjacency matrix is

$$||A_{ij}|| = \begin{bmatrix} 0 & 1 & 1 \\ 0 & 0 & 0 \\ 0 & 1 & 0 \end{bmatrix}. \tag{16}$$

f_{ij} and B_{ij} take the same form as (16) for this example. Then (11) reads

$$\begin{bmatrix} 2 & -1 & -1 \\ -1 & 2 & -1 \\ -1 & -1 & 2 \end{bmatrix} \begin{bmatrix} \phi_1 \\ \phi_2 \\ \phi_3 \end{bmatrix} = \begin{bmatrix} 2 \\ -2 \\ 0 \end{bmatrix}. \tag{17}$$

The solution for the Hodge potentials satisfying the constraint (15) is obtained by

$$\phi_1 = 2/3, \quad \phi_2 = -2/3, \quad \phi_3 = 0. \tag{18}$$

According to the potential, the nodes 1, 2 and 3 can be located from upstream to downstream in this order. Each of the original flow is decomposed into the gradient flow and the circular flow. Note that the former is rotation-free or irrotational, while the latter is divergence-free or solenoidal.

In Appendix 2, we briefly describe another way to look at the Hodge decomposition from a mathematical viewpoint of simplicial complex and de Rham cohomology.

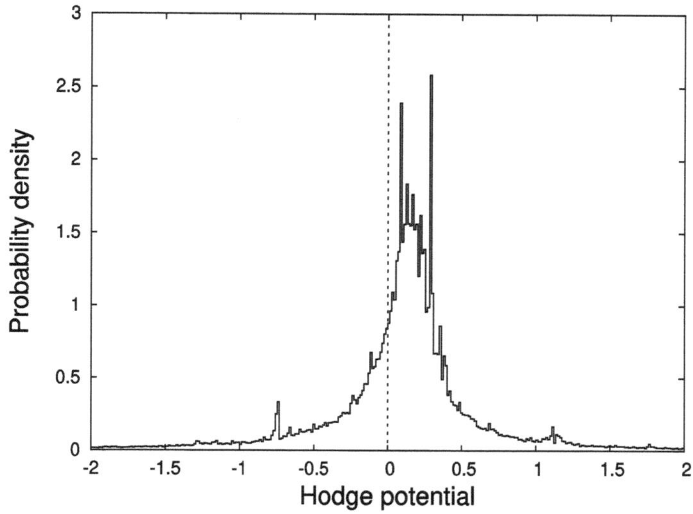

Fig. 6 Probability distribution function (PDF) for the Hodge potential calculated for the network of money flow (data: October 10, 2017). Tendrils in the bow-tie structure are removed from the network. Average of potential is set to zero. Note that the PDF has skewness toward positive

4.2 Result

Let us first take a look at the distribution for the Hodge potential of individual user. Figure 6 shows the probability distribution function for ϕ_i of users. The calculation was done for the GWCC with all the tendrils removed from the network, so comprising of GSCC, IN, and OUT so as to see how ϕ_i depends on the user i's location in the upstream and downstream in the network. Note that the distribution has skewness toward positive showing that relatively large number of users has positive values of potential, while a small number of users has negative values of potential with relatively large absolute value, because phi_i's satisfy (15). It would be an interesting issue to quantify the skewness to compare it with the level of demand or supply by examining daily price change in the currency exchange markets, although it is beyond the present manuscript.

We then proceed to examine how individual user's Hodge potential and location in the bow-tie structure, in particular the position of upstream and downstream, are related to one another. Figure 7 is a scatter plot for each user's Hodge potential (horizontal) and the user's shortest distance from the core or GSCC. If the user is in the GSCC, the distance is defined to be zero. If the user is in the upstream or IN, her potential is mostly positive, while the potential is mostly negative for the downstream or OUT users. Note, however, that the potential can tell us more information than what the bow-tie structure can do. For example, even if the user is in the core, the potential of the user takes a certain range of values from positive and negative (horizontally scattered points along the line corresponding to the distance 0).

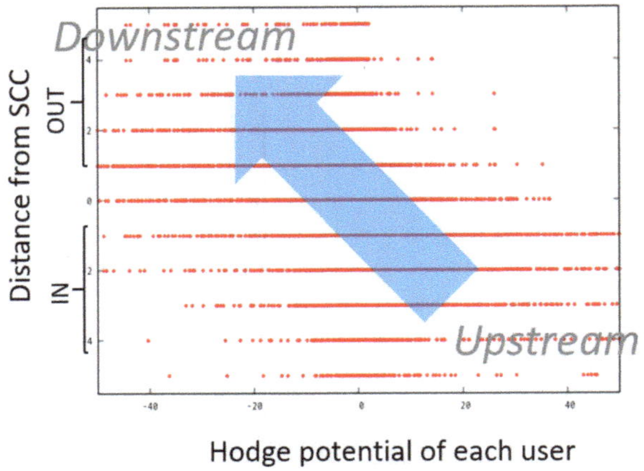

Fig. 7 Individual user's Hodge potential (horizontal axis) and her shortest distance (vertical) from or to the "core" or the GSCC (see Fig. 4) in a scatter plot (data: October 10, 2017). The shortest distance is defined to be 0 if the user is located in the GSCC; otherwise it is defined as indicated. If the user is located in the upstream or "IN", its potential is mostly positive; for the downstream or "OUT", it is mostly negative. Note, however, Hodge potential tells more than what the topological information of bow-tie structure can show

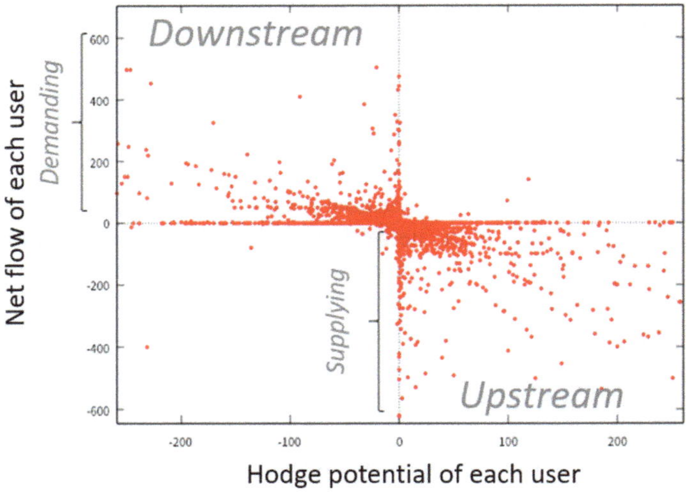

Fig. 8 Each user's Hodge potential (horizontal axis) and her net flow (vertical) in a scatter plot (data: October 10, 2017). The net flow is defined to be the amount of in-coming money minus that of out-going money from the user; it is positive when the user is demanding, while it is negative when supplying. There is obviously a correlation between the value of potential and demanding/supplying property of the user, while one can see fine structures in the scatter plot

On the other hand, the demand/supply by each user i can be measured by the net flow:

$$\text{net flow of user } i = \sum_j f_{ji} - \sum_k f_{ik}, \tag{19}$$

where the first term on the right-hand side is the total amount of in-coming money into the user i, and the second term is the total of out-going money from i. If the user has more demand than supply, (19) is positive, while it is negative for the user with relatively more supply. One can expect that the net demand is likely to be negative (supplying) for the users with larger Hodge potential; and vice versa for the demanding users. Figure 8 is a scatter plot of individual user's Hodge potential (horizontal) and the net flow (vertical). It is obvious that there is a correlation between the value of potential and demanding/supplying property of the user. Moreover, one can observe interesting structures such as several diagonal alignments of users, which presumably correspond to some topologically non-trivial fine structures of connectivity and flow among users.

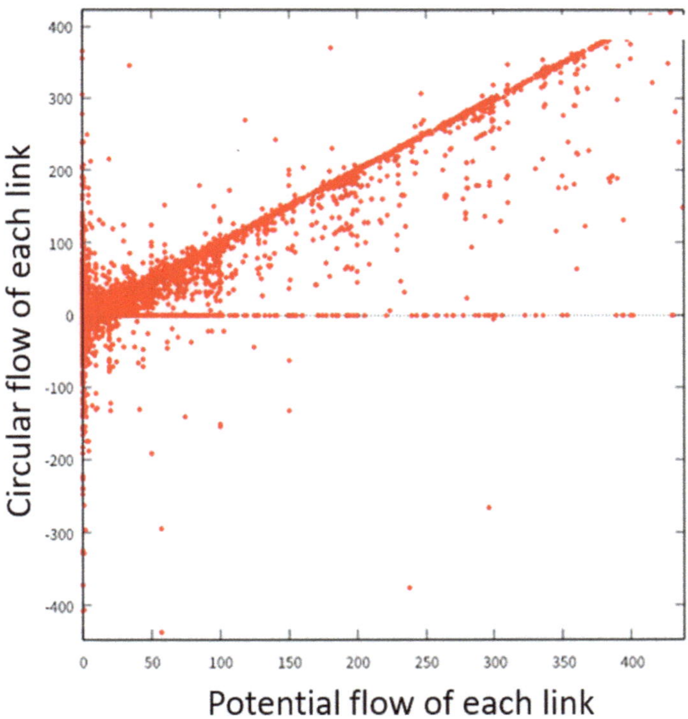

Fig. 9 Each link's original flow is decomposed into gradient flow (horizontal) and circular flow (vertical) according to the Hodge decomposition (data: October 10, 2017). See Fig. 5 for an illustration. While there are links without circular flow (scattered along the horizontal line), one can see that many links have both of gradient and circular flows with comparable magnitude (scattered along the diagonal line)

Finally, the Hodge decomposition (9) allows us to decompose the flow of individual *link* into a gradient flow, or the difference between the potentials at the head and tail of the link, and a circular flow. It would be interesting to see such decompositions in order to see how money is simply circulating among users. Figure 9 is a scatter plot of individual link with its gradient flow (horizontal) and circular flow (vertical). A horizontal alignment of points (circulation $= 0$) is a group of links with vanishing circular flow, implying that those links do not play any role as the circulation of money flow, but simply as the flow from upstream to downstream. A vertical alignment of points (gradient flow $= 0$) corresponds to the links that are circulating money, presumably in the core of the network. Interestingly, there is a diagonal alignment of points that are the links with comparable amount of gradient flow and circular flow. These links can be considered to have the largest share among all the links, although we will study in a future work.

5 Summary

We studied the daily transactions of cryptoasset of Bitcoin among users by using the Hungary research group's dataset based on a way of identifying users from addresses. The daily transactions comprise a directed and weighted graph or network with users as nodes and money flow as links. We employed two methods in order to study how money flows in the entire network. The first method is the so-called bowtie structure analysis, based merely on the connectivity or topology without taking into account of weights. As a result, one can identify individual user's location in the upstream/downstream or the core of the network. The second method is the Hodge decomposition that enables one to decompose the flow into a gradient flow and a circular flow in a unique way. The gradient flow is essentially a difference of potentials at the head and tail of the link. The resulting Hodge potential can measure the location of individual users in the entire flow of network. We examined the relationship between the bow-tie structure and the Hodge potential, studied how the potential is related to each user's net flow or demand/supply, and performed quantification of circular flow in the system. It would be an interesting issue in the future to investigate how the flow is related to the currency exchange market dynamics of price/volume.

Acknowledgements The authors would like to thank Hideaki Aoyama, Yuichi Ikeda, Naoyuki Iwashita, Shinya Kawata, Hiwon Yoon for discussions. We are grateful to the editors who invited us to make this contribution, in particular to Lukas Pichl and Taisei Kaizoji. This work is supported by JSPS KAKENHI Grant Numbers, 17H02041 and 19K22032, by the Nomura Foundation (Grants for Social Science), and also by Kyoto University and Ripple's collaboration scheme.

Appendix 1: Proof of the Uniqueness of Hodge Potential

Consider a directed network with an adjacency matrix A_{ij} given by (2). Denote the number of nodes by N. Represent the flow on the network as (3). Then define F_{ij} or "net flow" by (5), and w_{ij} or "net weight" by (6). The Hodge decomposition is given by (9), where ϕ_i is the Hodge potential. The potential can be obtained by solving (11), where L_{ij} is defined by (12).

We use such a notation that $\mathbf{L}$ is a matrix whose (i, j) element is L_{ij}; $\boldsymbol{\phi}$ is a vector whose i component is ϕ_i.

In this appendix, we shall prove that for a weakly connected network, i.e. connected when regarded as an undirected network, the Hodge potential for each node is uniquely determined up to addition of a constant.

Let us consider the eigenvalues and eigenvectors of $\mathbf{L}$:

$$\mathbf{L}\boldsymbol{v}^{(a)} = \lambda_a \boldsymbol{v}^{(a)}, \tag{20}$$

for $a = 1, \ldots, N$. Because $\mathbf{L}$ is symmetric, we have the following consequences:

- eigenvalues, λ_a, are real;
- eigenvectors form an orthonormal set of bases:

$$\sum_i v_i^{(a)} v_i^{(b)} = \delta_{ab}, \tag{21}$$

  for any pair of a and b;
- eigenvectors form a complete set of bases:

$$\sum_a v_i^{(a)} v_j^{(a)} = \delta_{ij}, \tag{22}$$

  for any pair of i and j.

We assume, without loss of generality, that the indices, a, are ordered such that the eigenvalues are in the ascending order of values:

$$\lambda_1 \leq \lambda_2 \leq \cdots \leq \lambda_N \tag{23}$$

One of the eigenvalues is zero with its corresponding eigenvector being a multiple of $\boldsymbol{v} = \mathbf{1}$, as one can easily confirm.[2] Due to the existence of this eigenvector, the linear equation (11) has a solution $\boldsymbol{\phi}$ only up to the addition of a multiple of the trivial eigenvector $\mathbf{1}$. In other words, one can choose the origin of potential in an arbitrary way.

Now we show that the other eigenvalues are all positive, that is

[2] $\mathbf{1}$ is the vector with all the components equal to 1.

$$0 = \lambda_1 < \lambda_2 \leq \cdots \leq \lambda_N \tag{24}$$

The solution of the linear equation (11), therefore, is uniquely determined up to the addition of a multiple of the trivial eigenvector.

For an arbitrary function $\boldsymbol{f}$, which is not a zero vector, consider a quadratic form, $\boldsymbol{f}^{\mathrm{t}}\mathbf{L}\boldsymbol{f}$. One can easily show that

$$\begin{aligned}
\boldsymbol{f}^{\mathrm{t}}\mathbf{L}\boldsymbol{f} &= \sum_{i,j} L_{ij} f_i f_j = \sum_{i,j} (\delta_{ij} \sum_k w_{ik} - w_{ij}) f_i f_j \\
&= \sum_{i,j} w_{ij} (f_i^2 - f_i f_j) \\
&= \frac{1}{2} \sum_{i,j} w_{ij} (2 f_i^2 - 2 f_i f_j) \\
&= \frac{1}{2} \sum_{i,j} w_{ij} (f_i - f_j)^2 \geq 0
\end{aligned} \tag{25}$$

In the last line, we used the symmetry (7). The inequality follows from the non-negativity (8).

If the equality holds in (25), it follows that for any i and j such that $w_{ij} > 0$, $f_i = f_j$. Because the network is weakly connected, this means that f_i is constant for all the nodes. Conversely, if f_i is constant, the equality holds in (25).

If one considers the case $f_i = v_i^{(k)}$ for a fixed k, one has

$$\boldsymbol{f}^{\mathrm{t}}\mathbf{L}\boldsymbol{f} = \lambda_k \tag{26}$$

Because the inequality (25) holds for any $\boldsymbol{f}$, it follows that $\lambda_k \geq 0$ for any k. But we have shown above that the equality holds in (25) if and only if $\boldsymbol{f} = \mathbf{1}$, i.e. the trivial eigenvector, we have $\lambda_k > 0$ for $k = 2, \ldots, N$. This proves (24).

Appendix 2: Simplicial Complex and de Rham Cohomology

It would be interesting to see that Hodge decomposition is related to what is known as *de Rham cohomology* if the network under consideration, or in general, a graph is regarded as *simplicial complex*. Let us recapitulate it in this appendix (see Johnson 2013 for a lucid introduction).

Consider a graph $G = (V, E)$ with V a set of nodes and E as a set of edges. A directed graph can be regarded as a "flow" on an undirected graph, as we shall see, so let us assume that G is undirected with a possibly positive, zero, or negative value associated with each edge. Let the total number of nodes be n. Suppose that the nodes are indexed by $1, \ldots, n$.

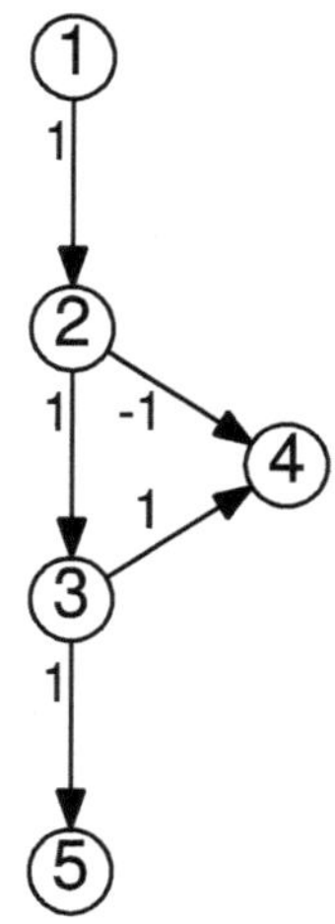

Fig. 10 A simple example of graph comprising 5 nodes. Note that by definition in this appendix, the direction of edges is define as $i \to j$ so that the index of node is increasing, that is, $i < j$. Value associated with each edge represents "flow". The edge $2 \to 4$ has a negative flow of -1, which means that there is a flow of $+1$ from the node 4 to 2, by the definition

k-simplex Σ_k in G: a fully connected subgraph of G with $(k+1)$ nodes. A node is a 0-simplex: an edge is a 1-simplex: an triangle is a 2-simplex. In general, G can be uniquely expressed by a collection of Σ_k, the so-called a simplicial complex.

Figure 10 is a simple example with $n = 6$ (taken from Miura and Aoki 2015).

$$\Sigma_0 : 1, 2, 3, 4, 5, 6 \tag{27}$$
$$\Sigma_1 : 12, 23, 24, 34, 35 \tag{28}$$
$$\Sigma_2 : 234 \tag{29}$$

Σ_{k-1} can be expressed by a sequence $i_1 \ldots i_k$ where i_p is a node's index. The triangle (234) can also be designated as (324). We adopt the notation $i_1 \ldots i_k$ for an index sequence that may or may not be in ascending order, whereas $\overline{i_1 \ldots i_k}$ means $i_1 < \cdots < i_k$.

Vector spaces, V_k:

$$V_k = \left\{ \sum_{\overline{i_1 \ldots i_{k+1}} \in \Sigma_k} a_{\overline{i_1 \ldots i_{k+1}}} (\overline{i_1 \ldots i_{k+1}}) \text{ with } a_{\overline{i_1 \ldots i_{k+1}}} \in R \right\} \tag{30}$$

We introduce a calculus

$$(j_1 \ldots j_k) = \begin{cases} +(\overline{i_1 \ldots i_k}) & \text{if } j_1 \ldots j_k \text{ is an even permutation of } i_1 \ldots i_k \\ -(\overline{i_1 \ldots i_k}) & \text{if } j_1 \ldots j_k \text{ is an odd permutation of } i_1 \ldots i_k \end{cases} \tag{31}$$

For the example in Fig. 10, $\alpha \in V_1$ can be represented by

$$\alpha = a_{12}(12) + a_{23}(23) + a_{24}(24) + a_{34}(34) + a_{35}(35) \tag{32}$$

Σ_1 can be regarded as a natural basis of V_1.

Figure 10 is a "flow network"; each edge has a flow indicated by a value on it. The flow can be regarded as a vector $\omega \in V_1$:

$$\omega = (12) + (23) - (24) + (34) + (35) \tag{33}$$

One can introduce an inner product in which the natural bases form a complete set of orthonormal bases. For example, the inner product between (32) and $\beta = b_{12}(12) + \cdots + b_{35}(35)$ is

$$\langle \alpha, \beta \rangle = a_{12}b_{12} + a_{23}b_{23} + a_{24}b_{24} + a_{34}b_{34} + a_{35}b_{35} \tag{34}$$

Linear operator $\delta_k : V_k \to V_{k+1}$

$$\delta_k(i_1 \dots i_k) = \sum_{(j\overline{i_1 \dots i_{k+1}}) \in \Sigma_{k+1}} (j\overline{i_1 \dots i_{k+1}}) \tag{35}$$

For the example in Fig. 10,

$$\delta_0(1) = -(12) \tag{36}$$
$$\delta_0(2) = (12) - (23) - (24) \tag{37}$$
$$\delta_0(3) = (23) - (34) - (35) \tag{38}$$
$$\delta_0(4) = (24) + (34) \tag{39}$$
$$\delta_0(5) = (35) \tag{40}$$
$$\delta_1(12) = 0 \tag{41}$$
$$\delta_1(23) = (234) \tag{42}$$
$$\delta_1(24) = -(234) \tag{43}$$
$$\delta_1(34) = (234) \tag{44}$$
$$\delta_1(35) = 0 \tag{45}$$
$$\delta_2(234) = 0 \tag{46}$$

For the flow (33), we have

$$\delta_1(\omega) = 3(234) \tag{47}$$

Note that the coefficient 3 of (234) is a rotation or curl in the triangle (234).

Define a linear operator $\delta_k^* : V_{k+1} \to V_k$

For $\beta \in V_{k+1}$, $\delta_k^*(\beta)$ is defined by

$$\langle \alpha, \delta_k^*(\beta) \rangle = \langle \delta_k(\alpha), \beta \rangle \tag{48}$$

for all $\alpha \in V_k$. One can prove that

$$\delta_k^*(\overline{i_1 \dots i_{k+2}}) = \sum_{q=1}^{k+2} (-1)^1 (\overline{i_1 \dots \hat{i_q} \dots i_{k+2}}) \tag{49}$$

where $\hat{i_q}$ denotes the index i_q is removed from the sequence $\overline{i_1 \dots i_{k+2}}$.

For the example in Fig. 10,

$$\delta_0^*(12) = (2) - (1) \tag{50}$$
$$\delta_0^*(23) = (3) - (2) \tag{51}$$
$$\delta_0^*(24) = (4) - (2) \tag{52}$$
$$\delta_0^*(34) = (4) - (3) \tag{53}$$
$$\delta_0^*(35) = (5) - (3) \tag{54}$$
$$\delta_1^*(234) = (34) - (24) + (23) \tag{55}$$

Define subspaces G_k and S_k of V_k:

$$G_k = \text{Image}(\delta_{k-1}) = \{\alpha \in V_k : \text{Some } \beta \in V_{k-1} \text{ exists s.t. } \delta_{k-1}(\beta) = \alpha\} \tag{56}$$

$$S_k = \text{Image}(\delta_k^*) = \{\alpha \in V_k : \text{Some } \beta \in V_{k+1} \text{ exists s.t. } \delta_k^*(\beta) = \alpha\} \tag{57}$$

One can prove what follows.

1. For any $\alpha \in V_k$, $\delta_{k+1}(\delta_k(\alpha)) = 0$. For any $\beta \in V_{k+1}$, $\delta_{k-1}^*(\delta_k^*(\beta)) = 0$.
2. G_k and S_k are orthogonal subspaces of V_k.
3. *Define* a subspace
$$H_k = (G_k \oplus S_k)^\perp \tag{58}$$

   Then we have $V_k = G_k \oplus S_k \oplus H_k$
4. $G_k^\perp = \text{Kernel}(\delta_{k-1}^*)$ and $S_k^\perp = \text{Kernel}(\delta_k)$
5. $S_k = \delta_{k-1}^*(G_{k+1})$ and $G_k = \delta_{k-1}(S_{k-1})$
6. Any $\omega \in V_k$ has a unique decomposition

$$\omega = \omega_g + \omega_s + \omega_h \tag{59}$$

   where

$$\omega_g \in G_k = \delta_{k-1}(V_{k-1}) \tag{60}$$
$$\omega_s \in S_k = \delta_k^*(V_{k+1}) \tag{61}$$
$$\omega_h \in H_k = \text{Kernel}(\delta_{k-1}^*) \cap \text{Kernel}(\delta^k) \tag{62}$$

   This is called Hodge decomposition (Jiang et al. 2008).

References

Alvarez-Pereira, B., Matthew Ayres, M. A., Gómez López, A. M., Gorsky, S., Hayes, S. W., Qiao, Z., & Santana, J. (2014). Network and conversation analyses of bitcoin. In *2014 complex systems summer school proceedings*.

Androulaki, E., Karame, G. O., Roeschlin, M., Scherer, T., & Capkun, S. (2013). Evaluating user privacy in bitcoin. In *International conference on financial cryptography and data security* (pp. 34–51). Springer.

Antonopoulos, A. M. (2017). *Mastering bitcoin: Programming the open blockchain* (2nd edn). O'Reilly Media.

Bartoletti, M., Bracciali, A., Lande, S., & Pompianu, L. (2017). A general framework for bitcoin analytics. http://arxiv.org/abs/1707.01021.

Baumann, A., Fabian, B., & Lischke, M. (2014). Exploring the bitcoin network. In *Proceedings of the 10th international conference on web information systems and technologies—Volume 2: WEBIST*. https://doi.org/10.5220/0004937303690374.

Broder, A., Kumar, R., Maghoul, F., Raghavan, P., Rajagopalan, S., Stata, R., et al. (2000). Graph structure in the web. *Computer Networks*, *33*(1–6), 309–320.

Cazabet, R., Rym, B., & Latapy, M. (2017). Tracking bitcoin users activity using community detection on a network of weak signals. http://arxiv.org/abs/1710.08158.

Chakraborty, A., Kichikawa, Y., Iino, T., Iyetomi, H., Inoue, H., Fujiwara, Y., et al. (2018). Hierarchical communities in the walnut structure of the Japanese production network. *PLOS ONE*, *13*(8), 1–25.

Christian Cachin, Angelo De Caro, Pedro Moreno-Sanchez, Björn Tackmann, and Marko Vukolić. The transaction graph for modeling blockchain semantics. https://eprint.iacr.org/2017/1070, 2017.

Cormen, T. H., Leiserson, C. E., Rivest, R. L., & Stein, C. (2001). *Introduction to algorithms*. Cambridge, MA: MIT Press.

Fleder, M., Kester, M. S., & Pillai, S. (2015). Bitcoin transaction graph analysis. http://arxiv.org/abs/1502.01657.

Gurcan Akcora, C., Gel, Y. R., & Kantarcioglu, M. (2017). Blockchain: A graph primer. http://arxiv.org/abs/1708.08749.

Hungary research group: Elte bitcoin project. Retrieved January 3, 2020 from, http://www.vo.elte.hu/bitcoin/, https://senseable2015-6.mit.edu/bitcoin/.

Islam, R., Fujiwara, Y., Kawata, S., & Yoon, H. (2020). Unfolding identity of financial institutions in bitcoin blockchain by weekly pattern of network flows (in preparation).

Islam, R., Fujiwara, Y., Kawata, S., & Yoon, Hiwon. (2019). Analyzing outliers activity from the time-series transaction pattern of bitcoin blockchain. *Evolutionary and Institutional Economics Review*, *16*(1), 239–257.

Jiang, X., Lim, L.-H., Yao, Y., & Ye, Y. (2008). Learning to rank with combinatorial Hodge theory (Accessed in, 2020).

Jiang, X., Lim, L.-H., Yao, Y., & Ye, Y. (2011). Statistical ranking and combinatorial hodge theory. *Mathematical Programming*, *127*(1), 203–244.

Johnson, J. L. (2013). Discrete hodge theory on graphs: A tutorial. *Computing in Science & Engineering*, *15*(5), 42–55.

Juháaz, P., Stéger, J., Kondor, D., & Vattay, G. (2018). A bayesian approach to identify bitcoin users. *PLoS ONE*, *13*(12), e0207000.

Kichikawa, Y., Iyetomi, H., Iino, T., & Inoue, H. (2018). Hierarchical and circular flow structure of interfirm transaction networks in Japan (Vol. 4). https://ssrn.com/abstract=3173955.

Kondor, D., Csabai, I., Szüle, J., Pósfai, M., & Vattay, G. (2014). Inferring the interplay between network structure and market effects in bitcoin. *New Journal of Physics*, *16*(12), 125003.

Kondor, D., Pósfai, M., Csabai, I., & Vattay, G. (2014). Do the rich get richer? An empirical analysis of the bitcoin transaction network. *PLoS ONE*, *9*(2), e86197.

Lischke, M., & Fabian, Benjamin. (2016). Analyzing the bitcoin network: The first four years. *Future Internet*, *8*(1), 7.

Maesa, D., Marino, A., & Ricci, L. (2016). Uncovering the bitcoin blockchain: An analysis of the full users graph. In *Conference: 2016 IEEE international conference on data science and advanced analytics (DSAA)*. https://doi.org/10.1109/DSAA.2016.52.

Maesa, D., Marino, A., & Ricci, L. (2017). Data-driven analysis of bitcoin properties: exploiting the users graph. *International Journal of Data Science and Analytics*. https://doi.org/10.1007/s41060-017-0074-x.

Martin, F. (2014). *Money: The unauthorized biography*. Knopf.

Miura, K., & Aoki, T. (2015). Scaling of hodge-kodaira decomposition distinguishes learning rules of neural networks. *IFAC-Papers OnLine*, *48*(18), 175–180.

Ober, M., Katzenbeisser, S., & Hamacher, Kay. (2013). Structure and anonymity of the bitcoin transaction graph. *Future Internet*, *5*(2), 237–250.

Ranshous, S., Joslyn, C., Kreyling, S., Nowak, K., Samatova, N. F., West, C. L., et al. (2017). Exchange pattern mining in the bitcoin transaction directed hypergraph. In *Financial cryptography workshops*. https://doi.org/10.1007/978-3-319-70278-0_16.

Reid, F., & Harrigan, M. (2013). An analysis of anonymity in the bitcoin system. In *Security and privacy in social networks* (pp. 197–223). Springer.

Reid, F., & Harrigan, M. (2013). An analysis of anonymity in the bitcoin system. In Y. Altshuler, Y. Elovici, A. Cremers, N. Aharony, & A. Pentland (Eds.), *Security and privacy in social networks* (pp. 197–223). New York: Springer.

Ron, D., & Shamir, A. (2013). Quantitative analysis of the full bitcoin transaction graph. In *Financial cryptography and data security*. https://doi.org/10.1007/978-3-642-39884-1_2.

Time Series Analysis of Relationships Among Crypto-asset Exchange Rates

Takeshi Yoshihara, Tomoo Inoue, and Taisei Kaizoji

Abstract There are several previous empirical analyses for Bitcoin pricing; however, only a few pieces of research can be found in terms of the relationships among major crypto assets, such as Ethereum, and Ripple. Here, we apply a method proposed by Nan and Kaizoji (Int Rev Fin Anal 64:273–281, 2019), which calculates an indirect exchange rate to consider the possibility of a cointegrating relationship between a crypto-asset exchange rate and a direct FX spot rate. We investigate market efficiency in crypto-asset exchange rates through the application of several kinds of unit root tests and the Johansen procedure. The results suggest that the weak form of market efficiency does not seem to hold for all pairs; however, one of the prerequisites for semi-strong form of market efficiency holds for several pairs. Additionally, we focus on the dynamic relationships by applying the impulse response function for a four-variable VECM. Remarkably, the Bitcoin exchange rate can slightly affect the EUR/USD spot rate.

Keywords Crypto asset · Efficient market hypothesis · Cointegration · Impulse response function

1 Introduction

In recent years, crypto assets (or cryptocurrencies) have become more integrated into the world economy. Transactions in crypto-asset markets are done using a decentralized online platform called "blockchain," and its well-designed cryptographic system is at the underlying technology. As the market capitalization of crypto assets expands, increasing numbers of researchers in economics and finance have recently started paying attention to the issues related to crypto-asset markets. For instance,

T. Yoshihara · T. Kaizoji (✉)
International Christian University, Osawa 3-10-2, Mitaka, Tokyo 181-8585, Japan
e-mail: kaizoji@icu.ac.jp

T. Inoue
Faculty of Economics Organization, Seikei University, 3-3-1 Kichijoji Kitamachi, Musashino, Tokyo 180-8633, Japan
e-mail: inoue@econ.seikei.ac.jp

L. Pichl et al. (eds.), *Advanced Studies of Financial Technologies and Cryptocurrency Markets*, https://doi.org/10.1007/978-981-15-4498-9_8

the problem of whether or not crypto assets can become a currency is a point of contention in economics and finance research.

There are several studies on Bitcoin and its efficiency in econometrics. On the one hand, Cheah and Fry (2015) suggested that the price instability of Bitcoin was a speculative bubble. Corbet et al. (2018) reported that there were periods of bubble behavior in Bitcoin and Ethereum pricing. On the other hand, Urquhart (2016) investigated the market efficiency of Bitcoin and suggested that the markets would become more efficient. Nadarajah and Chu (2017) showed that a power transformation model of Bitcoin returns might be weakly efficient. Tiwari et al. (2018) analyzed Bitcoin price data by using robust long-range dependence estimators, and reported that the market was efficient. Nan and Kaizoji (2019) compared Bitcoin with EUR/USD spot, future, and forward rates, and concluded that weak and semi-strong efficiency of Bitcoin held in the long term.

Following these empirical investigations, we focus on the efficiency of Bitcoin, Ethereum, and Ripple by Nan and Kaizoji's methodology that compares exchange rates in the real markets to indirect crypto-asset exchange rates (*CER*). Its equation is given by

$$CER = \frac{CRP\_EUR}{CRP\_USD}$$

where *CRP_EUR* and *CRP_USD* are the crypto-asset prices in Euros and U.S. Dollars, respectively. The aim of this method is not only to eliminate the influence of the exponential growth of crypto-asset markets, but also to compare those markets with FX markets (See Figs. 1 and 2).

The rest of this paper is structured as follows. In the second chapter, we present the theoretical backgrounds of this research. In the third chapter, we show the results of empirical study and describe some implications for our findings. Conclusions are provided in the last chapter.

2 Data and Methodology

2.1 *Efficient Market Hypothesis*

The efficient market hypothesis proposed by Fama (1970) assumed that a price in the market was always fully reflective of all available information. When we consider how information availability is defined, market efficiency can be classified into three forms: weak, semi-strong, and strong forms. Weak-form efficiency considers historical price data to be all the available information; semi-strong-form efficiency includes not only historical price data but also publicly available new information; strong-form efficiency requires all the investors in the market to access not only public but private information related to pricing. This paper focuses only on the weak and semi-strong forms because Fama (1991) admitted that the strong form was impossible in the real world. In a general efficiency test, a dependent variable of one spot rate is examined toward an explanatory variable of a forward rate. However,

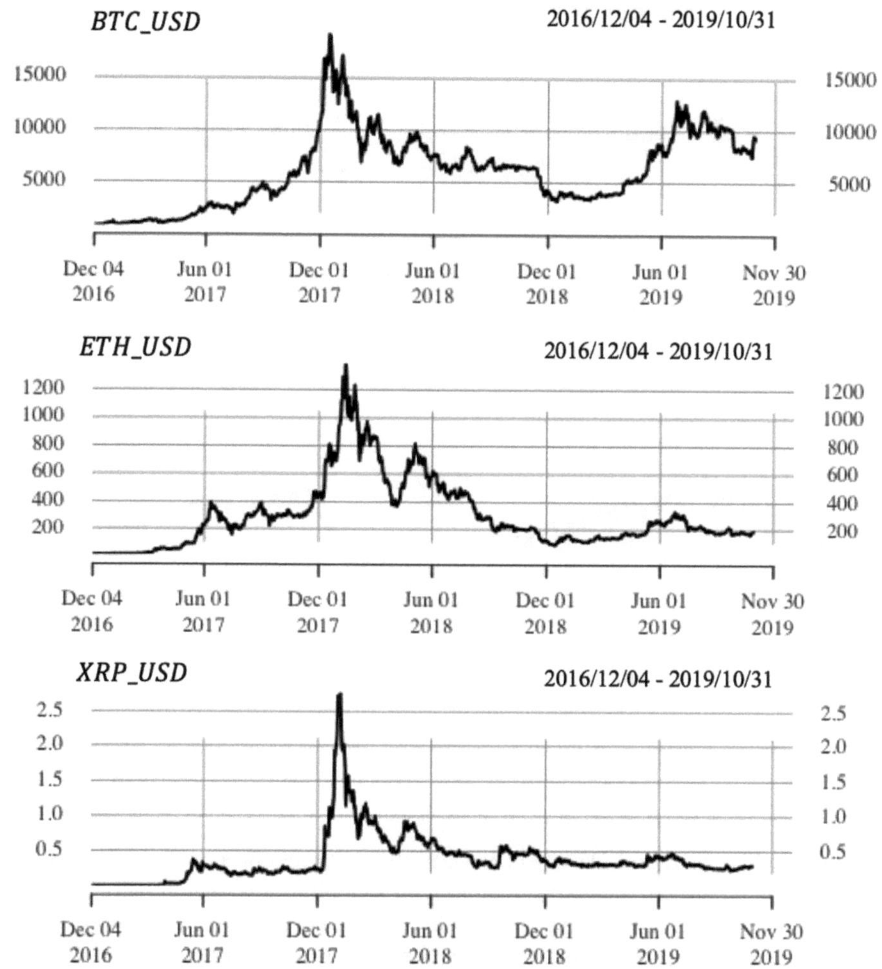

Fig. 1 Historical price data of Bitcoin, Ethereum, and Ripple in *USD*

we compare the crypto-asset exchange rates, which are considered to function as a kind of spot rates, with the EUR/USD spot rate, since our aim is not only to test the efficiency of Bitcoin but also to compare it with that of Ethereum and Ripple.

2.2 Unit Root Tests

For testing the hypothesis of weak-form efficiency on the four exchange rates, we first check whether or not the process has a unit root using the Augmented Dickey-Fuller (ADF), Kwiatkowski-Phillips-Schmidt-Shin (KPSS), and Zivot-Andrews (ZA) tests.

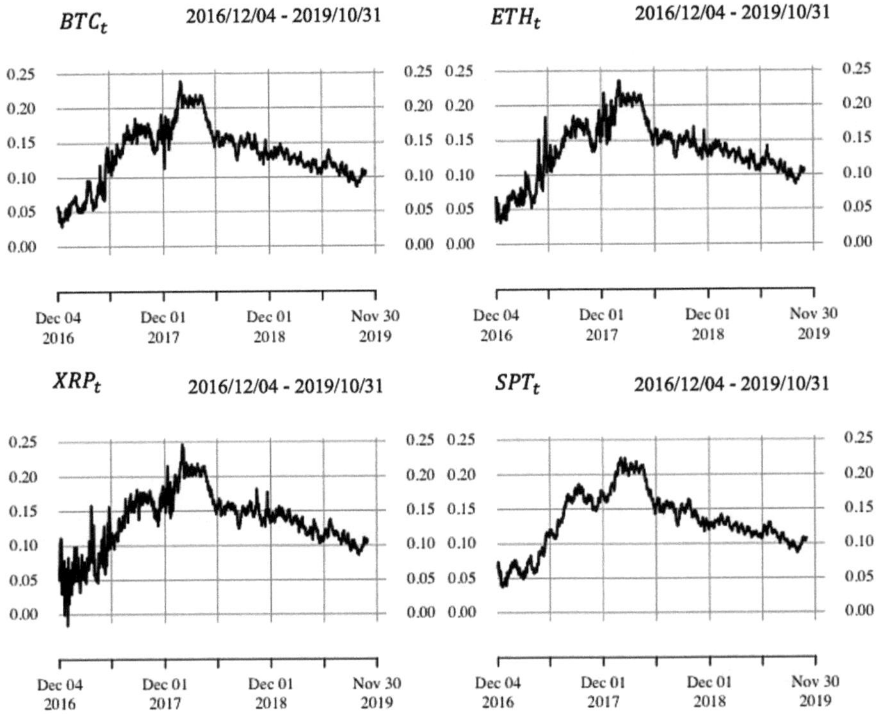

Fig. 2 Historical price data of the three crypto-asset exchange rates and the FX spot rate of EUR/USD

As noted by Said and Dickey (1984), in the ADF test proposed by Dickey and Fuller (1979) there are three specifications for modeling; (a) one with constant and trend, (b) one with constant, and (c) one with neither. For example, when we consider the crypto-asset exchange rates, CER_t, as an AR (ρ) process, the three specifications can be written as

(a) $CER_t = \rho_1 CER_{t-1} + \rho_2 CER_{t-2} + \cdots + \rho_p CER_{t-p} + \varepsilon_t$
(b) $CER_t = \alpha + \delta t + \rho_1 CER_{t-1} + \rho_2 CER_{t-2} + \cdots + \rho_p CER_{t-p} + \varepsilon_t$
(c) $CER_t = \alpha + \rho_1 CER_{t-1} + \rho_2 CER_{t-2} + \cdots + \rho_p CER_{t-p} + \varepsilon_t$

where α denotes the constant term, δ denotes the drift term, and ε_t denotes a stationary error. For these cases, the null and alternative hypotheses of the ADF test are

$$H_0 : \sum_{s=1}^{p} \rho_s - 1 = 0$$

$$H_1 : \sum_{s=1}^{p} \rho_s - 1 < 0.$$

In terms of hypothesis testing, it is not recommended to do the t-test as the distribution does not necessarily follow the Student's t-distribution if the data has a unit root (Dickey and Fuller 1979). MacKinnon (1996) proposed to utilize a τ distribution and its statistics instead of the Student's t-distribution and t-value. We follow this methodology in the unit root tests.

Second, the KPSS test also checks whether the process has a unit root; however, this tests the null hypothesis of stationarity against a unit root (Kwiatkowski et al. 1992). There are two specifications to test stationarity;

(d) $CER_t = \alpha + r_t + \varepsilon_t$
(e) $CER_t = \alpha + \delta t + r_t + \varepsilon_t$

where α denotes the constant term, r_t denotes the random walk, δ denotes the drift term, ε_t denotes stationary error, and u_t is iid $\left(0, \sigma_u^2\right)$. The set of the null and alternative hypotheses is contradictory to those of the ADF;

$$H_0 : \sigma_u^2 = 0 \quad \left[\text{the series is stationary}\right]$$
$$H_1 : \sigma_u^2 > 0 \quad [\text{the series has a unit root}].$$

The last approach for checking a unit root is the Zivot and Andrews (1992) test. This method allows us to test the existence of a unit root with a structural break. All three models of this test are considered to be "trend and drift" specification as with the model (c) of the ADF. Consider AR (1) processes,

(f) $CER_t = \alpha + \theta DU_t + \delta t + \rho CER_{t-1} + \sum_{j=1}^{k} \Delta c_j CER_{t-j} + \varepsilon_t$

(g) $CER_t = \alpha + \delta t + \gamma DT_t + \rho CER_{t-1} + \sum_{j=1}^{k} \Delta c_j CER_{t-j} + \varepsilon_t$

(h) $CER_t = \alpha + \theta DU_t + \delta t + \gamma DT_t + \rho CER_{t-1} + \sum_{j=1}^{k} \Delta c_j CER_{t-j} + \varepsilon_t$

$$\left(DU_t = \begin{cases} 1 & \text{if } t > bp \\ 0 & \text{otherwise} \end{cases}, \quad DT_t = \begin{cases} t - bp & \text{if } t > bp \\ 0 & \text{otherwise} \end{cases} \right)$$

where DU_t is a dummy variable for a mean shift, and DT_t is that for a trend shift occurring on a breakpoint day bp. θ and γ are corresponding coefficients for each dummy variable. The term $\sum_{j=1}^{k} \Delta c_j CER_{t-j}$ is to eliminate nuisance-parameter dependencies. In the case of an AR (p) process, the null and alternative hypotheses of this test are

$$H_0 : \sum_{s=1}^{p} \rho_s - 1 = 0$$

$$H_1 : \sum_{s=1}^{p} \rho_s - 1 < 0.$$

If the results suggest that a process has a unit root in these three tests, it implies that the process behaves like a random walk, and this is one of the prerequisites for the weak-form market efficiency.

2.3 Johansen Test for Cointegration

Johansen (1988, 1991) and Johansen and Juselius (1990) introduced a procedure for hypothesis testing of cointegration among two or more variables whose process had a unit root. Additionally, a cointegrating vector and its coefficients of the model can be obtained through this procedure.

In the multivariate time series analysis, the AR process is generalized to a vector autoregressive (VAR) process. For simplicity, consider a bivariate VAR (1) model,

$$\boldsymbol{y}_t = \boldsymbol{\gamma} + \boldsymbol{\Pi}\boldsymbol{y}_{t-1} + \boldsymbol{\varepsilon}_t \tag{1}$$

where $\boldsymbol{y}_t$ is $(v_t, w_t)'$, $\boldsymbol{\Pi}$ is a 2×2 matrix, $\boldsymbol{\gamma}$ is a constant term which is a 2×1 vector, and $\boldsymbol{\varepsilon}_t$ is a vector of residuals that are $W.N.(\Sigma)$. Equation (1) also can be written as the combination of two AR (1) processes:

$$\begin{cases} v_t = \gamma_1 + \Pi_{11}v_{t-1} + \Pi_{12}w_{t-1} + \varepsilon_{1t} \\ w_t = \gamma_2 + \Pi_{21}v_{t-1} + \Pi_{22}w_{t-1} + \varepsilon_{2t} \end{cases}, \begin{pmatrix} \varepsilon_{1t} \\ \varepsilon_{2t} \end{pmatrix} \sim W.N.(\Sigma)$$

$$\boldsymbol{\Sigma} = \begin{pmatrix} \sigma_1^2 & \rho\sigma_1\sigma_2 \\ \rho\sigma_1\sigma_2 & \sigma_2^2 \end{pmatrix}, \begin{pmatrix} \varepsilon_{1t} \\ \varepsilon_{2t} \end{pmatrix} \sim W.N.(\boldsymbol{\Sigma})$$

The n-variable VAR (ρ) model can be represented as

$$\boldsymbol{y}_t = \boldsymbol{\gamma} + \boldsymbol{\Pi}_1\boldsymbol{y}_{t-1} + \cdots + \boldsymbol{\Pi}_p\boldsymbol{y}_{t-p} + \boldsymbol{\varepsilon}_t \tag{2}$$

where $\boldsymbol{\gamma}$ denotes a $n \times 1$ vector of the constant term, and $\boldsymbol{\Pi}_i$ denotes a $n \times n$ vector of the coefficient matrix. Suppose $E(\boldsymbol{y}_t) = \mu$, the equation $\mu = \boldsymbol{\gamma} + \boldsymbol{\Pi}_1\mu + \cdots + \boldsymbol{\Pi}_p\mu$ can be obtained. And where $\boldsymbol{\Pi}(i) = 1 - \boldsymbol{\Pi}_1 i - \cdots - \boldsymbol{\Pi}_p i^p$ is defined, the equation $\boldsymbol{\gamma} = (1 - \boldsymbol{\Pi}_1 - \cdots - \boldsymbol{\Pi}_p)\mu = \boldsymbol{\Pi}(1)\mu$ is obtained. Therefore, we can get the following equation converted from the Eq. (1):

$$\Delta\boldsymbol{y}_t = -\boldsymbol{\Pi}(1)(\boldsymbol{y}_{t-1} - \mu) + \sum_{h=1}^{p-1} \boldsymbol{\Pi}_h \Delta\boldsymbol{y}_{t-h} + \boldsymbol{\varepsilon}_t.$$

This equation is called a vector error correction model (VECM), which represents that the term $-\boldsymbol{\Pi}(1)$ corrects the divergence from the long-term average $\boldsymbol{y}_{t-1} - \mu$.

As this paper mainly focuses on two-variable relationships, we consider, for simplicity, a bivariate VAR (ρ) model to explain how the VECM works. Consider the VAR (ρ) model:

$$y_t = \gamma + \Pi_1 y_{t-1} + \cdots + \Pi_p y_{t-p} + \varepsilon_t,$$

and which can be converted to

$$\Delta y_t = \gamma + \Pi y_{t-1} + \Gamma_1 \Delta y_{t-1} + \cdots + \Gamma_{p-1} \Delta y_{t-p+1} + \varepsilon_t \quad (3)$$

where

$$\begin{aligned} \Pi &= \Pi_1 + \cdots + \Pi_p - 1 \\ \Gamma_g &= -(\Pi_{g+1} + \cdots + \Pi_p) \quad (g = 1, 2, \ldots p - 2) \\ \Gamma_{p-1} &= -\Pi_p. \end{aligned}$$

Because the original VAR model has two variables, there are three possibilities of how many ranks of Π exist in the Eq. (3):

(i) If the rank of Π is zero, the two processes follow a random walk model;
(ii) If the rank is two, the two processes are stationary;
(iii) If the rank is one, the two variables have one common stochastic trend.

Π is a 2×2 matrix because the sum of 2×2 matrices, $\Pi_1 + \cdots + \Pi_p$, is also a 2×2 matrix. Therefore, there are two eigenvalues λ_1 and λ_2 $(0 \le \lambda_2 \le \lambda_1 \le 1)$ for the matrix Π. Utilizing the two eigenvalues, we can specify the rank of Π. This estimation can be examined using two cointegration tests; a trace test and a maximum-eigenvalue test (Osterwald-Lenum 1992; MacKinnon et al. 1999). Let us denote the rank of Π by r. We do the trace test twice to check whether the two processes have one cointegration. The first trace test assumes the hypotheses as

$$H_{0.1} : r = 0$$

$$H_{1.1} : r \ge 1,$$

the second trace test assumes that

$$H_{0.2} : r = 1$$

$$H_{1.2} : r \ge 2.$$

On the other hand, the first maximum-eigenvalue test assumes the hypotheses as

$$H_{0.3} : r = 0$$

$$H_{1.3} : r = 1,$$

the second maximum-eigenvalue test assumes that

$$H_{0.4} : r \leq 1$$

$$H_{1.4} : r = 2.$$

When $H_{0.1}$ is rejected and $H_{0.2}$ is not rejected, the result suggests that the rank of $\mathbf{\Pi}$ is one in the trace tests. Additionally, when $H_{0.3}$ is rejected and $H_{0.4}$ is not, the result suggests that the rank is one in the maximum-eigenvalue tests. If the two tests show different results, the result of the trace test is generally prioritized, because it is known that the test produces more robust results than the maximum-eigenvalue test (Lütkepohl et al. 2001). In addition, if there is one cointegration, it is indicative of the existence of a single common stochastic trend between the variables. This means that the markets are not weak-form efficient because the price is influenced by not only the historical price data but also other information. However, the possibility still exists that they are efficient in terms of the semi-strong form because that includes not only historical price data but also current open information.

The 2×2 matrix $\mathbf{\Pi}$ can be represented as

$$\mathbf{\Pi} = \begin{pmatrix} \alpha_1\beta_1 & \alpha_1\beta_2 \\ \alpha_2\beta_1 & \alpha_2\beta_2 \end{pmatrix} = \boldsymbol{\alpha}'\boldsymbol{\beta}$$

where $\boldsymbol{\alpha}' = (\alpha_1, \alpha_2)$, and $\boldsymbol{\beta} = (\beta_1, \beta_2)$. As we also have to consider an intercept in the model, we include the term β_0, and define the new 2×3 matrix $\mathbf{\Pi}$ as

$$\mathbf{\Pi} = \begin{pmatrix} \alpha_1\beta_1 & \alpha_1\beta_2 & \alpha_1\beta_0 \\ \alpha_2\beta_1 & \alpha_2\beta_2 & \alpha_2\beta_0 \end{pmatrix} = \boldsymbol{\alpha}'\boldsymbol{\beta}.$$

As $\boldsymbol{y}_t$ is $(v_t, w_t)'$, the VECM can be represented by

$$\Delta v_t = \alpha_1(\beta_1 v_{t-1} + \beta_2 w_{t-1} + \beta_0) + \sum_{i=1}^{p} \left(\gamma_{11,i}\Delta v_{t-i} + \gamma_{21,i}\Delta w_{t-i}\right) + \varepsilon_{1t} \quad (4)$$

$$\Delta w_t = \alpha_2(\beta_1 v_{t-1} + \beta_2 w_{t-1} + \beta_0) + \sum_{i=1}^{p} \left(\gamma_{21,i}\Delta v_{t-i} + \gamma_{22,i}\Delta w_{t-i}\right) + \varepsilon_{2t} \quad (5)$$

where v_t and w_t are non-stationary but $\beta_1 v_{t-1} + \beta_2 w_{t-1} + \beta_0$ is stationary. $\beta_1 v_{t-1} + \beta_2 w_{t-1} + \beta_0$ represents the relationship of one cointegration, and it refers to a relationship of long-term equilibrium between the two variables. Additionally, $\boldsymbol{\beta} = (\beta_1, \beta_2, \beta_0)$ represents a cointegrating vector; α_1 and α_2 represent coefficients of the speed of adjustment.

After checking whether the processes have one cointegration or not, Nan and Kaizoji (2019) tried to clarify the long-term relationship between an FX rate and the Bitcoin exchange rate by focusing on the estimated coefficients, $\hat{\boldsymbol{\alpha}}$ and $\hat{\boldsymbol{\beta}}$. We follow this procedure to check whether the relationship between variables is a perfect linear correlation and whether one variable is weakly exogenous in the bivariate system.

We define $H_{2.1}$, $H_{2.2}$, and $H_{2.3}$ for restrictions on $\hat{\boldsymbol{\beta}}$; $H_{3.1}$ and $H_{3.2}$ for those on $\hat{\boldsymbol{\alpha}}$ as

$$\begin{aligned}
H_{2.1} &: \hat{\beta}_1 = -\hat{\beta}_2 \\
H_{2.2} &: \hat{\beta}_0 = 0 \\
H_{2.3} &: \hat{\beta}_1 = -\hat{\beta}_2, \hat{\beta}_0 = 0 \\
H_{3.1} &: \hat{\alpha}_1 = 0 \\
H_{3.2} &: \hat{\alpha}_2 = 0.
\end{aligned}$$

Additionally, we restrict both $\hat{\boldsymbol{\alpha}}$ and $\hat{\beta}$ in H_4 as

$$H_4 : \hat{\beta}_1 = -\hat{\beta}_2, \hat{\beta}_0 = 0, \hat{\alpha}_1 = 0.$$

Also, it should be noted that H_4 represents $H_{2.3} \cap H_{3.1}$. Based on the Eqs. (4) and (5), we can obtain an equation which represents the relationship between the two variables with the coefficients assumed in H_4:

$$\begin{pmatrix} \Delta v_t \\ \Delta w_t \end{pmatrix} = \begin{pmatrix} 0 \\ \hat{\alpha}_2 \end{pmatrix} (v_{t-1} - w_{t-1}) + \sum_{i=1}^{p} \left(\gamma_{1,i} \Delta v_{t-i} + \gamma_{2,i} \Delta w_{t-i} \right) + \varepsilon_t.$$

Here, Nan and Kaizoji (2019) tested whether the Bitcoin exchange rate was semi-strongly efficient by the Johansen cointegration tests with forward rates. They considered a VECM

$$\begin{aligned}
\Delta BX_t &= \alpha_1(\beta_1 BX_{t-1} + \beta_2 FW_{t-1} + \beta_0) \\
&\quad + \sum_{i=1}^{p} \left(\gamma_{11,i} \Delta BX_{t-i} + \gamma_{21,i} \Delta FX_{t-i} \right) + \varepsilon_{1t} \\
\Delta FW_t &= \alpha_2(\beta_1 BX_{t-1} + \beta_2 FW_{t-1} + \beta_0) \\
&\quad + \sum_{i=1}^{p} \left(\gamma_{12,i} \Delta BX_{t-i} + \gamma_{22,i} \Delta FX_{t-i} \right) + \varepsilon_{2t}
\end{aligned}$$

where BX_t was the Bitcoin exchange rate, and FW_t was the direct forward rate. In this test, the existence of a cointegration supports semi-strong efficiency in the markets. Nan and Kaizoji found the existence of semi-strong form of market efficiency in some pairs. However, it should be noted that this study assumes that BX_t behaves like the direct spot rate

$$BX_t = SPT_t + r \,(r: \text{ risk premium}). \tag{6}$$

We assess the adequacy of this assumption by extending it not only for Bitcoin but for Ethereum and Ripple. If the assumption is applicable, it more likely supports the existence of the semi-strong form of market efficiency in the crypto-asset markets.

2.4 Dynamic Relationships Among the Four Exchange Rates

We also consider a VAR model including all four exchange rates to look at the dynamic relationships among them. First, we convert the four-variable VAR to a VECM, and check the rank of the VECM by following the Johansen procedure. Second, we analyze the dynamic relationships among the four variables by applying the impulse response functions (IRF) for the VECM.

The IRF can analyze quantitative effects among the variables when a one-standard-deviation shock for one of the endogenous variables occurs. According to Hamilton (1994), in the n-variate VAR model, Eq. (2), the variance-covariance matrix $\mathbf{\Sigma}$ of the disturbance term $\boldsymbol{\varepsilon}_t$ is a positive definite matrix; therefore, it can be written as

$$\mathbf{\Sigma} = \boldsymbol{A}\boldsymbol{D}\boldsymbol{A}'$$

where $\boldsymbol{A}$ is a lower triangular matrix whose diagonal components are equal to 1, and $\boldsymbol{D}$ is a diagonal matrix. Here, the orthogonalized disturbance term $\boldsymbol{u}_t$ can be defined as

$$\boldsymbol{u}_t = \boldsymbol{A}^{-1}\boldsymbol{\varepsilon}_t,$$

and the impulse response function for a one-unit shock can be computed as

$$IRF_{l,m}(k) = \partial y_{l,t+k}/\partial u_{mt} \quad (k = 1, 2, 3, \ldots).$$

The IRF for a one-standard-deviation can be obtained if the disturbance term is decomposed by the Cholesky factorization instead of LU decomposition.

2.5 Data and Software

Crypto-asset data, *BTC_USD*, *BTC_EUR*, *ETH_USD*, *ETH_EUR*, *XRP_USD*, and *XRP_EUR*, in this paper were close[1] price from Yahoo! Finance. The EUR/USD spot rate data was close price from the Bank of England.[2] All statistical analyses proceeded with *R* (R Core Team 2019).

[1] Latest data in the Coordinated Universal Time (UTC) time range.

[2] To eliminate the influence of arbitrage opportunity, we use crypto-asset and FX data in the same time zone.

3 Empirical Results

3.1 Unit Root Tests on the Four Exchange Rates

The time-series data of the four exchange rates were examined to determine whether each process had a unit root. First, we tested the original time series by the ADF and KPSS tests. Appropriate lag lengths for the four processes were selected by Schwartz Information Criterion (SIC) (Schwartz 1978) for the ADF test, and those for the KPSS test were selected as seven by a predetermined mathematical method proposed by Kwiatkowski et al. (1992).

Table 4 shows the result for the four series. According to the hypothesis testing, H_0 could not be rejected in terms of all the test statistics. It was suggested that all four series had a unit root. Second, the ADF and KPSS tests were also held on the first-difference series. Table 5 shows the result for the four first-difference series. According to the hypothesis testing, H_1 was rejected in terms of all the test statistics on the 1% level of significance. It was suggested that all four first-difference series did not have a unit root. These two results of hypothesis testing indicated that all the original series, BTC_t, ETH_t, XRP_t, and SPT_t, each had a unit root. The result of the ZA test is shown in Table 5. It was suggested that, even if we considered a structural break in the four processes, each time series had a unit root at the 1% level of significance.

3.2 Cointegration Tests on the Six Pairs

In the section of cointegration tests, we first selected an appropriate lag length for each serial pair. We used four information criteria: Akaike Information Criterion (Akaike 1974), SIC, Hannan-Quinn Criterion (Hannan and Quinn 1979), and Akaike's Final Prediction Error (Akaike 1969). Table 5 shows four lags selected for each pair by these information criteria. In the latter part, we used SIC for lag selection; the lag lengths for the pairs (SPT_t, BTC_t), (SPT_t, ETH_t), and (BTC_t, ETH_t) were selected as two; those of (SPT_t, XRP_t), (BTC_t, XRP_t), and (ETH_t, XRP_t) were selected as three.

Second, we calculated the two eigenvalues $\hat{\lambda}_1$ and $\hat{\lambda}_2$. Using the selected lag lengths, we examined the six pairs by the two cointegration tests. We checked the four null hypotheses for all the pairs and obtained test statistics: $\hat{\lambda}_{\text{trace}}$ and $\hat{\lambda}_{\text{eigen}}$. Table 6 shows the results of the hypothesis testing of cointegration for the six pairs.

For all the pairs, the hypothesis $r = 0$ was rejected at the 1% significance level and the hypothesis $r \leq 1$ could not be rejected in the two tests. This means that the two variables appear to have one cointegrating relationship. It should be noted this is one of the prerequisites for the semi-strong form of market efficiency.

3.3 Estimation of the Coefficients

From Eqs. (4) and (5), we can obtain an equation

$$\begin{pmatrix} \Delta v_t \\ \Delta w_t \end{pmatrix} = \begin{pmatrix} \alpha_1 \\ \alpha_2 \end{pmatrix} (\beta_1 v_{t-1} + \beta_2 w_{t-1} + \beta_0) + \sum_{i=1}^{p} (\gamma_{1,i} \Delta v_{t-i} + \gamma_{2,i} \Delta w_{t-i}) + \boldsymbol{\varepsilon}_t \quad (7)$$

that represents the VECM for the two variables. Using Eq. (7) with the estimated values, we can understand how the change of one variable at the current time t declines by a deviation from an equilibrium at the previous time $t-1$. In Eq. (7), $\begin{pmatrix} \alpha_1 \\ \alpha_2 \end{pmatrix}$ is the speed-of-adjustment coefficients, $(\beta_1 v_{t-1} + \beta_2 w_{t-1} + \beta_0)$ is the lagged deviation, and $\begin{pmatrix} \alpha_1 \\ \alpha_2 \end{pmatrix} (\beta_1 v_{t-1} + \beta_2 w_{t-1} + \beta_0)$ represents the error correction term. Let us denote the estimates of (α_1, α_2) by $\hat{\boldsymbol{\alpha}}$, and those of $(\beta_1, \beta_2, \beta_0)$ by $\hat{\boldsymbol{\beta}}^*$. Table 8 describes the values of $\hat{\boldsymbol{\alpha}}$ and $\hat{\boldsymbol{\beta}}^*$.

For the pair $(\Delta SPT_t, \Delta BTC_t)$, the error correction term is

$$\begin{pmatrix} -0.102 \\ 0.221 \end{pmatrix} (SPT_{t-1} - 1.002 BTC_{t-1} + 0.001).$$

ΔSPT_t declines by 10.2% from the equilibrium of the previous-period deviation; furthermore, ΔBTC_t increases by 22.1%. These changes seem to correct the imbalance.

For the second pair $(\Delta SPT_t, \Delta ETH_t)$, the error correction term is

$$\begin{pmatrix} -0.063 \\ 0.241 \end{pmatrix} (SPT_{t-1} - 1.038 ETH_{t-1} + 0.007).$$

ΔSPT_t declines by 6.3% from the equilibrium of the previous-period deviation, while ΔETH_t increases by 24.1%. These changes seem to correct the imbalance.

For the third pair $(\Delta SPT_t, \Delta XRP_t)$, the error correction term is

$$\begin{pmatrix} -0.035 \\ 0.426 \end{pmatrix} (SPT_{t-1} - 1.027 XRP_{t-1} + 0.006).$$

ΔSPT_t declines by 3.5% from the equilibrium of the previous-period deviation; additionally, ΔXRP_t increases by 42.6%. These changes appear to reduce the imbalance.

For the fourth pair $(\Delta BTC_t, \Delta ETH_t)$, the error correction term is

$$\begin{pmatrix} -0.020 \\ 0.276 \end{pmatrix} (BTC_{t-1} - 1.036 ETH_{t-1} + 0.006).$$

ΔBTC_t declines by 2.0% from the equilibrium of the previous-period deviation, while ΔETH_t increases by 27.6%. These changes appear to reduce the imbalance.

For the fifth pair (ΔBTC_t, ΔXRP_t), the error correction term is

$$\begin{pmatrix} 0.027 \\ 0.528 \end{pmatrix} (BTC_{t-1} - 1.026XRP_{t-1} + 0.005).$$

ΔBTC_t increases by 2.7% from the equilibrium of the previous-period deviation; and ΔXRP_t increases by 52.8%. Both variables seem to increase; however, the overall changes are to correct the imbalance, as the estimated coefficient $\hat{\alpha}_1$ is relatively small. Here, the hypothesis testing of the weak exogeneity need to be considered in the latter section.

For the last pair (ΔETH_t, ΔXRP_t), the error correction term is

$$\begin{pmatrix} -0.022 \\ 0.547 \end{pmatrix} (ETH_{t-1} - 0.994XRP_{t-1} - 0.001).$$

ΔETH_t declines by 2.2% from the equilibrium of the previous-period deviation, while ΔXRP_t increases by 54.7%. These changes appear to correct the imbalance.

Further, if $\hat{\beta}_2$ is close to -1, and $\hat{\beta}_0$ is close to zero, where $\hat{\beta}_1$ is normalized to 1, all six pairs appear to be at long-term equilibria, because $\beta_1 v_t = -\beta_2 w_t + \beta_0$. Table 8 shows that all six $\hat{\beta}_2$ seem to be close to -1, and all six $\hat{\beta}_0$ seem to be close to zero.

As all six pairs appeared to have one cointegration for each, hypotheses for the estimated parameters were tested to check whether the six relationships were perfectly linear and whether weak exogeneity existed. We examined the null hypotheses of linear restrictions, $H_{2.1}$, $H_{2.2}$, $H_{2.3}$, $H_{3.1}$, $H_{3.2}$, and H_4, against the alternative hypothesis H_1 that assumed $r = 1$. The method for this hypothesis testing is a likelihood ratio χ^2 test. In this test, the null hypothesis is rejected if a test statistic is greater than a predetermined critical value.

3.4 Inference on the Parameters

Table 7 summarizes the result of hypothesis testing for the estimated coefficients of the pair (ΔSPT_t, ΔBTC_t). The null hypotheses, $H_{2.1}$, $H_{2.2}$, and $H_{2.3}$, could not be rejected. This illustrates that the assumption of no risk premium and agents' rational use of open information will hold in the long term. Using the coefficients assumed in $H_{2.3}$, we obtain

$$\begin{pmatrix} -0.102 \\ 0.218 \end{pmatrix} (SPT_{t-1} - BTC_{t-1}).$$

This indicates that ΔSPT_t declines by 10.2% from the equilibrium of the previous-period deviation, while ΔBTC_t increases by 21.8%.

Table 8 summarizes the result for the pair (ΔSPT_t, ΔETH_t). It indicates that $H_{2.1}$ could not be rejected at 1% significance level. Using the coefficients assumed in $H_{2.1}$, we obtain

$$\begin{pmatrix} -0.067 \\ 0.235 \end{pmatrix} (SPT_{t-1} - ETH_{t-1} + 0.002).$$

This indicates that ΔSPT_t declines by 6.7% from the equilibrium of the previous-period deviation, while ΔETH_t increases by 23.5%.

Table 9 summarizes the result for the pair (ΔSPT_t, ΔXRP_t). $H_{2.1}$ could not be rejected at 5% significance level. Using the coefficients assumed in $H_{2.1}$, we obtain

$$\begin{pmatrix} -0.037 \\ 0.429 \end{pmatrix} (SPT_{t-1} - XRP_{t-1} + 0.002).$$

This indicates that ΔSPT_t declines by 3.7% from the equilibrium of the previous-period deviation, while ΔXRP increases by 42.9%.

Table 10 summarizes the result for the pair (ΔBTC_t, ΔETH_t). $H_{3.1}$ could not be rejected at 5% significance level. The acceptance of $H_{3.1}$ refers to weak exogeneity of BTC_t. Using the coefficients assumed in $H_{3.1}$, we obtain

$$\begin{pmatrix} 0 \\ 0.294 \end{pmatrix} (BTC_{t-1} - 1.037ETH_{t-1} + 0.007).$$

This indicates that, while ΔBTC_t remains steady, ΔETH_t increases by 29.4% from the equilibrium of the previous-period deviation. Therefore, the change of ΔETH_t corrects the imbalance.

Table 11 summarizes the result for the pair (ΔBTC_t, ΔXRP_t). $H_{2.1}$ and $H_{3.1}$ could not be rejected at 1% significance level. Using the coefficients assumed in $H_{3.1}$, we obtain

$$\begin{pmatrix} 0 \\ 0.507 \end{pmatrix} (BTC_{t-1} - 1.024XRP_{t-1} + 0.005).$$

This indicates that, while ΔBTC_t remains steady, ΔXRP_t increases by 50.7% from the equilibrium of the previous-period deviation. Therefore, the change of ΔXRP_t corrects the imbalance.

Table 12 summarizes the result for the pair (ΔETH_t, ΔXRP_t). All the null hypotheses excluding $H_{3.2}$ could not be rejected. The acceptance of H_4 indicates that the assumption of no risk premium and agents' rational use of open information will hold in the long term, and that ETH_t is weakly exogeneous. Using the coefficients assumed in H_4, we obtain

$$\begin{pmatrix} 0 \\ 0.558 \end{pmatrix}(ETH_{t-1} - XRP_{t-1}).$$

This indicates that, while ΔETH_t remains steady, ΔXRP_t increases by 55.8 from the equilibrium of the previous-period deviation. Therefore, the change of ΔXRP_t corrects the imbalance.

Overall, perfect linear correlation was found in the four pairs; (ΔSPT_t, ΔBTC_t), (ΔSPT_t, ΔBTC_t), (ΔSPT_t, ΔBTC_t), and (ΔETH_t, ΔXRP_t). This supports the adequacy of the assumption of Eq. (6) and it is the evidence that the crypto-asset markets are efficient in terms of the semi-strong form. The existence of risk premium was found in the two pairs; (ΔSPT_t, ΔETH_t), and (ΔSPT_t, ΔXRP_t) under the condition of perfect linear relationships. It indicates that traders are risk-loving in the Ethereum and Ripple markets. Additionally, for the three pairs; (ΔBTC_t, ΔETH_t), (ΔBTC_t, ΔXRP_t), and (ΔETH_t, ΔXRP_t), we found weak exogeneity of ΔBTC_t, ΔBTC_t, and ΔETH_t, respectively.

3.5 Analysis of the Dynamic Relationships Among the Four Variables

3.5.1 Cointegration Test for the Four-Variable VECM

The result of the cointegration test for the four-variable VECM is shown in Table 14. It is suggested that the rank of the VECM is three by both trace and maximum eigenvalue tests. This supports that the four variables have three cointegrations, and it is indicative of the semi-strong efficiency.

3.5.2 Impulse Response Functions Among the Four Exchange Rates

In an analysis by the orthogonal IRF, we must determine the order of the variables. In general, the order of variables of financial markets is determined by the order of their market-open time. However, we cannot set the order by that method, since the crypto-asset markets are open 24 h and all year around. In this analysis, the order of the four variables was determined by considering their market capitalization and the weak exogeneity in the six pairwise VECMs. The order of their market capitalizations was $\Delta SPT_t \rightarrow \Delta BTC_t \rightarrow \Delta ETH_t \rightarrow \Delta XRP_t$, as of November 25, 2019. This order was also supported by the consideration of the weak exogeneity. For example, ΔBTC_t, ΔBTC_t, and ΔETH_t seemed weakly exogeneous in each pair; (ΔBTC_t, ΔETH_t), (ΔBTC_t, ΔXRP_t), and (ΔETH_t, ΔXRP_t). This suggests that the order among the three crypto assets is $\Delta BTC_t \rightarrow \Delta ETH_t \rightarrow \Delta XRP_t$. Taking these two ordering methods into account, we determined the order $\Delta SPT_t \rightarrow \Delta BTC_t \rightarrow \Delta ETH_t \rightarrow \Delta XRP_t$ as the appropriate one for the following IRF.

Figure 3 shows the results of the IRF by 1,000 runs of bootstrapping. For the unexpected one-standard-deviation shock of ΔSPT_t, ΔSPT_t itself was affected permanently. Other variables, ΔBTC_t, ΔETH_t, and ΔXRP_t, were gradually affected in a week, and the effect remained permanently. For the shock of ΔBTC_t, it is remarkable that ΔSPT_t was slightly affected in a day and its effect remained permanently. ΔBTC_t, ΔETH_t, and ΔXRP_t were affected immediately, and the effect gradually declined; however, it remained at some degree in two weeks. For the ΔETH_t shock,

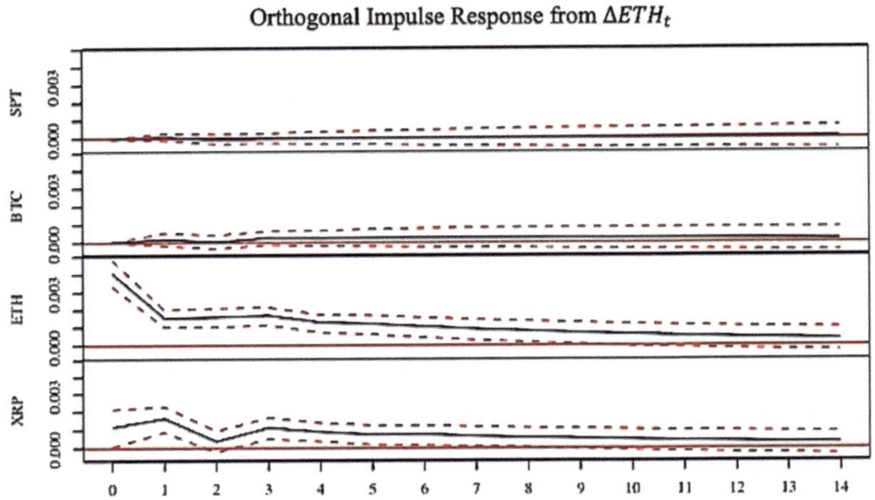

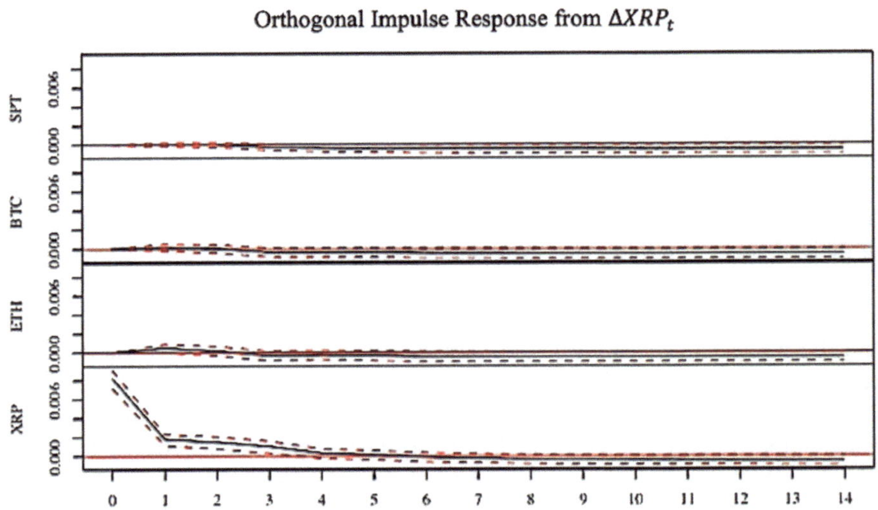

Fig. 3 Results of the impulse response function of the four-variable VECM. *Note* The dashed lines show a 95% confidence band

ΔSPT_t and ΔBTC_t did not seem affected; on the other hand, ΔETH_t, and ΔXRP_t were affected immediately, and the effect diminished in two weeks. For the ΔXRP_t shock, other variables, ΔSPT_t, ΔBTC_t, and ΔETH_t did not seem to be affected. It only affected ΔXRP_t itself, and the effect diminished in four days.

4 Conclusion

Based on the results of the unit root tests, we found that the current change of all four exchange rates was not dependent of historical price data. This is indicative of the weak form of market efficiency for the four processes. Second, we found one cointegrating relationship for each pair; cointegration is a prerequisite of the semi-strong form of market efficiency. Third, restrictions on the speed-of-adjustment and long-term-equilibrium coefficients were examined for each VECM. In terms of weak exogeneity, the results showed that one variable was weakly exogenous in the three pairs; (ΔBTC_t, ΔETH_t), (ΔBTC_t, ΔXRP_t), and (ΔETH_t, ΔXRP_t). We also found perfect linear correlations in the four pairs; (ΔSPT_t, ΔBTC_t), (ΔSPT_t, ΔETH_t), (ΔSPT_t, ΔXRP_t), and (ΔETH_t, ΔXRP_t). This implies that these four pairs are semi-strongly efficient. Further, for the two pairs (ΔSPT_t, ΔBTC_t) and (ΔETH_t, ΔXRP_t), the long-term equilibria seem to exist without premium. Finally, we examined the dynamic relationships through the analysis of the IRF. As expected, the results suggested that ΔSPT_t affected all three crypto-asset exchange rates. Additionally, it was notable that the price shock of ΔBTC_t slightly affected ΔSPT_t within a day, whereas, that of ΔETH_t and ΔXRP_t did not.

In conclusion, the existence of the semi-strong form of market efficiency was suggested in the Bitcoin, Ethereum, and Ripple markets. On the other hand, Bitcoin seems more influential than Ethereum and Ripple; the unexpected price shock of Bitcoin exchange rate can slightly affect the EUR/USD spot rate.

Acknowledgements This work was supported by JSPS KAKENHI Grant Number 17K01270, 20K01752 and NOMURA Foundation.

Appendix

See Figs. 1, 2 and 3; Tables 1, 2, 3, 4, 5, 6, 7, 8, 9, 10, 11, 12, 13 and 14.

Table 1 Some descriptive statistics

Variables	VN	Min	Q1	Median	Mean	Q3	Max	S.D.	Skewness	Kurtosis
Original SPT_t	735	0.04	0.11	0.13	0.13	0.16	0.22	0.04	−0.02	−0.42
Weekend filled SPT_t	1062	0.04	0.11	0.13	0.13	0.16	0.22	0.04	−0.04	−0.45
BTC_t	1062	0.03	0.11	0.13	0.13	0.16	0.24	0.04	−0.15	−0.23
ETH_t	1062	0.03	0.11	0.14	0.14	0.16	0.24	0.04	−0.15	−0.22
XRP_t	1062	−0.02	0.11	0.14	0.14	0.16	0.25	0.04	−0.26	0.00

Note Original SPT_t is the original data without filling the weekend missing values. Weekend-filled SPT_t is the data whose missing values are complemented by close prices on Fridays. The original and complemented data of SPT_t show close numbers in summary statistics, and it is indicative of unbiasedness by this complementation. The following tests including SPT_t are analyzed by Weekend-filled SPT_t

Table 2 Results of the ADF and KPSS tests on the original series

Variables	ADF		KPSS	
	Lag lengths	Test statistics	Lag length	Test statistics
SPT_t	1	−1.914	7	2.710***
BTC_t	2	−2.250	7	2.722***
ETH_t	2	−2.403	7	2.706***
XRP_t	3	−2.132	7	2.780***

Note *** denotes significance at 1% level. We consider the constant model specifications, (b) and (d), for the two tests, because the estimate of a trend term is small and insignificant when we examine the four processes as the trend model in the ADF tests

Table 3 Results of the ADF and KPSS tests on the first-difference series

Variables	ADF		KPSS	
	Lag lengths	Test statistics	Lag lengths	Test statistics
SPT_t	1	−24.313***	7	0.352
BTC_t	1	−28.164***	7	0.231
ETH_t	1	−30.350***	7	0.150
XRP_t	2	−27.670***	7	0.143

Note *** denotes significance at 1% level. We consider the constant model specifications, (b) and (d), for the two tests

Table 4 Result of the ZA tests

Variables	Lag lengths	Test statistics	Dates of Break point
SPT_t	1	−3.88	15-04-2017
BTC_t	1	−4.83**	13-05-2017
ETH_t	2	−4.43	13-05-2017
XRP_t	5	−4.37	14-05-2017

Note ** denotes significance at 5% level. We consider the break-in-intercept model specification (f) for this test, because we do not consider the four processes as the trend model in the ADF and KPSS tests. Therefore, we eliminate the influence of a trend term when finding a date of the break point in this test

Table 5 Results of lag selections using information criteria

Variables	N	AIC	SIC	HQ	FPE
(SPT_t, BTC_t)	1062	3	2	3	3
(SPT_t, ETH_t)	1062	3	2	3	3
(SPT_t, XRP_t)	1062	9	3	3	9
(BTC_t, ETH_t)	1062	8	2	5	8
(BTC_t, XRP_t)	1062	10	3	9	10
(ETH_t, XRP_t)	1062	10	3	10	10
$(SPT_t, BTC_t, ETH_t, XRP_t)$	1062	10	2	3	10

Note The maximum lag length is predetermined as ten when we select an appropriate lag length by each information criterion

Table 6 Results of Johansen cointegrating tests for the six pairs

Vectors	Lag lengths	Eigenvalues	Hypotheses	Statistics	
		$\hat{\lambda}_1$ and $\hat{\lambda}_2$	H_0 and H_1	$\hat{\lambda}_{\text{trace}}$	$\hat{\lambda}_{\text{eigen}}$
$(\Delta SPT_t, \Delta BTC_t)$	2	0.085	$r = 0$	140.18***	137.16***
		0.003	$r \leq 1$	3.01	3.01
$(\Delta SPT_t, \Delta ETH_t)$	2	0.080	$r = 0$	134.50***	131.28***
		0.003	$r \leq 1$	3.22	3.22
$(\Delta SPT_t, \Delta XRP_t)$	3	0.119	$r = 0$	197.28***	194.53***
		0.003	$r \leq 1$	2.75	2.75
$(\Delta BTC_t, \Delta ETH_t)$	2	0.106	$r = 0$	123.99***	118.53***
		0.005	$r \leq 1$	5.47	5.47
$(\Delta BTC_t, \Delta XRP_t)$	3	0.139	$r = 0$	163.77***	158.99***
		0.004	$r \leq 1$	4.77	4.77
$(\Delta ETH_t, \Delta XRP_t)$	3	0.149	$r = 0$	176.75***	171.28***
		0.005	$r \leq 1$	5.47	5.47

Note *** denotes significance at 1% level

Table 7 Results of the cointegrating vectors $\hat{\boldsymbol{\beta}}$ and the speed-of-adjustment coefficients $\boldsymbol{\alpha}$ of the six pairs

Pairs y_t	Eigenvalues					
	$\hat{\lambda}_1$	$\hat{\beta}_1$	$\hat{\beta}_2$	$\hat{\beta}_0$	$\hat{\alpha}_1$	
$(\Delta SPT_t, \Delta BTC_t)$	0.121	1	−1.002	0.001	−0.121	0.221
$(\Delta SPT_t, \Delta ETH_t)$	0.116	1	−1.038	0.007	−0.063	0.241
$(\Delta SPT_t, \Delta XRP_t)$	0.168	1	−1.027	0.006	−0.035	0.426
$(\Delta BTC_t, \Delta ETH_t)$	0.106	1	−1.036	0.006	−0.020	0.276
$(\Delta BTC_t, \Delta XRP_t)$	0.139	1	−1.026	0.005	0.027	0.528
$(\Delta ETH_t, \Delta XRP_t)$	0.149	1	−0.994	−0.001	−0.022	0.547

Table 8 Inferences on $\hat{\boldsymbol{\alpha}}$ and $\hat{\boldsymbol{\beta}}$ of $(\Delta SPT_t, \Delta BTC_t)$

	H_1	$H_{2.1}$	$H_{2.2}$	$H_{2.3}$	$H_{3.1}$	$H_{3.2}$	H_4
Restrictions on $\hat{\beta}$	–	$\hat{\beta}_1 = -\hat{\beta}_2$	$\hat{\beta}_0 = 0$	$\hat{\beta}_1 = -\hat{\beta}_2$, $\hat{\beta}_0 = 0$	–	–	$\hat{\beta}_1 = -\hat{\beta}_2$, $\hat{\beta}_0 = 0$,
Restrictions on $\hat{\alpha}$	–	–	–	–	$\hat{\alpha}_1 = 0$	$\hat{\alpha}_2 = 0$	$\hat{\alpha}_1 = 0$
LR test statistics		0.03	0.27	1.49	45.4	59.62	48.06
Degree of freedom		1	1	2	1	1	2
p-value		0.87	0.60	0.48	0.00	0.00	0.00
$\hat{\beta}_1$	1	1	1	1	1	1	1
$\hat{\beta}_2$	−1.002	−1	−0.996	−1	−1.017	−0.984	−1
$\hat{\beta}_0$	0.001	0.001	0	0	0.003	−0.002	0
$\hat{\alpha}_1$	−0.102	−0.103	−0.104	−0.102	0	−0.134	0
$\hat{\alpha}_2$	0.221	0.221	0.220	0.218	0.265	0	0.266

Table 9 Inferences on $\hat{\boldsymbol{\alpha}}$ and $\hat{\boldsymbol{\beta}}$ of $(\Delta SPT_t, \Delta ETH_t)$

	H_1	$H_{2.1}$	$H_{2.2}$	$H_{2.3}$	$H_{3.1}$	$H_{3.2}$	H_4
Restrictions on $\hat{\beta}$	–	$\hat{\beta}_1 = -\hat{\beta}_2$	$\hat{\beta}_0 = 0$	$\hat{\beta}_1 = -\hat{\beta}_2$, $\hat{\beta}_0 = 0$	–	–	$\hat{\beta}_1 = -\hat{\beta}_2$, $\hat{\beta}_0 = 0$,
Restrictions on $\hat{\alpha}$	–	–	–	–	$\hat{\alpha}_1 = 0$	$\hat{\alpha}_2 = 0$	$\hat{\alpha}_1 = 0$
LR test statistics		5.06	9.28	14.21	25.48	79.25	41.51
Degree of freedom		1	1	2	1	1	2
p-value		0.02	0.00	0.00	0.00	0.00	0.00
$\hat{\beta}_1$	1	1	1	1	1	1	1
$\hat{\beta}_2$	−1.038	−1	−0.989	−1	−1.053	−1.003	−1
$\hat{\beta}_0$	0.007	0.002	0	0	0.009	0.002	0
$\hat{\alpha}_1$	−0.063	−0.067	−0.067	−0.064	0	−0.092	0
$\hat{\alpha}_2$	0.241	0.235	0.228	0.218	0.268	0	0.249

Table 10 Inferences on $\hat{\boldsymbol{\alpha}}$ and $\hat{\boldsymbol{\beta}}$ of $(\Delta SPT_t, \Delta XRP_t)$

	H_1	$H_{2.1}$	$H_{2.2}$	$H_{2.3}$	$H_{3.1}$	$H_{3.2}$	H_4
Restrictions on $\hat{\beta}$	–	$\hat{\beta}_1 = -\hat{\beta}_2$	$\hat{\beta}_0 = 0$	$\hat{\beta}_1 = -\hat{\beta}_2$, $\hat{\beta}_0 = 0$	–	–	$\hat{\beta}_1 = -\hat{\beta}_2$, $\hat{\beta}_0 = 0$,
Restrictions on $\hat{\alpha}$	–	–	–	–	$\hat{\alpha}_1 = 0$	$\hat{\alpha}_2 = 0$	$\hat{\alpha}_1 = 0$
LR test statistics		2.88	6.67	13.11	10.38	165.88	24.63
Degree of freedom		1	1	2	1	1	2
p-value		0.09	0.01	0.00	0.00	0.00	0.00
$\hat{\beta}_1$	1	1	1	1	1	1	1
$\hat{\beta}_2$	−1.027	−1	−0.989	−1	−1.033	−0.967	−1
$\hat{\beta}_0$	0.006	0.002	0	0	0.007	−0.003	0
$\hat{\alpha}_1$	−0.035	−0.037	−0.038	−0.036	0	−0.063	0
$\hat{\alpha}_2$	0.426	0.429	0.425	0.408	0.441	0	0.425

Table 11 Inferences on $\hat{\boldsymbol{\alpha}}$ and $\hat{\boldsymbol{\beta}}$ of $(\Delta BTC_t, \Delta ETH_t)$

	H_1	$H_{2.1}$	$H_{2.2}$	$H_{2.3}$	$H_{3.1}$	$H_{3.2}$	H_4
Restrictions on $\hat{\beta}$	–	$\hat{\beta}_1 = -\hat{\beta}_2$	$\hat{\beta}_0 = 0$	$\hat{\beta}_1 = -\hat{\beta}_2$, $\hat{\beta}_0 = 0$	–	–	$\hat{\beta}_1 = -\hat{\beta}_2$, $\hat{\beta}_0 = 0$,
Restrictions on $\hat{\alpha}$	–	–	–	–	$\hat{\alpha}_1 = 0$	$\hat{\alpha}_2 = 0$	$\hat{\alpha}_1 = 0$
LR test statistics		10.98	16.57	20.70	0.27	35.84	22.28
Degree of freedom		1	1	2	1	1	2
p-value		0.00	0.00	0.00	0.60	0.00	0.00
$\hat{\beta}_1$	1	1	1	1	1	1	1
$\hat{\beta}_2$	−1.036	−1	−0.993	−1	−1.037	−1.020	−1
$\hat{\beta}_0$	0.006	0.002	0	0	0.007	0.004	0
$\hat{\alpha}_1$	−0.020	−0.046	−0.051	−0.046	0	−0.215	0
$\hat{\alpha}_2$	0.276	0.235	0.219	0.212	0.294	0	0.255

Table 12 Inferences on $\hat{\boldsymbol{\alpha}}$ and $\hat{\boldsymbol{\beta}}$ of $(\Delta BTC_t, \Delta XRP_t)$

	H_1	$H_{2.1}$	$H_{2.2}$	$H_{2.3}$	$H_{3.1}$	$H_{3.2}$	H_4
Restrictions on $\hat{\beta}$	–	$\hat{\beta}_1 = -\hat{\beta}_2$	$\hat{\beta}_0 = 0$	$\hat{\beta}_1 = -\hat{\beta}_2$, $\hat{\beta}_0 = 0$	–	–	$\hat{\beta}_1 = -\hat{\beta}_2$, $\hat{\beta}_0 = 0$,
Restrictions on $\hat{\alpha}$	–	–	–	–	$\hat{\alpha}_1 = 0$	$\hat{\alpha}_2 = 0$	$\hat{\alpha}_1 = 0$
LR test statistics		4.23	7.86	12.22	0.92	127.07	12.49
Degree of freedom		1	1	2	1	1	2
p-value		0.04	0.01	0.00	0.34	0.00	0.00
$\hat{\beta}_1$	1	1	1	1	1	1	1
$\hat{\beta}_2$	−1.026	−1	−0.992	−1	−1.024	−0.973	−1
$\hat{\beta}_0$	0.005	0.002	0	0	0.005	−0.003	0
$\hat{\alpha}_1$	0.027	0.017	0.013	0.014	0	−0.142	0
$\hat{\alpha}_2$	0.528	0.521	0.511	0.494	0.507	0	0.482

Table 13 Inferences on $\hat{\boldsymbol{\alpha}}$ and $\hat{\boldsymbol{\beta}}$ of $(\Delta ETH_t, \Delta XRP_t)$

	H_1	$H_{2.1}$	$H_{2.2}$	$H_{2.3}$	$H_{3.1}$	$H_{3.2}$	H_4
Restrictions on $\hat{\beta}$	–	$\hat{\beta}_1 = -\hat{\beta}_2$	$\hat{\beta}_0 = 0$	$\hat{\beta}_1 = -\hat{\beta}_2$, $\hat{\beta}_0 = 0$	–	–	$\hat{\beta}_1 = -\hat{\beta}_2$, $\hat{\beta}_0 = 0$,
Restrictions on $\hat{\alpha}$	–	–	–	–	$\hat{\alpha}_1 = 0$	$\hat{\alpha}_2 = 0$	$\hat{\alpha}_1 = 0$
LR test statistics		0.26	0.22	0.26	0.40	122.75	0.58
Degree of freedom		1	1	2	1	1	2
p-value		0.61	0.64	0.88	0.53	0.00	0.75
$\hat{\beta}_1$	1	1	1	1	1	1	1
$\hat{\beta}_2$	−0.994	−1	−0.999	−1	−0.995	−0.953	−1
$\hat{\beta}_0$	−0.001	0.000	0	0	−0.001	−0.007	0
$\hat{\alpha}_1$	−0.022	−0.019	−0.019	−0.019	0	−0.221	0
$\hat{\alpha}_2$	0.547	0.546	0.546	0.545	0.561	0	0.558

Table 14 Results of the Johansen cointegrating test for $(\Delta SPT_t, \Delta BTC_t, \Delta ETH_t, \Delta XRP_t)$

y_t	Lag length	Eigen values	Ranks	Statistics	
		$\hat{\lambda}_1, \hat{\lambda}_2, \hat{\lambda}_3, \hat{\lambda}_4$		$\hat{\lambda}_{trace}$	$\hat{\lambda}_{eigen}$
$(SPT_t, BTC_t, ETH_t, XRP_t)$	2	0.228	$r = 0$	537.03***	274.79***
		0.123	$r \leq 1$	262.25***	139.18***
		0.107	$r \leq 2$	123.07***	120.01***
		0.003	$r \leq 3$	3.06	3.06

Note *** denotes significance at 1% level

References

Akaike, H. (1969). Fitting autoregressive models for prediction. *Annals of the Institute of Statistical Mathematics, 21*(1), 243–247.

Akaike, H. (1974). A new look at the statistical model identification. *IEEE Transactions on Automatic Control, AC-19,* 716–723.

Cheah, E. T., & Fry, J. (2015). Speculative bubbles in Bitcoin markets? An empirical investigation into the fundamental value of Bitcoin. *Economics Letters, 130,* 32–36.

Corbet, S., Lucey, B., & Yarovaya, L. (2018). Datestamping the Bitcoin and Ethereum bubbles. *Finance Research Letters, 26,* 81–88.

Dickey, D., & Fuller, W. (1979). Distribution of the estimators for autoregressive time series with a unit root. *Journal of the American Statistical Association, 74*(366), 427–431.

Fama, E. F. (1970). Efficient capital markets: a review of theory and empirical work. *The Journal of Finance, 25*(2), 383–417.

Fama, E. F. (1991). Efficient capital markets: II. *The Journal of Finance, 46*(5), 1575–1617.

Hamilton, J. D. (1994). *Time series analysis*. Princeton, NJ: Princeton University Press.

Hannan, E. J., & Quinn, B. G. (1979). The determination of the order of an autoregression. *Journal of the Royal Statistical Society, B41,* 190–195.

Johansen, S. (1988). Statistical analysis of cointegration vectors. *Journal of Economic Dynamics and Control, 12*(2), 231–254.

Johansen, S. (1991). Estimation and hypothesis testing of cointegration vectors in gaussian vector autoregressive models. *Econometrica, 59*(6), 1551–1580.

Johansen, S., & Juselius, K. (1990). Maximum likelihood estimation and inference on cointegration–with applications to the demand for money. *Oxford Bulletin of Economics and Statistics, 52*(2), 169–210.

Kwiatkowski, D., Phillips, P. C., Schmidt, P., & Shin, Y. (1992). Testing the null hypothesis of stationarity against the alternative of a unit root: how sure are we that economic time series have a unit root? *Journal of econometrics, 54*(1–3), 159–178.

Lütkepohl, H., Saikkonen, P., & Trenkler, C. (2001). Maximum eigenvalue versus trace tests for the cointegrating rank of a VAR process. *The Econometrics Journal, 4*(2), 287–310.

MacKinnon, J. G. (1996). Numerical distribution functions for unit root and cointegration tests. *Journal of Applied Econometrics, 11*(6), 601–618.

MacKinnon, J. G., Haug, A. A., & Michelis, L. (1999). Numerical distribution functions of likelihood ratio tests for cointegration. *Journal of Applied Econometrics, 14*(5), 563–577.

Nadarajah, S., & Chu, J. (2017). On the inefficiency of Bitcoin. *Economics Letters, 150,* 6–9.

Nan, Z., & Kaizoji, T. (2019). Market efficiency of the Bitcoin exchange rate: weak and semi-strong form tests with the spot, futures and forward foreign exchange rates. *International Review of Financial Analysis, 64,* 273–281.

Osterwald-Lenum, M. (1992). A note with quantiles of the asymptotic distribution of the maximum likelihood cointegration rank test statistics. *Oxford Bulletin of Economics and Statistics, 54*(3), 461–472.

R Core Team. (2019). *R: A language and environment for statistical computing*. R Foundation for Statistical Computing, Vienna, Austria. URL https://www.R-project.org/.

Said, S. E., & Dickey, D. (1984). Testing for unit roots in autoregressive-moving average models of unknown order. *Biometrika, 71*(3), 599–607.

Schwarz, G. (1978). Estimating the dimension of a model. *The Annals of Statistics, 6*(2), 461–464.

Tiwari, A. K., Jana, R. K., Das, D., & Roubaud, D. (2018). Informational efficiency of Bitcoin—An extension. *Economics Letters, 163,* 106–109.

Urquhart, A. (2016). The inefficiency of Bitcoin. *Economics Letters, 148,* 80–82.

Zivot, E., & Andrews, D. W. K. (1992). Further evidence on the great crash, the oil-price shock, and the unit-root hypothesis. *Journal of Business and Economic Statistics, 10*(3), 251–270.

The Optimal Foreign Exchange Futures Hedge on the Bitcoin Exchange Rate: An Application to the U.S. Dollar and the Euro

Zheng Nan and Taisei Kaizoji

Abstract This study proposes utilizing FX futures to hedge the risk of currency exchanges based on the bitcoin exchange rate. The time-dependent optimal hedge ratio for the resulting portfolio can be calculated from the conditional covariance matrix of the two returns. To model the conditional joint density, a VECM plus DCC-GARCH model is suggested due to the existence of co-integration between the bitcoin exchange rate and FX futures. Comparisons suggest that this framework is superior to the commonly used naïve and conventional hedging strategies in several important aspects.

Keywords Bitcoin · Bitcoin exchange rate · FX futures · Optimal hedge ratio · VECM · DCC GARCH

1 Introduction

Bitcoin is the first cryptocurrency to be widely used in a decentralized peer-to-peer network. The marketization of bitcoin and its popularity have turned the bitcoin into a unique investment traded with a number of currencies in worldwide bitcoin markets (Briere et al. 2013). In these markets, one currency can be exchanged for another using bitcoin as the medium. From this perspective, bitcoin markets have become a new form of foreign exchange market. Nan and Kaizoji (2019b) have investigated the weak- and semi-strong form bitcoin market efficiency in terms of the U.S. dollar and Euro. Their work finds that the bitcoin markets present a long-run equilibrium relationship with the FX exchange rate of USD/EUR but mean-reverting short-run deviations happen all the time. In the Ethereum markets, similar results regarding the market equilibrium and its adjustment dynamics have been found by Pichl et al. (2020). These short-run deviations from the long-run market equilibrium could bring profitable chances for arbitraging. Hence, bitcoin-based foreign currency trading appears to be competitive against the direct investment in bitcoins in risk management and hedging due to plenty of finance tools existing in the FX markets.

Z. Nan · T. Kaizoji (✉)
International Christian University, 3-10-2-Osawa, Mitaka, Tokyo 181-8585, Japan
e-mail: kaizoji@icu.ac.jp

L. Pichl et al. (eds.), *Advanced Studies of Financial Technologies and Cryptocurrency Markets*, https://doi.org/10.1007/978-981-15-4498-9_9

This study proposes an effective arbitraging strategy in bitcoin markets whereby the user engages in currency trading rather than holding the bitcoin and hedging the trading risk with foreign exchange (FX) futures contracts. The price between two currencies trading in a bitcoin market is defined as the bitcoin exchange rate. Hedging the risk of currency trading based on the bitcoin exchange rate has substantial practical importance. The purpose is to find the optimal hedge ratio; that is, the ratio that would minimize risk and maximize user utility. Importantly, it is better for the optimal hedge ratio to be time-varying so that when the market goes up, a smaller hedge ratio will not discourage speculators from accepting the risk premium, and when the market goes down, a larger hedge ratio will offer greater compensation due to the profitability of short futures (Cecchetti et al. 1988).

Currency trading in bitcoin markets is assumed to follow the process C1 –> BTC –> C2, where C1 and C2 denote the two currencies being traded, and BTC denotes the bitcoin. Several advantages related to bitcoin transactions, such as freedom, low trading cost and instantaneity, make this trading strategy attractive. Moreover, since the two successive transactions in the process are assumed to be accomplished quickly, the risk exposure to holding bitcoins is minimized (Cheah and Fry 2015).

The price of C1 in C2 in a bitcoin market, defined as the bitcoin exchange rate of C2/C1 (Nan and Kaizoji 2017), is given by

$$BX_{C2/C1} = \frac{C2/BTC}{C1/BTC} = (C2/C1)_{BX} \tag{1}$$

where $BX_{C2/C1}$ denotes the bitcoin exchange rate of $C2/C1$; $C1/BTC$ and $C2/BTC$ denote the respective prices of bitcoin in $C1$ or $C2$; and the BX subscript in $(C2/C1)_{BX}$ is used to distinguish the bitcoin exchange rate from the FX exchange rate.

Naturally, since the bitcoin exchange rate represents the "cross rate" between C1 and C2 over the base currency, bitcoin and currency trading can be implemented from any direction. A European speculator, for instance, may think that the USD has been depreciated in the bitcoin market and believes the situation will change soon, or perhaps in a month. Consequently, he trades his EURs for USDs through the bitcoin exchange rate, $(USD/EUR)_{BX}$. To hedge the risk of his investment, the speculator uses an FX 3-month futures contract to purchase b EURs. Suppose the speculator has a one-unit fixed long position in the bitcoin market and a $-b$-unit fixed short position in the futures market. The return of the portfolio, X, is given by

$$X = R_{BX} - bR_{FU} \tag{2}$$

where R_{BX} denotes the return of the bitcoin exchange rate of USD/EUR, R_{FU} denotes the return of the relative futures, and b is the hedge ratio.

There are several approaches to selecting the magnitude of b. The *naïve hedge ratio* assumes that $b = 1$. The *conventional hedge ratio* is obtained by regressing the return of the asset being hedged (here, the bitcoin exchange rate) on the return of the FX futures:

$$R_{BX,t} = a + bR_{FU,t} + \varepsilon_t \tag{3}$$

where $R_{BX,t}$ and $R_{FU,t}$ denote the time series of the two returns, respectively, and a is the intercept and b is the coefficient calculated using Ordinary Least Squares (OLS), which minimizes the sum of squared errors.

The *optimal hedge ratio* is the ratio that minimizes risk and maximizes the user's utility. The process of identifying the optimal hedge ratio can be illustrated as follows:

One measure of risk is variance. The variance of portfolio X returns is given by

$$Var(X) = Var(R_{BX}) + b^2 Var(R_{FU}) - 2bCov(R_{BX}, R_{FU}) \tag{4}$$

where $Cov(\cdot)$ denotes the covariance operator. Optimization involves setting the derivative of (4) with respect to b equal to zero. The risk-minimizing hedge ratio can then be calculated as

$$b' = \frac{Cov(R_{BX}, R_{FU})}{Var(R_{FU})}; \tag{5}$$

Meanwhile, if the speculator has a mean-variance expected utility function, denoted $EU(\cdot)$, Kroner and Sultan (1993), given by

$$EU(X) = E(X) - \gamma Var(X) \tag{6}$$

where $\gamma > 0$ denotes the user's degree of risk aversion, then the maximization of (6) with respect to b is shown as

$$\max_b EU(X) = \max_b \{E(R_{BX}) - b\mathrm{E}(\mathrm{R_{FU}}) - \gamma [Var(R_{BX}) + b^2 Var(R_{FU}) - 2bCov(R_{BX}, R_{FU})]\}. \tag{7}$$

Note that the maximization here is equivalent to the minimization of the variance of the portfolio in (3). Let the derivative of (6) with respect b be set equal to zero and the utility-maximizing hedge ratio be given by

$$b'' = \frac{2\gamma Cov(R_{BX}, R_{FU}) - E(R_{FU})}{2\gamma Var(R_{FU})}. \tag{8}$$

If the futures rate follows a martingale where $E(R_{FU}) = 0$, (5) is equal to (8), we get

$$b^* = b' = b'' = \frac{Cov(R_{BX}, R_{FU})}{Var(R_{FU})} \tag{9}$$

where b^* denotes the optimal hedge ratio, featuring both minimum risk and maximum mean-variance expected utility.

The naïve hedge ratio is intuitively simple, but this fully hedged position faces the problem of ex-ante selection and over hedging (Cecchetti et al. 1988). The OLS-based conventional hedge ratio is easy to compute and straightforward to understand, i.e., the squared errors involve unconditional variances; specifically, OLS minimizes the unconditional variances over the sample period. This model, however, can be criticized on three grounds (Engle and Granger 1987; Kroner and Sultan 1993): (i) using the unconditional variance implies that the speculator holds his/her portfolio over the entire sample period; (ii) the constant variance indicates a time-invariant risk, so that the hedged position remains unchanged according to that risk; and (iii) there is model misspecification when there exists co-integration between the bitcoin exchange rate and the FX futures rate and the variables are over-differenced in (3), where $R_{BX,t} = \Delta BX_t = BX_t - BX_{t-1}$ and $R_{FU,t} = \Delta FU_t = FU_t - FU_{t-1}$, and FU_t denotes the time series of the futures rate. The daily USD/EUR bitcoin exchange rate has previously been found to be co-integrated with the corresponding FX futures rate (Nan and Kaizoji 2019b).

The present paper demonstrates an FX futures hedge on the bitcoin exchange rate and calculates the optimal hedge ratio to effectively address the aforementioned problems with the naïve and conventional hedge ratios. A bivariate Dynamic Conditional Correlation Generalized Autoregressive Conditional Heteroskedastic (DCC-GARCH) model (Engle 2002) was implemented to compute the time-varying variance-covariance matrix containing the conditional variance and the conditional covariance series of the two returns—$R_{BX,t}$ and $R_{FU,t}$. To address the model misspecification resulting from the presence of co-integration, an error correcting term (ECT) is incorporated according to Kroner and Sultan's (1993) suggestion; in the bivariate environment, the model becomes a two-dimensional vector error correction model (VECM) working to capture the conditional mean of the joint distribution of the two returns. Estimated together, the VECM plus bivariate GARCH model provides a description of the time-varying conditional joint distribution. Hence, a time-dependent hedge ratio can be calculated from the estimated variance-covariance matrix by invoking (9). Moreover, a time-dependent correlation series is produced by this model. Based on these findings, the proposed model is superior to the naïve and conventional methods in terms of both risk management and utility enhancement. [Note: All analyses were conducted in R (R Core Team 2018)].

The remainder of the paper is organized as follows: Sect. 2 describes the data and illustrates the methodology; Sect. 3 gives empirical results; and Sect. 4 concludes the paper.

2 Methodology

Knowledge of the distribution of returns is highly important in forming optimal hedging and trading strategies, as financial returns are usually found to have leptokurtic or fat-tailed distributions (Baillie and Myers 1991). It has been pointed out that these non-normal distributions are the result of weak dependence in the return series and that the GARCH framework (Engle 1982; Bollerslev 1986) with Student's t distribution works well for capturing time-varying conditional variances and the excess kurtosis in the unconditional distribution of returns. In addition, the autocorrelation structure of returns needs to be accounted for by the model. Therefore, a model combining an Autoregressive Moving Average (ARMA) component and a univariate GARCH component is employed for both the bitcoin exchange rates and futures series.

The universal representation of the ARMA (1, 1) plus GARCH (1, 1) model is given by

$$R_t = a_0 + a_1 R_{t-1} + \varepsilon_t + b_1 \varepsilon_{t-1} \quad (10)$$

$$\varepsilon_t | \Omega_{t-1} \sim \ std(0, h_t, v) \quad (11)$$

$$h_t = \omega + \alpha \varepsilon_{t-1}^2 + \beta h_{t-1} \quad (12)$$

where R_t denotes the return of either the bitcoin exchange rate or the futures; $\varepsilon_t|\Omega_{t-1}$ indicates that the current innovation in (10) is conditioned on the one-period-ahead information set Ω_{t-1}; $std(0, h_t, v)$ denotes a Student's t density function with mean zero, conditional variance h_t and degrees of freedom v; and h_t denotes the time-dependent conditional variance. Equation (10) accounts for the autoregressive structure of the return series; (11) emphasizes that the innovation has time-dependent variances and that the leptokurtosis in its unconditional density should be described as a Student's t density function, with parameter v accounting for its shape; (12) is used to represent time-varying heteroskedasticity (Baillie and Myers 1991). The three equations can be estimated simultaneously by maximizing the log-likelihood using the augmented Lagrange method in the 'rugarch' package in R (Ghalanos 2018).

The next step is to measure the joint conditional distribution of the bitcoin exchange rate and the futures using a bivariate GARCH model. The framework for the bivariate case is similar to the univariate case in (10)–(12), with the vector of series being substituted for the series.

The model in (10) is replaced by a vector autoregressive (VAR) model with the series in first-order differences. This specification becomes problematic if there exists co-integration between the series in level, as it involves over-differencing (Baillie and Myers 1991; Kroner and Sultan 1993). Indeed, the USD/EUR bitcoin exchange rate and the USD/EUR FX futures, each possessing a unit root, have been previously found to be co-integrated, i.e., they are in long-run equilibrium and any deviations from the equilibrium are adjusted by the error correction mechanism (Nan and Kaizoji 2019b). Therefore, the VAR model needs to incorporate an error correcting term (ECT) to ensure that the long-run equilibrium is maintained in the bivariate system (Kroner and Sultan 1993), which becomes the bivariate vector error correction model (VECM) (Engle and Granger 1987) as shown in (13) and (14). The joint distribution of innovations is assumed to follow multivariate normal density in (11b).

As for the bivariate GARCH model, there are several options, including the BEKK model (Engle and Kroner 1995) and the GJR model (Glosten et al. 1993). The BEKK model is simple to apply, but it is difficult to find a financial interpretation of the coefficient matrices. The GJR model is more appropriate for an asymmetric distribution, and because trading on the bitcoin exchange rate can start from any direction (or currency), the leverage effect is not a substantial problem. We propose to apply the dynamic conditional correlation (DCC-) GARCH model (Engle and Sheppard 2001; Engle 2002) to capture the variance-covariance matrix. This model contains two parametric parts: one for the conditional GARCH effect and the other for the time-dependent correlations. It can be estimated with a two-step method starting from the univariate GARCH model for each return, then estimating them as a whole based on likelihood functions. This means that computations can be easily made and that the method can be readily extended to a large portfolio. Although the method is nonlinear, the meaning of the estimated coefficients is straightforward: one set of estimates is for the univariate GARCH environment and the other is for the time-dependent correlations (Engle 2002).

The framework is as follows:

(i) VECM

$$R_{BX,t} = a_{0B} + a_{1B}(BX_{t-1} + b_1 FU_{t-1} + b_0) + \sum_{i=1}^{p} c_{iB} R_{BX,t-i} + e_{BX,t} \tag{13}$$

$$R_{FU,t} = a_{0F} + a_{1F}(BX_{t-1} + b_1 FU_{t-1} + b_0) + \sum_{i=1}^{p} c_{iF} R_{FU,t-i} + e_{FU,t} \tag{14}$$

where $R_{BX,t} = \Delta BX_t = BX_t - BX_{t-1}$ and $R_{FU,t} = \Delta FU_t = FU_t - FU_{t-1}$ are the returns of the bitcoin exchange rate and FX futures, respectively. Let $b = (1, b_1, b_0)'$, where vector b denotes the cointegrating vector that causes the variable vector, say, $y_t = (BX_t, FU_t, 1)'$, to become stationary (or to be in long-run equilibrium). Hence $b'y_{t-1}$ represents the one-period-before deviation from the equilibrium. Let $a = (a_{1B}, a_{1F})'$, where vector a denotes the speed-of-adjustment coefficients indicating which return will respond to a discrepancy at what speed and from which direction. The product $ab'y_{t-1}$ represents the error correction term (ECT) (Granger 1986). We can rewrite (13) and (14) in the matrix

$$R_t = a_0 + ab'y_{t-1} + \sum_{i=1}^{p} c_i R_{t-i} + e_t \tag{15}$$

where r_t denotes the return vector.

(ii) Probability density assumptions

$$e_t|\Omega_{t-1} \sim MN(0, H_t) \tag{16}$$

where MN denotes the multivariate normal density function with mean zero and conditional variance-covariance matrix H_t. For the elements in vector e_t, each $e_{BX,t}$ and $e_{FU,t}$ follows Student's t density as specified in (11).

(iii) DCC-GARCH (Engle and Sheppard 2001; Engle 2002)

$$H_t \equiv D_t P_t D_t \tag{17}$$

$$D_t^2 = diag(\omega) + diag(\alpha)e_t e_t' + diag(\beta)D_{t-1}^2 \tag{18}$$

$$\varepsilon_t = D_t^{-1} e_t \tag{19}$$

$$Q_t = \bar{Q}(u' - \Phi - \Psi) + \Phi\varepsilon_{t-1}\varepsilon_{t-1}' + \Psi Q_{t-1} \tag{20}$$

$$\mathrm{P}_t = diag\left(Q_t^{1/2}\right)^{-1} Q_t diag\left(Q_t^{1/2}\right)^{-1} \tag{21}$$

Equation (17) shows that the conditional variance-covariance matrix can be decomposed into $D_t \mathrm{P}_t D_t$ where P_t is the time-dependent conditional correlation matrix with unities on its diagonals, and D_t is the diagonal matrix of time-varying standard deviations from the univariate GARCH models described in (18). The operator $diag(\cdot)$ creates a diagonal matrix from a vector. Vector ε_t in (19) is the standardized innovations in (15). Equation (20) gives the dynamic structure of the conditional correlation matrix using a proxy process Q_t, where u is a vector of unities and $\bar{Q}$ is the unconditional correlation matrix of the standardized innovations in (19). This specification assumes that Q_t is integrated and has an exponential smoothing structure. Ding and Engle (2001) shows that restrictions on $(u' - \Phi - \Psi)$, Φ and Ψ can make Q_t positive semi-definite or positive definite. The conditional correlation matrix P_t is then exacted by rescaling Q_t as shown in (21). In the sample case where the univariate GARCH (1, 1) model is used for parameterizing the time varying conditional correlation, vector Φ and Ψ become scalar φ and ψ.

Under the multivariate normal density in (17), the log-likelihood function for this estimator is given by

$$LL = -\frac{1}{2}\sum_{t=1}^{T}\left(N\log(2\pi) + \log|H_t| + e_t' H_t^{-1} e_t\right)$$

$$= -\frac{1}{2}\sum_{t=1}^{T}\left(N\log(2\pi) + \log|D_t \mathrm{P}_t D_t| + e_t' D_t^{-1}\mathrm{P}_t^{-1}D_t^{-1}e_t\right)$$

$$= -\frac{1}{2}\sum_{t=1}^{T}\left(N\log(2\pi) + 2\log|D_t| + \log|\mathrm{P}_t| + \varepsilon_t'\mathrm{P}_t^{-1}\varepsilon_t\right) \tag{22}$$

where (17) and (19) have been invoked and N is the number of assets.

We can add and subtract $\varepsilon_t'\varepsilon_t$ in (22) and decompose (22) into two parts (volatility and correlation):

$$LL_V(\theta) = -\frac{1}{2}\sum_{t=1}^{T}\left(N\log(2\pi) + \log|D_t|^2 + \varepsilon_t'\varepsilon_t\right)$$

$$= -\frac{1}{2}\sum_{t=1}^{T}\left(N\log(2\pi) + \log|D_t|^2 + e_t' D_t^{-2}e_t\right)$$

$$= -\frac{1}{2}\sum_{t=1}^{T}\sum_{i=1}^{N}\left(\log(2\pi) + \log\left(h_{i,t}\right) + \frac{e_{i,t}^2}{h_{i,t}}\right) \tag{23}$$

where LL_V is the log-likelihood function for the volatility part and θ denotes the parameters associated with D_t in (18). Equation (23) shows that LL_V is the sum of the individual GARCH likelihoods in (12), which will be jointly maximized by separately maximizing each of them (Engle 2002).

The correlation part log-likelihood function, denoted as LL_C, is given by

$$LL_C(\theta, \varphi) = -\frac{1}{2}\sum_{t=1}^{T}\left(\log|\mathrm{P}_t| + \varepsilon_t'\mathrm{P}_t^{-1}\varepsilon_t - \varepsilon_t^{\text{prime}}\varepsilon_t\right) \tag{24}$$

where φ denotes the parameters associated with Q_t in (21).

Hence, the log-likelihood function in (22) is the sum of the volatility part and the correlation part:

$$LL(\theta, \varphi) = LL_V(\theta) + LL_C(\theta, \varphi) \tag{25}$$

which can be maximized using a two-step approach—first finding the estimates of θ, then passing the values of $\hat{\theta}$ to $LL_C(\theta, \varphi)$ and maximizing the function with respect to φ. This two-step approach can be fitted into the GMM framework to produce a consistent solution as long as the maximum function in the second step is continuous in the neighborhood of the true parameters (Newey and McFadden 1994; Engle 2002).

3 Empirical Results

Before employing the VECM + DCC-GARCH model, we first produce a statistical summary of the prices and changes in prices of both the bitcoin and the FX futures included in the study. We then apply the univariate GARCH model to the respective returns. Finally, comparisons of the various hedging strategies are made in order evaluate the effectiveness of our optimal hedge.

3.1 Data and Statistic Summary

The daily-basis data set is composed of two bitcoin index series—the USD/BTC series and the EUR/BTC series—and one USD/EUR futures series covering the period from May 1, 2014 to November 21, 2017, as provided by Bloomberg. The USD/EUR bitcoin exchange rate was constructed by invoking (1). The future contract is for the March quarterly cycle (March, June, September, December) listed on the Chicago Mercantile Exchange. After using timestamps to match the bitcoin exchange rate with the futures series, there were 894 observations in each of the series. Using natural logarithmic transformations, we represent the USD/EUR bitcoin exchange rate as BX_t (the subscript representing currencies is omitted for brevity) and the futures as FU_t. Their returns are approximated by taking the first-order differences of the logarithmic rates: $R_{BX,t} = \Delta BX_t = BX_t - BX_{t-1}$ and $R_{FU,t} = \Delta FU_t = FU_t - FU_{t-1}$ (see Fig. 1).

Table 1 gives the relevant summary statistics. As indicated, the two returns have an equal sample mean; however, the returns of the bitcoin exchange rate show a much greater deviation from the mean than the returns of the FX futures, indicating a much greater risk. Looking at the minimum and maximum values suggests a daily

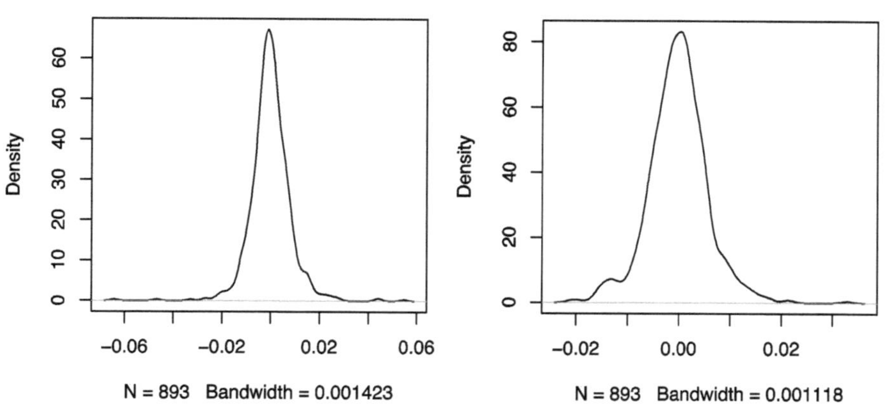

Fig. 1 The logarithmic returns of the USD/EUR bitcoin exchange rate (BX) and FX futures rate (FU)

Table 1 Summary statistics

Variables	Obvs.	Mean	Median	Min	Max	S.D.	Skewness	kurtosis
BX_t	894	0.136	0.115	0.012	0.333	0.072	1.189	3.533
FU_t	894	0.138	0.117	0.042	0.332	0.071	1.184	3.464
$R_{BX,t}$	893	−0.0002	−0.0005	−0.0643	0.0546	0.0082	0.033	9.299
$R_{FU,t}$	893	−0.0002	−0.0001	−0.0209	0.0328	0.0057	0.205	2.248

Note BX_t denotes the USD/EUR bitcoin exchange rate series and FU_t denotes the FX futures rate series. $R_{BX,t} = \Delta BX_t = BX_t - BX_{t-1}$ and $R_{FU,t} = \Delta FU_t = FU_t - FU_{t-1}$
All series are in natural logarithms (Period: May 1, 2014–November 21, 2017). The kurtosis column gives the excess kurtosis

loss and gain over the sample period for the bitcoin exchange rate of −6.43% and 5.46%, respectively. In contrast, the corresponding FX futures values were −2.09% and 3.28%, respectively. In addition, the unconditional standard deviation of the bitcoin exchange rate returns was larger than that of the FX futures returns. The skewness of the bitcoin exchange rate returns is slightly positive, indicating the absence of a leverage effect. Both returns present excess kurtosis in their probability density, which implies the existence of the GARCH effect and the appropriateness of Student's t density function (Baillie and Myers 1991).

Results from the Ljung-Box test on both return series with 20 lags show that serial autocorrelation exists in the returns of the bitcoin exchange rate but not in the returns of the FX futures. As an autoregressive model with a first and fifth lag [AR (1, 5)] was plausible for capturing this autocorrelation structure, the residual of the AR (1, 5) can be used in the univariate GARCH model. On the other hand, the returns of the FX futures can be used directly in the univariate GARCH model, as no autocorrelation was found. Jarque-Bera tests tended to reject the null hypothesis of normality for both sets of returns.

3.2 *Univariate GARCH Models*

The framework for the univariate GARCH model is the ARMA (1, 1) + GARCH (1, 1) model suggested in (10), (11), and (12). Some fine-tuning adjustments have been made to accommodate the autocorrelation structure, such as AR (1, 5) + GARCH (1, 1) for the returns of the bitcoin exchange rate and Mean + GARCH (1, 1) for the returns of the FX futures. The framework is estimated using maximum likelihood estimation; standard errors and robust standard errors are also calculated using this method. Estimation results and model diagnoses are listed in Table 2.

A comparison of the ARMA (1, 1) + GARCH (1, 1) and AR (1, 5) + GARCH (1, 1) models suggests that AR (1, 5) is more appropriate for modeling the autocorrelation structure of the mean of the bitcoin exchange rate returns. Although ARMA (1, 1) might be considered something of a universal model for this purpose, the a_1 and b_1 coefficients for the AR and MA terms here tend not to be significantly different from

Table 2 Estimation of univariate GARCH models for returns of the bitcoin exchange rate and the FX futures

	$R_{BX,t}$		$R_{FU,t}$	
Model	ARMA (1, 1)	AR (1, 5)	ARMA (1, 1)	Mean
a_0	−0.0003 (0.0002), (0.0002)	−0.0003 (0.0001), (0.0001)	−0.0003* (0.0001), (0.0002)	−0.0003* (0.0002), (0.0002)
a_1	0.0152 (0.1968), (0.1680)	−0.1401*** (0.0363), (0.0365)	0.2828 (0.5204), (0.4118)	
a_5		−0.0534* (0.0296), (0.0322)		
b_1	−0.1589 (0.1932), (0.1638)		−0.3269 (0.5120), (0.4064)	
ω	0.0000*** (0.0000), (0.0000)	0.0000*** (0.0000), (0.0000)	0.0000 (0.0000), (0.0000)	0.0000 (0.0000), (0.0000)
α	0.2626*** (0.0644), (0.0675)	0.2596*** (0.0616), (0.0620)	0.0542*** (0.0090), (0.0849)	0.0542*** (0.0092), (0.086)
β	0.4678*** (0.0857), (0.0926)	0.4803*** (0.0847), (0.0866)	0.9447*** (0.0074), (0.0726)	0.9447*** (0.0076)
v	4.8826*** (0.7939), (0.8684)	4.8346*** (0.7721), (0.8545)	5.4823*** (0.8717), (2.9958)	5.6193*** (0.8879), (3.0336)
LL	3163.2480	3164.3040	3419.7660	3418.7740
AIC	−7.0689	−7.0712	−7.6434	−7.6456
$Q(9)$	7.8840*	13.141 ($Q(24)$)	3.8527	2.1965 ($Q(5)$)
$Q^2(9)$	0.9689	0.9321	2.7844	2.7631
LM (7)	0.3511	0.3482	2.0387	2.0212

Note The ARMA (1, 1) + GARCH (1, 1) framework is specified as $R_t = a_0 + a_1 R_{t-1} + \varepsilon_t + b_1 \varepsilon_{t-1}$, $\varepsilon_t|\Omega_{t-1} \sim std(0, h_t, v)$, and $h_t = \omega + \alpha\varepsilon_{t-1}^2 + \beta h_{t-1}$, where R_t denotes one of the $R_{BX,t}$ and $R_{FU,t}$. Only the ARMA part was modified according to the autocorrelation structure of the return and the GARCH (1, 1) part remains unchanged. a_5 denotes the coefficient of the fifth lag of R_t
LL denotes the Log-Likelihood; *AIC* is the Akaike Information Criterion; $Q(9)$ is the Weighted Ljung-Box statistic for ninth-order autocorrelation in the standardized residuals, and $Q(5)$ and $Q(24)$ indicate the fifth-order and 24th-order correlation; $Q^2(9)$ is the Weighted Ljung-Box statistic for ninth-order serial correlation in the squared standardized residuals; and *LM* (7) is the Engle's Lagrange Multiplier test on the seventh-order squared innovations (ε_t^2)
The standard errors and the robust standard errors are listed in parentheses beneath each of the estimates
*significant at 10%, **significant at 5%, and ***significant at 1%

zero. Moreover, the $Q(9)$ statistic, which examines ninth-order serial correlation in the residuals of the ARMA (1, 1) model, is significant at the 6.36% level, indicating a weak autocorrelation in the residuals. On the other hand, the AR (1, 5) + GARCH (1, 1) model has significant coefficients a_1 and a_5 and a higher log-likelihood, and thus appears to provide better explanation. Coefficients α and β for the AR (1, 5) + GARCH (1, 1) model show the dynamic structure of the volatility of the bitcoin exchange rate returns, and their sum of roughly 0.7399 is indicative of the mean-reverting feature of this volatility. Furthermore, $Q^2(9)$ and $LM(7)$ tests indicate the absence of any GARCH effect in the model's standardized residuals.

For the FX futures returns, the mean + GARCH (1, 1) is competitive with the ARMA (1, 1) + GARCH (1, 1) model where $R_{FU,t} = a_0 + \varepsilon_t$. The 0.9989 sum of α and β appears to suggest an integrated process for the volatility of the FX futures returns. Diagnostic tests tend to support the appropriateness of this framework.

Finally, our results imply that the assumption of Student's t density, rather than normal density, is appropriate for highly significant values of v.

3.3 Multivariate GARCH Model

The DCC-GARCH framework is used for modelling the conditional joint density of the returns of both the bitcoin exchange rate and the FX futures. Results are presented in Table 3.

In the VECM model, coefficients b_0 and b_1 are obtained by OLS regression: $BX_t = b_0^{'} + b_1^{'}FU_t + \varepsilon_t^{'}$, with $b_0 = -b_0^{'} and b_1 = -b_1^{'}$. The lag length is determined by the Akaike Information Criterion (AIC) through an unrestricted VAR model of BX_t and FU_t. Term $(BX_{t-1} - 1.004FU_{t-1} + 0.0024)$ indicates a historical deviation from the long-run equilibrium in which BX_t and FU_t meander together in the same proportion, with a constant difference equal to 0.0024 (the risk premium). The values of coefficients a_{1B} and a_{1F} indicate that the current return of the bitcoin exchange rate appears to decrease by 40.68—eliminate the historical deviation, while the current return of the FX future tends to decrease 2.26% to enlarge the discrepancy. However, because the speed of the changes in the bitcoin rate is much faster than the speed of the changes in the FX futures, the deviation can be finally adjusted. The values of a_{0B} and a_{0F} suggest that both returns have a slightly negative sample mean.

After the VECM filtration of the unconditional mean, autoregression in the first moment, and the error correcting term, the volatility part of the DCC-GARCH model shows the mean-reverting pattern of the volatility of the bitcoin exchange rate returns, with $\alpha_B + \beta_B = 0.8076$, and the integrated pattern of the volatility of the FX futures returns, with $\alpha_F + \beta_F = 0.9985$. The estimated shape coefficients of Student's t density suggest that $v_B = 4.8828$ and $v_F = 5.6665$. Generally, the values of the estimated coefficients from the DCC-GARCH model were quite similar to the results of the univariate GARCH models; the differences come from the VECM filtration, i.e., because of the error correction mechanism, the volatility of the returns of the bitcoin exchange rate becomes less persistent and involves faster mean-reverting patterns.

The conditional proxy process Q_t appears to be persistent, as well, according to the magnitudes of φ and ψ, with $\varphi + \psi = 0.9835$. Thus the conditional correlation matrix P_t can be extracted by rescaling Q_t shown in (21). The diagonal of P_t is filled with unities, while the off-diagonal values are the conditional correlations between the two returns filtered by the VECM (see Fig. 2).

Table 3 Estimation of the bivariate VECM plus DCC-GARCH model

VECM		Bivariate GARCH (1, 1)		Conditional correlation	
b_0	0.0024	ω_B	0.0000*** (0.0000)	φ	0.0763*** (0.0328)
b_1	−1.0040	ω_F	0.0000 (0.0000)	ψ	0.9072*** (0.0470)
lags	4	α_B	0.1291*** (0.0160)		
a_{0B}	−0.0002	α_F	0.0528*** (0.0073)	*LL*	6747.5220
a_{0F}	−0.0002	β_B	0.6785*** (0.0317)	*AIC*	−15.0430
a_{1B}	−0.4068	β_F	0.9457*** (0.0087)		
a_{1F}	−0.0227	v_B	4.8828*** (o.6579)		
		v_F	5.6665*** (1.0251)		

Note In the VECM model given by $R_{BX,t} = a_{0B} + a_{1B}(BX_{t-1} + b_1 FU_{t-1} + b_0) + \sum_{i=1}^{p} c_{iB} R_{BX,t-i} + e_{BX,t}$ and $R_{FU,t} = a_{0F} + a_{1F}(BX_{t-1} + b_1 FU_{t-1} + b_0) + \sum_{i=1}^{p} c_{iF} R_{FU,t-i} + e_{FU,t}$, where coefficients b_0 and b_1 are obtained by the OLS regression $BX_t = b_0 + b_1 FU_t + \varepsilon_t$. The lag length is determined by the Akaike Information Criterion (AIC) through the unrestricted VAR model of BX_t and FU_t

The bivariate GARCH (1, 1) component is specified as $D_t^2 = diag(\omega) + diag(a) e_t e_t' + diag(\beta) D_{t-1}^2$. Subscript B denotes that the coefficient concerns the returns of the bitcoin exchange rate, while subscript F concerns the returns of the FX futures. Each univariate GARCH (1, 1) model is assumed to follow Student's t density, so that v_B and v_F are shape coefficients representing the respective degrees of freedom for the distribution

The conditional correlation is modelled by $Q_t = \bar{Q}(1 - \varphi - \psi) + \varphi \varepsilon_{t-1} \varepsilon_{t-1}' + \psi Q_{t-1}$

LL denotes Log-Likelihood,and *AIC* denotes the Akaike Information Criterion for the framework
***significant at 1%

The conditional variance-covariance matrix H_t is then constructed by invoking (17), with the conditional variances of the returns of the bitcoin exchange rate and the returns of the FX futures in the diagonal, denoted $h_{bb,t}$ and $h_{ff,t}$, and the conditional covariances in the off-diagonal, denoted $h_{bf,t}$. As plotted in Fig. 3, the graph of $h_{bb,t}$ shows mean-reverting and volatility clustering features, while the graph of $h_{ff,t}$ appears to show a random walk process. The conditional covariance remains generally positive except for the dramatic negative spike that occurred on 3 March 2017.

According to Eq. (9), the conditional optimal hedge ratio b_t^* can be obtained by taking the ratio of the conditional covariance to the conditional variance of the returns of the FX futures. The plot of b_t^* (see Fig. 4) shows a time-varying pattern, moving up and down around the red dashed line, which represents the conventional

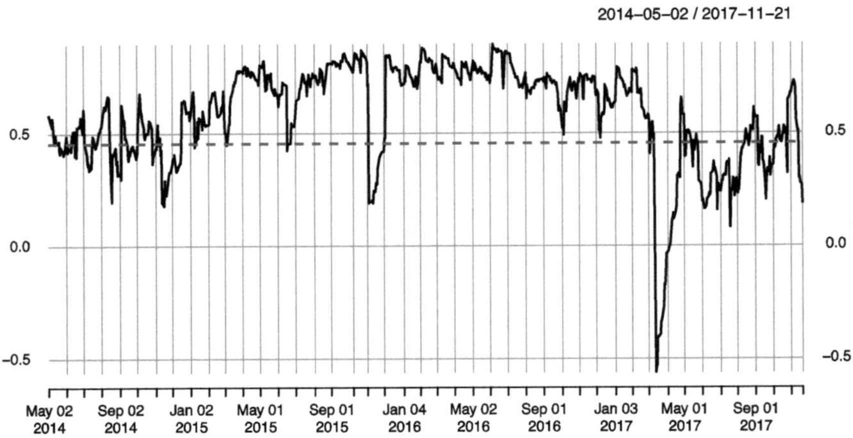

Fig. 2 The conditional correlation (corr.bf) between the return of the bitcoin exchange rate and the return of the FX futures (*Note* The red dashed line is the unconditional correlation between the two returns)

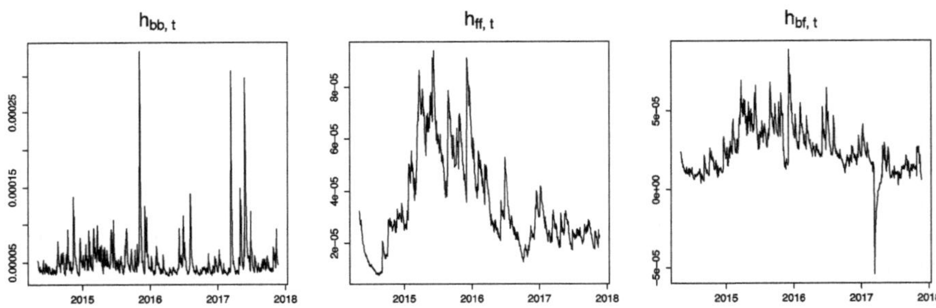

Fig. 3 The conditional variance of the return of the bitcoin exchange rate $\left(h_{bb,t}\right)$, the conditional variance of the FX futures $\left(h_{ff,t}\right)$ and the conditional covariance $\left(h_{bf,t}\right)$

variance-minimized hedge ratio calculated by the OLS method ($b_c = 0.6589$). As shown, the values of b_t^*, range from -1.77 to 1.54; they are positive for the most part, but become negative around March 2017.

3.4 Hedging Strategy Comparison

We can compare the conditional optimal hedging strategy based on the VECM + DCC-GARCH model to the naïve and conventional strategies.

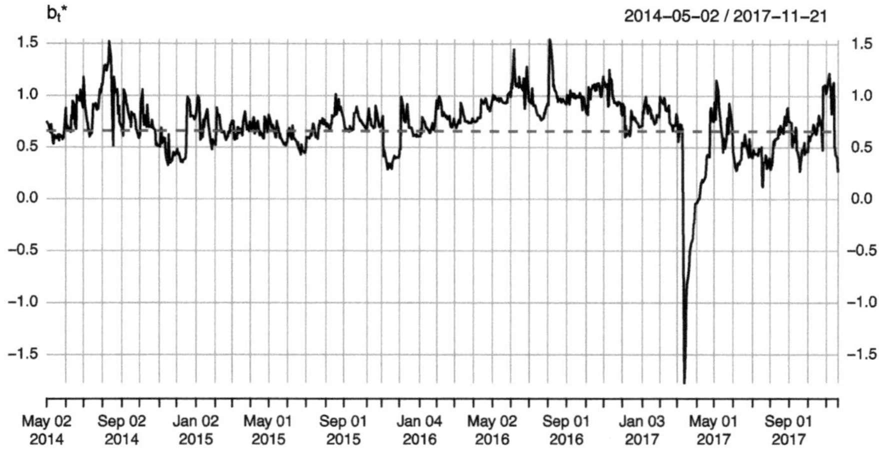

Fig. 4 The conditional optimal hedge ratio $\left(b_t^*\right)$. (*Note* The red dashed line is the conventional variance-minimized hedge ratio given by the OLS method)

Table 4 The log-likelihood and the Akaike Information Criterion for the different models nested in the VECM + DCC-GARCH model

	The conventional hedging model	The VECM hedging model	The conditional optimal hedging model
LL	6580.797	6676.798	6747.522
AIC	−14.557	−14.893	−15.043

Note *LL* denotes Log-Likelihood and *AIC* denotes the Akaike Information Criterion

3.4.1 Model Log-Likelihood

One of the conveniences of the VECM + DCC-GARCH model is that within the model are nested other hedging strategies that can be implemented by imposing restrictions on specific coefficients of the model. For example, imposing $\alpha_B = \alpha_F = \beta_B = \beta_F = \upsilon_B = \upsilon_F = 0$ gives the VECM model used to capture co-integration in the first moment where the variance is assumed to be constant. Imposing $\alpha_B = \alpha_F = \beta_B = \beta_F = \upsilon_B = \upsilon_F = a_{1B} = a_{1F} = c_{iB} = c_{iF} = 0$ gives the conventional hedging model. The results in Table 4 show that the conditional optimal hedging model has the highest log-likelihood and the lowest AIC score as compared to the other two models.

3.4.2 Unconditional Variances of Portfolios

By invoking Eq. (2), the portfolios are formed according to the various values of b. With $X_N = R_{BX,t} - R_{FU,t}$ denoting the portfolio based on naïve hedging, where $b = 1$; and $X_C = R_{BX,t} - b_C R_{FU,t}$ denoting the portfolio based on conventional

Table 5 Comparison of portfolios based on the naïve, conventional and conditional optimal hedge ratios

Portfolios	$X_N = R_{BX,t} - R_{FU,t}$	$X_C = R_{BX,t} - b_C R_{FU,t}$	$X_O = R_{BX,t} - b_t^* R_{FU,t}$
Variances	5.7277E−05	5.3491E−05	5.3024E−05
Historical VaR (1%)	−0.0215	−0.0199	−0.0190
Historical VaR (0.5%)	−0.0250	−0.0250	−0.0238
Gaussian VaR (1%)	−0.0176	−0.0171	−0.0169
Gaussian VaR (0.5%)	−0.0195	−0.0189	−0.0188
Modified VaR (1%)	−0.0525	−0.0509	−0.0487
Modified VaR (0.5%)	−0.0773	−0.0751	−0.0712
Mean-variance utilities	−0.2046	−0.1911	−0.1246 ($C = 0.0005$) (2) −0.1223 ($C = 0.0001$) (10) −0.1221 ($C = 0.00005$) (22)

Note X_N, X_C and X_O denote the portfolios based on the naïve hedge ratio, the conventional hedge ratio and the conditional optimal hedge ratio, respectively. Modified VaR concerns the Cornish-Fisher estimate of VaR. Constant C denotes the percentage losses in returns as the transaction cost; the number in the parentheses following C is the number of rebalances

hedging, where $b_C = 0.6589$; and $X_O = R_{BX,t} - b_t^* R_{FU,t}$ denoting the portfolio based on the conditional optimal hedge, where b_t^* is obtained from the VECM + DCC-GARCH model, the results in the first row of Table 5 show that portfolio X_O had the smallest unconditional variances during the sample period.

3.4.3 Value-at-Risk (VaR)

The 1 and 0.5% VaRs are calculated to estimate the negative values of the returns. Estimates are made using three analytic methods, producing a historical estimate, a Gaussian estimate, and a Cornish-Fisher (modified) estimate, which is more appropriate in cases involving a skewed and/or leptokurtic density of returns. The results from row 2 to row 7 in Table 5 indicate that risks are reduced in the distribution tail when the portfolio is based on the conditional optimal hedge ratio.

3.4.4 User Utility

For brevity, the mean-variance utility can be reduced to the variance component $[-N\gamma Var(X)]$, where N is the number of observations. In this expression, the smaller the variance, the greater is the user's utility. It we let U_n denote this type of user utility for the portfolio based on the naïve hedge ratio, we get $U_N = -4 \times 893 \times 0.000057277 = -0.2046$, where $N = 893$ *and* $\gamma = 4$. For the conventional hedging portfolio, user utility U_C is calculated as $U_C = -4 \times 893 \times 0.00005391 = -0.1911$. For the conditional optimal hedging portfolio, we follow the method proposed by Kroner and Sultan (1993) to construct a conditional user utility using the conditional variances obtained from the VECM + DCC GARCH model and consider transaction costs. The idea is that when the utility gained from changes in the variances is insufficient to offset the transaction cost, the user remains in his previous position; when the gain is greater than the cost, the user rebalances. The scenario is expressed by

$$\begin{aligned} &- C - \gamma\left(h_{bb,t+1} - 2b^*_{t+1}h_{bf,t+1} + b^{*2}_{t+1}h_{ff,t+1}\right) \\ &> -\gamma\left(h_{bb,t+1} - 2b^*_t h_{bf,t+1} + b^{*2}_t h_{ff,t+1}\right) \end{aligned} \tag{26}$$

where $h_{bb,t+1} - 2b^*_{t+1}h_{bf,t+1} + b^{*2}_{t+1}h_{ff,t+1}$ is the conditional variance of the optimal hedging portfolio at time t + 1 and C denotes the percentage return that the user pays as a cost of the transaction. Only if inequality (26) holds does the user rebalance his/her position. The mean-variance utility is calculated by summing each individual utility. The results (see Table 5) show that if $C = 0.0005$ (meaning the transaction cost is \$5 per \$1000), the utility is equal to −0.1246, and the number of rebalances is 2. When C decreases to 0.0001, the utility is equal to −0.1223 and the user needs to rebalance 22 times during the sample period. Nevertheless, the conditional mean-variance utility is nearly 40% greater than the utility of the other two methods that use constant hedging strategies.

4 Conclusion

This study investigated the effect of using the conditional optimal hedge ratio to construct portfolios consisting of the USD/EUR bitcoin exchange rate and the USD/EUR FX futures rate.

The optimal hedge ratio is the ratio that minimizes variance and maximizes user utility; it can often be obtained from the conditional variance-covariance matrix of the joint density of the two assets. The investigation began by addressing the univariate autoregressive structure and volatility of the return series. The AR (1, 5) + GARCH (1, 1) model was suggested for modelling the time-dependent density of the bitcoin exchange rate returns, while the Mean + GARCH (1, 1) model was suggested for modelling the density of the FX futures returns. The volatility of the bitcoin exchange rate returns has a mean-reverting feature, while the volatility of the FX futures returns appears to be integrated. In addition, the Student's t density function appears appropriate for describing both sets of returns according to a statistical test based on the log-likelihood ratio. The DCC-GARCH model was used to capture the time-varying joint density of the two assets. However, due to the existence of co-integration between the USD/EUR bitcoin exchange rate and the USD/EUR futures, the VECM term needs to be incorporated in order to avoid the over-differencing problem in model specification. The conditional optimal hedge ratio was calculated using this VECM + DCC-GARCH framework. In addition to the conditional variance-covariance matrix, a time-dependent conditional correlation series was obtained as a byproduct.

A comparison of the portfolios based on the naïve, conventional and conditional optimal hedge ratios showed that the conditional optimal hedging portfolio is superior to the other two portfolios in a number of aspects: maximum log-likelihood for model estimation, minimum unconditional variance of the portfolio, minimum Value-at-Risk of the portfolio, and maximum mean-variance utility.

The Bitcoin-based U.S. dollar and Euro trading strategy is effective regarding risk management and hedging, but this strategy is not satisfactory for its continuity—the user who bought Euros and sold dollars at the bitcoin markets must wait for the reverse market to change her Euros back into dollars. In a sense, the triangular arbitrage between the bitcoin and FX markets (Nan and Kaizoji 2019a; Pichl et al. 2020) tends to be more realistic. Obviously, many considerations of the trading strategies deserve the further effort.

Acknowledgements This work was supported by JSPS KAKENHI Grant Number 17K01270, 20K01752 and NOMURA Fundation.

References

Baillie, R. T., & Myers, R. J. (1991). Bivariate GARCH estimation of the optimal commodity futures hedge. *Journal of Applied Econometrics, 6*(2), 109–124.

Bollerslev, T. (1986). Generalized autoregressive conditional heteroskedasticity. *Journal of Econometrics, 31*(3), 307–327.

Briere, M., Oosterlinck, K., & Szafarz, A. (2013). *Virtual currency, tangible return: Portfolio diversification with bitcoins* (SSRN Scholarly Paper ID 2324780). Social Science Research Network.

Cecchetti, S. G., Cumby, R. E., & Figlewski, S. (1988). Estimation of the optimal futures hedge. *The Review of Economics and Statistics*, 623–630.

Cheah, E.-T., & Fry, J. (2015). Speculative bubbles in Bitcoin markets? An empirical investigation into the fundamental value of Bitcoin. *Economics Letters, 130,* 32–36.

Ding, Z., & Engle, R. F. (2001). *Large scale conditional covariance matrix modeling, estimation and testing.*

Engle, R. (2002). Dynamic conditional correlation: A simple class of multivariate generalized autoregressive conditional heteroskedasticity models. *Journal of Business & Economic Statistics, 20*(3), 339–350.

Engle, R. F. (1982). Autoregressive conditional heteroscedasticity with estimates of the variance of United Kingdom inflation. *Econometrica, 50*(4), 987–1007.

Engle, R. F., & Granger, C. W. (1987). Co-integration and error correction: Representation, estimation, and testing. *Econometrica: Journal of the Econometric Society*, 251–276.

Engle, R. F., & Kroner, K. F. (1995). Multivariate simultaneous generalized arch. *Econometric Theory, 11*(1), 122–150.

Engle, R. F., & Sheppard, K. (2001). *Theoretical and empirical properties of dynamic conditional correlation multivariate GARCH*. National Bureau of Economic Research.

Ghalanos, A. (2018). Introduction to the rugarch package. *R vignette*. (Version 1.3-8).

Glosten, L. R., Jagannathan, R., & Runkle, D. E. (1993). On the relation between the expected value and the volatility of the nominal excess return on stocks. *The Journal of Finance, 48*(5), 1779–1801.

Granger, C. W. (1986). Developments in the study of cointegrated economic variables. *Oxford Bulletin of Economics and Statistics, 48*(3), 213–228.

Kroner, K. F., & Sultan, J. (1993). Time-varying distributions and dynamic hedging with foreign currency futures. *Journal of Financial and Quantitative Analysis, 28*(4), 535–551.

Nan, Z., & Kaizoji, T. (2017). Market efficiency of the bitcoin exchange rate: Evidence from co-integration tests. Working paper. Available at SSRN 3179981

Nan, Z., & Kaizoji, T. (2019a). Bitcoin-based triangular arbitrage with the Euro/US dollar as a foreign futures hedge: Modeling with a bivariate GARCH model. *Quantitative Finance and Economics, 3*(2), 347–365.

Nan, Z., & Kaizoji, T. (2019b). Market efficiency of the bitcoin exchange rate: Weak and semi-strong form tests with the spot, futures and forward foreign exchange rates. *International Review of Financial Analysis, 64*(2019), 273–281.

Newey, W. K., & McFadden, D. (1994). Large sample estimation and hypothesis testing. *Handbook of Econometrics, 4*, 2111–2245.

Pichl, L., Nan, Z., & Kaizoji, T. (2020). Time series analysis of ether cryptocurrency prices: Efficiency, predictability, and arbitrage on exchange rates. In *Advanced studies of financial technologies and cryptocurrency markets*. Japan: Springer.

R Core Team. (2018). *R: A language and environment for statistical computing. R Foundation for Statistical Computing*. Vienna, Austria. https://www.R-project.org/.

Time Series Analysis of Ether Cryptocurrency Prices: Efficiency, Predictability, and Arbitrage on Exchange Rates

Lukáš Pichl, Zheng Nan, and Taisei Kaizoji

Abstract The Ether cryptocurrency, based on the blockchain of the Ethereum project for smart contracts, has long had the 2nd market capitalization, next to the Bitcoin. Despite its importance and the innovative features of the entire Ethereum ledger ecosystem, Ether has attracted far less attention than Bitcoin in terms of the time series analysis. This work provides an analysis of the R/S Hurst Exponent for the Ether time series in order to test to what extent the price dynamics may be predictable by deterministic methods including machine learning. Daily log returns, volatility time series, and transaction count sequences are analyzed. Support Vector Machine algorithm is used for testing the marginal predictability level. Ether-mediated triangular arbitrage between six major fiat currencies is also studied—we provide the distributions of the logarithmic rate of arbitrage transaction return for the 15 currency pair combinations. We also study the cointegration process of Ether-exchange rates with the foreign exchange rates that are the cause and driving force of the adjustment process towards dynamic market equilibrium eliminating arbitrage windows. The efficiency of the Ether market is found to increase with time.

Keywords Ether · ETH · Ethereum · Hurst exponent · Triangular arbitrage · Volatility · Ether exchange rates · Time series prediction

1 Introduction

Since Bitcoin was released as the first open source distributed cryptocurrency in 2009, it has been followed by a number of altcoins, derivatives of the original encrypted distributed ledger concept, and other block-chain based cryptocurrencies emerged,

L. Pichl (✉) · Z. Nan · T. Kaizoji
Graduate School of Arts and Sciences, International Christian University, Osawa 3-10-2, Mitaka, Tokyo 181-8585, Japan
e-mail: lukas@icu.ac.jp

Z. Nan
e-mail: nijelnan@gmail.com

T. Kaizoji
e-mail: kaizoji@icu.ac.jp

L. Pichl et al. (eds.), *Advanced Studies of Financial Technologies and Cryptocurrency Markets*, https://doi.org/10.1007/978-981-15-4498-9_10

such as Ethereum. As of the writing of this article (January 16, 2020), the market capitalization of all cryptocurrencies is about 237 USD billion, with the share of Bitcoin in USD 158 billion, followed by Ethereum (USD 18 billion; Coinmarketcap 2020). Standard economics treats cryptocurrencies as digital assets with no intrinsic value; the extent of market capitalization of the entire cryptocurrency enterprise is therefore remarkable for such a marginal project. The main valuation is still largely speculative, due to betting on the cryptocurrencies' chance of becoming a major means of payment with the potential of gradually disrupting the national currency systems. It is somewhat ironical that cryptocurrencies, this far with no intrinsic economic value in behind whatsoever, gained popularity in the years after the 2008 financial crisis, which showed that also financial products and the monetary supply can be created out of nothing by policies of central banks known as quantitative easing leading to such extremes as the negative interest rates.

According to the Ethereum project, "Ethereum is a decentralized platform that runs smart contracts". The system rules out the possibilities of inaccessibility, censorship, fraud (provided certain security precaution measures observed on the user side) or any regulatory interference. Ether is a digital asset built on top of Ethereum blockchain used as a form of payment within the Ethereum ecosystem. It is the second major cryptocurrency as mentioned above, which can be obtained at cryptocurrency exchanges in return for fiat currencies or gained through mining process that insures the integrity of the ever-growing encrypted distributed transaction ledger. The economic incentive for the mining process for Ether varies considering the current mining difficulty, hash rate, hardware and electrical power cost parameters. The mining profitability varies according to the cryptocurrency; e.g. in case of Bitcoin, CNBC spread the news that the Bitcoin mining was no longer profitable with the prices that were current on March 15, 2018.

The Ethereum project brought substantial innovations to cryptocurrencies, such as the Turing-complete scripting ability or much shorter block time (15 s) compared to Bitcoin (10 min). Ethereum is often used as the platform for initial coin offerings (ICOs). Ether currency has gradually gained mass popularity, and in 2017 its price in USD has increased by a 90-fold factor. At present, Ether has a market capitalization of about 18 billion US dollars.

Whether cryptocurrencies will find a stable role in the global financial system or turn out to be one of the largest Ponzi scheme events is still an open question since their adoption as regular means of payment for goods and services is still marginal; in this work we handle Ether as a digital asset traded in numerous fiat currencies in a market featuring many extreme events such as bubbles and crashes. The efficient market hypothesis by Fama applied to Ether should rule out arbitrage opportunities. In this work, we will explore the statistical characteristics of the time series of Ether prices to find out to what extend a deterministic prediction based on the past data is possible, and quantify the degree of market efficiency.

1.1 Statistical Properties

In this paper, we study the property of Ether time series, using the logarithmic return of ETHUSD prices, the intraday volatility measure (derived as the ratio of maximum and minimum prices in the trading period), and the transaction count measure. For all these three time series we compute the Hurst exponent by the classical R/S method and using 2 variants of Detrended Fluctuation Analysis (DFA). Despite the limited size of the moving window of 256 days, we argue below that the R/S values are appropriate rather than the DFA estimates, in contrary to similar studies applied not to Ether, but to Bitcoin (Bariviera et al. 2017).

The central question addressed in this article is whether the Ether USD market is efficient (Fama 1970 and Fama 1991), and to what extent we can predict the log returns, intraday volatility time series, and the log returns of the transaction count time series. To that aim, we first compute Hurst exponents, $0 <= H <= 1$, for each of the series. For H close to 0.5, we have unpredictable Brownian motion dynamics; for H well below 0.5 we have anti-persistent, mean reverting dynamics, whereas for H well above 0.5 the dynamics is persistent, with clusters of bearish and bullish behavior. Once the Hurst exponent is known, we try to classify the trend of each time series by using two methods: Support Vector Regression (SVR), which in facts fits the magnitudes of the time series, and Support Vector Machine (SVM), which is a binary classifier trained on the binary class of -1 (negative return) and $+1$ (positive return). Extremely rare cases of 0 return (no change in the market) are excluded from the analysis. It indeed turns up that the time series of intraday volatility differences can be predicted to the largest extent in accord with their value of Hurst exponent. We also apply a simple mean reverting strategy (next day trend prediction is the opposite of today's trend sign) which performs well in the anti-persistent regime of $H \ll 0.5$. To our knowledge, none of such analysis has been applied to Ether cryptocurrency yet.

1.2 Triangular Arbitrage

It will be shown in what follows that based on the particular currency pairs, arbitrage windows for Ether-based transactions range from negligible (USDEUR) to substantial (JPYCNY). Nevertheless, a long-term disparity cannot exist between major markets even though the cryptocurrency trade volumes still compare to a minor volume fraction at the FX markets. It is therefore plausible to investigate how the long-term trend of FX foreign exchange rates integrates into the dynamics of Ether-derived exchange rate time series. In what follows, we adopt the following notation: ETH stands for Ether; CR1CR2 represents the exchange rate of 1 unit of CR1 into CR1CR2 units of CR2, ECR1CR2 is defined as ETHCR2/ETHCR1, and rate variables printed in the lower case denote the natural logarithms, e.g. ethusd = log (ETHUSD). We may also use FX for CR1CR2 to shorten the notation provided the context is clear.

2 Summary of the Contribution

Compared to Bitcoin, Ether has received relatively low attention in cryptocurrency research thus far. This study reports in the first part the classical R/S Hurst exponent values for the time period from 8 July 2015 to 9 March 2018 using moving windows with the time lag length of 256 days. The daily results oscillate near values of 0.5, indicating Brownian motion dynamics, but are substantially lower, if de-trended fluctuation analysis is applied, which would correspond to anti-persistent character of the time series. Support vector regression and a binary support vector classifier are applied to the time series of Ether logarithmic returns, Ether intraday volatility series, and Ether transaction count log return time series. The latter data are further used to represent an information criterion of Ether popularity in an attempt to enhance the performance of the Support Vector techniques. It is shown that a simple reverse prediction for next-day trend is accurate by 51% for daily log return, by 64% for volatility time series, and by 56% for transaction count time series. The SV-techniques are not found to exceed these margins.

In the second part, we focus on Ether efficiency from the viewpoint of arbitrage opportunities across markets trading Ether in various fiat currencies. Using daily closing values for ETH prices in the last 2 years (2017/01/01–2019/02/26) we provide triangular arbitrage log profit rate distributions for conversion transactions of the type CR1-ETH-CR2-CR1, where CR1 and CR2 are arbitrary fiat currencies drawn from among CAD, CNY, BGP, EUR, JPY and USD. Co-integration between the 15 Ether-derived exchanged rates and the actual FX time series is estimated by the VECM model using the Engle-Granger and Johansen methods. One-way Granger causality is found in which the daily foreign-exchange rate changes drive the subsequent adjustments of Ether-derived exchange rate. Cointegration vector parameters and coefficients for the error correction term (ECT) are provided. In addition, cointegration with the error correction term expressed as the plain difference of the two time series is studied by the Engle Granger method. Standard deviation values of logarithmic profit rate in triangular arbitrage are found to vary from 1.0% (USDEUR) to 9.0% (JPYCNY). The efficiency of the Ether market increases with time.

3 Literature Review

The scientific literature on cryptocurrencies has become abundant just recently, and most of it deals with Bitcoin. As of present, we are not aware of any article that would report Ether's Hurst exponents or predict Ether-related time series by means of machine learning.

The blockchain technology underlying cryptocurrency design is summarized in the work of Huckle et al. (2016). In a recent research work, Gkillas and Katsiampa (2018) have studied the behavior of returns of five major cryptocurrencies using extreme value analysis, finding out that Ether is in the middle of the risk region. In a statistical study by Phillip et al. (2018) diverse stylized facts such as long memory and heteroscedasticity have been explored for 224 different cryptocurrencies, which are found to "exhibit leverage effects and Student-error distributions". Bariviera et al. (2017) studied the statistical features and long-range dependence of Bitcoin returns, focusing on the behavior of the Hurst exponent computed in sliding windows, showing that it has a similar behavior at different time scales. We closely follow this work on the methodological side, applying the Hurst exponent estimation to Ether instead of Bitcoin. Alabi (2017) studies the applicability of Metcalf's law to cryptocurrency networks and finds that the network's value is related to the exponential of the root of its active users. Ciaian et al. (2018) study the Bitcoin and Altcoin market relations on several time scales, finding out substantial interdependence between Bitcoin and Altcoin markets, which is more pronounced in the short-term run relative to the long time scales. Corbet et al. (2018) study, in the time and frequency domains, the relationships between popular cryptocurrencies and a variety of other financial assets, revealing the evidence of relative isolation of cryptocurrency assets from the economic assets, which may be used in favor of cryptocurrencies, if applying the portfolio diversification argument. Hayes (2017) offers an interesting insight into the valuation of Bitcoin using the cost of production. In an article by Phillip et al. (2018), diverse stylized facts of cryptocurrencies are studied; it is found that Ethereum has a smaller kurtosis than Bitcoin, a fact which is ascribed to the ease of Ether transactions compared to Bitcoin. Remaining available literature on cryptocurrencies focuses solely on Bitcoin or excludes Ether and thus will not be reviewed here.

4 Theoretical Method

First, we briefly outline the original procedure to estimate the Hurst exponent following closely (Bariviera et al. 2017). We also start with the sequence of continuously compounded returns, $\{\mathrm{r}_1, \ldots, \mathrm{r}_t\}$ with mean $\bar{\mathrm{r}}_t$ and standard deviation s_t, defining the R/S values at time t as

$$(\mathrm{R/S})_t = \frac{1}{s_t}\left[\max_{1\le t'\le t}\sum_{t''=1}^{t'}(\mathrm{r}_{t''}-\bar{\mathrm{r}}_t) - \min_{1\le t'\le t}\sum_{t''=1}^{t'}(\mathrm{r}_{t''}-\bar{\mathrm{r}}_t)\right] \tag{1}$$

which, according to Hurst (1951), obey the following statistical distribution,

$$(\mathrm{R/S})_t = \left[\frac{t}{2}\right]^H \tag{2}$$

where H is the value of the Hurst exponent. Peng et al. (1995) developed the method of the De-trended Fluctuation Analysis (DFA) that is claimed to avoid the possible effect of spurious detection of long term dependence, resulting thus typically in lower values of DFA-estimated Hurst exponent *H*. Since there remain some controversies on the use of DFA (Bryce and Sprague 2012), in particular "(1) it introduces uncontrolled bias; (2) is computationally more expensive than the unbiased estimator; and (3) cannot provide generic or useful protection against nonstationaries," we will not generally adopt nor describe the DFA method. Primarily for the sake of magnitude comparison, Fig. 2 provides the Hurst exponent estimates in moving windows of length of 256 days for the ETHUSD time series (see Fig. 1), computed by the R/S method above along with 2 implementations of the DFA method in R: function dfa in package nonlinearTseries and function DFA in package fractal. We can see that for the period of the 1st year in the ETHUSD dataset covering the time interval of 8 July 2015–9 March 2018, the DFA techniques tend to decrease the values of H; then the trend reverses. Since there are also substantial differences between the implementations, we do not consider the DFA technique reliable for the present dataset in view of the discussion by Bryce and Sprague (2012).

In order to predict the future behavior of r_{t+1} given the past values of r_i up to r_t, we use the following procedures. First, a simple anti-persistent strategy (motivated by low values of DFA based estimate for Hurst exponent of ETHUSD time series, or the lower values of R/S estimate for the remaining two time series of intraday volatility and transaction count series), we test the assumption that the sign of r_{t+1} is opposite to the sign of r_t. If the values of H are very much below 0.5, anti-persistent dynamics may indeed take the form of such oscillations. This is of course a toy-model check. Next, we apply the Support Vector based algorithms of machine learning, namely the binary classifier for the sign of the logarithmic return (daily trend: up or down) by means of SVM, or the continuous version trying to fit the magnitude of the logarithmic return with the continuous regression technique of SVR.

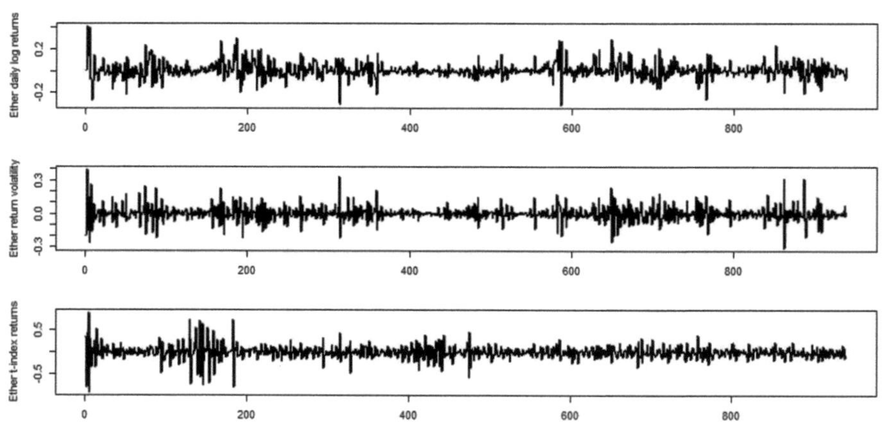

Fig. 1 Time series of ETH over a period of 946 days, starting 8 July 2015. The first panel indicates the log return of the daily close price, the second differences in intraday volatility, and the third panel shows the logarithmic return of the daily count of Ether transactions from (data retrieved https://coinmarketcap.com/currencies/ethereum/historical-data/ and https://etherscan.io/chart/tx)

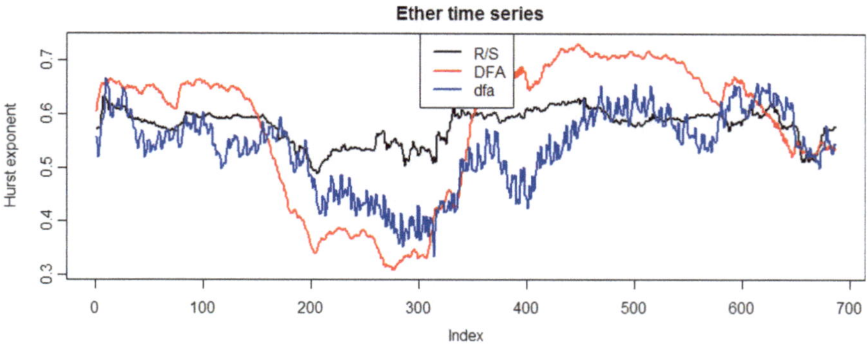

Fig. 2 Hurst exponent estimated for the log returns of ETHUSD time series by 3 different methods (see text for details)

The implementation of the SV-based techniques is based on the R package kernlab (Karatzoglou et al. 2004). We use past data in a moving window of the size of 10 days as the dimension of the input space. In addition, it is found that the inclusion of the returns on the transaction count time series improves the prediction accuracy, therefore it is added as an extra predictor. 60% of the data is used for training, 10% of the data for validation of model parameters (which includes manual screening for the reasonable value of miss-classification penalty C), and remaining 30% is used for testing. Radial basis functions with automatic parameter selection are applied in order to represent the nonlinear boundary between the +1 and −1 classes. A detailed description of SV-techniques can e.g. be found in the book by the inventor of these methods (Vapnik 2000). SVR results are transferred to the binary results by taking the sign of the predicted logarithmic return. Standard information measures are applied for the evaluation of the results.

To evaluate the applicability of the above approaches, we use accuracy, precision, recall and F-measure. Since the value of the F-measure may depend on the initial setting for the positive category (+1 or −1), we evaluate the F-measure in both cases, and combine it together by the same relation that is used in F-measure definition, i.e. $(F = 2F_1F_2/(F_1 + F_2))$.

In case of the Ethereum mediated triangular arbitrage, we proceed as follows. All cryptocurrency data used for analysis are retrieved from Yahoo finance database. Foreign exchange rates are taken from the Pacific Exchange Rate service. Cryptocurrency prices are obtained as daily time series for each date between 2017/1/1 and 2019/2/26 for fiat currencies of USD, JPY, EUR, GBP, CNY and CAD. The 15 exchange rates correspond to the combination pairs among the 6 currencies.

For the sake of triangular arbitrage analysis, we assume the following multiple conversion transactions: CR1-ETH-CR2-CR1. The rates for each of the three steps are ETHCR1 (buy ETH), CR2ETH (sell ETH), CR1CR2 (convert CR2 back to CR1). Thus the logarithmic return of the transaction chain reads

Table 1 Prediction results (F-measure) for the 3 time series by several methods

Method/data series	ETHUSD log return (%)	Intraday volatility (%)	Transaction count (%)
Reverse trend	51.5	63.7	55.7
SV binary classifier	51.9	56.3	52.3
SV regression sign	50.5	58.4	53.8

$$\mathrm{r} = \log\left(\frac{ETHCR1}{ETHCR2}/CR2CR1\right) = \log(EFX/FX) = efx - fx \tag{3}$$

We remark that r(CR1CR2) = −r(CR2CR1). The distribution of r-values is computed for the relevant time series and summarized in Table 1.

The cointegration of the time series of order 1 with lag 1 (unit root non-stationary processes where efx + βfx stands for the error term proxy between the two time series) is modeled by the following equations,

$$\begin{aligned} \Delta \mathrm{efx}_t &= \alpha + \sigma \Delta \mathrm{efx}_{t-1} + \omega \Delta \mathrm{fx}_{t-1} + \gamma(\mathrm{efx}_{t-1} + \beta \mathrm{fx}_{t-1}) + \varepsilon_1 \\ \Delta \mathrm{fx}_t &= \alpha' + \sigma' \Delta \mathrm{efx}_{t-1} + \omega' \Delta \mathrm{fx}_{t-1} + \gamma'(\mathrm{efx}_{t-1} + \beta \mathrm{fx}_{t-1}) + \varepsilon_2 \end{aligned} \tag{4}$$

where the coefficients beta and gamma are estimated by the method of maximum likelihood by Johansen (1998) and Johansen and Juselius (1990). Next, we set $\beta = -1$ and estimate the remaining coefficients by the method of Engle and Granger (1987) for comparison. All coefficients are statistically significant at the 1% level. Index 1 is used for the method of direct error correction term computed as $\mathrm{efx}_{t-1} - \mathrm{fx}_{t-1}$. Adjustment to long-term equilibrium is represented by negative values of the coefficient γ. Figure 4 shows the r-distribution for JPYCNY currency pair. The secondary peak at negative values corresponds to over-pricing episodes of Ether in Japan compared to China which has taken place during 2017 (the trend largely reversed in 2018, though).

5 Results and Discussions

Table 1 summarizes the reverse trend toy model and the SV-techniques results for the time series of (1) log return of ETHUSD prices on daily sampling grid, (2) daily differences of intraday volatility computed as the logarithm of the intraday High/Low ratio, and (3) log return of the ETH daily transaction count. Figure 3 provides the moving window based estimates of the Hurst exponent for each of the three time series using the original R/S estimates. By comparing Table 1 and Fig. 3, it can be seen that the ETHUSD time series are near the Brownian motion regime, the market is near to efficient, and the F-measure of the success of the prediction is very close to the statistical limit of equal odds ratio of 50%. For the remaining two time series,

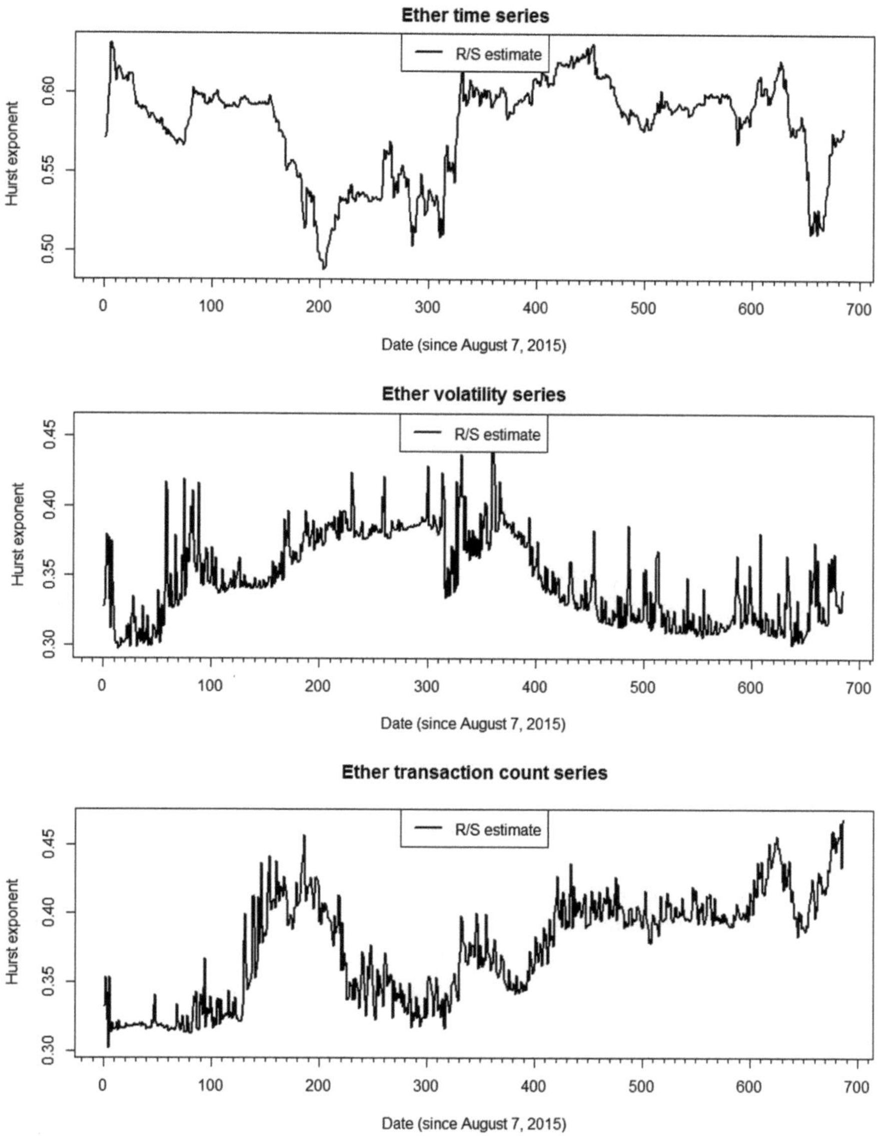

Fig. 3 Results for the Hurst exponent using the classical R/S method of estimation

the Hurst exponent by R/S method (and the more the DFA estimates, not shown in the paper) suggest anti-persistent dynamics with H substantially below the value of 0.5, especially for the volatility time series. Consequently, deterministic mode can be observed and predicted, which is consistent especially with the higher values of the F-measure in the 2nd numerical column for the intraday volatility time series. It can also be seen in Table 1 that the "Reverse trend" strategy is surprisingly successful, and presents an upper bound for the present application of the Support Vector based methods. Since we are working with non-linear kernels in highly-dimensional spaces, even for the modest data set of the present size, it is difficult to find the optimal values of the parameters. It remains a task for the future work to find which machine learning algorithms would perform the best. However, the present results conform to a reasonable degree of Ethereum market efficiency, and probably may not be easily improved.

The standard R/S estimate of the Hurst exponent for the Ether time series is relatively close to the value of 0.5 within the entire period studied (2015–2018) thus supporting the martingale behavior of the pricing process, market efficiency, and resulting in a very limited applicability of machine learning methods, including the support vector based algorithms, for trend and future value prediction. De-trended fluctuation analysis based estimates of Hurst exponent would result in anti-persistent dynamics for the first half of the time period studied, inverting then to the persistent dynamics in the latter half. The differences from the R/S estimates are substantial; however, since there is still a controversy on the use of DFA for Hurst exponent estimation, and because the deterministic dynamics is not confirmed by the Support Vector prediction results, we opt to provide the R/S estimates of Hurst exponent as the main result of the present work. In addition, Ether intraday volatility time series and transaction count time series to a lesser extent indicate anti-persistent dynamics and can be estimated to a significant degree of 58–63% of trend prediction accuracy based on the particular method. Future work may provide more efficient implementation of the machine learning techniques; however, the present results are in reasonable accord with the dynamical regime classified by the Hurst exponent.

Using the methods described in the previous section, we have estimated the r-distributions of logarithmic profit rate from triangular arbitrage transactions for all 15 currency pairs with results shown in Table 1. Sample distribution for the most volatile currency pair is also provided in Fig. 4. All analysis was performed in R (R Core Team 2018). The results provide insight into the validity of the Efficient Market Hypothesis and the mechanism of establishing the long-term balance relation between the Ether-based exchange rates and the foreign exchange rates. For the currency of Ether, such

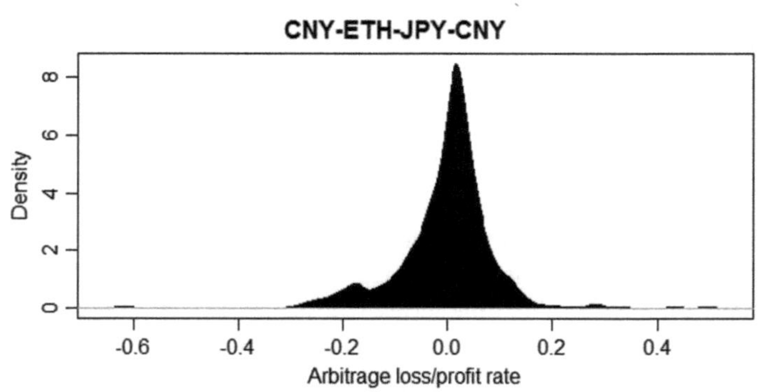

Fig. 4 Distribution of triangular transaction loss/profit rates r for JPYCNY (daily data basis)

results have not been obtained yet. The Ether-related literature is relatively scarce, most of it dating up to less than 2 years ago. For instance, the altcoin markets have been studied in the short-term and long-term run by Ciaian et al. (2018); the relation of cryptocurrencies to other financial assets has been examined by Corbet et al. (2018). Extreme value theory was applied to cryptocurrencies including Ether by Gkillas and Katsiampa (2018) who ranked Ether in the middle of the risk-ranking list of 5 digital currencies. Phillip et al. (2018) found that "being easier to transact, Ethereum has a smaller kurtosis than Bitcoin".

Our results in Table 2 show that ETH in the past 2 years exhibits substantial variation among exchange rates to the 6 fiat currencies considered in this work. On one hand, the relation of the USD and EUR exchanges is quite efficient, with the mean and median of the r-distribution close to 0, and standard deviation of only 1.0%. On the other side of the scale there are currency pairs that involve CNY with standard deviation ranging between 6 and 9%. This is more than what is found for Bitcoin-mediated exchange rates. The r-distributions show considerable skews and kurtosis corresponding to side peaks of far-from-equilibrium events. The cointegration estimates are also the closest to the efficient market hypothesis for the case of USDEUR currency pair.

6 Conclusion

The standard R/S estimate of the Hurst exponent for the Ether time series is relatively close to the value of 0.5 within the entire period studied (2015–2018) thus supporting the martingale behavior of the pricing process, market efficiency, and resulting in a very limited applicability of machine learning methods, including the support vector based algorithms, for trend and future value prediction. De-trended fluctuation analysis-based estimates of Hurst exponent would result in anti-persistent dynamics for the first half of the time period studied, inverting then to the persistent dynamics in the latter half. The differences from the R/S estimates are substantial; however, since there is still a controversy on the use of DFA for Hurst exponent estimation, and because the deterministic dynamics is not confirmed by the Support Vector prediction results, we opt to provide the R/S estimates of Hurst exponent as one of the main results of the present work. In addition, Ether intraday volatility time series and transaction count time series to a lesser extent indicate anti-persistent dynamics and can be estimated to a significant degree of 58–63% of trend prediction accuracy based on the method. Future work may provide more efficient implementation of the machine learning techniques; however, the present results are in reasonable accord with the dynamical regime classified by the Hurst exponent.

We have also provided a novel view on the efficiency of the Ether exchanges to several fiat currencies. It was found that whereas the USDEUR pair is close to the efficient market hypothesis with a fast adjustment mechanism for deviations from the equilibrium, other currency pairs involving CNY are integrated to a lesser degree. The cointegration results improve for more recent subsets of the time series, showing

Table 2 Triangular arbitrage distribution parameters and estimated cointegration coefficients

FX Pair	Min	Max	Mean	Median	St. Dev.	Skewness	Kurtosis	Beta	Beta1	Gamma	Gamma1
USDJPY	−0.1855	0.1860	0.0107	0.0041	0.0336	0.9386	10.1467	−1.1542	−1.0000	−0.5695	−0.4871
USDGBP	−0.3569	0.2385	−0.0042	0.0019	0.0500	−1.9230	14.3632	−0.9460	−1.0000	−0.4706	−0.4636
USDEUR	−0.0707	0.0296	−0.0021	−0.0015	0.0101	−1.6757	12.2852	−0.9514	−1.0000	−0.2812	−0.2245
USDCNY	−0.5687	0.4930	0.0083	0.0118	0.0833	0.0627	11.5142	−0.2666	−1.0000	−0.3582	−0.3247
USDCAD	−0.0642	0.1460	0.0213	0.0178	0.0296	0.3578	3.9774	−1.2104	−1.0000	−0.2483	−0.1508
JPYGBP	−0.3785	0.2246	−0.0149	−0.0023	0.0586	−1.5855	9.8495	−0.8943	−1.0000	−0.5150	−0.4668
JPYEUR	−0.2001	0.1845	−0.0124	−0.0041	0.0349	−1.2460	10.6874	−0.7811	−1.0000	−0.5548	−0.4322
JPYCNY	−0.6180	0.4952	−0.0024	0.0099	0.0904	−0.4579	10.1356	−0.1633	−1.0000	−0.3513	−0.3308
JPYCAD	−0.1844	0.1932	0.0107	0.0128	0.0460	−0.3129	4.6073	−1.0680	−1.0000	−0.3360	−0.3120
GBPEUR	−0.2351	0.3824	0.0024	−0.0052	0.0486	2.2276	16.6215	−0.7722	−1.0000	−0.4825	−0.4721
GBPCNY	−0.6671	0.5320	0.0125	0.0108	0.0965	0.3528	12.4333	−1.2551	−1.0000	−0.3927	−0.3832
GBPCAD	−0.2281	0.3870	0.0256	0.0251	0.0550	1.0065	9.4868	−0.6699	−1.0000	−0.4824	−0.3482
EURCNY	−0.5745	0.4991	0.0101	0.0133	0.0828	0.0666	11.9889	−1.9861	−1.0000	−0.3605	−0.3244
EURCAD	−0.0757	0.1503	0.0231	0.0195	0.0301	0.6384	4.1938	−1.0670	−1.0000	−0.2236	−0.1304
CNYCAD	−0.4473	0.5265	0.0131	0.0103	0.0857	−0.3812	9.0186	−0.3169	−1.0000	−0.3376	−0.3089

that a gradual transition to a higher degree of market efficiency occurs recently in the Ether market. The two methods examined in this work provide similar results; the adjustment coefficient is consistently somewhat smaller in magnitude when the error correction term is represented as the difference of the ether-based exchange rate from the foreign exchange rate by fixing $\beta = -1$. Comparison of the ratios between the two exchange rates, i.e. deviations of exp(r) from 1, indicate that the Ether market efficiency increases in time, despite the recent bubble burst in all cryptocurrency markets.

Acknowledgements This research was supported by JSPS Grants-in-Aid Nos. 2538404, 2628089, 19K01738, 20K01752 and NOMURA Fundation.

References

Alabi, K. (2017). Digital blockchain networks appear to be following Metcalfe's Law. *Electronic Commerce Research and Applications, 24,* 23–29.

Bariviera, A. F., Basgall, M. J., Hasperue, W., & Naiouf, M. (2017). Some stylized facts of the bitcoin market. *Physica A, 484,* 82–90.

Bryce, R. M., & Sprague, K. B. (2012). Revisiting detrended fluctuation analysis. *Scientific Reports, 2*(315).

Ciaian, P., Rajcaniova, M., & Kancs, d'A. (2018). Virtual relationships: Short- and long-run evidence from BitCoin and altcoin markets. *Journal of International Financial Markets, Institutions and Money, 52*, 173–195.

Coinmarketcap. (2020). Cryptocurrency Market Capitalizations. https://coinmarketcap.com/. Accessed 16 January 2020.

Corbet, S., Meegan, A., Larkin, C., Lucey, B., & Yarovaya, L. (2018). Exploring the dynamic relationships between cryptocurrencies and other financial assets. *Economics Letters, 165,* 28–34.

Engle, R. F., & Granger, C. W. (1987). Co-integration and error correction: representation, estimation, and testing. *Econometrica. Journal of the Econometric Society*, 251–276.

Fama, E. F. (1970). Efficient capital markets: A review of theory and empirical work. *The Journal of Finance, 25,* 383–417.

Fama, E. F. (1991). Efficient capital markets: II. *The Journal of Finance, 46,* 1575–1617.

Gkillas, K., & Katsiampa, P. (2018). An application of extreme value theory to cryptocurrencies. *Economics Letters, 164,* 109–111.

Hayes, A. S. (2017). Cryptocurrency value formation: An empirical study leading to a cost of production model for valuing bitcoin. *Telematics and Informatics, 34*(7), 1308–1321.

Huckle, S., Bhattacharya, R., White, M., & Beloff, N. (2016). Internet of things, blockchain and shared economy applications. *Procedia Computer Science, 98,* 461–466.

Hurst, H. E. (1951). Long-term storage capacity of reservoirs. *Transactions of the American Society of Civil Engineers, 116,* 770–808.

Johansen, S., & Juselius, K. (1990). Maximum likelihood estimation and inferences on cointegration with applications to the demand for money. *Oxford Bulletin of Economics and Statistics, 52,* 169–210.

Johansen, S. (1998). Statistical analysis of cointegration vectors. *Journal of Economic Dynamics and Control, 12,* 231–254.

Karatzoglou, A., Smola, A., Hornik, K., & Zeileis, A. (2004). Kernlab—An S4 package for kernel methods in {R}. *Journal of Statistical Software, 11*(9), 1–20.

Peng, C.-K., Havlin, S., Stanley, H. E., & Goldberger, A. L. (1995). Quantification of scaling exponents and crossover phenomena in nonstationary heart-beat time series. *Chaos: An Interdisciplinary Journal of Nonlinear Science, 5*(1), 82–87.

Phillip, A., Chan, J. S. K., & Peiris, S. (2018). A new look at cryptocurrencies. *Economics Letters, 163,* 6–9.

R Core Team. (2018). R: A language and environment for statistical computing. In R Foundation for Statistical Computing, Vienna, Austria. URL https://www.R-project.org/.

Vapnik, V. (2000). The Nature of Statistical Learning Theory. Berlin: Springer.

Estimating the Proportion of Informed Traders in BTC-USD Market Using Spread and Range

Ping Chen Tsai and Shou Huang Dai

Abstract The proportion of informed traders in financial markets is seen as a measure for the degree of information asymmetry and has been used to explain the existence of Bid-Ask spread. We identify a proxy—a spread-to-range ratio—for the unobserved proportion of informed traders in a market from the classic Glosten-Milgrom (1985) model. It can be shown that this ratio is the minimum of the proportion of informed traders, and the respective dynamics of spread and range motivate the conditional modelling of the ratio. Empirical results are given for the BTC-USD data over an 1186-day period, which indicate that the estimated proportion of informed traders can be as high as 6% in the cryptocurrency market.

Keywords Bid-Ask spread · Information asymmetry · Informed trading · Range

1 Introduction

Over the past few years, crypto-currencies have arisen as a popular investment tool and the focus of research as well. Conventional theory and methods for financial assets have been studied to see if they also hold for the cryptocurrency market[1]. In this study the focus is on the degree of information asymmetry as captured by the proportion of informed traders in cryptocurrency market. Specifically, we work under the classic Glosten-Milgrom (1985) framework and consider the estimation of the proportion of informed traders for Bitcoin.

[1] For example, Momtaz (2019) evaluates the pricing and performance of cryptocurrency market, and Tiwari et al. (2019) compare GARCH and Stochastic Volatility model for the dynamics of Bitcoin and Litecoin.

P. C. Tsai (✉)
Department of Finance, Southern Taiwan University of Science and Technology, No. 1, Nan-Tai Street, 71005 Yungkang District, Tainan City, Taiwan
e-mail: vincenttsai@stust.edu.tw

S. H. Dai
Center for General Education, Southern Taiwan University of Science and Technology, No. 1, Nan-Tai Street, 71005 Yungkang District, Tainan City, Taiwan
e-mail: shdai@stust.edu.tw

L. Pichl et al. (eds.), *Advanced Studies of Financial Technologies and Cryptocurrency Markets*, https://doi.org/10.1007/978-981-15-4498-9_11

The Glosten-Milgrom (1985) model explains the existence of Bid-Ask spread by assuming that there are two types of traders in a market: the informed and uninformed or liquidity traders. The assumptions made in this model are pragmatic: there is one asset traded in the economy, whose value can only go up to a high level $\overline{V}$ with some probability π or down to a low level $\underline{V}$ with probability $(1 - \pi)$. Under these assumptions and a no-arbitrage condition for market makers, the Glosten-Milgrom (1985) model derives simple solutions to the Bid and Ask price for the asset. In this chapter, we first show that the Bid-Ask spread can be obtained as a linear function of price range $\left(\overline{V} - \underline{V}\right)$. The ratio of spread-to-range is then considered a proxy for the unobserved proportion of informed traders. This is one of the contributions made by this chapter to the existing literature.

A conditional modelling approach for the dynamics of the spread-to-range ratio is done following Chou (2005) and Brandt and Jones (2006). Specifically, Chou (2005) gives the conditional autoregressive range (CARR) model and Brandt and Jones (2006) estimate an EGARCH model for log-range data. We adapt the CARR model for the spread-to-range ratio with an exponential and a Weibull distribution. We also specify a conditional autoregressive model for the log-ratio (CARLR). The modelling of log-ratio is also supported by the empirical properties of spread and range data, which has close-to-normal distributions after a log-transformation.

Our empirical results are obtained for BTC-USD price data over the sample period Sept 01, 2016–Nov 30, 2019, a total of 1186 trading days. We choose this sample period as BTC-USD saw a dramatic change in its price level. Estimation results suggest that a CARR(1, 1) model with Weibull distribution significantly outperforms its counterpart with exponential distribution. On the other hand, the CARLR model fits the log-ratio data very well as is evidenced by the small values of standard errors of the model parameters. We also consider a CARLR(2, 2) model versus CARLR(1, 1) model; the former can further capture the strong self-dependence in the log-ratio with two extra parameters. We plot the estimated spread-to-range ratio as proxy of proportion of informed traders in BTC-USD market. Over the sample period, the ratio can be as high as 6% in the beginning of sample period but remains at less than 1% afterwards. This result suggests to model the proportion of informed traders with an alternative two-state approach.

The chapter is organized as follows. In Sect. 2 we review the Glosten-Milgrom model and derive the linear relationship between Bid-Ask spread and price range $\left(\overline{V} - \underline{V}\right)$. We then consider the CARR model of Chou (2005) for the spread-to-range ratio. In Sect. 3 we provide summary statistics of BTC-USD spread and range data. Section 4 gives the estimation results, and the CARLR model for log-ratio. Section 5 concludes.

2 Model Specification

We begin with the classic Glosten-Milgrom (1985) model for the Bid and Ask prices of a single asset in an economy with informed and uninformed traders:

$$Bid = \frac{\pi(1-\mu)\overline{V} + (1-\pi)(1+\mu)\underline{V}}{1-(2\pi-1)\mu}$$

$$Ask = \frac{\pi(1+\mu)\overline{V} + (1-\pi)(1-\mu)\underline{V}}{1+(2\pi-1)\mu}$$

where π is the probability that the asset's price will increase to a higher level $\overline{V}$, and $(1-\pi)$ is the probability that it declines to $\underline{V}$. A detailed derivation of the Bid and Ask formula is given in Koch (2007). The proportion of informed traders in the market is given by μ, and the rest $(1-\mu)$ is the proportion of uninformed traders. By definition, the condition must hold $\mu \ll 1-\mu$ which implies $\mu \ll 0.5$.

The spread $S = Ask - Bid$ of Glosten-Milgrom (1985) del can be shown to have a linear relationship with the range of asset price $\left(\overline{V} - \underline{V}\right)$. First, when holding μ constant, we have the following conditions:

$$\begin{cases} \pi = 0 \\ \pi = 0.5 \\ \pi = 1 \end{cases} \Rightarrow \begin{cases} S = 0 \\ S = \mu\left(\overline{V} - \underline{V}\right) \\ S = 0 \end{cases}$$

When $\pi = 0.5$, the result $S = \mu\left(\overline{V} - \underline{V}\right)$ has an intuitive interpretation. From the market maker's perspective, the expected loss in dealing with an informed trader is:

$$\mu\left(\frac{\overline{V} + \underline{V}}{2} - \overline{V}\right) + \mu\left(-\frac{\overline{V} + \underline{V}}{2} + \underline{V}\right) = \mu\left(\underline{V} - \overline{V}\right)$$

where $\frac{\overline{V}+\underline{V}}{2}$ is the equilibrium price. To breakeven, the market maker needs to set a Bid-Ask spread with 100% probability to offset the expected loss from trading with an informed trader. Hence we have $S = \mu\left(\overline{V} - \underline{V}\right)$. This process may also be seen as a hedging activity by the market maker.

For other values of π, it can be assumed that S is a function of π which must satisfy the above conditions. One can consider a linear approximation:

$$\begin{cases} S = 2\mu\left(\overline{V} - \underline{V}\right)\pi, & for\, \pi \le 0.5 \\ S = 2\mu\left(\overline{V} - \underline{V}\right)(1-\pi), & for\, \pi > 0.5 \end{cases}$$

Alternatively, it is sensible to take $\mu\left(\overline{V} - \underline{V}\right)$ as the maximum of S at $\pi = 0.5$; consequently the spread S as a function of π is of the form:

$$S = S(\pi) = 2\mu\left(\overline{V} - \underline{V}\right)\left(\pi - \pi^2\right) \tag{1}$$

Thus, the Bid-Ask spread S in Glosten-Milgrom model is proportional to the range of asset price $\left(\overline{V} - \underline{V}\right)$. The function in (1) is consistent with the well-known facts in the literature: spread should increase with the degree of asymmetric information as captured by the proportion of informed traders μ, and it also increases with the range of price $(\overline{V} - \underline{V})$ which is a proxy of volatility.

A parallel analysis can be done by holding the probability π constant; the spread is then a function of μ:

$$\begin{cases} \mu = 0 \\ \mu = 0.5 \\ \mu = 1 \end{cases} \Rightarrow \begin{cases} S = 0 \\ S = c_1(\overline{V} - \underline{V}) \\ S = (\overline{V} - \underline{V}) \end{cases}$$

where

$$0 < c_1 = \frac{8\pi^2 - 8\pi}{(2\pi + 1)(2\pi - 3)} \leq 0.5$$

As mentioned earlier, the proportion μ should be less than 50%, and thus the case $\mu = 1$ is only theoretically plausible. The spread S again has a linear relationship with the price range $(\overline{V} - \underline{V})$. This linear result also holds when the Glosten-Milgrom model is extended to have a speculator as in Tsai and Tsai (2018)[2].

In the literature, there have been many studies on the relationship between spread and daily price range. For example, Corwin and Schultz (2012) and Abdi and Ranaldo (2017) propose to estimate spread using daily price range. In this study we utilize the proportionality between spread and price range and consider the conditional autoregressive range (CARR) model of Chou (2005):

$$\begin{aligned} R_t &= \lambda_t \epsilon_t, \ \epsilon_t | I_{t-1} \sim f\left(1, \sigma_\epsilon^2\right) \\ \lambda_t &= \omega + \alpha R_{t-1} + \beta \lambda_{t-1} \end{aligned} \tag{2}$$

where R_t is the range of day t, λ_t is the conditional mean of R_t given information up to day t and $\epsilon_t > 0$ has a distribution $f(\cdot)$ with unit mean. The parameters ω, α and β are all positive. Common choices for ϵ_t include Exponential distribution and Weibull distribution. A stationary condition on λ_t is $(\alpha + \beta) < 1$, which is obtained in the vein of GARCH-type models. In Chou (2005), it is mentioned that some exogenous variables can be added to the equation of λ_t:

$$\lambda_t = \omega + \alpha R_{t-1} + \beta \lambda_{t-1} + \gamma X_{t-1}$$

In particular, the exogenous variables X_{t-1} can be the trading volume on day $(t - 1)$. However, this will not be considered in the following analysis, but will left in future research.

[2]It can be shown that when $\pi = 0.5$, $S = [\mu_i + (2p - 1)\mu_s](\overline{V} - \underline{V})$, where μ_i is the proportion of informed traders, μ_s is the proportion of speculators and p is the probability of speculators in making a correct investment decision.

From the analysis on Glosten-Milgrom model, we confirm the linear relationship between spread and price range. Therefore, if price range can be described by the CARR model of Chou (2005), spread should evolve with a similar dynamics. One can then specify a model for daily spread S_t, whose conditional mean has a recursive form as in (2). In this study, however, the interest is on the proportion of informed traders μ, which from the above analysis on Glosten-Milgrom model is related to the ratio of spread-to-range:

$$\mu_t \propto Q_t = \frac{S_t}{\left(\overline{V_t} - \underline{V_t}\right)}$$

In this study, we will assume the spread-to-range ratio Q_t is a proxy of μ_t, and consider:

$$Q_t = m_t u_t, \; u_t | I_{t-1} \sim g\left(1, \sigma_u^2\right)$$
$$m_t = \omega + \alpha Q_{t-1} + \beta m_{t-1}$$

Here we maintain the same notation for parameters ω, α and β. The ratio Q_t can be seen as the lower bound of μ_t, since μ_t has an inverse relationship with the quadratic function $\left(\pi - \pi^2\right)$ in (1). Thus, μ_t has minimum Q_t when $\pi = 0.5$. The ratio Q_t is by construction a small value, which is consistent with the natural property of $\mu_t \ll 0.5$.

3 Data

Our data in this study is the traded price, spread and range of Bitcoin (BTC-USD), downloaded from the exchange Bitfinex and Yahoo Finance. The sample period is from Sept 01, 2016 to Nov 30, 2019, a total of 1186 trading days. We choose this period to avoid some data inconsistency between the two data sources. The spread data provided by Bitfinex is given as the ratio:

$$\frac{Ask - Bid}{Ask}$$

Thus, the spread used in our analysis is obtained by multiplying the above ratio by the traded price also provided by Bitfinex. The effect of this adjustment is an under-estimation of Q_t, or the proportion of informed traders. On the other hand, daily range of BTC-USD is given by the daily High and Low prices from Yahoo Finance. We provide the time-series plots of BTC-USD traded price, spread and range in Figs. 1, 2 and 3. It can be seen that the price level of BTC-USD has experienced a dramatic change over the sample period. The spread and range display a pattern which corresponds to the price level. In particular, the range can be seen as a proxy for volatility.

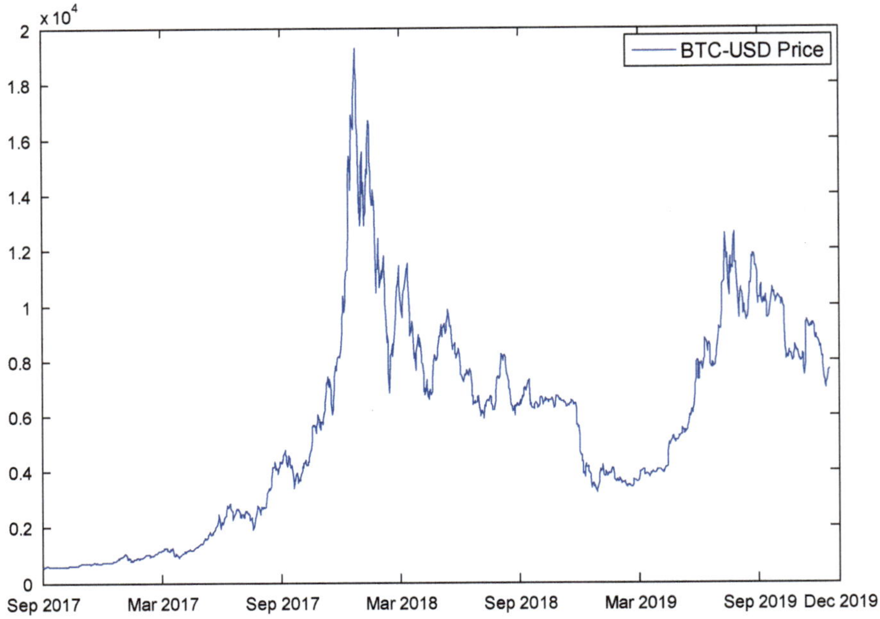

Fig. 1 BTC-USD traded price, Sept 01, 2016–Nov 30, 2019

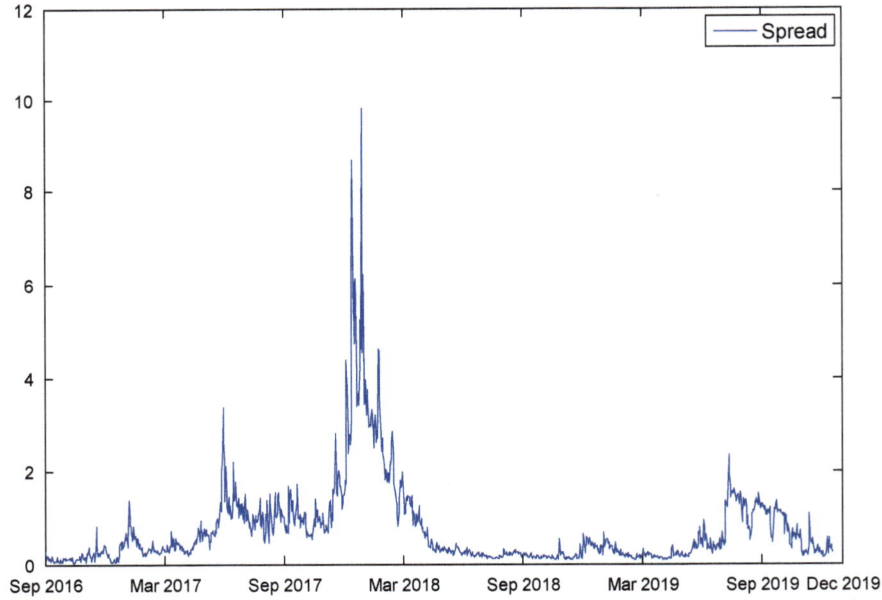

Fig. 2 BTC-USD price spread, Sept 01, 2016–Nov 30, 2019

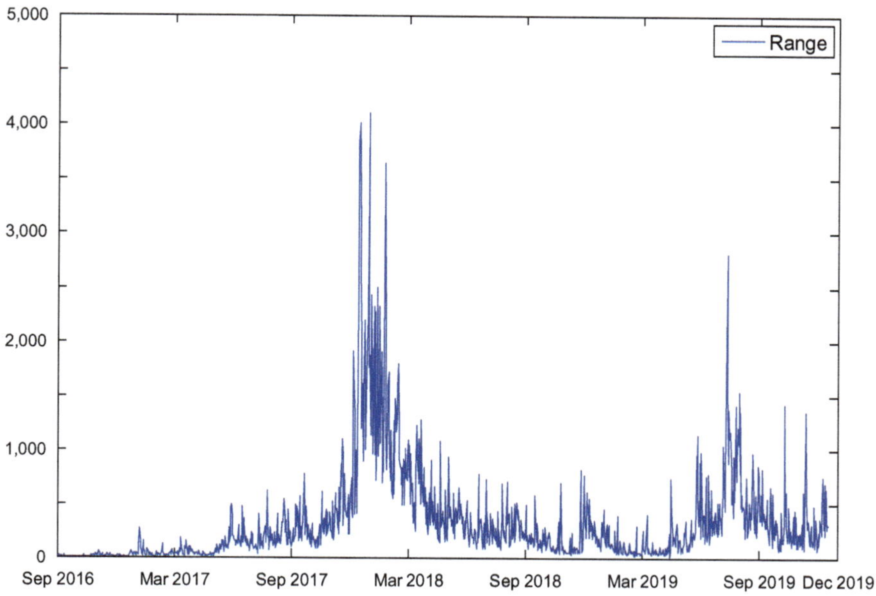

Fig. 3 BTC-USD range, Sept 01, 2016–Nov 30, 2019

Summary statistics of BTC-USD are given in Table 1. The distributions of spread and range are all skewed to the right, with skewness value being larger than 3. Consequently, the Jarque-Bera test rejects a normal distribution at very small p value. On the other hand, the two quantities display strong persistence, as can be seen by the reported auto-correlation function (ACF) up to lag 5. Specifically, the spread of BTC-USD shows a higher degree of persistence than the range, which can also be observed by comparing Fig. 2 with Fig. 3.

In the right panel of Table 1, we report the summary statistics of ln(spread) and ln(range) of BTC-USD. The log-transformation helps to make the distributions close to Gaussian, as indicated by the values of skewness and kurtosis, which are close to zero and three respectively. Nevertheless, the Jarque-Bera test still rejects a Gaussian distribution for the two quantities at small p value, but the test statistics has decreased significantly. The log-transformation also makes the ACF higher. This result is consistent with the vast literature on log-volatility models; in particular, Brandt and Jones (2006) consider an EGARCH model for log-range data. This approach will also be followed in the subsequent analysis on the spread-to-range ratio Q_t in Sect. 4.2.

Table 1 Summary statistics of BTC-USD data, Sept 01, 2016–Nov 30, 2019

	Spread	Range	ln(Spread)	ln(Range)
Mean	0.745	332.894	– 0.786	4.992
Median	0.410	191.060	– 0.892	5.253
Maximum	9.840	4110.400	2.287	8.321
Minimum	0.030	1.590	– 3.507	0.464
Standard deviation	0.914	458.70	0.968	1.480
Skewness	3.617	3.475	0.308	– 0.686
Kurtosis	23.187	20.256	2.485	3.245
Jarque-Bera	2272.4	1710.2	31.825	95.903
Probability	<0.001	<0.001	<0.001	<0.001
ACF(1)	0.923	0.783	0.955	0.882
ACF(2)	0.897	0.715	0.930	0.856
ACF(3)	0.860	0.687	0.919	0.856
ACF(4)	0.845	0.655	0.912	0.855
ACF(5)	0.831	0.647	0.904	0.841
Ljung-Box (20)	1492.9	955.1	1738.3	1561.4

4 Results

4.1 Estimation of CARR Model

In this subsection we provide the estimation results of the CARR model of Chou (2005) for the spread-to-range ratio Q_t as a proxy for the proportion of informed traders in the market. Given the daily values of Q_t, the parameters of CARR model can be obtained by maximizing the log-likelihood function:

$$L(\boldsymbol{\theta}|Q_1, Q_2, \ldots, Q_T) = -\sum_{t=1}^{T}\left[\ln(m_t) + \frac{Q_t}{m_t}\right]$$

where $\boldsymbol{\theta} = \{\omega, \alpha, \beta\}$ and the residual term $u_t|I_{t-1} \sim g$ is assumed to have an exponential density with unit mean. More generally, the distribution $g(\cdot)$ can be assumed to be a Weibull distribution with parameter $\psi > 0$:

$$g(Q_t|m_t) = \left(\frac{\psi}{Q_t}\right)\left(\frac{Q_t\Gamma(1+\psi^{-1})}{m_t}\right)^{\psi} \exp\left(-\left(\frac{Q_t\Gamma(1+\psi^{-1})}{m_t}\right)^{\psi}\right),$$

where $\Gamma(\cdot)$ is the gamma function with $\Gamma(1) = 1$ and $\Gamma(n) = (n-1)!$ for $n \in \mathbb{P}$. When the parameter $\psi = 1$, the Weibull density reduces to the exponential density.

The log-likelihood function for the Weibull distribution is:

$$L(\boldsymbol{\theta}|Q_1, Q_2, \ldots, Q_T) = \sum_{t=1}^{T}\left[\ln\left(\frac{\psi}{Q_t}\right) + \psi \ln\left(\frac{Q_t\,\Gamma(1+\psi^{-1})}{m_t}\right) - \left(\frac{Q_t\,\Gamma(1+\psi^{-1})}{m_t}\right)^{\psi}\right],$$

with $\boldsymbol{\theta} = \{\omega, \alpha, \beta, \psi\}$. The two models are called ECARR and WCARR model in Chou (2005).

In Table 2, we report the estimation results of ECARR(1, 1) and WCARR(1, 1) model. The parameter ω is estimated at 0.0017% and 0.0003% respectively; both models obtain α around 0.22 and β around 0.77. These values are consistent with the very high ACF values in Table 1. Note that in WCARR(1, 1) model, $(\alpha + \beta) = 1$, which corresponds to an Integrated-GARCH situation. The ψ parameter of Weibull distribution is estimated at 1.7683 with standard error 0.1566, indicating that $\psi = 1$ can be soundly rejected. The increase in log-likelihood value of WCARR model relative to that of ECARR model confirms the significance of ψ. A likelihood ratio (LR) test is obtained with very small p value.

In Fig. 4, we plot the estimated conditional spread-to-range ratio, m_t, from WCARR(1, 1) model (blue circle) over our sample period. It can be seen that the estimated m_t displays some variation in the first year of sample period, and can be as high as 6%. After Sept 2017, however, the conditional spread-to-range ratio remains at a very low level, mostly less than 1%, despite the BTC-USD price, spread and range all experience large fluctuations after Sept 2017. The plot of m_t therefore suggests a change in state from a high m_t state to a low m_t state during the sample period.

Table 2 Estimation of ECARR and WCARR model

	ECARR(1, 1)	WCARR(1, 1)
ω	0.0017%	0.0003%
	(0.0020%)	(0.0232%)
α	0.2166	0.2230
	(0.0474)	(0.1565)
β	0.7805	0.7770
	(0.0465)	(0.0313)
ψ		1.7683
		(0.1566)
Log-likelihood	5487.09	5776.37
Likelihood ratio test		578.56
Probability		<0.001

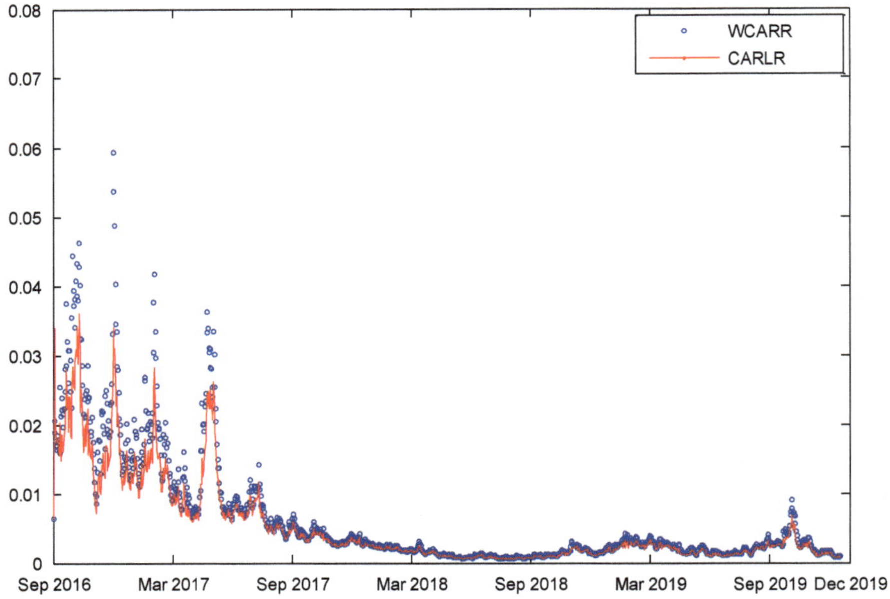

Fig. 4 Conditional spread-to-range ratio as proportion of informed traders, WCARR and CARLR model

4.2 Estimation of Conditional Log-Ratio Model

The CARR model of Chou (2005) is designed for modelling the daily range of stock price data, which is assumed to follow an exponential or a Weibull distribution. The spread-to-range ratio Q_t, which is assumed to be a proxy for the proportion of informed traders in this study, however, may not share this distributional property. An alternative approach is provided by Brandt and Jones (2006), who consider an EGARCH model for the log-range data. This is also considered for Q_t as follows:

$$\ln(Q_t) = \ln(m_t) + z_t,\, z_t|I_{t-1} \sim N\left(0, \sigma_z^2\right),$$
$$\ln(m_t) = \omega' + \alpha' \ln(Q_{t-1}) + \beta' \ln(m_{t-1}).$$

In the first equation, we assume $\ln(Q_t)$ has an innovation z_t which is i.i.d. $N\left(0, \sigma_z^2\right)$. This assumption is motivated by the close-to-normal distributions of ln(Spread) and ln(Range) in Table 1. In the second equation, $\ln(m_t)$ has a recursive specification and the parameters are now denoted by ω', α' and β'. This model is called Conditional Autoregressive Log-Ratio (CARLR) model. It also has four parameters as in the WCARR(1, 1) model.

The estimation result of CARLR(1, 1) model is reported in Table 3. In general, the log-transformation improves the statistical properties of maximum log-likelihood estimation, as the parameters of CARLR(1, 1) all have smaller standard errors than

Table 3 Estimation of CARLR model

	CARLR(1, 1)	CARLR(2, 2)
ω'	– 0.0338	– 0.0407
	(0.0189)	(0.0220)
α_1'	0.1866	0.2090
	(0.0202)	(0.0296)
α_2'		0.0000*
		(0.0375)
β_1'	0.8079	0.5478
	(0.0211)	(0.0112)
β_2'		0.2367
		(0.0312)
σ_z	0.5498	0.2305
	(0.0109)	(1.0000)
Log-likelihood	116.53	121.21
Likelihood ratio test		9.36
Probability		<0.01

those of WCARR(1, 1) model. In particular, α_1' is estimated at 0.1866 and β_1' at 0.8079, which indicate a very persistent $\ln(m_t)$. To further explore the dependence of $\ln(m_t)$ on its past values, we also estimate a CARLR(2, 2) model. It can be seen that most parameters in this model are still significant (except for α_2' which is estimated at boundary); the parameter σ_z also decreases from 0.5498 to 0.2305. A likelihood ratio test has statistic 9.36, which is significant with p value smaller than 1%. In Fig. 4, we plot the estimated conditional spread-to-range ratio as the red dashed line from CARLR(2, 2) model. It can be seen that the red dashed line is mostly below the blue circle. The two-state phenomenon is still prominent across the sample period.

From the above analysis, we can describe and estimate the spread-to-range ratio as a proxy for the proportion of informed traders μ in the cryptocurrency market. To the best of our knowledge, this study is the first to consider the spread-to-range ratio and relate it to the proportion of informed traders. This result, however, is based on the assumption that there are only informed and uninformed traders in the market, and the single asset's value will either increase to $\overline{V}$ or decrease to $\underline{V}$. Also, as mentioned in Sect. 2, the spread-to-range ratio is the lower bound of μ. It is possible to give a non-parametric estimate of probability π of price increase using trade directions and trading volume, as in Lee and Ready (1991) and Ellis et al. (2000), to recover the full distribution of μ.

5 Conclusion

In this chapter, we are interested in estimating the proportion of informed traders in the BTC-USD market. The informed traders are not directly observable and their proportion is obtained by a proxy which is the spread-to-range ratio under the framework of Glosten-Milgrom (1985) model. The spread-to-range ratio has an intuitive interpretation from a market maker's perspective when the asset's value is equally likely to increase and decrease, and the ratio is shown to be the lower bound of its target the proportion of informed traders in the market. We estimate the temporal dynamics of spread-to-range ratio using the CARR model of Chou (2005) and the approach in Brandt and Jones (2006). The modelling approach is very general and can be applied to other financial assets/markets.

Our empirical results suggest that the proportion of informed traders in BTC-USD market changes over time, and can be as high as 6% in the first year of our sample period. It then subsequently remains at less than 1% for the rest of the period. This result is robust for both modelling approach. Informed trading can have an important effect on a firm's cost of capital (Easley and O'Hara 2004; Brennan et al. 2015). Our study can be related to the work of Zhang et al. (2008) which investigates the determinants of Bid and Ask prices. Moreover, our approach is a new attempt in the probability of informed-trading (PIN) literature, which originates from Easley (1996) and Easley et al. (2012). Finally, our empirical findings suggest a two-state phenomenon for the proportion of informed traders in BTC-USD market; this finding speaks to the hidden Markov model (HMM) approach of Yin and Zhao (2014) and can serve as an auxiliary method in the HMM approach for informed-trading.

Acknowledgements We thank the organizers and participants of the 23rd WEHIA conference in International Christian University, Tokyo, Japan.

Appendix

Figure 1 plots the daily price of BTC-USD over our sample period during Sept 01, 2016–Nov 30, 2019, a total of 1186 complete trading days. It can be seen that the BTC-USD price has seen a dramatic increase from below \$1000 up to more than \$18,000 in early 2018. The price then decreases to below \$10,000 for most of the time during 2018 and 2019.

Figure 2 plots the daily value of spread $(Ask - Bid)$ in BTC-USD price, given by the exchange Bitfinex. The spread was given as a ratio in Bitfinex:

$$\frac{Ask - Bid}{Ask}$$

We make a pragmatic adjustment and multiply this ratio by the traded BTC-USD price also given by Bitfinex to recover the spread as the difference $(Ask - Bid)$. This adjustment will cause a downward bias in the reported value of spread, and subsequently a downward bias in our estimate of the proportion of informed traders which is the spread-to-range ratio.

Figure 3 plots the daily value of BTC-USD price range over our sample period, which is represented by $(\overline{V} - \underline{V})$ in the Glosten-Milgrom model. The range data displays many large and sudden increases and is less persistent than the spread data. This property can be confirmed by the values of auto-correlation function (ACF) of spread and range in Table 1.

Figure 4 plots the estimated conditional spread-to-range ratio which is taken as the proxy for the proportion of informed traders in BTC-USD market. The conditional estimates are given by the Conditional Autoregressive Range model with Weibull (WCARR) distribution of Chou (2005), in blue circle, and by the Conditional Autoregressive Log-Ratio model (CARLR) adapted from Brandt and Jones (2006), in red dashed line. It can be seen that before Sept, 2017, the estimated proportion of informed traders are in general higher than the rest of sample period, and can be as high as 6% by the WCARR model. The CARLR model gives lower estimated values than WCARR model. After Sept 2017, both models give estimated proportion of informed traders below 1%.

Table 1 reports summary statistics of BTC-USD spread and range data over our sample period. Both spread and range data have positive skewness and high kurtosis; after a log-transformation, however, the distributions are close to normal, although a Jarque-Bera test still rejects normality. The spread and range of BTC-USD are also very persistent, with ACF value above 0.83 and 0.64 at lag 5. The log-transformation makes the ACF value even higher.

Table 2 reports the maximum log-likelihood estimation of CARR model for the spread-to-range ratio Q_t of BTC-USD price:

$$Q_t = m_t u_t,\, u_t | I_{t-1} \sim g\left(1, \sigma_u^2\right)$$
$$m_t = \omega + \alpha Q_{t-1} + \beta m_{t-1}$$

The model is termed ECARR and WCARR when the conditional distribution of u_t is an exponential or a Weibull distribution. The WCARR model reduces to ECARR if the parameter $\psi = 1$, in which case $\sigma_u = 1$. The estimation result suggests that $\psi = 1$ can be rejected by a t test or by a likelihood ratio test at very small p value. The estimated values of α and β are consistent with the high ACF values of spread and range in Table 1, with a measure of persistence $(\alpha + \beta)$ close to 1. The very small estimated value of ω with relatively large standard error is a challenge to the model estimation task.

Table 3 reports the maximum log-likelihood estimation of CARLR model for the log of spread-to-range ratio $\ln Q_t$ of BTC-USD price:

$$\ln(Q_t) = \ln(m_t) + z_t,\, z_t | I_{t-1} \sim N\left(0, \sigma_z^2\right),$$

$$\ln(m_t) = \omega' + \alpha' \ln(Q_{t-1}) + \beta' \ln(m_{t-1}).$$

The conditional distribution of $z_t = \ln(Q_t) - \ln(m_t)$ is assumed to be normal, which can be justified by the close-to-normal distributions of spread and range data in Table 1. The parameters of CARLR(1, 1) model can be estimated with small standard errors, indicating that the log-transformation help to improve the overall fit of the model. The sum $(\alpha_1' + \beta_1')$ is also very close to 1, whereas ω' can be estimated with significant value. We also estimate a CARLR(2, 2) model, which gives a smaller standard deviation of standardized error σ_z.

References

Abdi, F., & Ranaldo, A. (2017). A simple estimation of Bid-Ask spreads from daily close, high, and low prices. *The Review of Financial Studies, 30,* 4437–4480.

Brandt, M. W., & Jones, C. S. (2006). Volatility forecasting with range-based EGARCH models. *Journal of Business & Economic Statistics, 24,* 470–486.

Brennan, M. J., Huh, S.-W., & Subrahmanyam, A. (2015). Asymmetric effects of informed trading on the cost of equity capital. *Management Science, 62,* 2457–2764.

Chou, R. Y. (2005). Forecasting financial volatilities with extreme values: The conditional autoregressive range (CARR) model. *Journal of Money, Credit, and Banking, 37,* 561–582.

Corwin, S. A., & Schultz, P. (2012). A simple way to estimate bid-ask spreads from daily high and low prices. *The Journal of Finance, 67,* 719–759.

Easley, D., & O'Hara, M. (2004). Information and the cost of capital. *The Journal of Finance, 59,* 1553–1583.

Easley, D., Kiefer, N. M., O'Hara, M., & Paperman, J. B. (1996). Liquidity, information, and infrequently traded stocks. *The Journal of Finance, 51,* 1405–1436.

Easley, D., López de Prado, M. M., & O'Hara, M. (2012). Flow toxicity and liquidity in a high-frequency world. *The Review of Financial Studies, 25,* 1457–1493.

Ellis, K., Michaely, R., & O'Hara, M. (2000). The accuracy of trade classification rules: Evidence from NASDAQ. *Journal of Financial and Quantitative Analysis, 35,* 529–551.

Glosten, L. R., & Milgrom, M. R. (1985). Bid, Ask and Transaction Prices in a specialist market with heterogeneously informed traders. *Journal of Financial Economics, 14*, 71–100.

Koch, A. K. (2007). *Adverse selection in financial markets*. Royal Holloway, University of London.

Lee, C. M. C., & Ready, M. J. (1991). Inferring trade direction from intraday data. *The Journal of Finance, 46,* 733–746.

Momtaz, P. P. (2019). The pricing and performance of cryptocurrency. *The European Journal of Finance,* 1–14.

Tiwari, A. K., Kumar, S., & Pathak, R. (2019). Modelling the dynamics of Bitcoin and Litecoin: GARCH versus stochastic volatility models. *Applied Economics, 51* (37): 4073–4082.

Tsai, P. C., & Tsai , C. M. (2018). *Estimating the proportion of informed and speculative traders in financial markets: Evidence from CHF/EUR exchange rates*. Southern Taiwan University of Science and Technology working paper.

Yin, X., & Zhao, J. (2014). A hidden Markov model approach to information-based trading: Theory and applications. *Journal of Applied Econometrics, 30,* 1210–1234.

Zhang, M. Y., Russell, J. R., & Tsay, R. S. (2008). Determinants of Bid and Ask quotes and implications for the cost of trading. *Journal of Empirical Finance, 15,* 656–678.

Forecasting of Cryptocurrency Prices Using Machine Learning

Vasily Derbentsev, Andriy Matviychuk, and Vladimir N. Soloviev

Abstract Our study is devoted to the problems of the short-term forecasting cryptocurrency time series using machine learning (ML) approach. Focus on studying of the financial time series allows to analyze the methodological principles, including the advantages and disadvantages of using ML algorithms. The 90-day time horizon of the dynamics of the three most capitalized cryptocurrencies (Bitcoin, Ethereum, Ripple) was estimated using the Binary Autoregressive Tree model (BART), Neural Networks (multilayer perceptron, MLP) and an ensemble of Classification and Regression Trees models—Random Forest (RF). The advantange of the developed models is that their application does not impose rigid restrictions on the statistical properties of the studied cryptocurrencies time series, with only the past values of the target variable being used as predictors. Comparative analysis of the predictive ability of the constructed models showed that all the models adequately describe the dynamics of the cryptocurrencies with the mean absolute persentage error (MAPE) for the BART and MLP models averaging 3.5%, and for RF models within 5%. Since for trading perspective it is of interest to predict the direction of a change in price or trend, rather than its numerical value, the practical application of BART model was also demonstrated in the forecasting of the direction of change in price for a 90-day period. To this end, a model of binary classification was used in the methodology for assessing the degree of attractiveness of cryptocurrencies as an innovative financial instrument. Conducted computer simulations have confirmed the feasibility of using the machine learning methods and models for the short-term forecasting of financial time series. Constructed models and their ensembles can be the basis for the algorithms for automated trading systems for Internet trading.

V. Derbentsev · A. Matviychuk
Kyiv National Economic University named after Vadym Hetman, 54/1 Prospect Peremogy, Kyiv 03057, Ukraine
e-mail: derbv@kneu.edu.ua

A. Matviychuk
e-mail: editor@nfmte.com

V. N. Soloviev (✉)
Kryvyi Rih State Pedagogical University, 54 Gagarina Ave, Kryvyi Rih 50086, Ukraine
e-mail: vnsoloviev2016@gmail.com

L. Pichl et al. (eds.), *Advanced Studies of Financial Technologies and Cryptocurrency Markets*, https://doi.org/10.1007/978-981-15-4498-9_12

Keywords Binary autoregressive tree model · Cryptocurrency prices · Financial time series · Machine learning · Neural network · Regression and classification tree ensemble · Short-term forecasting

1 Introduction

Current stage of the global development has been characterized by the widespread Information Technology (IT) innovation in all spheres of human activity, especially in business and finance. Probably, today the question about the role and prospects of widespread implementation of the blockchain technology and the first cryptographic currency (cryptocurrency) Bitcoin, which was developed in 2009, is the most controversial.

This problem is the focus of debate among leading economists, politicians and businessmen, whose views are often diametrically opposite: from full support ("digital gold" of the twenty-first Century and the future of the world currency reserve (Popper 2015; Vigna and Casey 2015)), to complete negation ("financial bubble", the biggest financial shady transaction (Krugman 2013; CNBC 2018)).

This controversy is not least due to the significant fluctuations in the exchange rate of cryptocurrencies and legal uncertainty of the transactions with them in most countries of the world, which led to significant risks of investment in these assets.

In this regard, the problem of developing adequate cryptocurrency prices forecasting approach is relevant to the scientific community as well as to financial analysts, investors and traders.

In order to make investment decisions in the crypto market, it is necessary to have efficient tools of prices forecasting, profitability and risk assessment, at least for the shortterm time horizon.

Analysis of recent theoretical and empirical studies shows that the price dynamics of cryptocurrencies are influenced by many latent factors. These key factors (drivers) have not been well understood and identified yet (Selmi et al. 2018; Cheah 2015; Ciaian 2016; Catania and Grassi 2017). The vast majority of researchers are inclined to believe that the fundamental factors do not have a significant influence on the cryptocurrency rate. Instead their prices are determined by the demand-supply ratio.

In our recent studies, we used the methods of the complex systems theory and demonstrated the possibility of constructing indicators of critical and crash phenomena in the volatile stock and cryptocurrency markets (Derbentsev et al. 2019b; Soloviev and Belinskij 2016, 2019; Soloviev et al. 2019a, b, c; Belinskyi et al. 2019). Our results show that cryptocurrency time series are characterized by complex dynamics, extreme observations and a high degree of volatility. They are also non-stationary, fractal and have non-Gaussian distributions (Belinskyi et al. 2019). These results are consistent with several other empirical studies which applied the statistical approach (Catania and Grassi 2017).

Therefore, the application of traditional forecasting methods based on the use of casual models, built within a certain theoretical macroeconomic concept, or classical time series models has proven to be ineffective.

In the last two decades the methods and algorithms of machine learning have been applied to forecasting financial and economic time series (Flach 2012; Bontempi et al. 2013; Persio and Honchar 2018), and various automated trading systems—bots built on these algorithms—began to be used for trading.

The main purpose of our research is to compare the prognostic properties for the short-term prediction task of the cryptocurrency exchange rates of several ML methods: the BART algorithm (Derbentsev et al. 2019a), Artificial Neural Networks (ANN) and decision trees ensemble—RF.

The paper is structured as follows. Section 2 describes previous studies in these fields. Section 3 presents ML approach in the context of financial time series forecasting. In this section we described the main aspects of applying BART, ANN and RF to prediction of cryptocurrency prices.

Section 4 describes the datasets used to test and simulation the models. The empirical results are reported in Sect. 5. In this section we presented the results of the short-term predictions obtained with BART, ANN and RF models for the prices of the three most capitalized cryptocurrencies (Bitcoin (BTC), Ethereum (ETH) and Ripple (XRP)), and their price direction changes. And finally, we discuss results of our study in Sect. 6.

2 Analysis of Previous Studies

Recently non-parametric methods within the Machine Learning (ML) and Deep Learning (DL) paradigms have been widely used for predicting financial time series, in particular, cryptocurrency prices dynamics (Varghade and Patel 2012; Boyacioglu and Baykan 2011; Okasha 2014; Kumar 2006; Peng et al. 2018; McNally 2016).

In this area the primary focus has been on the use of such methods as ANNs of different types and architectures, and Support Vector Machines (SVM). The application of these methods has proven to be more efficient for the forecasting tasks for both "traditional" (fiat currency, stock indices, commodities prices, etc.) (Varghade and Patel 2012; Boyacioglu and Baykan 2011; Okasha 2014; Kumar 2006) and innovative financial assets, including cryptocurrencies (Peng et al. 2018; McNally 2016; Saxena and Sukumar 2018; Amjad and Shah 2016; Alessandretti et al. 2018).

Thus, examples of effective use of SVM in forecasting volatility of fiat- and cryptocurrencies are given, in particular, by Peng et al. (2018).

Several studies (McNally 2016; Saxena and Sukumar 2018; Amjad and Shah 2016) presented the results of BTC exchange rate prediction by using ARIMA models, RF, Logistic Regressions (LR), Linear Discriminant Analysis approach (LDA) and such ANN as Long Short-Term Memory (LSTM). According to obtained results, the ML models proved to be more accurate in prediction both cryptocurrency prices, and their volatility than times series models.

Rebane and Karlsson (2018) presented a comparative analysis of the prognostic properties of ARIMA with Recurrent Neural Networks (RNN) for such cryptocurrencies as Bitcoin, DASH, Ethereum, Litecoin (LTC), Siacoin (SC), Stellar (STR), NEM (XEM), Monero (XMR) and Ripple (XRP). Their results also revealed better predictive properties of ANN than ARIMA models.

Comparative performance of ML algorithms for forecasting cryptocurrency prices has reported in the paper of Hitam and Ismail (2018). They tested ANNs, SVM and Deep Learning (Boosted NN) for such coins as BTC, ETH, LTC, XEM, XRP and XLM. Their results show that SVM has the best predictive accuracy in the terms of the lowest value of Mean Percentage Error.

Yao et al. (2018) proposed to predict cryptocurrency price by using more a wider dataset, which includes not only prices, but also market cap, volume, circulating and maximum supply. Based on their results obtained on deep learning techniques (RNN and LSTM) the prediction accuracy was within 59% (when using only prices) and up to 75% (on an extended dataset).

Another powerful class of ML methods are the Classification and Regression Tree (C&RT) and their ensembles proposed by Leo Breiman and colleagues (Breiman et al. 1984; Breiman 2001). It should be noted that much less attention has been paid to these algorithms in the field of modelling and forecasting financial times series (see, for example (Varghade and Patel 2012; Kumar 2006)).

In our recent work (Derbentsev et al. 2019a), we proposed BART algorithm, which is a generalization of C&RT models for the case of scalar time series. The application of BART to cryptocurrency exchange rate prediction task demonstrated that is was more efficient than the ARIMA-ARFIMA time series models.

Nowadays combined classical econometric methods as well as methods of machine learning (Albuquerque et al. 2018; Wang et al. 2018) and those which take into consideration the spirit of social networks regarding the state and tendency of cryptocurrency dynamics (Kennis 2018) are becoming more popular.

Another important aspect in the forecasting dynamics of financial time series is prediction of the price changes direction. For this purpose Kumar (2006) tested such ML classification models as LDA, LR, ANN, RF and SVM. His empirical results suggests that the SVM and RF outperforms the other classification methods for the prediction direction of the stock market movement.

Akyildirim et al. (2018) investigated predictability of the 12 cryptocurrencies on the both daily and minute datasets by using the ML classification algorithms (SVM, LR, ANN and RF) with the past price information and technical indicators as model features. Their results showed that the direction of returns in the cryptocurrency market can be predicted with averages accuracy around 55–60% with the daily or minute observation.

In our previous works (Matviychuk 2006, 2011) we also solved the problem of prediction of the price changes direction of financial time series. To this end we applied the Fuzzy Logic tools were for formation of a knowledge base we used rules of wave development from technical analysis and Elliott wave theory. And also the task of pattern recognition in the structure of price curves and prediction of their further development we had dealt with usage of Counterpropagation Neural Networks.

3 Methodology

3.1 Machine Learning Approach of Forecasting Cryptocurrency Prices

The main difference between ML and classical modeling is that the Machine Learning algorithms interpret the data themselves, so there is no need to perform their initial decomposition. Depending on the purpose of the analysis, these algorithms "build" logic modeling based on the available data. This avoids the complex and lengthy pre-model stage of statistical testing of various hypotheses.

The main purpose of our study is to determine the ability of ML methods to effectively analyse the time series data of cryptocurrencies (both scalar and vector), and to identify the patterns and time correlations that form the basis for the qualitative forecasts.

An important characteristic of ML is that the methods used to search for templates in the data do not imply a priori data structure, their statistical properties and the type of relationships.

Within the ML paradigm, a number of powerful approaches, methods and algorithms have been developed, such as ANNs, SVM, C&RT, RF Regression and Classification ensembles, Gradient Boosting (GBoost), Deep Neural Networks and Deep Learning, Kernel methods, etc. (Flach 2012).

Among ML methods, neural networks of different architecture, particularly deep networks, have gained the most popularity. Numerous empirical studies have shown the effectiveness of the application of ANN to pattern recognition, image and voice analysis, machine translation, etc. They are increasingly being used to analyse and forecast financial time series, in particular cryptocurrency data.

Several studies (Boyacioglu and Baykan 2011; Hitam and Ismail 2018; Matviychuk 2011) showed that ANNs have better predictive properties than time series models and other ML algorithms for financial time series forecasting.

Another type of ML models is C&RT and their ensembles. Both ANN and C&RT approaches have their own advantages and disadvantages. Their common advantages are the following:

- they do not impose strict a priori assumptions about the input data;
- they have a high level of automation, because required mathematical tools are built into majority data mining software;
- they are able to process data both quantitative (metric) and qualitative (categorical).

The common disadvantages of both ANN and C&RT are the overfitting problem, and a large number of hyperparameters that require tuning. The overfitting leads to significantly increasing forecast errors on new data.

As for ANNs, they are "Black Box" model which are characterized by the "opacity" of the hypothesis function (a function that describes the relationship between input and output). So ANNs don't have enough explanatory power and they require significant training time. In addition, choosing a network architecture, the number of input neurons, hidden layers and activation functions is generally a non-trivial task.

The major weaknesses of the C&RT models are their lower accuracy compared to ANNs (for the regression problems) and the ambiguity of choosing the best final tree (for the prediction problem). But their advantage is visibility, perspicuity for visualization and interpretation.

However, complex tree branches are also difficult to interpret in a meaningful way, therefore, using them, we have to find a compromise between the complexity of the tree and its accuracy. This problem is inherent in the vast majority of ML algorithms.

The RF algorithm consists of constructing an ensemble of simple classifiers (trees) and obtaining an average estimate of the prediction of each of the trees that are built on different subsets of features and randomly selected training subsamples of data. This approach is less subject to overfitting, but is also poorly interpreted.

The input data for our analysis is a time series of values for a certain cryptocurrency of length T, which we denote by $Y = (Y_1, Y_2, \ldots, Y_T)$. We will use supervised learning, so training and test samples contain a set of examples. In our case this is one-step ahead forecast Y_t with known values of the target variable in p previous time periods $Y_{t-1}, Y_{t-1}, \ldots, Y_{t-p}$.

We state our hypothesis in the following form

$$\Pr(Y_t|Y_1, Y_2, \ldots, Y_{t-1}, \theta) = f\left(Y_t|Y_{t-p}, Y_{t-p+1}, \ldots, Y_{t-1}, \theta\right), \quad p < t \leq T, \tag{1}$$

where $f(\cdot|\cdot, \theta)$—is a family of conditional probability distributions, and θ—are unknown model parameters.

The hypothesis function can be represented as

$$\widehat{Y}_t = \hat{f}\left(Y_{t-p}, Y_{t-p+1}, \ldots, Y_{t-1}, \theta\right) + \varepsilon_t. \tag{2}$$

Thereby we used only past values of the target variable as factors (features).

We investigated three different type of ML algorithms to predict cryptocurrency time series (short-term forecast) and compare their predictive properties: the Binary Auto Regressive Tree, the Multilayer Perceptron, and the Random Forest tree ensemble models.

It should be mentioned that when we applying ML methods, it is necessary to solve the problem of Bias-Variance trade-off. This is the problem of simultaneously minimizing two sources of error that prevent supervised learning algorithms from generalizing beyond their training set:

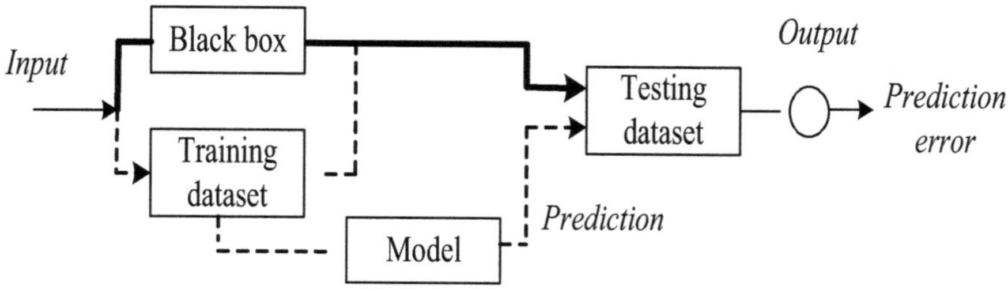

Fig. 1 Supervised machine learning prediction

- bias is error from erroneous assumptions in the learning algorithm, high bias can cause an algorithm to miss the relevant relations between features and target output (underfitting);
- variance is error from sensitivity to small fluctuations in the training set, high variance can cause overfitting, i.e., modelling the random noise in the training data, rather than the intended output.

Therefore, when adjusting the model parameters, we have to find a compromise between the forecast error caused by its bias and the unstable parameter values (high variance):

$$PE(Y_t) = \mathrm{E}\left[\left(Y_t - \hat{f}(Y_t)\right)^2\right] = \mathrm{Bias}^2\left(\hat{f}\right) + \mathrm{Var}\left(\hat{f}\right) + \sigma^2, \quad (3)$$

where $PE(Y_t)$—the total forecast error at time t; $\mathrm{E}(\cdot)$—mathematical expectation operator; $Y_t, \hat{f}(Y_t)$—the actual time series value and its predicted value; $\mathrm{Bias}(\cdot)$—the average bias across all datasets; $\mathrm{Var}(\cdot)$—error variance, which generally depends on the number of model parameters and their accuracy; σ^2—unavoidable error.

A general diagram of supervised ML prediction process is shown in Fig. 1.

3.2 *Binary Auto Regressive Tree (BART)*

Binary Auto Regressive Tree is a generalization of standard C&RT models, which is adapted to time series prediction tasks. BART combines the classic C&RT algorithm (Kumar 2006) and the ARIMA Box-Jenkins autoregressive models.

The target variable Y_t in this algorithm depends on p the previous values of the studied time series $Y_{t-1}, Y_{t-2}, \ldots, Y_{t-p}$. BART allows dividing the phase space into segments, with a subsequent development of a model for each, and a piecewise regression function presented in an intuitive and visual way. In such a tree, the inner nodes contain rules for splitting the space of explanatory variables; branches indicate conditions and transition between nodes; and the leaves are local ARIMA models.

When constructing BART a binary tree is constructed, therefore each node has two child nodes (i.e., number of branches is 2). An autoregressive tree is constructed sequentially (iteratively) and this process is described by the following algorithm (Derbentsev et al. 2019a; Breiman et al. 1984).

Step 1. The first step is to determine the threshold for splitting the initial (root) node, which is taken as the median *Me* (2-quantile $Q_{50\%}$) of the training series (sample) and is calculated by the formula

$$Me(Y) = Q_{50\%} = 0.5 \times \left(Y^{\min} + Y^{\max}\right), \tag{4}$$

The median of the time series is defined as the median of the distribution of the realization of a random variable at time t. For a stationary time series (or time series with a symmetric distribution), this value is independent of the observation time and then the sample median is equal to mean, i.e. $Me(Y) = \overline{Y}$.

Therefore, an autoregressive estimation of the tree at the first step of splitting will look like

$$f(Y_t) = Me(Y) I_R(Y_{t-1}), \tag{5}$$

where R is the dataset; $I_R(Y_{t-1})$—an indicator function of space, in fact it is a set of rules for getting variable Y_{t-1} into this space. So, in the first step, the dataset is divide into two subsets by criterion (5).

Step 2. The second step is to divide the data space in the selected node obtained in the first step into two parts. Some lag variable, for example, $Y_{t-k}, k \in (1, 2, \ldots, p)$ is selected and the left and right data subspaces R_{left}, R_{right} are defined:

$$R_{left} = \{Y_{t-k} \in R : Y_{t-k} \le \alpha\}, R_{right} = \{Y_{t-k} \in R : Y_{t-k} > \alpha\}, p < t \le T. \tag{6}$$

Then the regression estimation at the next step takes the form:

$$f(Y_t) = \left(\frac{1}{M} \sum_{I_1} Y_{t-k}^{(i)}\right) I_{R_{left}}(Y_{t-k}) + \left(\frac{1}{N} \sum_{I_2} Y_{t-k}^{(i)}\right) I_{R_{right}}(Y_{t-k}), \tag{7}$$

where $I_1 = \left\{i,\ Y_{t-k}^{(i)} \in R_{left}\right\}$, $I_2 = \left\{i,\ Y_{t-k}^{(i)} \in R_{right}\right\}$—sets of observation indices (i) falling into the subspaces R_{left} and R_{right} respectively; M, N are the number of elements in these subspaces.

Estimation of the best split is equal to the smallest sum of squares

$$R(\hat{f}) = \frac{1}{T} \sum_{t=p+1}^{T} \left(Y_t - \hat{f}(Y_{t-1}, Y_{t-2}, \ldots, Y_{t-p})\right)^2. \tag{8}$$

Step 3. For each untreated node, the best splitting is found. There are two arguments defined for this: the variable $Y_{t-k}, k \in (1, 2, \ldots, p)$ that will be splitting and the threshold value α of this variable.

We used as a threshold quintile the corresponding empirical distribution of the random variable Y (the value which random variable does not exceed with a certain probability) and limited the potential splitting on seven values of each predictor variable

$$\alpha \in \{Q_{10\%}, Q_{25\%}, Q_{40\%}, Q_{50\%}, Q_{60\%}, Q_{75\%}, Q_{90\%}\}. \tag{9}$$

Of the possible splitting options in this step, the "better" option is chosen by the adopted rule. These procedures are similar to the C&RT algorithm (Breiman et al. 1984). The difference is in the adopted rules, evaluation criteria and stop splitting. BART suggested an alternative criterion for selecting the best splitting based on the entropy (called Entropy Information Gain, IGain), because this reduces the complexity of the tree

$$IGain = \widehat{H}\,(M\,, N) - \widehat{H}\,(m, n), \tag{10}$$

where $\widehat{H}\,(M\,, N)$ is entropy of parent node, $\widehat{H}\,(m, n)$ is average entropy of children nodes.Thus, for each next splitting, algorithm selects node and lag variable (and, accordingly, the threshold value) that provide the maximum entropy reduction given by (10).

Step 4. In the next step it is necessary to evaluate the "value" of the tree, which characterizes the relationship between the accuracy of the approximation and the complexity (branching) of the constructed tree.

The value of the tree in BART is determined based on the early stop criterion. As such criterion, we used the Extended Bayesian Information Criterion (EBIC), which minimizes statistics:

$$EBIC = T \cdot \ln R\left(\hat{f}\right) + J \cdot [\ln(T) + 2\ln(b)], \tag{11}$$

where $R(\hat{f})$ is the root mean square error (8); J—number of model settings; T—number of samples in training set; b is the quantity that characterizes the complexity of the model space. It equals the product of the size of the tree (the number of branches in the tree) by the number of lag variables p.

In expression (11), the first term is the maximum value of the logarithmic function of the root mean square error, and the second is a penalty for the complexity of the model.

Step 5. Splitting nodes continues as long as the value of statistics EBIC decreases. If the selected splitting is effective at entropy gain (11), then it must be performed and the algorithm proceeds to step 3 (to evaluate other nodes). Otherwise, the final tree is selected and the BART algorithm is completed.

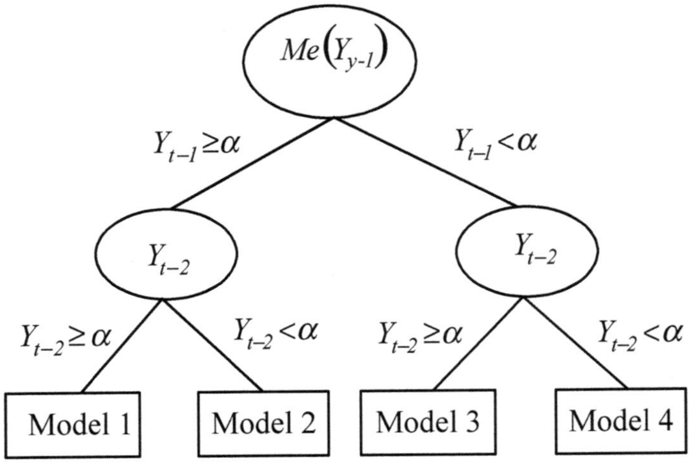

Fig. 2 Example of building BART with 2 split variables ($p = 2$)

Because the final target of the algorithm is prediction, we proposed to build Box-Jenkins ARIMA models on the each leaf nodes.

Fig. 2 shows a simple example of building BART with 2 split variables ($p = 2$), with local AIMA models located on leaf nodes.

Each of these models approximate thier own phase sub-space factor variables.

3.3 Random Forest

The random forest algorithm is based on the construction of an ensemble of classification (regression) trees, each of which is constructed from sub-samples of the original training sample using *bagging* (abbreviated from **b**ootstrap **agg**regat**ing**) (Breiman 2001). Bagging is a method of creating an ensemble of models based on various random samples from the original dataset. Samples are uniformly replaced and are called *bootstrap samples* (Flach 2012).

Bagging efficiency is achieved by training the basic algorithms in different sub-sets. These sub-sets will be significantly different from each other, and their errors are mutually compensated by "voting", as well as anomalous observations and time series jumps may not be included in some training sub-sets.

Bagging is especially useful in combination with tree models that are sensitive to changes in training data. In the RF algorithm, bagging is combined with the method of random subspaces: that is, each tree is built on different randomly selected subsets of features—this process is called *subspace sampling*.

The random subspaces method reduces the correlation between trees and avoids retraining because the basic algorithms are trained on different subsets of traits, which are also randomly selected.

As a result, the diversity of the ensemble will be even greater, reducing the learning time of each tree, which can be done in parallel. This ensemble is called a Random Forest.

The RF is used for both classification and regression problems, and RF can also be useful for selecting predictors and finding deviations in data analysis.

The prediction with RF algorithm is carried out by averaging the forecasts obtained by each ensemble tree (or by "voting" the trees for classification problems). Unlike individual trees, this algorithm is much less prone to overfitting and gives more sensitive (flexible) boundary to decision making.

3.4 Neural Network

As an ANN model, we used the simplest and most common Multilayer Perceptron architecture with one hidden layer of neurons, and an output layer containing only one neuron—estimation of the forecast of the studied time series by one step (Fig. 3).

According to Kolmogorov's theorem despite such a simple architecture, MLP can describe complex patterns in the data and modeled unknown nonlinear function of the time series with sufficient accuracy. This is achieved by using superposition of nonlinear activation functions on the hidden and output layers of the network.

Network output values depend on input and hidden neurons, weights, and activation functions

$$\widehat{Y}_{t+1} = g\left(\sum_{i=1}^{k} w_{i}f(s_i) + b_0\right), \tag{14}$$

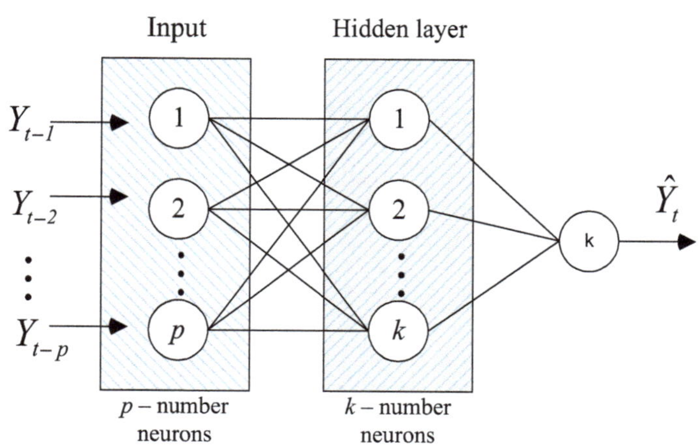

Fig. 3 Multilayer perceptron

where $f(\cdot), g(\cdot)$ are activation functions of the hidden and output layer neurons respectively; w_i—weights of links between hidden layer neurons and the output of the network; b_0, b_i—neurons bias of the output and hidden layers; $s_i = \sum_{j=1}^{p} \omega_{ji} Y_{t-j+1} + b_i$—sum of hidden layer neurons; ω_{ij}—weight of links between neurons of input and hidden layers.

MLP training consists in computing synaptic weights, and Error (Cost) Function (EF) is used to determine the difference between the target variable and the network output. Finding the minimum EF was performed using the gradient descent method.

We used a back-propagation algorithm. According to it the value of the EF is applied to the neurons of the hidden layer and the weights are adjusted. In the first step the input vector $Y_n, Y_{n+1}, \ldots, Y_{n+p}, (n = 1, 2, \ldots, t)$ propagates across the network from layer to layer in the forward direction with the fixed scales. In the next, reverse step, all synaptic weights are adjusted by the error correction rule.

4 Data

For numerical simulation of the short-term forecasting models (BART, RF and MLP) of cryptocurrency prices we selected data of daily exchanges of the three most capitalized coins: Bitcoin, Ethereum and Ripple. Data set includes 1583 observations for the period from August 1, 2015 to December 1, 2019 according to the Yahoo Finance (2019).

We chose closing prices both in absolute value and in natural log, which allows to stabilize the variability (variance) of the studied series (Fig. 4).

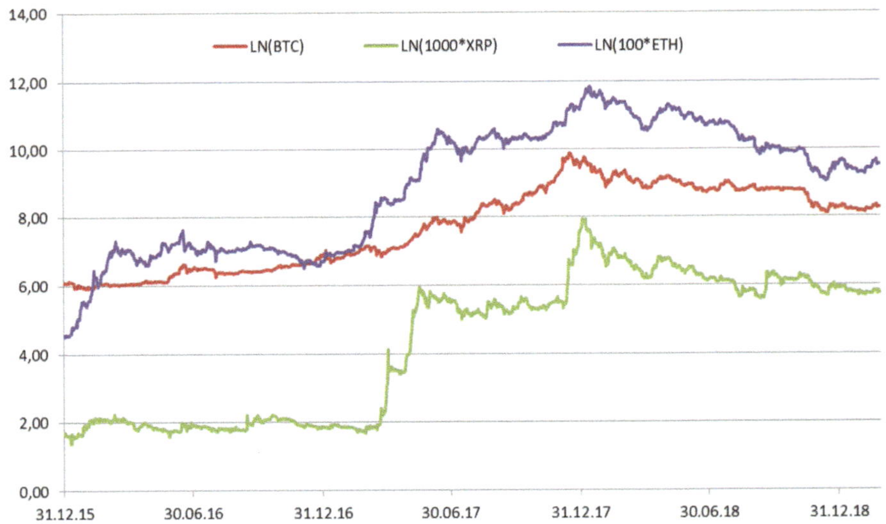

Fig. 4 Daily close prices of BTC, ETH and XRP (USD, log scale)

The first 1392 observations were divided into 80 and 20% between the training and test sets and were used to fit and train models and tuning their parameters, and the last 90 observations were reserved to estimate the quality of the forecast.

5 Empirical Result

Because all three types of models useses only past observations of the time series, the choice of the lag depth p is one of the main tasks for identifying them. According to many empirical studies (Boyacioglu and Baykan 2011; Okasha 2014; Matviychuk 2011), for "traditional" financial assets (fiat currencies, stock indices, commodity prices, etc.) that are traded for 5 days a week, there is a seasonal lag which is a multiple of 5 if we use daily observations.

Cryptocurrencies are traded 24/7, that's why it is expected a seasonal lag multiple of 7 days exists. Correlation analysis confirmed our hypothesis: for all 3 cryptocurrencies there are statistically significant correlations on lags 7, 14, 21, besides there are correlations on some other lags. Similar results were obtained in Catania and Grassi (2017), Alessandretti et al. (2018).

We tested 3 classes of models (BART, RF, MLP) with different lag depth for each cryptocurrency.

According to our hypothesis regarding lag depth for MLP models, we tested the following architectures:

- 7 inputs and 4–12 hidden layer neurons;
- 14 inputs and 5–15 hidden layer neurons;
- 21 inputs and 6–21 hidden layer neurons.

The most common functions such as logistic, hyperbolic tan, exponential and ReLu were selected as activation functions. Training MLP for each cryptocurrency and different lag values (number of input neurons) was conducted over 100 epochs, of which the best 5 architectures were selected for each case (in terms of minimum PE error (3) in the test sample and matching the model residuals to normal distribution).

The final prediction for each cryptocurrency was obtained as the prediction of the ensemble of networks, that is, average of the best 5 corresponding MLP models.

For RF simulation we used the following parameter settings: total number of trees—200, maximum tree depth—10, and number of predictors in each tree: 3, 5, 7 for RF-7, RF-14 and RF-21 models respectively.

For BART we chose two parameters: a maximum tree depth—15, a minimum number of examples (observations) per node—20.

Figure 5 shows the graphs that characterize the quality of approximation of BART models for training (a, c, e) and test (b, d, f) samples for 3 cryptocurrencies. The graphs (a, c, e) show the dependence of the predicted values (vertical axis) on the actual data (horizontal axis).

The short-term forecasts for each of the cryptocurrency were made for both absolute values of prices and their logs. It should be noted that according to our results

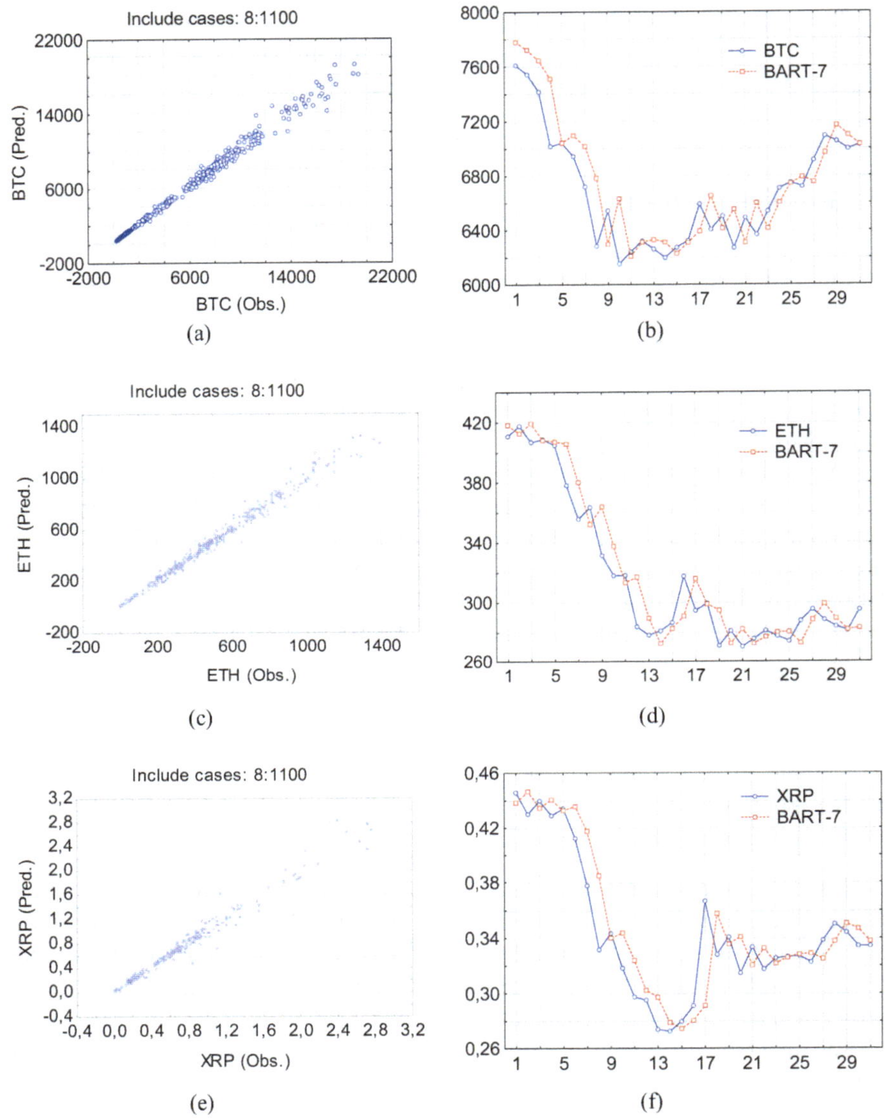

Fig. 5 Quality of approximation of BART models for training and test sets for BTC (**a**, **b**), ETH (**c**, **d**) and XRP (**e**, **f**)

the prediction accuracy by the metrics (15) defined below for the logs of prices was generally no better than for the absolute values.

This fact supports the argument that the ML algorithms (in particular, ANNs, C&RT and their ensembles) are much less sensitive to the time series statistical properties than classical statistical and econometric methods.

Figures 6, 7 and 8 show the final results of forecasting cryptocurrency prices for

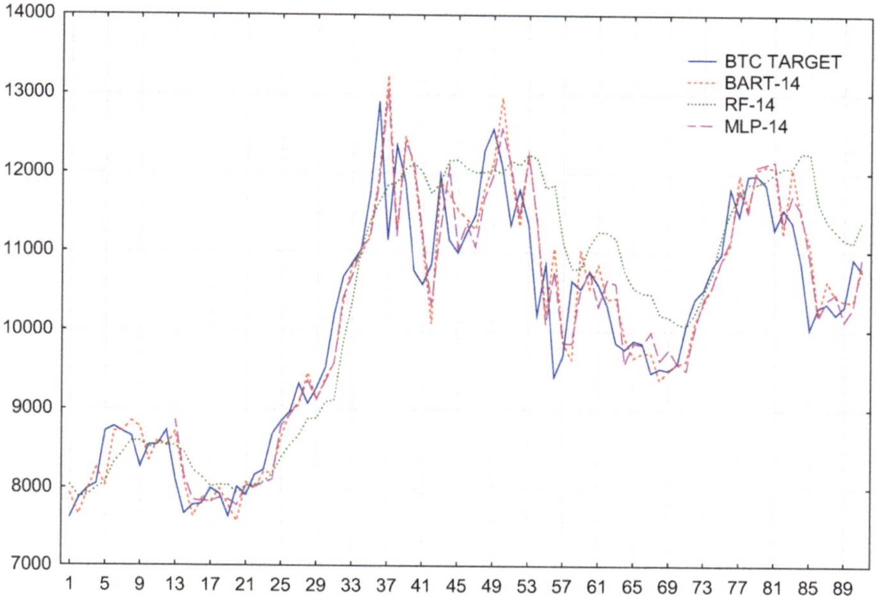

Fig. 6 90-day forecast of BTC prices (lag $p = 14$)

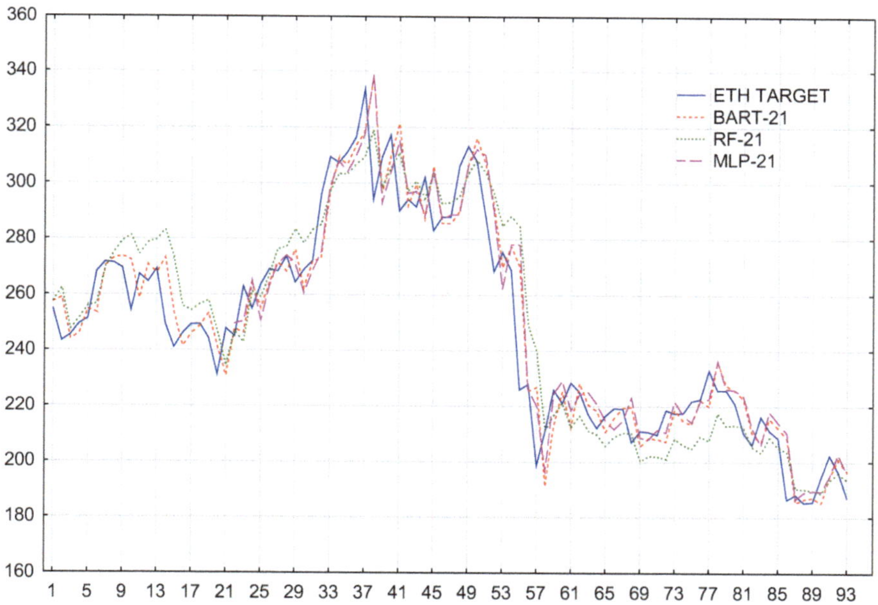

Fig. 7 90-day forecast of ETH prices (lag $p = 21$)

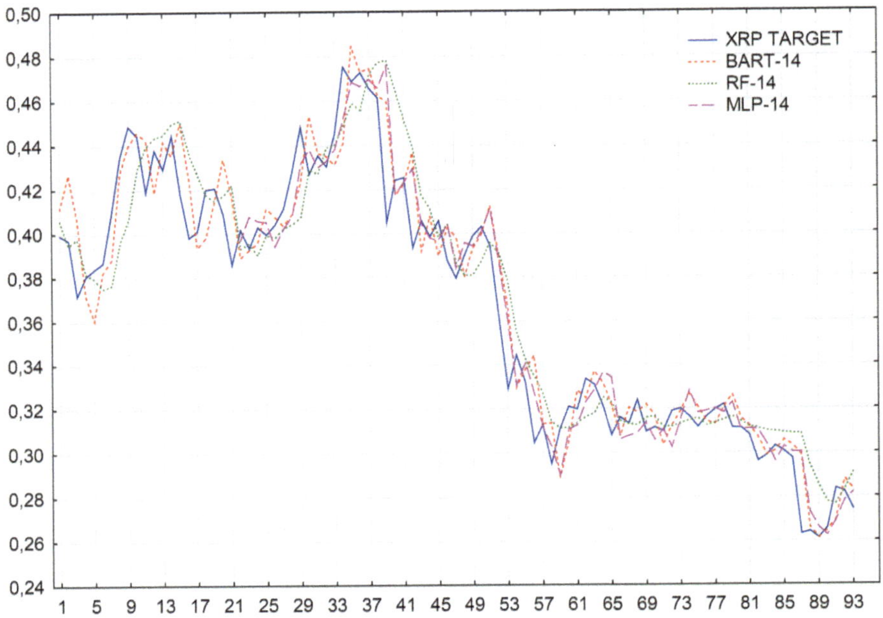

Fig. 8 90-day forecast of XRP prices (lag $p = 14$)

the 90-day time horizon, which was carried out using one-step forecasting technique without adjusting models parameters.

Analysis of the graphs allows us to conclude that the models fit the real data sufficiently well, taking into account the complex oscillating dynamic behavior of the studied series: an increasing trend for BTC and a decreasing one for ETH and XRP.

We can also observe that all models, despite the overall adequacy of the existing trends in the cryptocurrency dynamics, show some delay relative to the real data.

For estimating prediction accuracy we used metrics of Mean Percentage Absolute Error (MAPE) and Root Mean Square Error (RMSE):

$$MAPE = \frac{1}{n}\sum_{i=1}^{n}\frac{\left|Y_i - \hat{f}(Y_i)\right|}{Y_i} \times 100\%, \quad RMSE = \sqrt{\frac{1}{n}\sum_{i=1}^{n}\left(Y_i - \hat{f}(Y_i)\right)^2}. \qquad (15)$$

It should be noted that RMSE can only be used to evaluate the quality of different forecasts for one financial assets (time series). It provides information about the magnitude of the error. But RMSE does not characterize this error in comparison to the actual quote value.

In contrast, MAPE allows evaluating the forecasts performance of both individual models and their ensembles for different assets and compare them with each other.

Table 1 Out-of-sample accuracy performance results for different lags

	BTC		ETH		XRP	
	MAPE, %	RMSE	MAPE, %	RMSE	MAPE, %	RMSE
Lag $p = 7$						
BART-7	3.71	535.2	**3.39**	**11.74**	**3.07**	**0.0154**
RF-7	7.11	971.9	7.44	21.8	3.94	0.0196
MLP-7	**3.69**	**529.8**	3.53	12.17	**3.07**	**0.0153**
Lag $p = 14$						
BART-14	**3.83**	**541.9**	**3.37**	**11.86**	3.42	0.0167
RF-14	5.60	756.9	6.48	19.82	4.08	0.0203
MLP-14	3.95	559.1	3.51	12.16	**3.41**	**0.0162**
Lag $p = 21$						
BART-21	**3.94**	**558.5**	**3.69**	**12.55**	3.83	0.0183
RF-21	5.54	739.3	4.52	14.55	3.92	0.0212
MLP-21	4.28	610.8	3.84	13.17	**2.98**	**0.0151**

In our evaluation of predictive accuracy, we made a forecast of the dynamics of cryptocurrency prices over a 90-day horizon by using one-step forecasting technique.

The final out-of-sample accuracy results obtained from the BART, MLP and RF are shown in Table 1.

The accuracy obtained from both BART and MLP are significantly higher for all lags and cryptocurrencies than for the RF algorithm. The relatively low accuracy of RF may be due to the fact that a much larger number of factors are required for its effective implementation. It is worth noting that RF accuracy increases as the depth of the lag increases. Accuracy can also be improved by building more trees in the forest.

As for the comparison of the MLP and BART performance, the results in Figs. 6, 7 and 8 and Table 1 show similar accuracy of these models: the smallest error (MAPE) for BTC was 3.69% (MLP), for ETH—3.37% (BART), for XRP—2.98% (MLP).

Somewhat unexpected, there was a slight decrease in the accuracy of both the MLP and BART (at least for BTC and ETH) with increasing lag depth. In our opinion, this may be due to the overfitting problem.

From the trading point of view it is more valuable to predict the direction of price or trend change, rather than its numerical value. Since all three types of models can solve the classification problem we also performed prediction of the price change direction of BTC, ETH and XRP from August 1, 2019 to December 1, 2019 (123 observations).

To investigate this problem, we made forecast for growth (class positive, P) and falling (class negative, N) prices on the next day by using one-step forecasting technique without adjusting the model parameters.

However, a certain observation was classified as positive, P or negative, N if the price of the asset for that day increased (or decreased) by 1% or more, respectively.

Table 2 Prediction accuracy of the prices change direction of individual cryptocurrencies for the period 01/08/19–01/12/19

		Actual	BART		MLP		RF	
			Pred.	Accur. %	Pred.	Accur. %	Pred.	Accur. %
BTC	Rising, *P*	29	21	**64**	17	**62**	19	**57**
	Falling, *N*	53	31		28		29	
ETH	Rising, *P*	41	29	**62**	25	**59**	27	**59**
	Falling, *N*	49	27		24		26	
XRP	Rising, *P*	49	33	**59**	29	**61**	31	**56**
	Falling, *N*	52	26		25		25	

To measure forecasting performance, we used Accuracy metrics defined in (16) below, which represents the proportion of correctly predicted values among all predictions

$$Accuracy = \frac{TP + TN}{P + N}, \tag{16}$$

were TP and TN are the number of correctly predicted values of positive and negative classes, respectively; P and N are the actual number of values for each class. Table 2 shows the summary of the estimation accuracy of our models by using this metric.

As shown in Table 2, the prediction accuracy of the BART and MLP are higher for all time series than for the RF models. The average values of the Accuracy metric by the BART model are 62%, MLP 61%, RF 57%.

Note that for all models the proportion of correctly predicted values of the positive class (increase in price), turned out to be higher than the proportion of the correctly predicted values of the decrease in price, which must be taken into account in practical application of the models.

We can conclude based on the considered accuracy metrics defined in (15-16), that the models of the short-term forecast of the cryptocurrency prices dynamics in general have smaller errors than the "naive forecasts". During the periods of slow change, these models can be used to make a short-term forecasts for up to 30 days.

For traders with a longer investment horizon (90 days to a year) it is necessary to take into account the dynamics of nonlinear trends, and in our opinion, it would be advisable to use the models developed by us in combination with trend-cycles models.

6 Conclusion

The results of our modeling of short-term cryptocurrency dynamics and application of these models to real life data demonstrated the effectiveness of using machine learning approach, in particular, models of neural networks, regression (autoregressive) trees and their ensembles for forecasting tasks. Based on the results of the study, these models allow making short-term forecast with sufficient accuracy: within 3–4%.

Results of the binary classification of the direction of price changes showed, that BART and MLP models had an average accuracy of about 63% for the daily time series observations, which was higher than for the "naive" model.

It should be noted that we used a minimal dataset—only lag values of the studied series (closing prices). Forecast accuracy can be increased by using a more expanded dataset: including open, maximum, minimum and average prices, trading volume, etc. In addition, we can use a variety of indices, oscillators, in particular, moving averages of different types and time periods, taking into account the trend dynamics.

In this work we have applied a simple model of Neural Network—the Multilayer Perceptron with one hidden layer. Using networks with more complex architecture: recurrent, self-organized, deep, etc. should also improve the predictive accuracy. In summary, we note that the perspective approach for the financial time series forecasting is the construction of combined Classification and Regression Tree models and Neural Networks.

References

Akyildirim, E., Goncuy, A., & Sensoy, A. (2018). *Prediction of Cryptocurrency Returns Using Machine Learning*. https://www.researchgate.net/publication/329322600. Accessed November 15, 2019.

Albuquerque, Y., de Sá, J., Padula, A., & Montenegro, M. (2018). The best of two worlds: Forecasting high frequency volatility for cryptocurrencies and traditional currencies with support vector regression. *Expert Systems with Applications, 97,* 177–192. https://doi.org/10.1016/j.eswa.2017.12.004.

Alessandretti, L., ElBahrawy, A., Aiello, L., & Baronchelli, A. (2018). Anticipating cryptocurrency prices using machine learning. *Hindawi Complexity*. https://doi.org/10.1155/2018/8983590.

Amjad, M., & Shah, D. (2016). *Trading Bitcoin and online time series prediction*. NIPS 2016 Time Series Workshop. http://proceedings.mlr.press/v55/amjad16.pdf. Accessed November 15, 2019.

Belinskyi, A., Soloviev, V., Semerikov, S., & Solovieva, V. (2019). Detecting stock crashes using Levy distribution. In *CEUR Workshop Proceedings* (Vol. 2422, pp. 420–433). http://ceur-ws.org/Vol-2422/paper_34.pdf.

Bontempi, G., Taieb, S., & Borgne, Y. (2013). Machine learning strategies for time series forecasting. In *European Business Intelligence Summer School eBISS 2012* (pp. 62–77). Berlin, Heidelberg: Springer.

Boyacioglu, M., & Baykan, O. K. (2011). Predicting direction of stock price index movement using artificial neural networks and support vector machines: The sample of the Istanbul Stock. *Exchange Expert Systems with Applications, 38*(5), 5311–5319.

Breiman, L. (2001). Random forests. *Machine Learning, 45,* 5–32.

Breiman, L., Friedman, H., Olshen, R. A., & Stone, C. J. (1984). *Classification and regression trees*. Belmont, NJ: Wadsworth International Group.

Catania, L., & Grassi, S. (2017). *Modelling crypto-currencies financial time-series*. CEIS Research Paper (15(8), pp. 1–39). https://ideas.repec.org/p/rtv/ceisrp/417.html. Accessed November 15, 2019.

Cheah, E. (2015). Speculative bubbles in Bitcoin markets? An empirical investigation into the fundamental value of bitcoin. *Economic Letters, 130,* 32–36.

Ciaian, P. (2016). The economics of BitCoin price formation. *Applied Economics, 48*(19), 1799–1815.

CNBC. (2018). *Top Economists Stiglitz, Roubini and Rogoff Renew Bitcoin Doom Scenarios*. https://www.cnbc.com/2018/07/09/nobel-prize-winning-economist-joseph-stiglitz-criticizes-bitcoin.html. Accessed November 15, 2019.

Derbentsev, V., Datsenko, N., Stepanenko, O., & Bezkorovainyi, V. (2019a). Forecasting cryptocurrency prices time series using machine learning. In *CEUR Workshop Proceedings* (Vol. 2422, pp. 320–334).

Derbentsev, V., Kibalnyk, L., & Radzihovska, Y. (2019b). Modelling multifractal properties of cryptocurrency market using Hurst exponent and detrended fluctuation analysis. *PEN, 7*(2), 690–701.

Flach, P. (2012). *Machine learning: The art and science of algorithms that make sense of data*. Cambridge, UK: Cambridge University Press.

Hitam, N. A., & Ismail, A. R. (2018). *Comparative Performance of Machine Learning Algorithms for Cryptocurrency Forecasting*. https://www.researchgate.net/publication/327415267. Accessed November 15, 2019.

Kennis, M. (2018). *A Multi-channel Online Discourse as an Indicator for Bitcoin Price and Volume*. arXiv:1811.03146v1 [q-fin.ST]. Accessed November 6, 2018.

Krugman, P. (2013). *Bits and Barbarism*. http://www.nytimes.com/2013/12/23/opinion/krugmanbits-and-barbarism.html. Accessed November 15, 2019.

Kumar, M. (2006). *Forecasting stock index movement: A comparison of support vector machines and random forest*. SSRN Working Paper. https://papers.ssrn.com/sol3/papers.cfm?abstract_id=876544. Accessed November 15, 2019.

Matviychuk, A. (2006). Fuzzy logic approach to identification and forecasting of financial time series using Elliott wave theory. *Fuzzy Economic Review, 11*(2), 51–68.

Matviychuk, A. V. (2011). Shtuchnyi intelekt v ekonomitsi: neironni merezhi, nechitka logika (Artificial Intelligence in Economics: Neural Networks, Fuzzy Logic), Kyiv, KNEU (in Ukrainian).

McNally, S. (2016). *Predicting the price of Bitcoin using machine learning* (Doctoral dissertation). National College of Ireland, Dublin.

Okasha, M. K. (2014). Using support vector machines in financial time series forecasting. *Statistics, 4*(1), 28–39. https://doi.org/10.5923/j.statistics.20140401.03.

Peng, Y., Henrique, P., & Albuquerque, M. (2018). The best of two worlds: Forecasting high frequency volatility for cryptocurrencies and traditional currencies with support vector regression. *Expert Systems with Applications, 97,* 177–192.

Persio, L., & Honchar, O. (2018). Multitask machine learning for financial forecasting. *International Journal of Circuits, Systems and Signal Processing, 12*, 444–451.

Popper, N. (2015). *Digital gold: Bitcoin and the inside story of the misfits and millionaires trying to reinvent money*. New York, NY: Harper Collins Publisher.

Rebane, J., & Karlsson, I. (2018). Seq2Seq RNNs and ARIMA models for cryptocurrency prediction: A comparative study. In *SIGKDD Fintech'18*. https://doi.org/10.475/123_4.

Saxena, A., & Sukumar, T. (2018). Predicting bitcoin price using LSTM and compare its predictability with ARIMA model. *International Journal of Pure Applied Mathematics, 119*(17), 2591–2600.

Selmi, R., Tiwari, A., & Hammoudeh, S. (2018). Efficiency or speculation? A dynamic analysis of the Bitcoin market. *Economic Bulletin, 38*(4), 2037–2046.

Soloviev, V., & Belinskij, A. (2016). *Methods of Nonlinear Dynamics and the Construction of Cryptocurrency Crisis Phenomena Precursors*. arXiv:1807.05837; https://arxiv.org/abs/1807.05837. Accessed November 15, 2019.

Soloviev, V., & Belinskij, A. (2019). Complex systems theory and crashes of cryptocurrency market. In *Communications in Computer and Information Science* (Vol. 1007, pp. 276–297). https://link.springer.com/chapter/10.1007/978-3-030-13929-2_14.

Soloviev, V., Belinskij, A., & Solovieva, V. (2019a). Entropy analysis of crisis phenomena for DJIA index. In *CEUR Workshop Proceedings* (Vol. 2393, pp. 434–449). http://ceur-ws.org/Vol-2393/paper_375.pdf.

Soloviev, V., Serdiuk, O., Semerikov, S., & Kohut-Ferens, O. (2019b). Recurrence entropy and financial crashes. In *Proceedings of the 7th International Conference on Modeling, Development and Strategic Management of Economic System*, Ivano-Frankivsk, Ukraine, October 24–25, 2019. https://www.atlantis-press.com/proceedings/.

Soloviev, V., Solovieva, V., Tuliakova, A., & Ivanova, M. (2019c). Construction of crisis precursors in multiplex networks. In *Proceedings of the 7th International Conference on Modeling, Development and Strategic Management of Economic System*, Ivano-Frankivsk, Ukraine, October 24–25, 2019. https://www.atlantis-press.com/proceedings/.

Varghade, P., & Patel, R. (2012). Comparison of SVR and decision trees for financial series prediction. *IJACTE, 1*(1), 101–105.

Vigna, P., & Casey, M. J. (2015). *The age of cryptocurrency: How Bitcoin and digital money are challenging the global economic order*. New York, NY: St. Martin's Press.

Wang, M., Zhao, L., Du, R., Wang, C., Chen, L., Tian, L., et al. (2018). A novel hybrid method of forecasting crude oil prices using complex network science and artificial intelligence algorithms. *Applied Energy, 220,* 480–495. https://doi.org/10.1016/j.apenergy.2018.03.148.

Yahoo Finance. (2019). https://finance.yahoo.com. Accessed November 15, 2019.

Yao, Y., Yi, J., & Zhai, S. (2018). Predictive analysis of cryptocurrency price using deep learning. *International Journal of Engineering & Technology, 7*(3.27), 258–264.

Bitcoin and Its Offspring: A Volatility Risk Approach

Walter Bazán-Palomino

Abstract This study examines the relationship between the return on Bitcoin and the returns on its forks (Litecoin, Bitcoin Cash, Bitcoin Gold, Bitcoin Diamond, and Bitcoin Private). I obtain volatility series and time-varying correlation coefficients (Bitcoin with each of its forks) based on both univariate and multivariate GARCH models (EWMA, DCC, and BEKK). In terms of volatility, the gains of using a multivariate volatility approach are not substantial. However, the three multivariate volatility models offer a better estimation of the time-varying correlation. This study provides evidence that the volatility of Bitcoin forks and the volatility of Bitcoin are dynamically related, and there is a transmission of volatility risk from Bitcoin forks to Bitcoin. The results suggest that Bitcoin and its forks behave as crypto-currencies during bad times and as assets during good times. Also, for most of the sample period, Bitcoin forks do not offer a hedge against Bitcoin risk.

Keywords Bitcoin · Fork · Volatility risk · Time-varying correlation

JEL Classification: C22 · C5 · F3 · G15

1 Introduction

Since the creation of Bitcoin in October 2008, by Satoshi Nakamoto,[1] many new crypto-currencies have been created on top of Bitcoin technology (protocol). The proof-of-work is the Bitcoin consensus protocol which is open source, thus there is

[1] Satoshi Nakamoto is the nickname used by the person or persons who wrote Bitcoin white paper, and created Bitcoin protocol.

W. Bazán-Palomino (✉)
School of Economics and Finance, Universidad del Pacífico (University of the Pacific), 2141 Jr. Sanchez Cerro, Jesus Maria, 11, Lima, Peru
e-mail: wn.bazanp@up.edu.pe

Fordham University, The Center for International Policy Studies (CIPS), 441 East Fordham Road, Dealy Hall, Bronx, NY 10458, USA

L. Pichl et al. (eds.), *Advanced Studies of Financial Technologies and Cryptocurrency Markets*, https://doi.org/10.1007/978-981-15-4498-9_13

a natural incentive to copy this technology, or modify it and create a new peer-to-peer network. The latter is known as a fork. Generally speaking, a fork is a change in the set of rules of the original software (original blockchain) to develop a new version of it (new blockchain). Similar to Narayanan et al. (2016) and Antonopoulos (2017), I identify three main factors for a fork on the Bitcoin technology (details will be discussed in the next section). The first factor is the block size to store information. Bitcoin is a peer-to-peer decentralized and distributed public ledger, and each block of this ledger contains a record of all Bitcoin transactions. As Bitcoin became popular, the number of transactions increased and with it the problem of storing this information in a block. The restriction of storing this information leads us to the second factor: high transaction fees. The creator of any transaction has to pay a fee to a miner[2] in order to add her transaction into the block. Due to the fact that the block size is fixed and the number of transactions has increased over time, the creator of a transaction pays higher fees as an incentive for a miner to prioritize and add her transaction into the block. The third factor is mining centralization. That is, when a small number of miners or pool of miners control most of the computational power to process Bitcoin transactions.

As a result, Bitcoin blockchain has become a slow, expensive, and centralized payment system. To fix this problem, the Bitcoin community would need to adopt a new approach to establishing agreement on what transactions are valid in the ledger. As the Bitcoin technology stands at present, the only way to solve this problem is by a fork.

Forks create price volatility and increase uncertainty in the market, but their implications are not fully understood. This chapter tries to fill this gap by examining the relationship between the return on Bitcoin and the returns on its forks. I select the five major Bitcoin forks based on market capitalization and data availability: Litecoin (October 2011), Bitcoin Cash (August 2017), Bitcoin Gold (October 2017), Bitcoin Diamond (November 2017), and Bitcoin Private (February 2018). I also aim to provide an understanding of the transmission of the volatility risk after a fork occurs. The volatility risk transmission from a fork to Bitcoin could be direct through its conditional variance or indirect through its conditional covariances.

To that end, I proceed in two stages. In the first stage, I obtain the time-varying correlation based on univariate GARCH models. Earlier studies have used univariate GARCH models to calculate the volatility but not the dynamic correlation among virtual currency returns. Bouoiyour and Selmi (2015) compare two periods of Bitcoin volatility by estimating EGARCH and TGARCH models, whereas Dyhrberg (2016) uses an EGARCH to study the capabilities of Bitcoin in terms of risk management. Using several volatility models, Katsiampa (2017) makes a comparison of GARCH specifications for modeling Bitcoin volatility, and Chu et al. (2017) use twelve GARCH models to analyze the volatility of seven crypto-currencies; just to name a few.

In the second stage, I consider a multivariate volatility approach by using Exponentially Weighted Moving Average (EWMA), DCC-GARCH and BEKK-GARCH

[2] As discussed in the next section, a user is not necessarily a miner.

models. The benefit of the BEKK-GARCH method is that it allows dependence between the volatility series, something that cannot be done with univariate volatility models or with the other multivariate GARCH specifications (Bauwens et al. 2006). There are few studies which have used a multivariate GARCH methodology to study simultaneously the variances and covariances of crypto-currency returns. For instance, Bouri et al. (2017) employ a DCC-GARCH to claim that Bitcoin can act as a hedge for equity indices, bonds, oil, and gold. Likewise, Corbet et al. (2018) were among the first to measure the interrelation between the crypto-currency returns, but they only study Bitcoin, Ripple, and Litecoin. Beneki et al. (2019) apply the BEKK-GARCH methodology to investigate the volatility spillovers between Bitcoin and Ethereum.

The data used are the daily closing prices for Bitcoin, Litecoin, Bitcoin Cash, Bitcoin Gold, Bitcoin Diamond, and Bitcoin Private from April 28, 2013 (as the earliest date available for the other Bitcoin forks) to August 31, 2019. I think that the sample period is relevant because it includes the year 2017. During this year, Bitcoin pushed the market into a bubble (Corbet et al. 2018; Beneki et al. 2019), with prices reaching their peak in December 2017,[3] followed by a sharp decrease. Also, three Bitcoin forks (Bitcoin Cash, Bitcoin Gold, and Bitcoin Diamond) began to unfold in August 2017.

In this research, I contribute to existing literature in three ways. First, after explaining the economic factors behind Bitcoin forks, I find that (1) forks since 2017 were driven by the excess demand for storing Bitcoin transactions in a block, the highest transaction fees during the bubble period, and the fact that the block size hit the limit of 1 MB during the bubble period and remained around 0.9 MB thereafter; and (2) mining centralization evolved like a market entry dynamic game (huge investment in hardware as a barrier to entry the market). Second, I estimate in a novel way the time-varying correlation of each pair of crypto-currency returns (Bitcoin and each of its forks) using univariate volatility models, absent in previous literature. Third, I provide a robustness check of the estimated time-varying correlation by applying three multivariate GARCH models to each pair of crypto-currency returns. This is the first study to apply both univariate and multivariate volatility approaches to a particular consensus protocol (proof-of-work) and its forks; to the best of my knowledge.

If the forks are sharing the same technology, we would expect substitutability among crypto-currencies. My univariate and multivariate results show a negative correlation for the last two months of 2017, indicating that there was a substitutability among crypto-currencies during high risk times. However, the correlation became positive for the rest of the sample, suggesting that they behave more like stocks rather than currencies.

---

[3]Bitcoin went from USD 998.33 on January 1, 2017, to USD 19,497.4 (maximum historical price) on December 16, 2017. Over this year, Litecoin hit a record high price of USD 358.34 on December 18, 2017, representing a return of 7845.4% year-to-date. Bitcoin Cash started a precipitous rise shortly after its launch in August 2017, increasing from about USD 300 to a peak of USD 3,923 on December 20, 2017. Likewise, Bitcoin Gold was created in October 2017 and since then, its price meteorically raised from USD 142.92 to USD 453.45 on December 20, 2017, being its maximum level.

Regarding the multivariate approach, all volatility models produce higher correlations than my univariate results. Applying univariate volatility models to calculate the time-varying correlation between crypto-currency returns could lead to underestimating the mutual impact between Bitcoin and its forks. Also, the BEKK-GARCH(1, 1) offers more accurate modeling of the time-varying volatility and correlation which are of great importance for risk management and asset pricing. Since this method allows dependence between the volatility risk of crypto-currency returns, we can conclude that the volatilities of Bitcoin and each of its forks are dynamically related and this relationship is strong. Therefore, Bitcoin forks do not offer a hedge for Bitcoin risk.

The rest of the chapter is organized as follows. Section 2 provides precise descriptions of the Bitcoin network and the drivers behind Bitcoin forks. Section 3 shows the data and the univariate and multivariate volatility models I use to estimate both the volatilities of return on Bitcoin and returns on its forks and the correlation between them. I present the results and discuss the main findings in Sect. 4. Finally, Sect. 5 concludes my arguments.

2 The Bitcoin Network and the Drivers Behind Bitcoin Forks

In this section, I describe what a blockchain is, how the Bitcoin consensus protocol works, and the factors that caused and would cause Bitcoin forks.[4]

A blockchain is a public distributed ledger or a collection of transactions which is maintained by a network of users or computers, called nodes. Each of the nodes can store a copy of the blockchain, verify the authenticity of the blocks containing the transactions, and propose a new block. Here I make a distinction between a user and a miner. A user is a node or computer that can verify all transactions since the beginning and can do it in the future. On the other hand, a miner is a user with an additional feature, she can create a new block.

An important aspect of blockchain technology and, in particular, of Bitcoin is the consensus protocol or consensus mechanism. The main idea behind the consensus mechanism is how nodes agree to validate transactions and produce a new block of information (a set of new transactions) which is added to the chain. At every point in time, the majority of participants—51% of the users in most of the crypto-currency networks—must agree about the ownership rights to the tokens or coins. Because of network participants can remain anonymous, the consensus mechanism is the core for the functionality of any virtual currency.

[4]The source of information was crypto-currencies white papers and websites, and other online sources such as www.coinmarketcap.com, www.cointelegraph.com, www.coindesk.com, and www.coinbase.com.

Proof-of-work is the Bitcoin consensus algorithm for verifying transactions. Under this protocol,[5] miners compete against each other in a race for the right to add a new block of information (transactions) to the chain. To do so, miners have to solve a mathematical puzzle called the hash puzzle or hash algorithm. The winner reports both the new block and the solution of the hash puzzle, getting as a reward new Bitcoins and transaction fees included in the block. This process is also known as mining, and in this way, new Bitcoins are added to the money supply. The role of miners is crucial since they are responsible for securing and confirming transactions by adding blocks of transaction information to the chain. Unlike fiat money, Bitcoin does not depend on a central authority providing a clearinghouse service or a central bank that controls the money supply.

In a general sense, Bitcoins are just created from nowhere. The transactions in each block are messages to transfer coins from one address to another. These transactions are broadcast to the network, and the first miner who puts together new transactions in a new block and solves a mathematical puzzle gets new Bitcoins and transaction fees.

Having explained what Bitcoin is and how it works, let's talk about the underlying factors of Bitcoin forks. The first factor—and perhaps the most important—is the block size to store information. From its inception, Bitcoin has a block size of 1 MB,[6] limiting the amount and frequency of transactions that the network can process. The original consensus protocol allows 2–7 transactions per second and a block time of 10 min. With its increasing popularity over time, given the current technology, it is very difficult for Bitcoin to meet demand.

The excess of demand for Bitcoin technology leads us to the second cause of a fork: high transaction fees. In order to have her transaction processed by a miner, the creator of a transaction has to pay a transaction fee. In this way, miners are compensated for the services they provide. Over the years, the number of users sending transactions increased, but only a limited number of transactions could be added to the chain. Therefore, there is congestion in the available block space and there are pending transactions. If the creator of a transaction wants to move her transaction to the top of the list, she has to pay a higher transaction fee to incentivize the miner to do it. The creators of transactions know that to have priority, they have to offer a high transaction fee to a miner. Consequently, the cost for getting a transaction into the next Bitcoin block rises.

Panel (a) of Fig. 1 presents the Block Size which refers to data sent to legacy nodes. The Block Size hit the limit of 1MB during March 2016–December 2017. The following three months, it remained around 0.5 MB and ever since the data per block was above 0.9 MB on average. Similarly, Panel (b) of Fig. 1 shows the

[5]Antonopoulos (2017) mentions that Bitcoin consensus is based on four processes: (a) independent verification of each transaction by any node, (b) independent aggregation of Bitcoin transactions into a new block by a miner, (c) independent verification of a new block by all users in the network, and (d) independent selection of the chain with the highest proof-of-work (highest cumulative computational power) by any node.

[6]The block size was arbitrarily set to 1 MB and the reason was to prevent attack from hackers to the network.

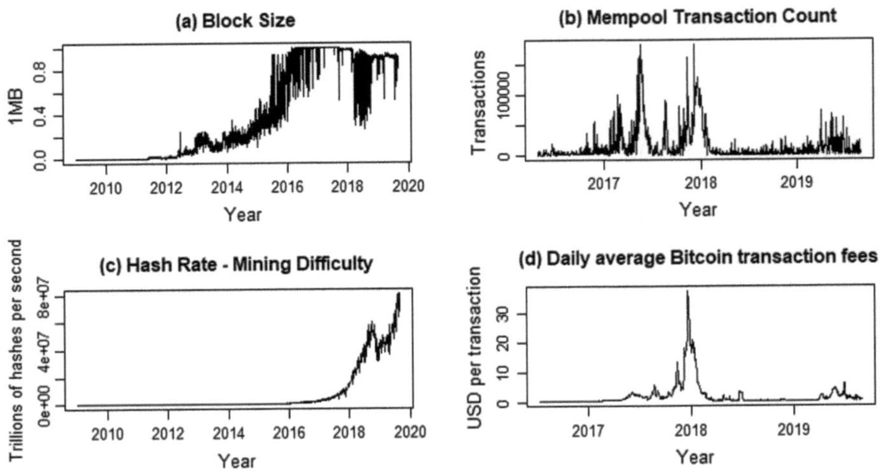

Fig. 1 Factors behind a Bitcoin fork. Block size: data sent to legacy nodes. Mempool: number of unconfirmed transactions that have been broadcast to the bitcoin network. Hash rate: he estimated number of tera hashes per second (trillions of hashes per second) the Bitcoin network is performing. Bitcoin transaction fees: daily average fees in USD per transaction. *Sources* Block Size—https://bitcoinvisuals.com, Mempool—https://www.blockchain.com, Transaction Fees—https://bitcoinfees.info, and Hash Rate and Mining Difficulty—https://www.blockchain.com

Mempool or memory pool which is the number of unconfirmed transactions that have been broadcast to the Bitcoin network. In simple words, this is a measure of excess demand for storing Bitcoin transactions in a block. Over the crypto-currency bubble year, the mempool reached four main peaks: February (100,125), May (184,101), November (161,450), and December (184,106).

This excess demand caused an adjustment in the hash algorithm. The Bitcoin network adjusts the hash algorithm every 2016 blocks based on a target time of 10 min per block. Valid blocks must have a hash below a preset target but if this target is adjusted, it is more difficult to find a block below the new hash target. As a result, more hash tries are needed to have the same probability of finding a block which in turn brings more chances of mining profitability. Hash Rate is the estimated number of tera hashes per second which means how many mathematical calculations a miner performs per second (Panel (c) of Fig. 1). This variable is a measure of mining difficulty. Finally, as explained before, the congestion in a block leads to an increase in the transaction fees (Panel (d) of Fig. 1). The daily average Bitcoin transaction fee started to rise in February 2017 and reached its peak on December 21, 2017, 5 days after the highest Bitcoin price.

Before moving on to the next problem, centralization, it is necessary to talk a little more about the consensus protocol. According to Narayanan et al. (2016), the Bitcoin community achieves proof-of-work using hash puzzles, and the nodes which propose a new block are selected based on their computing power. Bitcoin hash puzzle is SHA-256 which is a cryptographic hash function used for mining. The

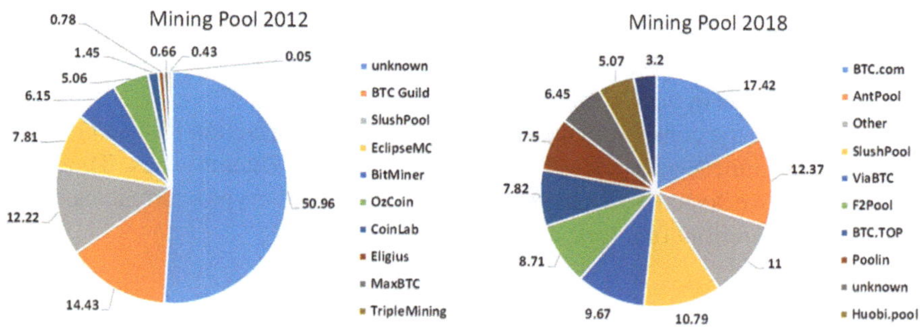

Fig. 2 Mining pool centralization

hash function could be adjusted by the network in order to keep the average time between successive blocks within 10 min.

As Bitcoin has become mainstream, the hash puzzle has become more complex. The increasing difficulty of the mathematical puzzle causes centralization.That is, more transactions in the network lead to a more difficult hash puzzle, and a more complicated puzzle leads to centralization because only a few miners can invest in more powerful hardware and electricity. By doing so, a miner increases her probability to be the next proposer of a block. As a result, small miners have left the market and those that remain have worked together to increase their likelihood of finding a block to offset their mining cost. They have congregated into mining pools, i.e., they pool their hashing power and split their rewards proportionally to the amount of work they have done (Antonopoulos 2017).

Figure 2 presents the biggest mining pools by the end of 2012 (left panel) and by the end of 2018 (right panel). In December 2012, more than 50% of the miners were unknown and small, and BTC Guild and SlushPool were the only miners with more than 10% of the mining hash power. Six years later, the story is quite different. Five miners—www.BTC.com (17.42%), AntPool (12.37%), SlushPool (10.79%), ViaBTC (9.67%), and F2Pool (8.71%)—control 69.75% of the mining hash power. Unknown (6.45%) and other (11%) miners only represent 17.45% of the mining hash. In addition, the vast majority of miners who were active in 2012 are no longer in 2018. Only SlushPool remains active with its market participation steady at around 10%. An implication of the mining centralization is the possibility that the biggest five miners could cooperate to control the Bitcoin network influencing the transaction fees, hash rate, and Bitcoin price. Along these lines, Hayes (2017) found that the level of competition in the network of producers could explain the value of Bitcoin.

To save money on energy, miners moved to countries where the cost of energy is cheaper.[7] By the end of 2018, 81% of the network hash rate was concentrated in China, followed by the Czech Republic (10%), Iceland (2%), Japan (2%), Georgia

[7] According to the Bitcoin Energy Consumption Index (https://digiconomist.net/bitcoin-energy-consumption), the global energy consumption of all Bitcoin mining is equivalent to the power usage of the Czech Republic.

(2%), and Russia (1%). Regarding the top miners in the network, www.BTC.com, Antpool, F2pool, ViaBTC, BTC.top, DPOOL, and 58COIN are located in China, while Slushpool is in the Czech Republic.

In summary, the constant block size, the increasing transaction fees and the centralization of miners have caused disagreements among Bitcoin users. These disagreements have fostered incentives to create alternative crypto-currencies. Thus, we are at the forefront of a fork.

2.1 *The Mining Game and Bitcoin Forks*

Inevitably, a hard fork is the solution to Bitcoin protocol problems. For the purpose of this chapter, I consider a hard fork to happen whenever there is a change in the core Bitcoin protocol which causes two candidate blocks competing to form the longest blockchain. In simple words, it is a change in the set of rules of the original software (original blockchain) to develop a new version of it (new blockchain). Every time there is a Bitcoin fork, the miners have to decide whether or not to continue supporting the original blockchain. Under proof-of-work, if a miner wants to support both the new and the original blockchain, she has to split her computational power between the two.

As an economic principle, if Bitcoin miners are rational, they will act "honestly" as long as the benefits exceed the costs. That is, if block rewards and transaction fees are higher than electricity and hardware costs, broadly speaking, then it is beneficial to be a miner. The behavior of each miner is a Nash Equilibrium and she will follow the rules of this game—the consensus mechanism—as long as there is no incentive to deviate from the equilibrium.

However, the incentives have changed over time. Note that a miner is like any other firm in the market, it has revenues and production costs and the miner's primary objective is to maximize profits. On the revenues side, the market value of the reward is denominated in Bitcoins, and due to the enormous increase in Bitcoin price, the reward does not seem to be a problem. On the cost side, there are a couple of complications. First, the variable costs (electricity) and the fixed costs (computers) are denominated in fiat money, for example, in U.S. Dollars. Thus, there is a balance sheet effect in terms of the exchange rate between Bitcoin and the U.S. Dollar. Second, the computers are the fixed costs for a miner; it is like investing in a new factory. But a miner's level of investment depends on the investment of its competitors. If a miner wants to stay in the market, i.e., wants to make profits, she has to invest systematically in more computer power. This market environment is closely related to market entry dynamic games, where the new player (new miner) desires to enter and the incumbent (the existing miner) threatens the entrant with a huge investment in a factory.

How does it evolve? If a miner has the most powerful computer in the network, the rest of the users would complicate the mathematical puzzle and in this way, try to keep even the probability to be the next proposer of a new block. This change in the parameters of the hash puzzle will demand more computational power. Like in any other equilibrium, if a miner incurs losses, she will leave the market. On the contrary, if a miner makes a lot of profits, then she could invest in more powerful computers and therefore discourage new miners from entering the market. A natural consequence is that the difficulty of the hash puzzle will increase (Panel (c) of Fig. 1), but only the miners who can afford new computers will stay in the market.

At the beginning, the variable costs (energy) did not constitute any immediate threat to current or new miners. Nevertheless, the electricity cost is not negligible because more computational power leads to higher consumption of energy.

But the story does not end here. The blockchain industry is a capital-intensive industry. After a while, miners who stay in the network can act strategically. Since the capital investment is so high, the lead miners would expect to earn an attractive return on their investment. If they produce (mining Bitcoin) at a low level, the Bitcoin price and transaction fees stay high protecting their long-run competitive position. Unfortunately, due to a lack of information, it is not possible to study the direct connection between mining and Bitcoin price.[8] Also, studying the determinants of Bitcoin price is not within the scope of this document. I only present the economic incentives that cause a fork.

Returning to the rules of the game, the consensus protocol must change in order to correct the misallocation in the market. One way that can be done is if users agree to change the rules such as changing the hash algorithm or increasing the block size. The latter is more complicated than it seems and would not solve the problem of centralization. Under proof-of-work, a bigger block means a higher computational power, and, as discussed before, a higher computational power means better and more expensive mining hardware. Another way to fix the disequilibrium is to "copy"[9] the Bitcoin technology to meet the demand, causing a fork.

Bitcoin (BTC) has experienced five major forks causing instability to the value of crypto-currencies.

- *Litecoin (LTC)*: In October 2011, a former Google engineer Charles Lee, created a Bitcoin clone which is considered a fork. Litecoin is based on Bitcoin protocol but differs in terms of the hashing algorithm (scrypt, instead of SHA-256), the total number of coins, and the time to generate a block. At the time of writing this document, according to CoinMarketCap and CoinBase, Litecoin reduced the time to generate a block from 10 to 2.5 min. The fork also lowered the transaction fees.
- *Bitcoin Cash (BCH)*: On August 1, 2017, the Bitcoin network finally agreed to update the protocol and increase the block size to 8 MB. This network agreement brought Bitcoin Cash (BCH) to life. According to Bitcoin website, the blockchain forked at block 478,558 and all Bitcoin holders as of block 478,558 are also owners

[8]In this sense, Hayes (2017) made an attempt to try to link these factors and found that the cost of mining influences the price of crypto-assets.

[9]In this context, copy means using almost the same consensus algorithm, but with slightly different rules. If the blockchain community wants to switch from proof-of-work to other protocol, for example, proof-of-stake, this is not considered as a fork. At least for the purpose of this research.

of Bitcoin Cash. The new block size allows nodes in the BCH network to process more transactions per second, and to reduce transaction fees.

- *Bitcoin Gold (BTG)*: Jack Liao founded Bitcoin Gold on October 24, 2017. The fork occurred at the block 419,406 and as in Bitcoin Cash, the owner of 1 BTC also gets 1 BTG. As expected, Bitcoin Gold reaches consensus using proof-of-work, but the main difference from the Bitcoin protocol is the hash algorithm (Equihash, instead of SHA-256). The cause of this fork was centralization since the Bitcoin community perceived mining to be under the control of a few mining pools.
- *Bitcoin Diamond (BCD)*: On November 11, 2017, a fork of Bitcoin happened at block 495,866 and as a result, Bitcoin Diamond was created. This fork seeks to add more transaction capacity to the network and lower transaction fees by slightly changing the proof-of-work algorithm. It is not clear what the main difference in the consensus algorithm is. Other differences are the algorithm of the transaction signatures and the money supply (10 times more than BTC).
- *Bitcoin Private (BTCP)*: Bitcoin Private is a special crypto-currency since it is a fork from both ZClassic and Bitcoin. In fact, ZClassic itself is a fork of ZCash. Officially, the fork took place at the blocks 511,346 for BTC and 272,991 for ZClassic on February 28, 2018. Bitcoin Private was designed to decrease centralization by increasing the block size to 2 MB and reducing the block time to 2.5 min.

As a side note, I could have included Bitcoin SV (November 15, 2018) in the sample, however, I was looking for crypto-currencies that had observations longer than a year. In addition, the fork list is large and it is not known with certainty how many coins have originated from Bitcoin technology. As of the time of writing this document, according to CoinDesk and CoinMarketCap, there are at least ten more forks: Bitcoin Atom, Bitcoin Scrypt, Bitcoin Uranium, Bitcoin Rhodium, Bitcoin Energy, Copper Bitcoin, Super Bitcoin, BitCore, Bitcoin Zero, and Bitvolt.

To conclude this section, most people in the crypto-industry agree that the current Bitcoin technology needs to be changed if the entire industry wants to overtake traditional financial institutions. There is an active discussion about increasing the block size and reducing transaction fees, in order to achieve real decentralization and a faster payment system. As Bitcoin is designed, these modifications can be done outside the underlying protocol, i.e., by a fork. But every time there is a fork, the price volatility tends to spike inducing investors to readjust their portfolios. The purpose of the next section is to present the volatility models I use to analyze whether the return on Bitcoin and the return on its forks are related, and how the volatility risk is transmitted among them.

3 The Data and Risk Models

The data set is from coinmarketcap.com which reports historical data for crypto-currency prices since April 28, 2013. The data contain daily closing prices for Bitcoin and Bitcoin forks: Bitcoin and Litecoin (April 2013–August 2019),

Bitcoin Cash (August 2017–August 2019), Bitcoin Gold (October 2017–August 2019), Bitcoin Diamond (November 2017–August 2019), and Bitcoin Private (February 2018–August 2019).

3.1 Univariate Models

To estimate the volatility of crypto-returns, I use three univariate Generalized Autoregressive Conditional Heteroskedastic (GARCH) models. I start with the most standard framework in empirical finance, the GARCH model proposed by Bollerslev (1986). According to Hansen and Lunden (2005), GARCH(1, 1) model performs well in most of the cases and the other GARCH specifications do not provide a significant gain in terms of goodness of fit. Nevertheless, I consider the exponential GARCH (EGARCH) model of Nelson (1991), and the threshold GARCH (TGARCH) model of Glosten et al. (1993) to capture a well-known feature of financial time series: the leverage effect. The leverage effect stems from the fact that volatility tends to respond asymmetrically to "bad news" (excess returns lower than expected) and to "good news" (excess returns higher than expected). Hansen and Lunden (2005) argue that the first order of any of the aforementioned GARCH specifications appears to be adequate to model the volatility of time series.

Let r_t be the logarithmic return on a crypto-currency. The conditional mean and variance of r_t given F_{t-1} are $\mu_t = E(r_t \mid F_{t-1})$ and $\sigma_t^2 = Var(r_t \mid F_{t-1}) = E((r_t - \mu_t)^2 \mid F_{t-1})$, where F_{t-1} denotes the information set available at time $t-1$ and typically consists of all linear functions of the past returns. Let $a_t = r_t - \mu_t$ be the residual of the mean equation or innovation at time t, and $\varepsilon_t = \frac{a_t}{\sigma_t}$ be the standardized residuals which is an independent and identically distributed (i.i.d.) random variable with mean 0 and variance 1.

To fix ideas, the equations for the conditional mean of r_t and the different specifications for modeling the volatility of r_t given F_{t-1}, are presented below.

$$r_t = \mu_t + a_t \tag{1}$$

$$\sigma_t^2 = \omega + \alpha a_{t-1}^2 + \beta \sigma_{t-1}^2 \tag{2}$$

$$\ln(\sigma_t^2) = \omega + + \alpha \left(|\varepsilon_{t-1}| - E(|\varepsilon_{t-1}|\right) + \gamma \varepsilon_{t-1} + \beta \ln(\sigma_{t-1}^2) \tag{3}$$

$$\sigma_t^2 = \omega + (\alpha + \gamma N_{t-1}) a_{t-1}^2 + \beta \sigma_{t-1}^2 \tag{4}$$

where ε_t is an i.i.d. standard normal process, $E(|\varepsilon_t|) = \sqrt{2/\pi}$, and ω, α, β, and γ are constants. Equation (1) describes the conditional mean of r_t which can be a constant or an ARMA model. For most asset returns the serial correlation is weak and a simple AR model might be enough (Zivot and Wang 2003).

Equations (2), (3), and (4) refer to the structure of the volatility model under GARCH(1, 1), EGARCH(1, 1) and TGARCH(1, 1) specifications, respectively. Note the standard restrictions on the parameters: $\omega \geqq 0, \alpha \geqq 0, \beta \geqq 0$ and $\alpha + \beta < 1$; the latter restriction implies that the variance is finite and not integrated. The benefit of Eq. (3) is that there is no need for further non-negative restrictions for the parameters. A positive a_{t-1} contributes $\alpha(1+\gamma)\,|\varepsilon_{t-1}|$ to the log volatility whereas a negative value of a_{t-1} increases the log volatility in $\alpha(1-\gamma)\,|\varepsilon_{t-1}|$ due to a value of $\gamma < 0$ is expected. Regarding Eq. (4), the coefficient γ has to be positive in order to capture the leverage effect where $N_{t-i} = 1$ if $a_{t-i} < 0$, and $N_{t-i} = 0$ otherwise.

3.2 Multivariate Models

I consider an approach to multivariate volatility modeling using the Exponentially Weighted Moving Average (EWMA), the BEKK-GARCH model of Engel and Kroner (1995), and the DCC-GARCH model of Engel (2002). All the models allow us to study the dynamic relationship between volatility processes of multiple asset returns. Consider a k-dimensional return series $\{r_t\}$

$$r_t = \mu_t + a_t \tag{5}$$

where $a_t = (a_{1t}, \ldots, a_{kt})'$ is the shock, or innovation, at time t. The mean equation μ_t could follow a multivariate linear model like a VARMA(p, q) structure, or multivariate nonlinear models. As Tsay (2010) argues, it is enough to employ a simple VARMA structure with exogenous variables.

The conditional covariance matrix of a_t given F_{t-1} is a $k \times k$ positive-definite matrix $\{\Sigma_t\}$ defined by $\Sigma_t = Cov(a_t \mid F_{t-1})$. The shock can be written as $a_t = \Sigma_t^{1/2}\epsilon_t$ where $\Sigma_t^{1/2}$ is the square-root matrix of Σ_t, and ϵ_t is a sequence of i.i.d. random vector such that $E(\epsilon_t) = 0$ and $Cov(\epsilon_t) = I_k$.

A simple multivariate volatility framework is the EWMA model. Let $\widehat{a}_t$ be the residuals of the mean equation. The model for the conditional covariance matrix is

$$\widehat{\Sigma}_t = \lambda\widehat{\Sigma}_{t-1} + (1-\lambda)\widehat{a}_{t-1}\widehat{a}'_{t-1} \tag{6}$$

where $0 < \lambda < 1$ denotes the decaying rate or the persistent parameter. For a given λ and initial estimate of covariance matrix $(\widehat{\Sigma}_0)$, $\widehat{\Sigma}_t$ can be computed recursively. A common choice of $\widehat{\Sigma}_0$ is the sample covariance matrix of $\widehat{a}_t$ which produces a positive-definite volatility matrix $(\widehat{\Sigma}_t)$ for all t. A major drawback with the EWMA model is that it tends to reject the diagnostic tests in empirical applications.

The second multivariate volatility method is the BEKK-GARCH model which is concerned with the dynamic evolution of Σ_t. For a k-dimensional time series r_t, the BEKK-GARCH(1, 1) specification assumes the form

$$\Sigma_t = A_0A_0' + A_1a_{t-1}a'_{t-1}A_1' + B_1\Sigma_{t-1}B_1' \tag{7}$$

where A_0 is a lower triangular matrix such that is $A_0 A_0'$ a posititve-definite matrix, and A_1 and B_1 are $k \times k$ matrices. The main advantage of this approach is that it allows dependence between the volatility series. In addition, the model solves the problem of positive-definite constraint, i.e., it provides positive-definite volatility matrix Σ_t for all t. On the other side, the main disadvantage of this model is that it contains too many parameters, $k^2 + [k(k+1)/2]$. Also, the parameters in A_1 and B_1 do not have a direct interpretation.

Finally, the dynamic conditional correlation (DCC) model is built on the idea of modeling the conditional variances and correlations instead of modeling Σ_t. Let the conditional correlations to be time-varying

$$\rho_t = D_t^{-1} \Sigma_t D_t^{-1} \tag{8}$$

where $D_t = diag\left\{\sigma_{11t}^{1/2}, \ldots, \sigma_{kkt}^{1/2}\right\}$ is the diagonal matrix of the k volatilities at time t, and ρ_t is the correlation matrix with $k(k-1)/2$ elements. To fit a DCC-GARCH model, we first estimate individually each element of D_t (σ_{iit}) using any univariate GARCH specification and form estimated standardized residuals, and then model the pairwise conditional correlations between the standardized residuals.

In this regard, Engel (2002) proposes the following correlation structure

$$Q_t = (1 - \theta_1 - \theta_2) Q + \theta_1 Q_{t-1} + \theta_2 \epsilon_{t-1} \epsilon_{t-1}' \tag{9}$$

where Q_t is the covariance matrix of standardized residuals, Q is the unconditional covariance matrix of standardized residuals, and θ_1 and θ_2 are non-negative real numbers satisfying $0 < \theta_1 + \theta_2 < 1$. The correlation matrix is defined as $\rho_t = J_t Q_t J_t$, where $J_t = diag\left\{q_{11t}^{-1/2}, \ldots, q_{kkt}^{-1/2}\right\}$ is a normalization matrix and q_{iit} denotes the (i, i)th element of Q_t. The parameters θ_1 and θ_2 describe the dynamic dependence of the correlation matrix, and make the DCC model very parsimonious. But it is hard to justify that all correlations evolve in the same manner regardless of the assets involved (Bauwens et al. 2006).

4 Results

I investigate the interdependencies in risk-return between the return on Bitcoin and the returns on its forks: Litecoin (LTC), Bitcoin Cash (BCH), Bitcoin Gold (BTG), Bitcoin Diamond (BTD), and Bitcoin Private (BTCP). This set of five forks are particularly interesting for examining the relationship between a specific consensus protocol (Bitcoin proof-of-work) and its forks.

With the exception of BTCP, all other crypto-returns have a weak serial correlation based on ACF and PACF. Also I estimate AR(p) model for each return series, and

Table 1 The p-values of the Ljung-box test and the Lagrange multiplier test for detecting conditional heteroscedasticity in crypto-currency returns

	BTC	LTC	BCH	BCD	BTCP	BTG
Ljung-box						
$Q(1)$	0.602	0.085	0.442	0.894	0.978	0.442
$Q(2)$	0.253	0.038	0.497	0.246	0.999	0.682
$Q(5)$	0.183	0.007	0.558	0.146	0.368	0.036
$Q(10)$	0.004	0.000	0.519	0.023	0.474	0.071
$Q(15)$	0.027	0.000	0.503	0.030	0.132	0.219
Lagrange multiplier						
$LM(1)$	0.000	0.000	0.000	0.000	0.000	0.000
$LM(2)$	0.000	0.000	0.000	0.000	0.000	0.000
$LM(5)$	0.000	0.000	0.000	0.000	0.000	0.000
$LM(10)$	0.000	0.000	0.000	0.000	0.000	0.000
$LM(15)$	0.000	0.000	0.000	0.000	0.000	0.000

Q(m) and LM(m) denote the Ljung-box test and the Lagrande multiplier test on the innovations of crypto-currency returns at lag m, respectively

only BTCP and BTD need an AR(1) specification.[10] The mean equation indicates that the lagged daily log returns of crypto-currencies are not relevant factors of current log returns, at least lagged values greater than one period. This result is in line with the empirical fact of a low serial correlation of asset returns (Zivot and Wang 2003). Also, the first-order autoregressive process could be a sign of violation of the efficient market hypothesis. By building a model for the conditional mean, I eliminate any linear dependence. However, the returns on tokens can still be serially non-linear dependent due to ARCH effects.

Table 1 shows the Ljung-Box test results for the innovations of log returns. One interesting finding is that the null hypothesis is rejected at 5% for lag values longer than 10. Except for Litecoin, there is no serial correlation at very short intervals of time. On the other hand, the LM test for ARCH effects reveals that the null hypothesis is rejected for all the time series and at different lag values. Therefore, the squared residuals are positively correlated even though the innovations themselves are not.

After testing for the presence of ARCH effects, the next step is to specify a univariate GARCH model for the crypto-returns. Table 2 gives the results for GARCH(1, 1), EGARCH(1, 1), and TGARCH(1, 1). The three estimated models are essentially the same and produce a high persistence of the variance, especially for BTG, BTD and BTCP. Based on the GARCH(1, 1), we can compute the half-life defined as the number of days it takes for half of the expected reversion back towards the long-run variance: BTC (25.32 days), LTC (22 days), BCH (4.39 days), BTG (86.29 days), BTD (40.43 days), and BTCP (692.8 days). It is clear that BTCP has a strong volatility persistence.

[10]The results are available upon request.

Table 2 Estimation results of GARCH-type models for crypto-currency returns

	BTC	LTC	BCH	BCD	BTCP	BTG
GARCH(1, 1)						
$Const(\mu)$	0.112*	−0.072	−0.160	−0.371	−0.953**	−0.394*
$AR(1)(\phi)$	–	–	–	−0.110***	−0.0118	–
$Const(\omega)$	0.538***	1.054***	7.268	1.280***	0.898*	0.227***
$ARCH(\alpha)$	0.111***	0.084***	0.100***	0.057***	0.069***	0.021**
$GARCH(\beta)$	0.862***	0.885***	0.754***	0.926***	0.930***	0.971***
LL	−6289.97	−7068.24	−2572.63	−2291.8	−2090.72	−2162.81
AIC	5.435	6.107	6.701	7.122	7.776	6.410
EGARCH(1, 1)						
$Const(\mu)$	0.131*	−0.024	−0.068	−0.330	−1.577***	−0.346
$AR(1)(\phi)$	–	–	–	−0.103***	−0.019	–
$Const(\omega)$	0.191***	0.188***	0.342***	0.230***	0.877*	0.009
$ARCH(\alpha)$	0.250***	0.174***	0.138***	0.245***	0.195***	0.039***
$GARCH(\beta)$	0.939***	0.951***	0.914***	0.954***	0.986***	0.990***
$Leverage(\gamma)$	−0.001	0.020***	0.041***	0.045***	−0.082***	0.017***
LL	−6276.14	−7071.43	−2573.31	−2286.71	−2083.19	−2163.79
AIC	5.424	6.111	6.704	7.110	7.752	6.4163
TGARCH(1, 1)						
$Const(\mu)$	0.122*	0.057	−0.122	−0.363	−1.164***	−0.381*
$AR(1)(\phi)$	–	–	–	−0.108**	−0.021	–
$Const(\omega)$	0.530***	1.054***	5.463	1.395**	0.929*	0.063
$ARCH(\alpha)$	0.117***	0.090***	0.100***	0.066***	0.023***	0.02***
$GARCH(\beta)$	0.863***	0.885***	0.807***	0.921***	0.928***	0.983***
$Leverage(\gamma)$	−0.012	−0.014	−0.037	−0.010	0.097***	−0.017
LL	−6289.72	−7067.72	−2571.98	−2291.72	−2081.29	−2161.42
AIC	5.536	6.108	6.702	7.124	7.745	6.410

(*) Represents the significance at the 10% level, (**) represents the significance at the 5% level, and (***) represents the significance at the 1% level

From Table 2, it can be noticed that the Akaike Information Criterion (AIC) is minimized and the log-likelihood function is maximized under the TGARCH(1, 1) model in most of the cases. Nevertheless, the difference in these information criteria between the EGARCH(1, 1) and TGARCH(1, 1) models is marginal. Note that the EGARCH(1, 1) produces a positive leverage parameter which is difficult to explain. Also, the AR(1)-TGARCH(1, 1) specification better fits the volatility dynamics for Bitcoin Diamond and Bitcoin Private. If we focus our attention only on Bitcoin (first column of Table 2), contrary to Bouoiyour and Selmi (2015) and Katsiampa (2017), my estimates do not include an AR(1) coefficient in the mean equation.

If AIC and log-likelihood function are used in model selection, one selects the TGARCH(1, 1) specification. The model checking confirms that the TGARCH(1, 1)

Table 3 Model checking of TGARCH specifications—the p-values of Ljung-box and Lagrange multiplier tests

	BTC	LTC	BCH	BCD	BTCP	BTG
Ljung-box						
$Q(1)$	0.931	0.629	0.250	0.054	0.021	0.991
$Q(5)$	0.806	0.951	0.661	0.070	0.096	0.814
$Q(10)$	0.865	0.989	0.518	0.163	0.207	0.749
Lagrange multiplier						
$LM(1)$	0.376	0.850	0.793	0.771	0.507	0.468
$LM(5)$	0.378	0.919	0.751	0.821	0.738	0.832
$LM(10)$	0.559	0.969	0.380	0.927	0.873	0.682

Q(m) and LM(m) denote the weighted Ljung-box test and the weighted ARCH LM test on standardized squared residuals at lag m, respectively

fits the data well and captures all ARCH effects. Table 3 presents the p-value of the Weighted Ljung-Box test and the Weighted ARCH LM test on standardized squared residuals. Both tests fail to reject the null hypothesis at different lags.

Figure 3 gives the fitted volatility series of the TGARCH(1, 1) model. From this figure, we can see that there are no jumps in the volatility of any of the return series, the volatility does not diverge to infinity, and the leverage effect is present. As expected, the volatility was high from the beginning of 2017 until mid-2018. It seems that the Bitcoin bubble in 2017 contributes significantly to the high volatility persistence of Bitcoin forks. The only crypto-currency that exhibits higher volatility in the second half of the sample (since November 2018) is Bitcoin Private.

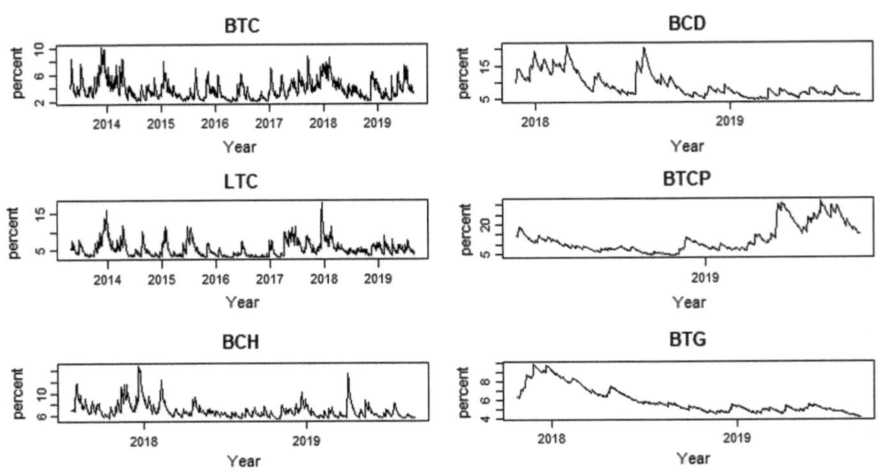

Fig. 3 TGARCH(1, 1) daily volatility of returns on crypto-currencies

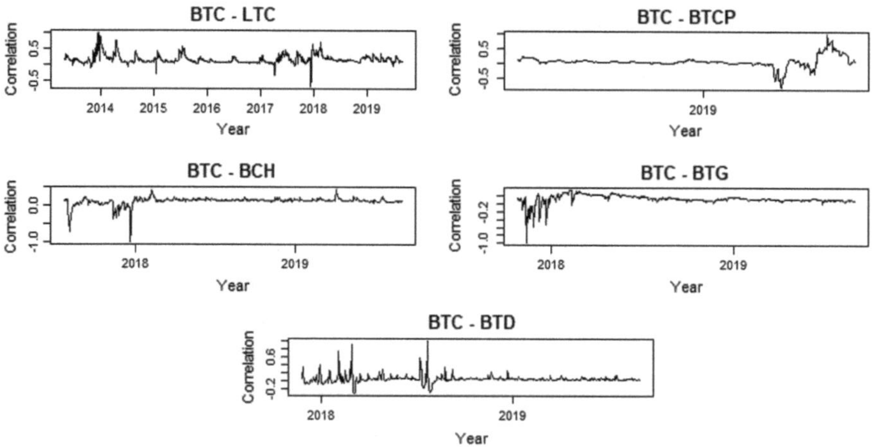

Fig. 4 TGARCH(1, 1) daily correlation between return on bitcoin and returns on bitcoin forks

Once the volatility model is selected, I carry out a time-varying correlation analysis in order to get a better understanding of the sign and the strength of the dynamic relationship between the return on Bitcoin and the returns on its forks (Fig. 4). The correlation between Bitcoin and Litecoin exhibits an interesting pattern. For the first part of the sample, the correlation was strong and positive. In fact, the highest positive correlation was in December 2013. After that, it decreased steadily and remained low until the beginning of the year 2017. During the bubble period, the correlation between these returns strengthened, increasing from about 0 in March 2017, to 0.7 on February 2018. Subsequently, it went back to the pre-bubble levels.

The most striking finding is related to Bitcoin Cash, the most popular Bitcoin fork. For the second half of the year 2017, the correlation between Bitcoin and Bitcoin Cash was negative, and they had a perfect negative correlation on December 21, 2017. Thereafter, the correlation stabilized around 0.2.

The results of the other three crypto-currency returns are remarkable too (Fig. 4). To begin with, the correlation of Bitcoin Gold with Bitcoin presents an expected dynamic. During the first two months after BTG's inception in October 2017, the statistical association between these two returns was negative. From that moment on, the correlation oscillated between 0 and 0.2. The story of Bitcoin Diamond is quite different. Its association with Bitcoin was unstable during the November 2017–August 2018 period, sometimes positive and sometimes negative. Afterwards, the correlation decreased to a low positive value. Finally, Bitcoin Private was not strongly correlated with Bitcoin until April 2019. In the next month, the correlation plunged to a negative value (−0.8), and two months later it reached its peak (1.0).

Turning now to the multivariate volatility approach, this paper uses the EWMA, BEKK-GARCH(1, 1) and DCC-GARCH(1, 1) specifications to examine whether these models produce results similar to those of the TGARCH(1, 1) model. Before applying the multivariate method, it is necessary to check for the presence of con-

Table 4 The p-values of the multivariate Ljung-box test and the multivariate Lagrange multiplier test for detecting the conditional heteroscedasticity in a vector of two crypto-currency returns

	BTC-LTC	BTC-BCH	BTC-BCD	BTC-BTCP	BTC-BTG
Ljung-box					
$Q(1)$	0.000	0.000	0.000	0.000	0.000
$Q(5)$	0.000	0.000	0.000	0.000	0.000
$Q(10)$	0.000	0.000	0.000	0.000	
Lagrange multiplier					
$LM(1)$	0.000	0.000	0.000	0.000	0.000
$LM(5)$	0.000	0.000	0.000	0.000	0.000
$LM(10)$	0.000	0.000	0.000	0.000	0.000

Q(m) and LM(m) denote the weighted Ljung-box test and the weighted ARCH LM test on standardized squared residuals at lag m, respectively

ditional heteroscedasticity in the two dimensional time series. It should be noted that each pair of returns has different number of observations. Thus, the tests are carried out based on the return with fewer observations. Table 4 displays the results of four tests for detecting conditional heteroscedasticity in the bivariate innovations. As we expect, the test statistics reject the null hypothesis confirming the presence of conditional heteroscedasticity.

Figure 5 provides time plots of the volatilities of the EWMA (blue line) and BEKK-GARCH(1, 1) (black line) models. As expected, the estimated volatility series

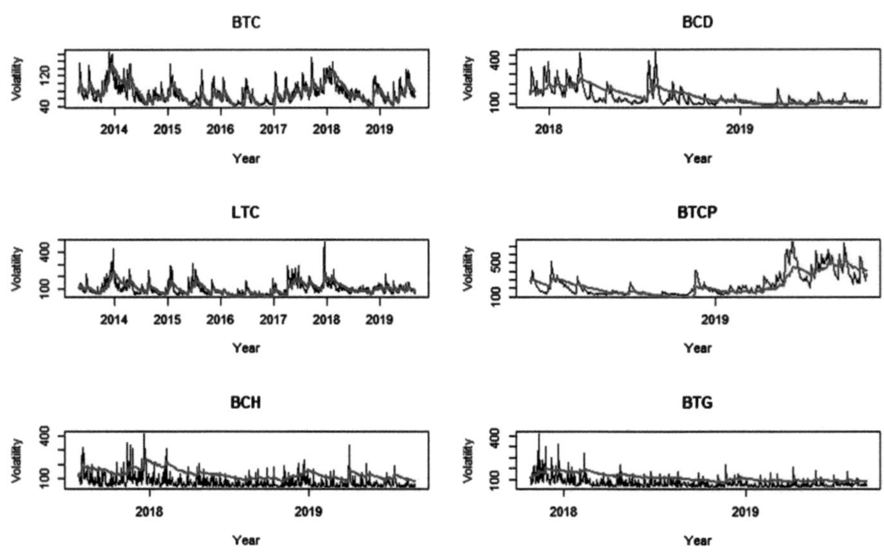

Fig. 5 Multivariate daily volatility of returns on crypto-currencies. The blue line is the EWMA estimated volatility and the black line is the BEKK-GARCH(1, 1) estimated volatility

produced by the EWMA approach are smoother than the volatility series produced by the BEKK model. Nevertheless, both time series share a similar pattern. What is surprising is that the estimated volatilities of BTC, LTC, and BTCP produced by the two multivariate methods are very close to the univariate results. On the other side, the volatilities of BCH, BTG, and BCD produced by the multivariate models are slightly higher than the volatilities of the TGARCH(1, 1) specification. It is important to bear in mind that I used the standardized residuals of the TGARCH(1, 1) estimation to fit the DCC-GARCH(1, 1) model. Thus, the DCC does not estimate the volatility return.

Equally significantly, the parameter λ that governs the time dynamics of the EWMA covariance matrix lies in the typical range commonly seen in practice. The estimated lambda is around 0.97 and is statistically significant at the 1% level: BTC-LTC (0.973), BTC-BCH (0.968), BTC-BTD (0.977), BTC-BTCP (0.970), and BTC-BTG (0.975).

On the question of the time-varying correlation, the benefits of applying multivariate volatility models are significant. Figures 6, 7, and 8 present the results of the estimated time-varying correlation by EWMA, BEKK, and DCC models, respectively. Contrary to the univariate case, the multivariate volatility methods produce high and positive correlations between the return on Bitcoin and the returns on its forks, for most of the sample. These figures are revealing in three ways. First, Bitcoin and its forks are negatively correlated during the bubble year. In particular, LTC, BCH, BTG, and BTD are negatively correlated with Bitcoin during the last two months of 2017, while the correlation of LTC with Bitcoin was negative in March, August, November, and December of the same year. Second, due to the fact that LTC is the only fork that happened before the bubble period, we can see that from May 2013 to December 2013, the correlation decreased from a high to a low value,

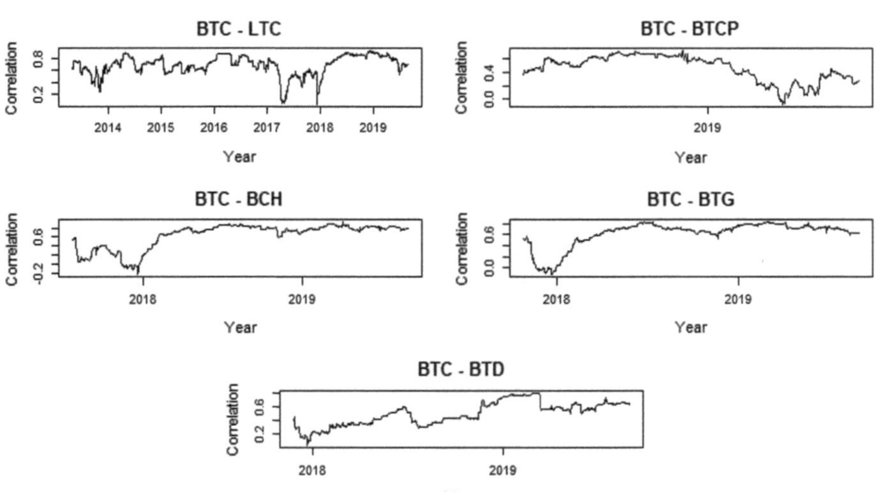

Fig. 6 EWMA estimated correlations

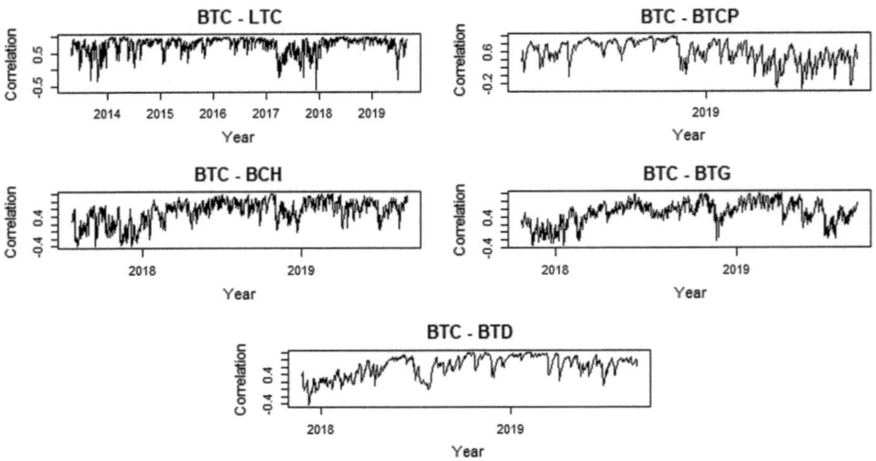

Fig. 7 BEKK-GARCH(1, 1) estimated correlations

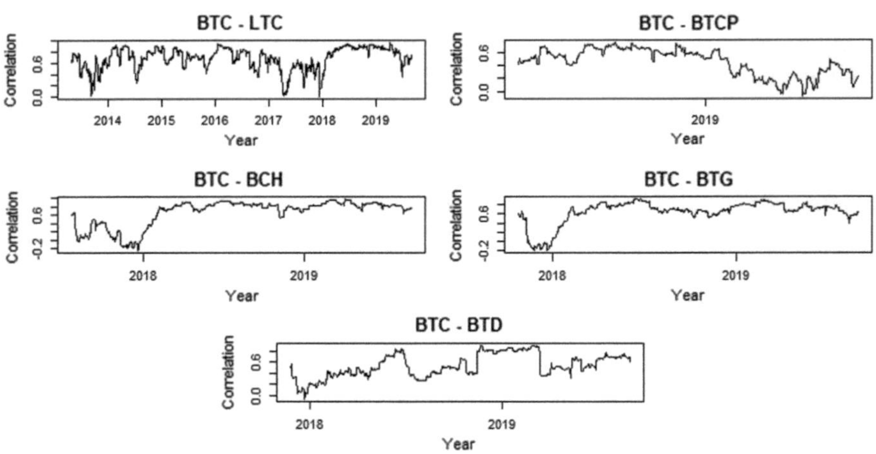

Fig. 8 DCC-GARCH(1, 1) estimated correlations

and was even negative in September and October of the same year. Thus, the 2017 correlation resembles the 2013 correlation. Third, BTCP, is highly correlated with Bitcoin, averaging 0.82 until November 2018, and 0.55 thereafter. The decreasing correlation over time is apparent, contrary to the increasing estimated correlation by the TGARCH(1, 1) model.

Finally, to check the adequacy of the fitted multivariate volatility models, this study employs two portmanteau test statistics: the multivariate Ljung-Box test and the multivariate Lagrange Multiplier (LM) test.[11] As expected, the standardized residuals

[11]For further details, see Tse, Y. K. (2002). Residual-based diagnostics for conditional heteroscedasticity models. The Econometrics Journal 5 (2), 358–374.

Table 5 Model checking of the multivariate volatility models—The p-values of the multivariate Ljung-box and the multivariate Lagrange multiplier tests

	BTC-LTC	BTC-BCH	BTC-BCD	BTC-BTCP	BTC-BTG
EWMA					
$Q(5)$	0.002	0.007	0.000	0.004	0.000
$Q(10)$	0.046	0.000	0.006	0.000	0.000
$LM(5)$	0.001	0.000	0.001	0.000	0.000
$LM(10)$	0.007	0.000	0.020	0.000	0.000
BEKK-GARCH(1, 1)					
$Q(5)$	0.983	–	–	0.000	–
$Q(10)$	0.995	–	–	0.000	–
$LM(5)$	0.828	0.207	0.986	0.000	0.085
$LM(10)$	0.798	0.430	0.643	0.000	0.069
DCC-GARCH(1, 1)					
$Q(5)$	0.534	0.003	0.497	0.488	0.000
$Q(10)$	0.621	0.080	0.841	0.011	0.000
$LM(5)$	0.338	0.001	0.329	0.633	0.050
$LM(10)$	0.436	0.001	0.644	0.432	0.084

Q(m) and LM(m) denote the weighted Ljung-box test and the weighted ARCH LM test on standardized squared residuals at lag m, respectively

of the EWMA model still have conditional heteroscedasticity, because both tests reject the null hypothesis (Table 5). Conversely, both statistics fail to reject the null hypothesis of serial correlation for the BEKK and DCC specifications.

4.1 Discussion

The empirical analysis of univariate GARCH models for the return on Bitcoin and the returns on its forks offers a starting point to study the volatility risk in cryptocurrency markets and how this kind of risk is transmitted from a Bitcoin fork to Bitcoin. In terms of volatility, the gains of using a multivariate volatility approach are not substantial. A closer inspection of Figs. 3 and 5 reveals that volatility changes are closely linked across crypto-currencies.

However, the three multivariate volatility models offer a better estimation of the time-varying correlation than the TGARCH(1, 1) results. All the models produce higher correlation coefficients between Bitcoin and each of its forks, and the overall pattern of the time-varying correlations based on the EWMA, BEKK, and DCC specifications seem similar to each other. In particular, the BEKK method appears to have stronger persistence in the time-varying relationship between crypto-currencies.

One of the most important findings that emerges from the time-varying correlation analysis is the negative value during times of high risk (November 2017–December

2017), but positive value in times of low risk (May 2018–July 2019). An implication of this is the possibility that Bitcoin is not only the leader of the crypto-market but also the most liquid token. In times of turmoil, investors prefer to invest in this crypto-currency rather than in Bitcoin forks. But the positive value for most of the sample suggests that Bitcoin and its forks behave like assets instead of currencies. Therefore, it is not possible to reduce the volatility risk of Bitcoin by taking opposite positions in one of its forks simultaneously. In other words, Bitcoin forks run on top of Bitcoin protocol and these tokens share the same risk as Bitcoin and consequently, Bitcoin forks do not provide benefits of diversification. Note that Litecoin—a crypto-currency that has been around longer than the other Bitcoin forks—is not more interconnected.

Another remarkable finding is that the 2017 bubble made more persistent volatility series, and this outcome is regardless of the method that was applied. Moreover, all crypto-currencies display the highest volatility in December 2017. It is somewhat surprising that the highest transaction fees, the highest BCH volatility, and the perfect negative correlation of BCH with BTC took place on December 21, 2017; 5 days after the highest Bitcoin price, and 1 day after the maximum Bitcoin Cash price.

Perhaps, Bitcoin Cash is the most popular and controversial Bitcoin fork. The relevance of BCH lies not only in the perfect negative correlation with Bitcoin in December 2017, but also in the shape of its volatility series in 2018. The BCH volatility risk increased between July and December 2018, and it could be explained by the Bitcoin SV fork. In early 2018, the Bitcoin Cash community was involved in a big disagreement related to its block size. In May 2018, the block size was increased from 8MB to 32MB. On August 16, 2018, a fork of BCH happened after Jimmy Nguyen, the former CEO of nChain, proposed Bitcoin SV as a new chain. In opposition, some members of the Bitcoin Cash community announced Bitcoin ABC as the real blockchain, which was very similar to BCH. Finally, on November 15, 2018, BCH forked into Bitcoin SV and Bitcoin ABC. For a period, both blockchains complete to take control of Bitcoin Cash. According to the Bitcoin Cash website, Bitcoin ABC took over the Bitcoin Cash chain and Bitcoin SV is listed as its own coin.

The relationship between BTC and LTC needs special attention during two periods of turmoil. The first period, October 2013-May 2014, was characterized by a high volatility and a decreasing correlation. One factor that could explain these findings is the collapse of Mt. Gox—the biggest Bitcoin exchange market—in February 2014. During this month, Mt. Gox suspended services and filed for bankruptcy protection from creditors, and two months later it liquidation proceedings. Likewise, the second period—the 2017 bubble—exhibits a high volatility but a low and even negative correlation. What is interesting is that the pattern of the time-varying correlation was qualitatively the same during these two episodes of high volatility risk.

Regarding Bitcoin return, it is important to note that my findings are different from Bouoiyour and Selmi (2015)'s and Katsiampa (2017)'s outcomes, because the AR(1) coefficient of the mean equation is absent in my estimates. It could suggest that, at the beginning, the crypto-market was Bitcoin and it was inefficient. But the crypto-market is becoming more efficient over time (Urquhart 2016 and Bariviera 2017). In this line of reasoning, the sample period is relevant because I extend it until

August 2019. While I include the 2017 bubble period, Bouoiyour and Selmi study Bitcoin volatility until June 2015 and Katsiampa's estimates are until July 2016.

Last but not least, I show that there is a serial dependence in the crypto-currency returns. However, during the modeling process, removing serial dependence by fitting an ARMA(p, q) model to the mean equation has hardly any effects on the estimated time-varying correlation. As a matter of fact, the time-varying correlations before and after fitting an AR(1) model for Bitcoin Diamond and Bitcoin Private are qualitatively the same. With respect to the volatility equation, any unusual volatility in the innovation (a_t) tends to persist, though not forever. The conditional variance tends to revert to its long-term value, so that the process is stationary with a finite variance.

5 Conclusions

The present study was designed to investigate the relationship between the return on Bitcoin and the returns on its forks. I provide evidence that the volatility of Bitcoin forks and the volatility of Bitcoin are dynamically related, and there is a transmission of the volatility risk from Bitcoin forks to Bitcoin. The BEKK-GARCH(1, 1) model produces a more accurate estimation of both the volatility and correlation series. In particular, the BEKK-GARCH(1, 1) results suggest that feedback between the volatility series has to be considered in future research.

The fact that the time-varying correlation is negative in times of high risk but positive in times of low risk has an important implication. Bitcoin and its forks behave like currencies (there is substitution among tokens) during episodes of turmoil, but behave like assets during calmer times. This shift from a negative to a positive correlation could induce a readjustment in investors' portfolio causing fluctuations in Bitcoin fork prices.

The time horizon is not relevant for the statistical association between Bitcoin and its forks because Litecoin is not more interconnected than the other forks. After the bubble period, Bitcoin and its forks are strongly positive correlated indicating that investors cannot reduce Bitcoin risk by taking opposite positions in Bitcoin forks.

References

Antonopoulos, A. M. (2017). *Mastering bitcoin: Programming the open blockchain* (2nd edn., pp. 187–207). O'Reilly Media, Inc.

Bariviera, A. F. (2017). The inefficiency of Bitcoin revisited: A dynamic approach. *Economic Letters*, *161*, 1–4.

Bauwens, L., Laurent, S., & Rombuts, J. V. K. (2006). Multivariate GARCH models: A survey. *Journal of Applied Econometrics*, *21*, 79–109.

Beneki, C., Koulis, A., Kyriazis, N. A., & Papadamou, S. T. (2019). Investigating volatility transmission and hedging properties between bitcoin and ethereum. *Research in International Business and Finance*, *48*, 219–227.

Bollerslev, T. (1986). Generalized autoregressive conditional heteroskedasticity. *Journal of Econometrics, 31*(3), 307–327.
Bouoiyour, J., & Selmi, R. (2015). *Bitcoin price: Is it really that new round of volatility can be on way?* (p. 6558). RePEc Arch: Munich Pers.
Bouri, E., Molnár, P., Azzi, G., Roubaud, D., & Hagfors, L. I. (2017). On the hedge and safe haven properties of Bitcoin: Is it really more than a diversifier? *Finance Research Letters*, *20*, 192–198.
Chu, J., Chan, S., Nadarajah, S., & Osterrieder, J. (2017). GARCH modelling of crypto-currencies. *Journal of Risk Financial Management*, *10*(4), 1–15.
Corbet, S., Meegan, A., Larkin, C., Lucey, B., & Yarovaya, L. (2018). Exploring the dynamic relationships between crypto-currencies and other financial assets. *Economics Letters*, *165*, 28–34.
Dyhrberg, A. H. (2016). Bitcoin, gold and the dollar—A GARCH volatility analysis. *Finance Research Letters*, *16*, 85–92.
Engel, R. H. (2002). Dynamic conditional correlations: A simple class of multivariate GARCH models. *Journal of Business and Economic Statistics*, *20*, 339–350.
Engel, R. F., & Kroner, K. F. (1995). Multivariate simultaneous generalized ARCH. *Econometric Theory*, *11*, 122–150.
Glosten, L. R., Jagannathan, R., & Runkle, D. E. (1993). On the relation between the expected value and the volatility of nominal excess return on stocks. *Journal of Finance, 48*(5), 1779–1801.
Hansen, P. R., & Lunde, A. (2005). A forecast comparison of volatility models: Does anything beat a GARCH(1,1)? *Journal of Applied Econometrics, 20*, 873–889.
Hayes, A. S. (2017). Crypto-currency value formation: An empirical study leading to a cost of production model for valuing bitcoin. *Telematics and Informatics*, *34*(7), 1308–1321.
Katsiampa, P. (2017). Volatility estimation for Bitcoin: A comparison of GARCH models. *Economics Letters*, *158*, 3–6.
Narayanan, A., Bonneau, J., Felten, E., Miller, A., & Goldfeder, S. (2016). Bitcoin and cryptocurrency Technologies. In *A comprehensive introduction* (pp. 51–98), Princeton University Press.
Nelson, D. B. (1991). Conditional heteroskedasticity in asset returns: A new approach. *Econometrica, 59*(2), 347–370.
Tsay, R. S. (2010). *Analysis of financial time series* (3rd edn). Wiley Inc.
Urquhart, A. (2016). The inefficiency of Bitcoin. *Economic Letters*, *148*, 80–82.
Zivot, E., & Wang, J. (2003). Multivariate GARCH modeling. In *Modeling financial time series with S-Plus®*. Springer.

MIX
Papier aus verantwortungsvollen Quellen
Paper from responsible sources
FSC® C105338

If you have any concerns about our products,
you can contact us on
ProductSafety@springernature.com

In case Publisher is established outside the EU,
the EU authorized representative is:
Springer Nature Customer Service Center GmbH
Europaplatz 3, 69115 Heidelberg, Germany

Printed by Libri Plureos GmbH
in Hamburg, Germany